T0093020

Blockchain for Cybersecurity and Privacy

Internal Audit and IT Audit

Series Editor: Dan Swanson, Dan Swanson and Associates, Ltd.,
Winnipeg, Manitoba, Canada.

The Internal Audit and IT Audit series publishes leading-edge books on critical subjects facing audit executives as well as internal and IT audit practitioners. Key topics include Audit Leadership, Cybersecurity, Strategic Risk Management, Auditing Various IT Activities and Processes, Audit Management, and Operational Auditing.

For more information about this series, please visit:
https://www.crcpress.com/Internal-Audit-and-IT-Audit/bookseries/CRCINTAUDITA

Blockchain for Cybersecurity and Privacy

Architectures, Challenges, and Applications

Edited by
Yassine Maleh
Mohammad Shojafar
Mamoun Alazab
Imed Romdhani

CRC Press
Taylor & Francis Group
Boca Raton London New York

CRC Press is an imprint of the
Taylor & Francis Group, an **informa** business

First edition published 2020
by CRC Press
6000 Broken Sound Parkway NW, Suite 300, Boca Raton, FL 33487-2742

and by CRC Press
2 Park Square, Milton Park, Abingdon, Oxon, OX14 4RN

Library of Congress Cataloging-in-Publication Data

Names: Maleh, Yassine, 1987- editor.
Title: Blockchain for cybersecurity and privacy : architectures,
challenges, and applications / edited by Yassine Maleh, Mohammad
Shojafar, Mamoun Alazab, and Imed Romdhani.
Description: First edition. | Boca Raton, FL : CRC Press, 2020. | Series:
Internal audit and it audit | Includes bibliographical references and
index.
Identifiers: LCCN 2020009460 | ISBN 9780367343101 (paperback) | ISBN
9780367473587 (hardback) | ISBN 9780429324932 (ebook)
Subjects: LCSH: Blockchains (Databases) | Computer security.
Classification: LCC QA76.9.B56 B56 2020 | DDC 005.8/3--dc23
LC record available at https://lccn.loc.gov/2020009460

ISBN: 9780367473587 (hbk)
ISBN: 9780367343101 (pbk)
ISBN: 9780429324932 (ebk)

Typeset in Times
by Lumina Datamatics Limited

This book is dedicated to the loving memory of my mother Fatima.

Yassine Maleh

Contents

SECTION I Blockchain for Cybersecurity: Architectures and Challenges

SECTION II   Blockchain for Cybersecurity and Privacy in IoT

SECTION III   Blockchain for Cybersecurity and Privacy in Healthcare

SECTION IV   Blockchain for Cybersecurity and Privacy in Payment Systems

SECTION V   Blockchain for Cybersecurity and Privacy in Digital Forensics

Foreword

Blockchain has moved beyond hype to real-world implementation in a broad range of industries (eg, finance, supply chain management, and Internet of Things) and applications (eg, cybersecurity and digital forensics), partly evidenced by its evolution over the last decade or so. At the time of writing this foreword, we are already in the fourth generation of blockchain (also known as Blockchain 4.0) and inching toward the fifth generation of blockchain.

Interest in blockchain among the academic community is also reflected by the growing number of conferences and initiatives such as the IEEE Blockchain Initiative (https://blockchain.ieee.org/), as well as this book entitled *Blockchain for Cybersecurity and Privacy: Architectures, Challenges and Applications.*

This book focuses on the applications of blockchain in cybersecurity, privacy, and digital forensics, for different industry sectors such as Internet of Things and healthcare. Specifically, the book comprises five sections, each covering a different theme. In Section I, the reader is introduced to the blockchain architectures and a number of associated research challenges. The next two sections then provide a more in-depth discussion of how blockchain can be utilized for cybersecurity and privacy in the IoT and healthcare sectors. The fourth section then discusses the potential of blockchain in facilitating payment system security and privacy. The last section, perhaps my favorite due to my professional bias, covers the potential utility of blockchain in digital forensic applications.

In summary, this book is a timely contribution to the literature and a quality addition to the reader's bookshelf and library.

Kim-Kwang Raymond Choo
The University of Texas at San Antonio

Preface

Since the creation of the first application in cryptocurrency, which is the Bitcoin in 2009 by Satoshi Nakamoto, blockchain technology has been presented as a revolution impacting the industrial and economic worlds.

Unlike most digital platforms, blockchain is a decentralized system that allows each participant with a regularly updated copy of the large register. There is no central server but a collaborative management, which is in principle a protection against falsifications and other attacks. This disintermediation must also be a factor in reducing costs.

The system is also completely transparent. The register and, therefore, the transaction history can be consulted at any time by any Internet user (or by all members of the network). It is thus possible to ensure the full traceability of an asset or product that has been traded via a blockchain. A participant operates under a pseudonym, but all his operations are traceable.

The blockchain is tamperproof and inviolable. Once recorded in the blocks, the information can no longer be changed or deleted. With this technology, the electronic document could have as much or more evidentiary value as the paper. The decentralized system, by multiplying the number of copies, also offers a guarantee against piracy.

Blockchain technology has infiltrated all areas of our lives, from manufacturing to healthcare and beyond. Cybersecurity is an industry that has been significantly affected by this technology and maybe more so in the future. Blockchain technology can be used to prevent any data breach, identity theft, cyberattacks, or criminal acts in transactions. This ensures that data remains private and secure. Indeed, it could improve cyberdefense by being a platform for preventing fraudulent activities through consensus mechanisms. The blockchain could also detect data falsification through its underlying characteristics such as operational resilience, data encryption, auditability, transparency, and immutability.

The key point that makes it possible to affirm that blockchain technology is an opportunity for cybersecurity is its infallibility. Indeed, while a centralized server allows porous entrances to be seen for the joy of the most experienced hackers, a distributed server is, on the contrary, an impassable wall. Unless you have almost infinite power, it is currently impossible to bring malware into it. In a few paragraphs, let us summarize the benefits that could bring the blockchain to cybersecurity.

Thanks to the blockchain technology, companies would be able to authenticate devices and users without the need for a password. This would eliminate human intervention from the authentication process, preventing it from becoming a potential attack vector.

The use of a centralized architecture and simple connections is the major weakness of conventional systems. No matter how much an organization invests in cybersecurity, all these efforts are in vain if employees and customers use passwords that are easy to steal or hack (the famous 123456). The blockchain would offer strong authentication and resolution of a single point of attack at the same time.

With the help of blockchain, a security system used in an organization could take advantage of a distributed public key infrastructure for device and user authentication. This security system would provide each device with a specific SSL certificate instead of a more vulnerable password. The management of certificate data would then be performed on the blockchain, making it virtually impossible for hackers to use fake certificates.

Each transaction added to a private or public blockchain is timestamped and digitally signed, and irreversibly so. This is one of the basic principles of technology. This means that companies can track back to a specific time for each transaction and locate the corresponding part on the blockchain via their public address.

This characteristic is similar to what is commonly referred to as non-repudiation. It means that the author of a declaration will not have the possibility to positively question the authorship of this declaration or the validity of an associated contract. The term is often used in a legal context where the authenticity of a signature is disputed. In such a case, the authenticity is called 'repudiated'. In practice, when a contract is signed on the Internet, it cannot be challenged by one of the parties. A blockchain would significantly increase the reliability of the system, because each transaction would then be cryptographically associated with a user. Non-repudiation would become null and void.

This book comprises a number of state-of-the-art contributions from both scientists and practitioners working in blockchain technology and cybersecurity It aspires to provide a relevant reference for students, researchers, engineers, and professionals working in this area or those interested in grasping its diverse More specifically, the book consists of 16 contributions classified into five pivotal sections. Section I Blockchain for Cybersecurity and Privacy: Architectures and challenges: Introducing the state-of-the-art blockchain architectures, the taxonomy of blockchain threats and vulnerabilities, and Blockchain security and potential future use cases. Section II Blockchain for Cybersecurity and privacy in IoT: Offering the latest architectures, challenges, and applications of blockchain for cybersecurity and privacy in IoT. Section III Blockchain for Cybersecurity and Privacy in Healthcare: Dealing with the application of blockchain for cybersecurity and privacy in healthcare. Section IV Blockchain for Cybersecurity and Privacy in payment systems: Exploring the exploitation of blockchain for mining cryptocurrencies, and the utilization of blockchain as an effective tool to secure e-transactions and payment projects. Section V Blockchain for Cybersecurity and Privacy in Digital Forensics: proposing some applications of blockchain in digital forensics and for avoiding fraudulence.

Editors

Yassine Maleh (http://orcid.org/0000-0003-4704-5364) is a cybersecurity professor and practitioner with industry and academic experience. He holds a PhD degree in computer sciences. Since 2019, He is working as a professor of cybersecurity at Sultan Moulay Slimane University, Morocco. He was working for the National Port agency (ANP) in Morocco as a senior security analyst from 2012 to 2019. He is senior member of IEEE, member of the International Association of Engineers and the Machine Intelligence Research Labs. Dr. Maleh has made contributions in the fields of information security and privacy, Internet of Things security, and wireless and constrained networks security. His research interests include information security and privacy, Internet of Things, networks security, information system and IT governance. He has published over 50 papers (book chapters, international journals, and conferences/workshops), 3 edited books, and 1 authored book. He is the editor in chief of the *International Journal of Smart Security Technologies*. He serves as an associate editor for *IEEE Access* (2019 Impact Factor 4.098), the *International Journal of Digital Crime and Forensics*, and the *International Journal of Information Security and Privacy*. He was also a guest editor of a special issue on 'Recent Advances on Cyber Security and Privacy for Cloud-of-Things' of the *International Journal of Digital Crime and Forensics*, Volume 10, Issue 3, July–September 2019. He has served and continues to serve on executive and technical program committees and as a reviewer of numerous international conference and journals such as *Elsevier Ad Hoc Networks, IEEE Network Magazine, IEEE Sensor Journal, ICT Express, and Springer Cluster Computing*. He was the publicity chair of BCCA 2019: International Symposium on Blockchain Computing and Applications and the general chair of the International Symposium on Machine Learning and Big Data Analytics For Cybersecurity and Privacy 2019.

Mamoun Alazab (https://orcid.org/0000-0002-1928-3704) is the associate professor in the College of Engineering, IT, and Environment at Charles Darwin University, Australia. He earned his PhD degree in computer science from the Federation University of Australia, School of Science, Information Technology, and Engineering. He is a cybersecurity researcher and practitioner with industry and academic experience. Dr. Alazab's research is multidisciplinary that focuses on cybersecurity and digital forensics of computer systems, including current and emerging issues in the cyber environment, such as cyber-physical systems and the Internet of Things, by taking into consideration the unique challenges present in these environments, with a focus on cybercrime detection and prevention. He looks into the intersection use of machine learning as an essential tool for cybersecurity, for example, for detecting attacks, analyzing malicious code, or uncovering vulnerabilities in software. He has more than 100 research papers. He is the recipient of short fellowship from Japan Society for the Promotion of Science, based on his nomination from the Australian Academy of Science. He delivered many invited and keynote speeches, 27 events in 2019 alone. He convened and chaired more than 50 conferences and workshops.

He is the founding chair of the IEEE Northern Territory Subsection: (February 2019–current). He is a senior member of the IEEE, cybersecurity academic ambassador for Oman's Information Technology Authority, member of the IEEE Computer Society's Technical Committee on Security and Privacy, and has worked closely with government and industry on many projects, including IBM, Trend Micro, the Australian Federal Police, the Australian Communications and Media Authority, Westpac, United Nations Office on Drugs and Crime (UNODC), and the Attorney General's department.

Mohammad Shojafar (https://orcid.org/0000-0003-3284-5086) earned his PhD in information communication and telecommunications (advisor Prof. Enzo Baccarelli) from Sapienza University of Rome, Italy, the second-ranked university in Quacquarelli Symonds (QS) Ranking in Italy and top 100 in the world, in May 2016. He is Intel innovator, senior IEEE member, and senior lecturer in the 5G Innovation Centre/ The Institute for Communication Systems (5GIC/ICS) at the University of Surrey, Guildford, UK. Before joint to 5GIC, he served as a senior member in the computer department at the University of Ryerson, Toronto, Canada. He was senior researcher (Researcher Grant B) and a Marie Curie fellow in the SPRITZ Security and Privacy Research group at the University of Padua, Italy. Also, he was a senior researcher in the Consorzio Nazionale Interuniversitario per le Telecomunicazioni partner at the University of Rome Tor Vergata and contributed to 5g PPP European H2020 "SUPERFLUIDITY" project for 14 months. Dr. Mohammad was principal investigator on PRISENODE project, a 275,000-euro Horizon 2020 Marie Curie project in the areas of network security and fog computing and resource scheduling collaborating between the University of Padua and University of Melbourne. He was also a principal investigator on an Italian SDN security and privacy (60,000 euro), supported by the University of Padua, in 2018. He contributed to some Italian projects in telecommunications such as GAUChO, a Green Adaptive Fog Computing and Networking Architecture (400,000 euro); S2C Secure, Software-defined Cloud (30,000 euro), and SAMMClouds, Secure and Adaptive Management of Multi-Clouds (30,000 euro), collaborating among Italian universities. His main research interest is in the area of network and network security and privacy. In this area, he published more than 100 papers in topmost international peer-reviewed journals and conferences, for example, *IEEE TCC, IEEE TNSM, IEEE TGCN, IEEE TSUSC, IEEE Network, IEEE SMC, IEEE PIMRC, and IEEE ICC/GLOBECOM*. He served as a Program Committee (PC) member of several prestigious conferences, including IEEE INFOCOM Workshops in 2019, IEEE GLOBECOM, IEEE ICC, IEEE ICCE, IEEE UCC, IEEE SC2, IEEE ScalCom, and IEEE SMC. He was a general chair in FMEC 2019, INCoS 2019, and INCoS 2018 and a technical program chair in IEEE FMEC 2020. He served as an associate editor in *IEEE Transactions on Consumer Electronics, IET Communication, Springer Cluster Computing, KSII – Transactions on Internet and Information Systems, Taylor & Francis International Journal of Computers and Applications*, and *Ad Hoc & Sensor Wireless Networks Journals*.

Imed Romdhani is a full-time associate professor in networking at Edinburgh Napier University since June 2005. He was awarded his PhD from the University of Technology of Compiegne, France, in May 2005. He also holds engineering and a master degree in networking, obtained in 1998 and 2001, respectively, from the National School of Computing (ENSI, Tunisia) and Louis Pasteur University (ULP, France). He worked extensively with Motorola Research Labs in Paris and authored four patents.

- Member of Huawei ICT Academy Advisory Board (https://www. huaweiacad.com)
- Member of Africa Universities Fund Advisory Board (https://aufusa.org)
- Module leader of a set of Advanced Networking modules
- Module leader of the MSc Dissertation Project module
- An active member of the Internet Engineering Task Force (IETF)
- Founder and CEO of Digital Tunisia
- Founder of the Student PPMS Project (www.studentppms.com)
- Higher education expert at E-Taalim (www.e-taalim.com)
- Specialities: IoT, IPv6, Wireless and Mobile Networking, Multicast Communication, Vehicular, and Mesh
- Networks, Wireless Sensor Networks, Fellowship of the UK Higher Education Academy, and PRINCE2 certified

Contributors

Kayode Adewole
Bournemouth University
United Kingdom

Salar Ahmadisheykhsarmast
Middle East Technical University
Ankara, Turkey

Mamoun Alazab
Charles Darwin University
Casuarina, Northern Territory,
    Australia

Zibouda Aliouat
Ferhat Abbas
University of Setif
Setif, Algeria

Ayman Alkhalifah
La Trobe University
Melbourne, Victoria, Australia

Junaid Arshad
University of West London
United Kingdom

Otman Basir
University of Waterloo
Waterloo, Ontario, Canada

Sudheer Kumar Battula
University of Tasmania
Hobart, Tasmania, Australia

Mohammed Benabdellah
Mohammed First University
Oujda, Morocco

Saumya Bhadauria
ABV-Indian IITM
Gwalior, India

Bertony Bornelus
Florida A&M University
Tallahassee, Florida

Yassine Chahid
Mohammed First University
Oujda, Morocco

Hongmei Chi
Florida A&M University
Tallahassee, Florida

Jabed Chowdhury
La Trobe University
Melbourne, Victoria, Australia

**Mohammad Jabed Morshed
Chowdhury**
La Trobe University
Melbourne, Victoria, Australia

Jack Curran
The Open University
United Kingdom

Kevin Curran
Ulster University
United Kingdom

Saurabh Garg
University of Tasmania
Hobart, Tasmania, Australia

G. Geetha
Lovely Professional University
Phagwara, India

Alireza Mokhtari Golpayegani
Islamic Azad University
Tehran, Iran

Hadjer Goumidi
Ferhat Abbas
University of Setif
Setif, Algeria

Khizar Hameed
University of Tasmania
Hobart, Tasmania, Australia

Yasmine Harbi
Ferhat Abbas
University of Setif
Setif, Algeria

Anis Herbadji
Ferhat Abbas
University of Setif
Setif, Algeria

Takia Islam
Daffodil International University
Dhaka, Bangladesh

Md. Ismail Jabiullah
Daffodil International University
Dhaka, Bangladesh

Byeong Kang
University of Tasmania
Hobart, Tasmania, Australia

Nabil Kannouf
Mohammed First University
Oujda, Morocco

A. S. M. Kayes
La Trobe University
Melbourne, Victoria, Australia

D. K. Tonoy Kumar
Daffodil International University
Dhaka, Bangladesh

Gulshan Kumar
Lovely Professional University
Phagwara, India

Manish Kumar
M S Ramaiah Institute of Technology
Bengaluru, India

Mohamed Labbi
Mohammed First University
Oujda, Morocco

Angela R. Martin
Florida A&M University
Tallahassee, FL 32307

Omaru Maruatona
La Trobe University
Melbourne, Victoria, Australia

Khadidja Medani
Ferhat Abbas
University of Setif
Setif, Algeria

Muhammad Mubashir Khan
University of Engineering and
   Technology
Karachi, Pakistan

Roopashree Munegowda
San Jose State University
San Jose, California

Ranesh Kumar Naha
University of Tasmania
Hobart, Tasmania, Australia

Karthika M. S. Nair
San Jose State University
San Jose, California

Alex Ng
La Trobe University
Melbourne, Victoria, Australia

Raza Nowrozy
La Trobe University
Melbourne, Victoria, Australia

Md Anwarul Kaium Patwary
University of Tasmania
Hobart, Tasmania, Australia

Sheikh Shah Mohammad Motiur Rahman
Daffodil International University
Dhaka, Bangladesh

Pavan H. Ramesh
San Jose State University
San Jose, California

Rahul Saha
Lovely Professional University
Phagwara, India

Gokay Saldamli
San Jose State University
San Jose, California

Neetesh Saxena
Cardiff University
United Kingdom

Ahmad Sghaier Omar
University of Waterloo
Waterloo, Ontario, Canada

Ferda Özdemir Sönmez
Middle East Technical University
Ankara, Turkey

Rifat Sönmez
Middle East Technical University
Ankara, Turkey

Alireza Souri
Islamic Azad University
Tehran, Iran

Lo'ai A. Tawalbeh
Texas A&M University
San Antonio, Texas

K. C. Ujjwal
University of Tasmania
Hobart, Tasmania, Australia

Jeevan Venkataramana
San Jose State University
San Jose, California

Paul A. Watters
La Trobe University
Melbourne, Victoria, Australia

Ariba Aslam Zahoor
University of Engineering and
    Technology
Karachi, Pakistan

Mani Zarei
Islamic Azad University
Tehran, Iran

Section I

Blockchain for Cybersecurity

Architectures and Challenges

1 A Taxonomy of Blockchain Threats and Vulnerabilities

*Ayman Alkhalifah, Alex Ng, A. S. M. Kayes,
Jabed Chowdhury, Mamoun Alazab,
and Paul A. Watters*

CONTENTS

1.1   INTRODUCTION

Blockchain technology (BT), which is the underlying technology of Bitcoin, has emerged with a number of promising potential applications. In less than a decade, BT has seen investment by many companies, stimulated the establishment of a range of consortia, and raised more than US$3.1 billion in total venture capital [1]. The cryptocurrency market created by BT is estimated to reach a total market capitalization of more than US$143 billion [2]. Furthermore, BT has been applied to the public sector and academic institutes [3], and governments have been planning and developing the use of blockchain in the public sector [4]. KPMG [5] reports that in the first half of 2018, investment in the US fintech companies is $14.2 billion. Furthermore, BT has been applied to the public and private sectors, and over 53% of Deloitte's survey respondents say that BT is a priority for their organizations [6].

Blockchain technology promises a new dimension of conducting business transactions among untrusted entities; its features that support verification, identification, authentication, integrity, and immutability are guaranteed through cryptography, transparency, and decentralized smart contracts and smart ledgers. Blockchain technology offers chronologically linked and replicated digital ledgers in a decentralized database and a sharing of transactions in an extensive network of untrusted entities. It also provides independent verification guarantees, which eliminate the need to rely on a central authority. Furthermore, given the absence of central authorities, blockchain services are able to provide better security properties for systems that are distributed among different entities and can apply immutability against abuse and supervision even if there is a malicious insider.

Given that BT is a cutting-edge technology with many promises, there are concerns about its robustness [7]. If such authority exists in a system, tampering with blockchain or interrupting the broadcast of its contents is possible with collusion between the most powerful entities. There have been many reported cyberattacks, and several cybersecurity vulnerabilities have been identified in blockchain implementations [8]. A recent example is a dusting attack on the Litecoin blockchain network, which shows that attackers are able to break the privacy and anonymity of Bitcoin (BTC) users by sending tiny amounts of dust coins to the personal wallets of the target victims. The attackers can track down the transnational activity of these wallets by performing a combined analysis of the addresses, which can identify the owner of each wallet [9].

These defects raise questions about whether BT can deliver the security guarantees – in practice – that it promises. The growing use of BT as a service delivered by governments or large firms, such as the financial technology industry, has raised users' concerns about its security. Recently, several reports have been published about cyber-attacks and cybersecurity vulnerabilities in BT. For instance, 8833 existing Ethereum smart contracts are vulnerable, and their total balance is 3,068,654 million Ethers, which is equal to about US$30 million [8]. Financial losses are possible because of the vulnerabilities in the smart contracts. For example, an attacker attacked Mt. Gox in 2014, the largest platform for BTC trading, and stole Bitcoins equal to US$450 million, which led to the collapse of Mt. Gox. Another example is when a hacker managed to exploit vulnerability and steal Ethers, which were equal to more than US$60 million in 2016 from the Decentralised Autonomous Organisation (DAO), a smart contract in Ethereum blockchain [10]. Taylor et al. [11] showed that recent researches on BT in terms of cybersecurity concept are mostly concerned with how blockchain can provide security to current and future systems. There is a paucity of studies on the cybersecurity vulnerabilities of BT. This research raises the following questions:

- Is blockchain a proven technology and delivers what it promises?
- What vulnerabilities are usually exhibited in the BT design?
- How have the theoretical vulnerabilities in blockchain been exploited between 2009 and 2019?

In this chapter, we extend the previous works from different entities and conduct a systematic analysis of identifiable incidents and vulnerabilities reported so far and as such establish a direction for the future development of BT. We adopted the following methodology to conduct our research:

- We started with reviewing news available from sources that specialize in Bitcoin, Ripple, Ethereum, and other digital currencies. The purpose was to collect information about incidents reported in news and blogs. Coin-Desk, CoinTelegraph, Bitcoin.com, and CCN are some of the sites that we have visited.
- The second stage was to analyze the incidents to look for clues that could lead us to the answers that we have set in the previous questions.
- The third stage was another round of review in search of any news and articles that explained those incidents, allowing us to conclude the questions set in this research.

The contributions of our study are as follows:

- We identified 65 blockchain-related cybersecurity incidents between 2011 and 2019.
- We conducted a detailed analysis of the attack vectors, victims, and damage in each incident and categorized the attack vectors.

- We identified a list of major concerns for blockchain system designers and developers to consider.
- We developed a taxonomy that classifies all the known threats and vulnerabilities identified so far under five main types of attack vectors.

The rest of this chapter is organized as follows. Section 1.2 introduces some of the distinctive features exhibited by BT. Section 1.3 studies the threats and incidents that have been happening on the blockchain network since 2011. Section 1.4 presents our findings in categorizing the threats and vulnerabilities of BT, and finally, future work and conclusions are presented in Section 1.5.

1.2 BLOCKCHAIN TECHNOLOGY EXPLAINED

Blockchain technology comprises tamper-proof and tamper-evident digital ledgers executed without a central repository, as a distributed system, and often without a central authority, such as a government, a bank, or a firm. It allows users in a community to store transactions in a shared ledger within that community. The transactions cannot be changed when they are published in the blockchain network's normal operation. A new cryptocurrency based on blockchain was created in 2008 by combining BT idea with other computing concepts and technologies. In 2009, BT became very famous following the start of the BTC cryptocurrency, which allowed digital cash to be transferred within a distributed ledger. In Bitcoin, users' digital rights can be digitally signed and transferred to another BTC user. The BTC blockchain announces this transfer publicly to all the network users to independently verify the transaction's validity; moreover, a distributed group of users independently manages and maintains the BTC blockchain, and this, together with cryptographic mechanisms, creates BT's resilience toward subsequent attempts to modify the ledger by counterfeiting the transaction or altering the blocks. Blockchain technology has enabled the development of numerous cryptocurrency systems, such as Ethereum and Bitcoin, and that is why some people tend to restrict BT to cryptocurrency solutions only; however, a range of different industry sectors are contemplating using BT in their applications [12].

The Nakamotos white paper [13] introduced the concept of electronic cash, and with the launch of the BTC cryptocurrency in 2009, BT became one of the widely talked-about technologies. Blockchain is a database of blocks that are linked together with a cryptography hash function, with replicated information stored in all participants' server. The data in the BT database is immutable. It can grow only by appending new block (data) at the end of the chain by authenticated users (miners) with strong cryptography capability, as they can add the new block through a competitive mining scheme. Bitcoin is not blockchain. Bitcoin is just one of the many applications utilizing BT to support the BTC cryptocurrency network, which allows digital cash to be transferred within a distributed ledger. There are many other cryptocurrencies such as Ripple (XRP), Ethereum (ETH), Bitcoin Cash (BCH), Litecoin (LTC), and Binance Coin (BNB). In BTC, users' ownership of a BTC can be digitally signed and transferred to another BTC user. The BTC blockchain announces this transfer publicly to all the network users to independently verify the transaction's validity;

moreover, a distributed group of users independently manages and maintains the BTC blockchain, and this, together with cryptographic mechanisms, creates BT's non-repudiation capability toward attempts to modify the ledger by counterfeiting the transaction or altering the blocks.

There are three main types of BT: private, public or permissionless, and federated or consortium blockchain. Both private and consortium blockchains are considered as permissioned; a permission management entity is required to grant access rights to trusted and known participants. Examples of private blockchain include Multichain, Monax, and Quorum. A consortium blockchain is controlled by more than one organization. The group of organizations that control the consensus mechanism have predetermined nodes in the network. Examples are Ripple, R3 (banks), and B3i (insurance). In contrast to the previous two types, public blockchain allows anyone to write or read the data stored in the blockchain network, without any permission from any authority, and the operation is entirely decentralized and anomalous. Some examples are Monero, Etherum, and Bitcoin. Public blockchain often uses a consensus-based system.

Consensus mechanisms determine which user submits the next block. Consensus mechanisms are designed to allow distrusting users in a blockchain network to cooperate. Many consensus mechanisms have been used in BT, and these include proof of work (PoW), proof of stake (PoS), round-robin, proof of authority (PoA) or proof of identity (PoI), and proof of elapsed time (PoET).

Figure 1.1 shows the BT categorization of private, consortium, public, and permission versus permissionless. The categorization is based on how many organizations are involved in maintaining the ledger and whether validated trusted participants are required or not.

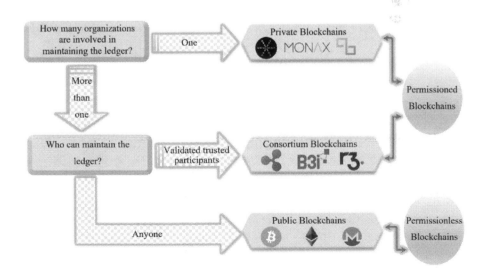

FIGURE 1.1 Blockchain categorization.

1.2.1 Blockchain Consensus Mechanism

The PoW mechanism is based on solving a computationally intensive puzzle that requires carrying out resource-intensive computations. A user who can solve this puzzle first can publish the next new block in the blockchain network. The checking of the correctness of the solution is done by all other miners to verify any new blocks before adding them to the blockchain and reject any block that does not satisfy the solution. In the PoW mechanism, it is hard to carry out a denial-of-service attack by flooding the blockchain network with malicious blocks. In theory, PoW enables an open non-monopoly environment for all participants to contribute; however, due to the difference in computational power and cost of electrical power, this creates an unfair situation among the users. The PoW implementation domain is a public cryptocurrency, such as BTC and Ethereum.

The PoS consensus mechanism is based on investors in a network. The likelihood that a PoS user will publish a new block in the network is based on the percentage of their stake in the total staked cryptocurrency in the blockchain network. When they invest in a huge stake, which is usually an amount of cryptocurrency, the possibility that they will destroy the network diminishes, and they will be more likely to help the system succeed. When the cryptocurrency is staked, the user will not be able to spend it. A user's stake is used by PoS blockchain networks to determine who can publish new blocks. The PoS mechanism has several advantages, one of which is that, compared with PoW, it is less computationally intensive. The PoS mechanism allows any interested user to stake on cryptocurrency; besides, the system that uses PoS is controlled by stakeholders, although this is sometimes considered a disadvantage if they format a pool to create a centralized power base. In contrast, the PoS mechanism is known for its unique issues, such as the 'nothing at stake' problem. This problem arises when, at some point, due to a temporary ledger conflict, multiple blockchains that are competing against one another appear. The appearance of these blockchains will cause different results from different blockchain versions to be published at almost the same time. In this case, the staked users can perform on every chain to increase their reward-earning likelihood, which might grow in different branches in the blockchain network for a period without rejoining a single branch. In addition, the PoS mechanism is vulnerable to a 51% attack by having sufficient financial power. The PoS implementation domain is public cryptocurrency, such as Casper and Krypton.

The round-robin mechanism allows each user to take his or her turn to create the next block, which might include a time limit for each user to avoid halting the publication of blocks. This mechanism is used by some private and federated blockchain networks. This mechanism prevents users from making the blocks plurality, which is easy to understand and does not require high computational power, due to a lack of cryptographic puzzles. On the other hand, this mechanism requires a considerable amount of trust between users; therefore, it is useless in the public blockchain domain, which dominates the majority of current blockchain implementations. The great need for trust in this mechanism is because a malicious user might increase the number of users contributing to the network to raise the likelihood of publishing malicious new blocks to ruin the network. The round-robin implementation domain is a private and federated blockchain, such as MultiChain.

The PoA mechanism is based on publishing users' partial trust, which relies on their real identities, which must be verified, proved, and included on the blockchain network. The central idea behind this mechanism is that a publishing user's reputation or identity is being staked to publish new blocks. A publishing user's reputation is affected by other users in the network based on his or her behavior. If the blockchain network users disagree with the actions of a publishing user, which must adhere to the agreed manner on the network, the user will lose reputation, minimizing the user's chance of publishing a block. The confirmation time in this mechanism is fast, and the block production rates are dynamic. Moreover, this mechanism can be used in hybrid systems, which draw on another consensus mechanism. In contrast, this mechanism assumes that the validating user is not compromised. In addition, the user's reputation is subject to possible high-risk exposure that can compromise the user at any time. This mechanism also leads to a single point of failure. The implementation domain of the PoA or PoI mechanism is a private and federated blockchain and includes hybrid systems such as Ethereum, Kovan Testnet, and POA Chain.

In the PoET mechanism, each publishing user requests a wait time within the network from a hardware time source, which is secured and installed in the user's computer system. The hardware produces a random wait time for the publishing user, and the user becomes inactive during the period of the wait time. When the publishing user is reactivated, the user creates and publishes a block on the network, and all the users who are in the inactive state will stop waiting, and the whole process will begin again. In this mechanism, the given wait time must be random; otherwise, the malicious user might dominate the system by keeping the wait time at a minimum amount. Besides, the publishing user in this mechanism must not start early by waiting for the actual given time. These challenges are resolved by executing an application in a trusted processing environment, such as Intel's Software Guard Extensions, which cannot be modified by external applications. This mechanism is computationally less expensive than PoW. However, the disadvantages of this mechanism are that it relies on hardware to produce random time and that it assumes that the hardware is not compromised. The implementation domain of the PoET mechanism is a private and federated blockchain, such as Hyperledger Sawtooth.

1.2.2 BLOCKCHAIN BLOCK

A block consists of a header and a list of transactions and events ledger. Figure 1.2 shows the structure of a block in a blockchain. It is explained in the following:

1.2.2.1 Block Header

The block header consists of three different sets of metadata.

1.2.2.1.1 Version and Previous Block Hash

The version field (4 bytes) is for the tracking of software and protocol updates. The previous block hash field (32 bytes) is a reference to the hash of the previous block. The cryptographic hash algorithm is by applying SHA256 twice each time. In a blockchain, every block is linked from the previous block. The previous block's hash is used to create the new block's hash. The first block in the blockchain is known as the genesis block.

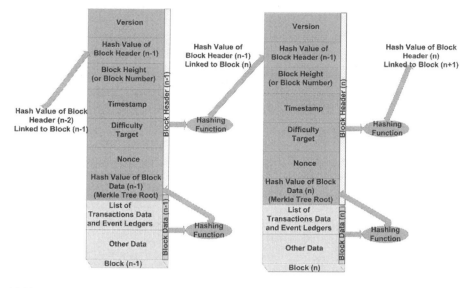

FIGURE 1.2   Blockchain chaining process.

1.2.2.1.2   The Mining Competition Scheme

This set of metadata contains the timestamp (4 bytes), the nonce (4 bytes), and the difficulty target (4 bytes). The timestamp is the creation time of the block. The nonce ('number only used once') is a number added to a hashed block that, when rehashed, meets the difficulty target level restrictions. The nonce is the first number a blockchain miner needs to discover before solving for a block in the blockchain.

1.2.2.1.3   The Merkle Tree Root (32 Bytes)

This is the hash of the root of the Merkle tree, which contains a data structure of the transactions in the block. The Merkle tree root is created by repeatedly hashing pairs of transaction nodes until only one hash is left. The process is performed from the bottom up, from hashes of individual transactions.

1.2.2.2   Block Data

A Merkle tree is a digital fingerprint of the entire set of transactions in a block, enabling a user to verify whether or not a transaction is included in a block. It helps to verify that later versions of the event log include all previous versions and that all data is recorded and presented in the chronological order. Block data contains a ledger of events and transactions list included inside the block as well as any other data for all authentic and validated transactions that have been published on the blockchain network.

1.2.2.3   Chaining of Blocks

The miners perform the adding of a new block. A block in the chain may come from any miner who gets the right to add the new block. The miner picks up the hash of the last block in the chain, combines it with its own set of messages, and creates a new hash for the newly created block.

This newly created block now becomes the new end for the chain. With this, transaction integrity and non-repudiation are guaranteed, as they can be rejected and detected by any altered blocks. Figure 1.2 shows the generic chaining process in BT.

1.2.3 SMART CONTRACTS

Ethereum was launched in 2015, and the virtual coin 'Ether' was proposed as the Ethereum cryptocurrency [14]. Similar to fiat currencies, Ether values and balances have standardized denominations for smaller units such as Wei, Kwei (1K Wei), and Mwei (Mega Wei), and one Ether is (10 ** 18 Wei). Ethereum miners maintain the state of the network and resolve possible conflicts due to, for example, attacks or failure by using a consensus mechanism. The current consensus mechanism used in Ethereum is the PoW consensus, which relies on the assumption that miners are willing to follow the mechanism rather than attacking it, because the mechanism will pay them for performing the computation needed to maintain the network and users will pay execution fees for every transaction [8]. Ethereum supports all types of computational structures, including loops, which can run any decentralized application (DApp) programming code utilizing the back end Ethereum 'smart contracts'.

Smart contracts are digital contracts that are executed by themselves when precise circumstances are met and can be developed and implemented on top of Ethereum blockchain. The smart contract can symbolize the digital property ownership and enable everything of value such as shares, property, and money to be exchangeable [15]. All the transactions are stored on the Ethereum blockchain, and the transactions sequence locates every user's balance and every smart contract's state on the blockchain. The state of smart contracts comprises the balance, which contains the amount of Ether they hold, private storage with 256-bit values, and a key-value storage with 256-bit keys. The storage is private, which means that it cannot be modified or read by other contracts. A transaction deploys the Ethereum Virtual Machine (EVM) bytecode to the Ethereum blockchain to create the primary state with the constructor and to transfer the code of the contract. Users of smart contracts utilize a contract-invoking transaction with the address of the target smart contract as a recipient to invoke the smart contract once the smart contract is deployed. Every smart contract obtains an independent address to interact within the Ethereum network. The contract is stored on the ledger if both the smart contract initiation and the deployment transaction succeed. There are two approaches to make one contract interact with another contract. The first approach is that one of the users directly creates transactions to the second contract, which has a known address carrying the contract required shape. The second approach is that one of the users makes a new instance of the second contract by creating a new contract account with the same functionality of the contract class [16].

PROGRAM LISTING 1: A SIMPLE SMART CONTRACT

```
pragma solidity ¿=0.4.0;
contract Aeth {
//"public" makes variables accessible from
other contracts
address public minter;
mapping (address =¿ uint) public balances;
// Events allow clients to react to specific
// declare contract changes
event Sent(address from, address to, uint amount);
// Constructor to create the contract
constructor() public {
minter = msg.sender;
}
// Sends an amount of newly created ETH to an address
// To be called by the contract creator
function mint(address receiver, uint amount) public {
require(msg.sender == minter);
require(amount ¡ 1e60); balances[receiver] += amount;
}
// Sends an amount of existing ETH
// from any caller to an address
function send(address receiver, uint amount) public {
require(amount ¡= balances[msg.
sender],"Insufficient balance.");
balances[msg.sender] -= amount;
balances[receiver] += amount;
emit Sent(msg.sender, receiver, amount);
}
}
```

In solidity, several primitives are provided to access the information of the block and the transaction. For instance, msg.value is used to access the Wei amount transmitted by a transaction, invoking the method. Another example is msg.sender, which is used to access the account address, which invoked the method. The exact signature of the smart contact's function must be indicated if anyone wants to call a specific function in the smart contract. Any smart contract has a fallback function that handles the request from transactions that indicate incompatible or no function. The transaction will be executed by executing the code of the smart contract in the contract instance context, and every instruction will consume a predefined amount of gas. The transaction's sender sets a gas limit, and if the gas limit exceeds or a runtime error occurs, the whole transaction is cancelled, and the ledger will not be affected, except that the sender will lose the used gas. The transaction is handled as an exception if the gas finishes before the transaction attains a regular stopping point. If one smart contract sends a message to another contract, a portion of the sender gas can only be offered to the receiver.

If the gas finishes from the receiver, the control will be returned to the sender, who can utilize its remaining gas to straighten and treat the exception [17]. Program Listing 1 shows a simple smart contract program.

1.3 CYBERSECURITY THREATS AND INCIDENTS ON BLOCKCHAIN NETWORK

We have identified that 65 real-world cybersecurity incidents occurred between 2011 and the first half of year 2019 that have adversely impacted blockchain systems. We calculate the impact figures reported from the source that are based on the price of the lost coins at the time the attacks were discovered. The reported cases may not be complete, since our research is based on publicly available information on forums, news feeds, and other journal articles. Most incidents are lacking in detail about the real circumstances surrounding the incidents. Thus, we provide a high-level classification of three types, namely hack, scam, and smart contract flaws. The total impact of the cybersecurity incidents between 2011 and 2019 has been more than US$3 billion. The highest loss relates to hacking, which is equal to more than US$1.6 billion, followed by scam, which is equal to more than US$1.1 billion, and smart contract flaws, which is equal to more than US$289 million.

Figure 1.3 shows that, on average, there are seven incidents per year, which gradually decreased and reached the bottom in 2015, with only two incidents. This drop coincides with the drop in the price of BTC in that year. The price of BTC gradually climbed up after 2015 and so did the number of attack incidents, which increased gradually to 12 incidents in 2018. The amount of loss to the incidents followed the same trend from US$7 million in 2015 to a peak of US$1.6 billion in 2018. The first 6 months in 2019 showed just seven incidents, with the amount of loss being US$131 million only.

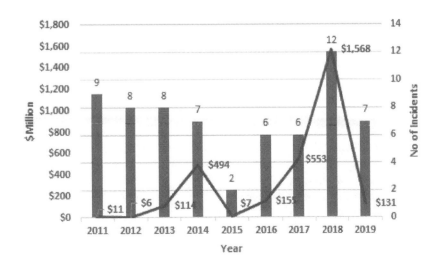

FIGURE 1.3 Blockchain incidents 2011–2019 (6 months).

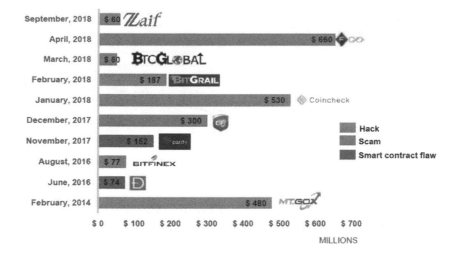

FIGURE 1.4 Top 10 most affected blockchain incidents.

Figure 1.4 shows the top 10 cybersecurity incidents that had happened on the blockchain networks between 2011 and 2019 in terms of financial loss. It shows that the highest loss was due to a Ponzi scam suffered by victims in Vietnam, where as many as 32,000 investors invested in Ifan and Pincoin in April 2018, with a loss of total US$660 million [12]. Victims were unable to withdraw their profits in cash. It is a typical pyramid scam, which boasts the investment as a risk-free activity with profits of up to 40% monthly through a range of bonus structures that allow early investors to gain profits over the later ones. The second-highest loss is due to Coincheck, suffered from an external hack into its system in January 2018 for a record loss of 530 million in cryptocurrency [18]. Coincheck provides BTC wallet and exchange service with 68% dominance in the BTC market. The Coincheck staff failed to implement the exchange's Its a proper name of crypto money platform multisig contract security feature recommended by the NEM developers and stored all NEM blocks in a single hot wallet. It is recommended for exchanges today to use a hybrid hot/cold wallet system, which stores the majority of the value in the cold wallets and secures it via multisig contract security.

The third-highest loss is the Mt. Gox hack, which happened in February 2014, with a loss of US$480 million and another US$27.4 million missing from its bank accounts. Hackers had broken into the Mt. Gox exchange and had taken a huge portion of the cryptocurrency money controlled by the company. The incident led Mt. Gox into insolvency [15]. Mt. Gox was the largest BTC exchange in the world at that time, which suffered three separate attacks in June 2011 (US$8.75 million), October 2011 (US$8.35 million), and February 2014 (US$480 million). The failure of Mt.Gox was ascribed to poor management and lack of software development and security control. Transaction malleability is a vulnerability in the BTC blockchain network, which enables the adversary to alter the transaction identifier (TXID) without revoking the transaction. Modifying the TXID will deceive the victim into believing that the transaction has failed, although it is later confirmed. Currency exchanges are the common targets for this attack. The adversary withdraws from an exchange and then republishes the same transaction with a different TXID, and one of them will show on the network. Because of delays, it is highly probable that the altered transaction will win rather than the original withdrawal. The currency exchange will not locate the original transaction on the network and will think that the transaction has failed if the exchange relies on TXIDs only. Thus, the adversary can continuously withdraw in the Mt. Gox attack; the attackers performed a transaction malleability attack to steal coins from the exchange, which forced the exchange to freeze users' account and halt withdrawals [19].

Table 1.1 shows that hacking fraud tops, with 48 incidents and a total loss of $1.6 billion. Based on the information from the source, hack vectors include compromising computer system, compromising cloud service, compromising email account, compromising private key, compromising third party, compromising server, compromising website, compromising cold and hot wallet, compromising platform, phishing attack, social engineering, masquerade attack, malicious insider, and Subscriber Identity Module (SIM) swapping attack. Coinbase successfully detected and blocked what would have been a hack on June 20. The hackers are believed to have exploited a Firefox zero-day bug, targeting employees by spear-phishing [20]. There are different types of flaws in blockchain users' software, such as runtime, concurrency, memory, security, performance, configuration, Graphical User Interface (GUI), compatibility, build and hard fork flaws. Flaws in the blockchain users' software, which is used in the blockchain network, might lead to the exposure of users' private keys. In 2014, Blockchain. info, which is a hybrid wallet provider, made a mistake during their software update in that when their users generated a new key pair on their local computer using the affected software, the Elliptic Curve Digital Signing Algorithm (ECDSA), inputs were not adequately random, which caused an adversary to operate the software to compromise the users' private keys by only viewing the public address. There are 0.0002% of users affected, and the issue was detected and resolved within two and a half hours, although some Bitcoins were stolen. Software flaws might lead to a leak of users' private keys [21]. The number of blockchain incidents due to scam is 10. The secrecy of identity property provided by blockchain has enabled itself to become the platform of choice for scams. The table shows that the second-highest loss is due to scams such as the Ponzi scheme and Pyramid scheme, causing a loss of 1 billion dollars. Scam includes all the incidents from which the target owner disappeared with the funds.

Table 1.2 shows that the victims of blockchain incidents range from individuals to BTC banks, BTC service providers such as Wallet service, currency trading platform, and exchange. Cryptocurrency exchanges are the prime targets of attack.

TABLE 1.1
Blockchain Incident Classification

Type	No. of Incident	Total Amount Loss ($ million)
Hack	48	1621
Scam	10	1126
Smart contract flaws	7	289

TABLE 1.2
Blockchain Fraud Victim Classification

Victim Type	No. of Incident	Amount Loss ($)
Bitcoin bank	1	502,029
Bitcoin payment service provider	1	1,800,000
Bitcoin stock market	2	6,741,039
Blockchain network	1	7,700,000
Cryptocurrency project	1	40,000
Blockchain project	1	500,000
Cloud services provider	1	228,845
Darknet market	1	100,000,000
Digital currency trading platform	1	4,100,000
Distributed autonomous organization	1	74,124,000
Exchange	36	1,568,184,876
Individual	4	6,646,944
Margin trading service	2	441,760
Mining marketplace	1	64,931,534
Online poker room	1	15,543
Ponzi scheme	4	1,014,500,000
Pyramid scheme	1	2,300,000
Smart contract coding company	2	182,210,733
Stock exchange	1	10,000
Bitcoin stock market	2	2,200,000

There are 36 incidents, with a total of $1.56 billion loss. The transaction malleability vulnerability in BT was the cause of the Mt. Gox incident in 2014. There are incidents where hackers make use of cryptojacking to install the malware in the target machine or mobile device to utilize their computational power to mine a block, which consumes a large amount of electricity and might compromise the target's system functionality. In February 2018 alone, researchers launched a cryptojacking campaign, which affected more than 4000 websites, including the UK and US government pages; the other campaign targeted millions of Android devices. In addition, Radiflow, a critical infrastructure security company, found cryptocurrency mining malware on the European water utility operational network, which had a huge impact on the systems [22].

1.4 CATEGORIZATION OF BLOCKCHAIN THREATS AND VULNERABILITIES

Figure 1.5 shows a taxonomy of blockchain threats and vulnerabilities that we have identified so far. This taxonomy is built upon the findings from 65 real-world cybersecurity incidents occurred between 2011 and the first half of year 2019 and produces a classification scheme according to the threat vectors and vulnerabilities of BT.

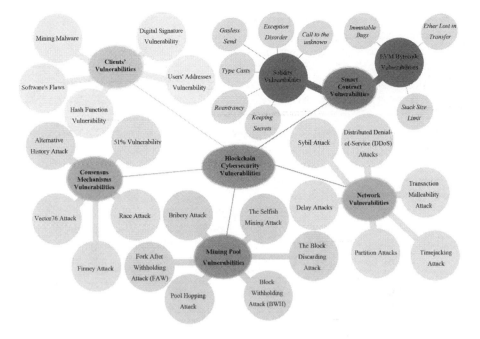

FIGURE 1.5 Classification of blockchain threats and vulnerabilities.

We classify BT threats and vulnerabilities into the following five categories:

- Clients vulnerabilities
- Consensus mechanism vulnerabilities
- Mining pool vulnerabilities
- Network vulnerabilities
- Smart contract vulnerabilities

Each of the threat and vulnerability types is discussed in the following sections.

1.4.1 CLIENTS' VULNERABILITIES

1.4.1.1 Digital Signature Vulnerability

All BTCs' asymmetric cryptography is based on elliptic curve cryptography (ECC). The addresses in BTC are derived from public keys of ECC, and the authentication of the transaction uses digital signatures, which are generated by the ECDSA. The use of ECC is inadequate, because it does not have the requisite randomness, which might compromise the user's private key. A random value must be used with the private key to create a digital signature, where the random value must be different for each transaction. For example, in BTC blockchain, 158 unique public keys were found, which used the same random value (nonce) in more than one signature, which made it possible to compromise the users' private keys [23].

1.4.1.2   Hash Function Vulnerability

The operation in some of the blockchain networks, such as BTC blockchain, relies on cryptographic primitives to ensure the correctness and accuracy of the operation. With the rapid development in the computational power and advanced crypt-analysis, these primitives have become breakable [24]. One of these primitives is the hash function. For example, SHA256 is the hash function used in BTC blockchain, which is vulnerable to different cybersecurity threats, such as preimage and collision attacks [25]. A preimage attack is when the attacker is given an output Y from hashing an input m; the attacker attempts to find an input m* so that hashing m* equals Y; however, the attacker's attempt to find two inputs providing the same hash is considered a collision attack [26]. The potential impact of performing the preimage attack on BTC blockchain might lead to uncovering an address or the complete failure of the blockchain, while the impact of the collision attack might be stolen to destroy coins or repudiate payment. Although enormous computation power is needed to perform such attacks, attacks might be possible if the adversary has quantum computing or dominates a huge mining pool [24].

1.4.1.3   Mining Malware

Cryptojacking is when the adversary installs the malware on the target machine or mobile device to utilize its computational power to mine a block, which consumes a large amount of electricity and might compromise the target's system functionality. In February 2018 alone, researchers launched a cryptojacking campaign, which affected more than 4000 websites, including the UK and US government pages; the other campaign targeted millions of Android devices. Venkatraman et al. [27,28] proposed a deep-learning image-based analysis for malware detection. In addition, a critical infrastructure security company found cryptocurrency mining malware on the European water utility operational network, which had a huge impact on the systems [22].

1.4.1.4   Software's Flaws

There are different types of flaws in blockchain users' software, such as runtime, concurrency, and hard fork flaws [29]. Flaws in the blockchain users' software, which is used in the blockchain network, might lead to the exposure of users' private keys. In 2014, Blockchain.info, which is a hybrid wallet provider, made a mistake during their software update in that when their users generated a new key pair on their local computer by using the affected software, the ECDSA inputs were not adequately random, which meant that an adversary could operate the software to compromise the users' private keys by only viewing the public address [21].

1.4.1.5   Users' Addresses Vulnerability

Addresses in BTC blockchain are vulnerable to identity theft threat because these addresses are not certified. For instance, a man-in-the-middle attack might be performed by an adversary to change the target BTC address to the adversary address. The adversary might vandalize the target website to obtain payments destined for the target. The impact of the attack is disastrous, because, in the BTC blockchain, it is impossible to return the payment if the nodes in the network accept and register it in the ledger [30].

1.4.2 CONSENSUS MECHANISMS VULNERABILITIES

1.4.2.1 51% Vulnerability

Establishing mutual trust in BT is based on the shared consensus mechanism. However, the attackers might control the whole blockchain network by exploiting the 51% vulnerability, which is built in the mechanism. For example, if a single user or a group of users have more than 50% of the total hashing power in the blockchain networks, which are based on the PoW mechanism, then the user or the group of users can exploit the 51% vulnerability. Therefore, gathering the mining power under a few mining pools might lead to this issue. Recently, GHash.io alone dominated 54% of all BTC network processing power for a day [19]. In addition, the blockchain networks, which are based on the PoS mechanism, also have the 51% vulnerability. The vulnerability can be exploited when a single miner has more than 50% of the total coins in the network; a 51% vulnerability leads to a 51% attack, which allows the attacker to do the following [31]:

- Injecting deceptive transactions
- Manipulating the blockchain network
- Outstripping all other users in the blockchain network
- Performing a double-spending fund
- Stealing other users' assets

1.4.2.2 Alternative History Attack

In this attack, the attacker sends a payment transaction to the target while he or she mines another blockchain fork, which includes a deceptive double-spending transaction. After the confirmation, a product or service will be received by the attacker from the target. If the attacker succeeds in finding more blocks than the genuine chain, he or she propagates his or her malicious fork and recovers the coins; otherwise, he or she must extend his or her malicious fork to reach the fork of the honest miners. If the attacker cannot catch up with the other nodes, the attack will fail [32].

1.4.2.3 Finney Attack

In this attack, one transaction is pre-mined in a block, and a duplicated version of this transaction is sent to a user by the attacker. After the transaction is accepted and the receiver delivers the product, the attacker propagates the block, which contains the initial transaction. Thus, the transaction, which is sent to the user, will be invalid, and the attacker will succeed in producing a double-spend transaction [33].

1.4.2.4 Race Attack

This attack is easy to launch in blockchain networks, which are based on the PoW mechanism; this is mainly because an attacker can exploit the time between the creation transaction and the confirmation transaction to carry out the attack. Before mining the confirmation transaction, the attacker has obtained the creation transaction results, which leads to double spending [34].

1.4.2.5   Vector76 Attack

This attack originally came from the BitcoinTalk forums, where a user named Vector76 described an attack against the MyBitcoin e-wallet, which resulted in double-spending issues. In this attack, the attacker does not need to mine two consecutive blocks; one block is sufficient to perform this attack. The attacker needs to observe the blockchain network to determine the timing of the propagating transactions of network nodes and how they are broadcasting over the network. The attacker then identifies the nodes that are earlier in the propagating transactions than the target and sets up a direct connection with the target. After that, the attacker initiates a transaction that makes a legitimate deposit into the target and mines it into a block, without broadcasting it to the network. The attacker mines the block like other nodes, except that he or she adds an extra transaction that is not broadcast. When the attacker succeeds in initiating a valid block, he or she does not broadcast it until some other nodes mine a block. Once a node mines a block, the attacker immediately broadcasts his or her block to the target, and if the target receives the attacker block before the other block, the target will accept the attacker block, and the transaction will gain one confirmation. In this situation, the blockchain and the target and other nodes connected to the target will be forked mainly because the target that passed on the transaction quickly will consider the attacker block legitimate, whereas the other nodes in the network will consider the other fork valid. The attacker directly transfers the coins to a different address that is controlled by the attacker, and the target will generate the transaction because the target believes that it is a legitimate transaction. The attacker also double spends the inputs by transferring the coin to himself or herself. The network nodes that did not receive the attacker's first block will accept the transaction as a genuine transaction, and they will include it in the next block. If the attacker's first block wins when the blockchain has forked, the attacker will not lose anything; however, if the first block loses, then the deposit to the target will become invalid, although the withdraw transaction will still be valid [35].

1.4.3   Mining Pool Vulnerabilities

1.4.3.1   Block Withholding Attack

In this attack, the attacker joins a mining pool to assist the pool members in mining blocks; however, the attacker will never broadcast any block to decline the pool anticipated income. This attack is also called a 'Sabotage Attack' because the scoundrel miner does not obtain anything but causes everyone to lose [36]. Although the attacker does not gain any revenue from this attack, Courtois et al [37] assert that the attacker might be able to earn income from this attack.

1.4.3.2   Bribery Attack

This attack is based on bribing miners to mine on precise forks or blocks. The attacker can validate random transactions and publish them because he or she has paid to dishonest nodes to verify them. The attacker might gain the majority of the computing resources by using three ways of bribing, namely out-of-band payment, negative-fee mining pool, and in-band payment. In the out-of-band payment, the computing resources owner is directly paid by the attacker to mine the attacker's blocks. In the negative-fee mining pool, the attacker creates a pool by rewarding the higher return. Finally, in in-band payment, the attacker pursues to bribe the blockchain itself by making a fork, which includes free bribe money to any miner endorsing the attacker fork [38].

1.4.3.3   Pool Hopping Attack

In this attack, the attacker mines based on the appeal rate. If the rate is high, the attacker mines; otherwise, the attacker leaves the pool. The attacker utilizes the information about the number of the submitted shares in the target mining pool to understand how many shares have been submitted and how many blocks have been found. Using this information, the attacker stops mining in the target pool and contributes elsewhere. The central idea behind this attack is that the attacker chooses various pools to mine to gain maximum income [36].

1.4.3.4   Block Discarding Attack

In this attack, compared with the honest nodes, the attacker must possess an adequate number of network connections and dominate multiple slave nodes to increase his or her network superiority. Once the attacker is informed of newly mined blocks, he or she immediately publish his or her own block, which must be faster than the rest in the network; therefore, when a node publishes a block, the attacker can instantly propagate his or her own blocks to discard honest nodes' blocks [39].

1.4.3.5   Selfish Mining Attack

In this attack, a group of attackers conspire to create a mining pool to negate the honest miners' work and acquire better income for themselves. The attackers mine in their private blockchain and broadcast it based on the length difference between the public and the private blockchains to influence the rewards [40].

1.4.3.6   Fork-After-Withholding Attack

The fork-after-withholding (FAW) attack income is equal or greater than a block withholding (BWH) attack income, and the attack is four times more fruitful, usually per poll, than the BWH attack. This attack has two types: single-pool FAW attack and multipool FAW attack. This attack combines the selfish mining attack and the BWH attack. In the single-pool FAW attack, the attacker joins the target mining pool and performs the attack against it, whereas, in the multipool FAW attack, the attacker aims to increase his or her income by expanding the attack against several pools. The attacker computing power is divided in this attack into infiltration mining and innocent mining. When the attacker infiltration part locates a full PoW, the attacker keeps the block and does not broadcast it. Based on the next steps, the attacker might publish his or her private block to the manager of the target pool, hoping that a fork is created identical to the selfish mining attack or the attacker discards the block, which is identical to the BWH attack [41].

1.4.4 Network Vulnerabilities

1.4.4.1 Partition Attacks

In this attack, the attacker isolates a group of nodes from the rest of the BTC block-chain network, and the network is partitioned into disjoint components. The adversary hijacks the most specific prefixes, which host each of the isolated nodes' IP address to redirect the traffic destined to them. The traffic is intercepted by the adversary when he or she is on the path and determines which connections cross the partition that the adversary attempts to create. If the connection does not cross the partition, the adversary drops the packets; otherwise, the connection is contained within the isolated nodes. The adversary tracks the exchanged messages to determine the leakage points; these are nodes in the isolated group, which maintain connections with the external nodes and the adversary cannot intercept. The adversary finally isolates the leakage points from other nodes in the isolated group [42].

1.4.4.2 Delay Attacks

In the previous attack, the adversary needed to gain full control over the target's traffic to perform the attack effectively. In contrast, the delay attack can cause significant delays in block publishing even when the adversary intercepts only one of the target's connections. First, the attacker alters the content of specific messages to delay the block delivery; this is achievable because of a lack of integrity checks and encryption of BTC messages. In addition, the adversary makes use of the fact that nodes first send block requests to the peer that propagated each block and wait for 20 minutes to deliver it before requesting it from another peer. Thus, the adversary delivers a block to a target node by a 20-minute interval, which makes the target unaware of the most recently mined blocks and makes the target unable to contribute to the network [42].

1.4.4.3 Distributed Denial-of-Service Attack

Nowadays, the distributed denial-of-service (DDoS) attack is one of the most common and inexpensive attacks on the Internet [19]. Despite being a peer-to-peer technology, BT is still vulnerable to the DDoS attack. The BT networks, such as Ethereum and Bitcoin, have frequently undergone these attacks. For instance, 40 BTC services have suffered from 142 DDoS attacks over 2 years, and the targets have included 7% of all popular operators [19]. Most of these attacks targeted large mining pools and currency exchange services because of a larger revenue possibility. These attacks have forced firms such as BitQuick and CoinWallet to shut down their service after a few months of their start [19].

1.4.4.4 Sybil Attack

In this attack, the adversary sets up fake assistant nodes and attempts to expose part of the blockchain network. The adversary might use a group of exposed nodes to perform the attack to isolate the target and disconnect the transactions created by the target, or the attacker will make the user choose only the blocks that are maintained by him or her [19]. The adversary with malicious nodes will surround the target. The target will think that he or she still connects to the network through different honest nodes; however, the reality is that the target has a limited access to the network because the adversary controls all the nodes to which he or she connects. Once the adversary surrounds the target, he or she can refuse to relay the target's transactions. Besides, the adversary can feed misleading information to the target of the network state [21]. A successful Sybil attack can incapacitate the consensus algorithm functionality and cause potential double-spending attack [19].

1.4.4.5 Time-Jacking Attack

This attack is a specific attack on the BTC blockchain network. The network time in this network is maintained by full nodes. The network time is acquired by obtaining a version message from the neighboring nodes. The median is calculated, and if the median time of all neighboring nodes exceeds 70 minutes, the network time counter returns to the node system time by default. When the adversary is connecting to the target node, he or she attempts to reveal imprecise timestamps. Once the adversary modifies the node network time counter, the misled node might adopt a substitute blockchain. This attack will isolate the target node from the network or decrease the transaction confirmation rate on the whole network [33].

1.4.4.6 Transaction Malleability Attack

Transaction malleability is a vulnerability in the BTC blockchain network that enables the adversary to alter the TXID without revoking the transaction. Modifying the TXID will deceive the victim into believing that the transaction has failed, although it is later confirmed. Currency exchanges are the common targets for this attack. The adversary withdraws from an exchange and then republishes the same transaction with a different TXID, and one of them will show on the network. Because of delays, it is highly probable that the altered transaction will win rather than the original withdrawal. The currency exchange will not locate the original transaction on the network and will think that the transaction has failed if the exchange relies on TXIDs only. Thus, the adversary can continuously withdraw [43]. Mt. Gox was one of the largest exchanges in BTC history; it declared bankruptcy due to losing coins valued over US$450 million. The attackers performed a transaction malleability attack to steal coins from the exchange, which forced the exchange to freeze users' account and halt withdrawals [19].

1.4.5 SMART CONTRACT VULNERABILITIES

Two of the major vulnerabilities of Ethereum are discussed in the following subsections.

1.4.5.1 Ethereum Virtual Machine Bytecode Vulnerabilities

The ethereum virtual machine (EVM) is a virtual machine that runs the bytecode, which is the result of compiling the source code of a smart contract. Each operation in the EVM expends a specific amount of gas. The gas represents the code execution cost. Table 1.3 shows three vulnerabilities under the EVM bytecode umbrella [44].

TABLE 1.3
EVM Bytecode Vulnerabilities

Vulnerability Name	Reason
Ether lost in transfer	Any ether sent to an orphan address, which is not associated with any user lost forever, and there is no way to check if the address is orphan or not.
Immutable bugs	Published smart contracts are immutable against any alteration.
Stack size limit	The call stack limitation, which can be leveraged by the attacker.

1.4.5.2   Solidity Vulnerabilities

Solidity is the smart contract high-level programming language in Ethereum, which the programmer uses to write the smart contract source code. There are six known vulnerability types in the smart contract source codes that are already exploited and represent the highest portion of the smart contracts' vulnerabilities number. Most of these vulnerabilities emanate from a misalignment between the programmers' insight and the Solidity semantics [44]. These vulnerabilities are shown in Table 1.4.

Ethereum Smart Contract Coding flaw represents the third-highest impact of the incident type. The main cause is due to the reentrancy vulnerability in smart contracts, as shown in the case of the DAO incident in 2016. Reentrancy is a kind of vulnerability exhibited in Ethereum Smart Contract only. As the name suggests, an attacker first deposits an amount X to a multiparty smart contract. The attacker then executes a function to withdraw an amount Y, which is more than X, before the balance of funds deposited and withdrawn has been settled. The effect is the attacker essentially stealing the money of other parties in the contract. Our study reveals that incidents related to Ethereum Smart Contract flaw have risen from being one incident in 2016 to two incidents in 2017 to four incidents in 2018.

TABLE 1.4
Solidity Vulnerabilities

Vulnerability Name	Reason
Call to the unknown	The recipient fallback function is invoked because the called function does not exist.
Exception disorder	Anomaly in exceptions handling.
Gasless send	Invoking the out-of-gas exception.
Keeping secrets	Compromise a private field in the smart contract.
Reentrancy	Reenter a non-recursive function before its termination.
Type casts	No exception is thrown when the caller made an error.

1.5 CONCLUSION

This chapter analyzed 65 cybersecurity incidents and discussed some of the attack mechanisms in BT, and developed a taxonomy for blockchain attack issues that have arisen because of concerns in blockchain conceptualization, blockchain network implementation, the functionality of smart contracts, the process of mining, and consensus mechanisms. Some of these vulnerabilities might become obsolete in the future, and new ones may be discovered; however, we believe that the taxonomy we have developed describes a more general set of vulnerabilities that are likely to persist into the future. In addition, this chapter also catalogued real cybersecurity incidents in the BT systems. The outcome of this chapter provides a clear direction for BT designers and implementers guidance on how to implement a more secure BT system.

The followings are suggested for the future research direction and guidance on how to implement secure BT:

- No actors on the blockchain network are immune to attacks. Blockchain exchanges are the prime targets that suffered most of the attacks, with a significant amount of loss. Apart from the NEM multisig security, enhanced cryptography techniques for integrity, dealing with malware, and other active threats are required in working toward future implementations of blockchain-based access control required for the exchanges and the network.
- Blockchain network is being used actively for scamming nowadays. Thus, there is an upward trend in attacks targeting the Ethereum Smart Contract flaw from 2016. We assert that the Ethereum smart contract vulnerability will be the next prime target for the attackers. Future researchers should improve blockchain by directly addressing these categories of vulnerability through the use of more advanced context-aware access control systems [45,46], working toward future implementations of blockchain-based access control for secure data access and maintaining data sharing between different parties [47,48].
- Fraud prevention and detection mechanisms are required as an add-on to BT to ensure that trustworthy and privacy-preserving attributes of the users are maintained [49].

REFERENCES

1. Coindesk: Bitcoin venture capital funding, www.coindesk.com/bitcoin-venture-capital, 17 July 2019.
2. CoinMarketCap: Cryptocurrency market capitalizations—Coinmarketcap, https://coinmarketcap.com/, 17 July 2019.
3. Chowdhury, M.J.M., Colman, A., Kabir, M.A., Han, J., Sarda, P.: Blockchain as a notarization service for data sharing with personal data store. In: Trust-Com/BigDataSE 2018, IEEE (2018) 1330–1335.
4. Berryhill, J.: New opsi guide to blockchain in the public sector—Observatory of public sector innovation observatory of public sector innovation, https://oecd-opsi.org/new-opsi-guide-to-blockchain-in-the-public-sector/, 17 July 2019.

5. Pollari, I., Ruddenklau, A.: The pulse of fintech 2018, biannual global analysis of investment in fintech, https://assets.kpmg/content/dam/kpmg/au/pdf/2018/pulse-of-fintech-h1-2018.pdf, 11 August 2019.

6. Deloitte's 2019 global blockchain survey, www2.deloitte.com/content/dam/insights/us/articles/2019-global-blockchain-survey/di-2019-global-blockchain-survey.pdf, 17 July 2019.

7. Natarajan, H., Krause, S.K., Gradstein, H.L.: Dis-tributed ledger technology (dlt) and blockchain, https://documents.worldbank.org/curated/en/177911513714062215/distributed-ledger-technology-dlt-and-blockchain, 17 July 2019.

8. Luu, L., Chu, D.H., Olickel, H., Saxena, P., Hobor, A.: Making smart contracts smarter. In: *Proceedings of the 2016 ACM SIGSAC Conference on Computer and Communications Security*. CCS'16, New York (2016) 254–269.

9. Omelchenko, D.: Litecoin experiencing dusting attack, https://ihodl.com/topnews/2019-08-10/litecoin-experiencing-dusting-attack/, 11 August 2019.

10. Castillo, M.D.: The dao attacked: Code issue leads to $60 million ether theft, www.coindesk.com/dao-attacked-code-issue-leads-60-million-ether-theft, 11 August 2019.

11. Taylor, P.J., Dargahi, T., Dehghantanha, A., Parizi, R.M., Choo, K.K.R.: A systematic literature review of blockchain cyber security. *Digital Communications and Networks* (2019).

12. Yaga, D., Mell, P., Roby, N., Scarfone, K.: Nistir 8202 blockchain technology overview. Retrieved from National Institute of Standards and Technology, US Department of Commerce (2018).

13. Nakamoto, S.: Bitcoin: A peer-to-peer electronic cash system. bitcoin.org., https://bitcoin.org/bitcoin.pdf, (2008), 21 May 2019.

14. Tikhomirov, S., Voskresenskaya, E., Ivanitskiy, I., Takhaviev, R., Marchenko, E., Alexandrov, Y.: Smartcheck: Static analysis of ethereum smart contracts. In: *2018 IEEE/ACM 1st International Workshop on Emerging Trends in Software Engineering for Blockchain* (WETSEB), IEEE (2018) 9–16.

15. Dannen, Chris. *Introducing Ethereum and Solidity*. Vol. 1. Berkeley, Apress (2017).

16. Destefanis, G., Marchesi, M., Ortu, M., Tonelli, R., Bracciali, A., Hierons, R.: Smart contracts vulnerabilities: A call for blockchain software engineering? In: *2018 International Workshop on Blockchain Oriented Software Engineering (IWBOSE)*, IEEE (2018) 19–25.

17. Hajdu, Á., Jovanović, D.: Solc-verify: A modular verifier for solidity smart contracts. arXiv preprint arXiv:1907.04262 (2019).

18. Curran, B.: The History of the coincheck Hack: One of the largest heists ever, https://blockonomi.com/coincheck-hack/, 21 December 2018.

19. Conti, M., Sandeep Kumar, E., Lal, C., Ruj, S.: A survey on security and privacy issues of bitcoin. *IEEE Communications Surveys Tutorials* 20(4) (2018) 3416–3452.

20. Das, L.: The most prominent crypto exchange hacks - all stocks network all-stocks.net/crypto-exchange-hacks/, 8 July 2019.

21. Lloyds: Bitcoin: Risk factors for insurance, www.lloyds.com/~/media/files/news-and-insight/risk-insight/2015/bitcoin--final.pdf, 11 August 2019.

22. ORourke, M.: Hackers hijack computers to mine cryptocurrency. *Risk Management* 65(3) (2018) 27.

23. Bos, J.W., Halderman, J.A., Heninger, N., Moore, J., Naehrig, M., Wustrow, E.: Elliptic curve cryptography in practice. In Christin, N., Safavi-Naini, R., eds.: *Financial Cryptography and Data Security*, Berlin, Germany, Springer Berlin Heidelberg (2014) 157–175.

24. Giechaskiel, I., Cremers, C., Rasmussen, K.B.: On bitcoin security in the presence of broken cryptographic primitives. In Askoxylakis, I., Ioannidis, S., Katsikas, S., Meadows, C., eds.: *Computer Security – ESORICS 2016*, Cham, Switzerland, Springer International Publishing (2016) 201–222.

25. Hoch, J.J., Shamir, A.: On the strength of the concatenated hash combiner when all the hash functions are weak. In Aceto, L., Damgård, I., Goldberg, L.A., Halldorsson, M.M., Ingólfsdóttir, A., Walukiewicz, I., eds.: *Automata, Languages and Programming*, Berlin, Germany, Springer Berlin Heidelberg (2008) 616–630.
26. Gauravaram, P., Kelsey, J., Knudsen, L.R., Thomsen, S.S.: On hash functions using checksums. *International Journal of Information Security* 9(2) (2010) 137–151.
27. Venkatraman, S., Alazab, M., Vinayakumar, R.: A hybrid deep learning image-based analysis for effective malware detection. *Journal of Information Security and Applications* 47 (2019) 377–389.
28. Vinayakumar, R., Alazab, M., Soman, K., Poornachandran, P., Venkatraman, S.: Robust intelligent malware detection using deep learning. *IEEE Access* 7 (2019) 46717–46738.
29. Wan, Z., Lo, D., Xia, X., Cai, L.: Bug characteristics in blockchain systems: A large-scale empirical study. In: *2017 IEEE/ACM 14th International Conference on Mining Software Repositories (MSR)* (2017) 413–424.
30. Ateniese, G., Faonio, A., Magri, B., de Medeiros, B.: Certified bitcoins. In Boure-anu, I., Owesarski, P., Vaudenay, S., eds.: *Applied Cryptography and Network Security*, Cham, Switzerland, Springer International Publishing (2014) 80–96.
31. Xu, J.J.: Are blockchains immune to all malicious attacks? *Financial Innovation* 2(1) (2016) 25.
32. Mechkaroska, D., Dimitrova, V., Popovska-Mitrovikj, A.: Analysis of the possibilities for improvement of blockchain technology. In: *2018 26th Telecommunications Forum (TELFOR)* (2018) 1–4.
33. Saad, M., Spaulding, J., Njilla, L., Kamhoua, C., Shetty, S., Nyang, D., Mohaisen, A.: Exploring the attack surface of blockchain: A systematic overview. arXiv preprint arXiv:1904.03487 (2019).
34. Li, X., Jiang, P., Chen, T., Luo, X., Wen, Q.: A survey on the security of blockchain systems. *Future Generation Computer Systems* 107 (2020) 841–853.
35. Fake bitcoins? https://bitcointalk.org/index.php?topic=36788.msg463391#msg463391, 11 August 2019.
36. Rosenfeld, M.: Analysis of bitcoin pooled mining reward systems. arXiv preprint arXiv:1112.4980 (2011).
37. Courtois, N.T., Bahack, L.: On subversive miner strategies and block withholding attack in bitcoin digital currency. arXiv preprint arXiv:1402.1718 (2014).
38. Bonneau, J., Felten, E.W., Goldfeder, S., Kroll, J.A., Narayanan, A.: Why buy when you can rent? In: *International Conference on Financial Cryptography and Data Security*, Springer (2016) 19–26.
39. Bahack, L.: Theoretical bitcoin attacks with less than half of the computational power (draft). arXiv preprint arXiv:1312.7013 (2013).
40. Sapirshtein, A., Sompolinsky, Y., Zohar, A.: Optimal selfish mining strategies in bitcoin. In Grossklags, J., Preneel, B., eds.: *Financial Cryptography and Data Security*, Berlin, Germany, Springer (2017).
41. Kwon, Y., Kim, D., Son, Y., Vasserman, E., Kim, Y.: Be selfish and avoid dilemmas: Fork after withholding (faw) attacks on bitcoin. In: *Proceedings of the 2017 ACM SIGSAC Conference on Computer and Communications Security.* CCS'17, New York (2017) 195–209.
42. Apostolaki, M., Zohar, A., Vanbever, L.: Hijacking bitcoin: Routing attacks on crypto-currencies. In: *2017 IEEE Symposium on Security and Privacy (SP)* (2017) 375–392.
43. Tschorsch, F., Scheuermann, B.: Bitcoin and beyond: A technical survey on decentralized digital currencies. *IEEE Communications Surveys Tutorials* 18(3) (2016) 2084–2123.
44. Atzei, N., Bartoletti, M., Cimoli, T.: A survey of attacks on ethereum smart contracts (sok). In Maffei, M., Ryan, M., eds.: *Principles of Security and Trust*, Berlin, Germany, Springer (2017).

45. Kayes, A., Han, J., Rahayu, W., Dillon, T., Islam, M.S., Colman, A.: A policy model and framework for context-aware access control to information resources. *The Computer Journal* 62(5) (2018) 670–705.
46. Kayes, A., Rahayu, W., Dillon, T.: Critical situation management utilizing iot-based data resources through dynamic contextual role modeling and activation. *Computing* 101(7) (2019) 743–772.
47. Kayes, A., Han, J., Colman, A., Islam, M.S.: Relboss: A relationship-aware access control framework for software services. In: *OTM Confederated International Conferences "On the Move to Meaningful Internet Systems."* Berlin, Heidelberg, Springer (2014) 258–276.
48. Kayes, A., Rahayu, W., Dillon, T., Chang, E., Han, J.: Context-aware access control with imprecise context characterization for cloud-based data resources. *Future Generation Computer Systems* 93 (2019) 237–255.
49. Sarda, P., Chowdhury, M.J.M., Colman, A., Kabir, M.A., Han, J.: Blockchain for fraud prevention: A work-history fraud prevention system. In: *Trust-Com/BigDataSE 2018*, IEEE (2018) 1858–1863.

2 A Comparative Study of Distributed Ledger Technologies
Blockchain vs. Hashgraph

Ariba Aslam Zahoor, Muhammad Mubashir Khan, and Junaid Arshad

CONTENTS

2.1 INTRODUCTION

Distributed ledger technologies (DLT) has gained significant attraction lately, as it is a state-of-the-art technology for distributed data storage, utilizing cutting-edge advancements in peer-to-peer networking and cryptography and has transformed the manner in which we store, process, and transfer digital assets. A *distributed ledger* is referred to as a digital ledger, which is different from traditional, centralized arrangements, primarily because the information is stored by all participants, the modifications are replicated to all the nodes in a network concurrently, and all transactions are verified by digital signatures to achieve non-repudiation and data integrity (Khan, Arshad, and Khan, 2019; Nizamuddin et al., 2019). Typically, DLTs represent decentralized databases, without the requirement for a central authority to authenticate and validate transactions. Blockchain technology is one such technology that provides a ledger of digital transactions that have been executed and validated by consensus of the majority of population (participants). It uses software, which processes on the order of the newly created and connected blocks via cryptographic means to ensure security and integrity. It has a verified record of each transaction that has been executed to date, which cannot be tampered with, thereby ensuring integrity of information. Although Bitcoin (Nakamoto, 2009) is the most popular application of blockchain, it has been used in diverse application domains such as healthcare, logistics, e-voting, and security, as highlighted by (Crosby, 2016; Khan, Arshad, and Khan, 2018; Nizamuddin et al., 2019). While Bitcoin enables fairness, integrity, and prevention from denial-of-service (DoS) attacks, it lacks efficiency with respect to transaction processing time (tps) as compared with credit cards and other online payment services. Hashgraph, another DLT, has emerged recently, which focuses on addressing this limitation, promising extraordinary improvement in tps (Schueffel, 2017). Although hashgraph was initially deployed in private settings, public deployment has been recently launched, enabling its adoption for wider application domains. Within this context, this chapter is focused on presenting a comparative study of these DLTs, identifying their individual strengths and weaknesses to highlight potential application domains.

The rest of the chapter is organized as follows. Section 2.1 presents an overview of the demand for DLTs and the potential of blockchain to influence cutting-edge technological developments. Section 2.2 introduces discussion of one of the important challenges within DLTs, i.e., consensus, followed by a discussion of gossip protocols and the challenge of consensus within this domain in Section 2.3. Section 2.4 introduces the performance evaluation of hashgraphs and their comparative evaluation with blockchain. Section 2.5 concludes this chapter, along with a description of potential future directions.

2.1.1 OVERVIEW

The digital economy currently relies on a particular third party on which they place their trust. Each transaction is based on the trusted authority's approval. For instance, the certification body ensures that digital certificates are reliable. The bank ensures that funds have been deposited in our account, and therefore, we depend and trust a third party to secure our digital possessions. However, these organizations could be hacked, or their data could be compromised. This is where blockchain can make an impact; i.e., it enables efficient verification of digital assets by consensus while ensuring security and privacy. Blockchain works anonymously and without the involvement of any third-party sources and has established a system where distributed consensus takes place for the digital environment. It ensures individuals that an event had taken place by adding that event in the public ledger, which becomes part of an immutable record. Owing to its significant popularity within the blockchain community, in this chapter, the term blockchain is used to represent the Bitcoin cryptocurrency system. Other DLT under consideration is hashgraph, which uses a protocol known as *gossiping* for its fundamental operation. A typical gossip protocol works by sending messages to different individuals in a system; if fair individuals attempt to match up, they will inevitably succeed in the event that they continue attempting to send messages, regardless of whether aggressors, who attempt to control the system; they will at last enable any two genuine individuals to convey. Gossip ensures that when one individual sends messages to another, the receiving individual will acknowledge the messages with a substantial mark and hashes. While hashgraph is also a DLT, which is fundamentally different from blockchain, the major differences are related to the information distribution and consensus formulation. Furthermore, as hashgraph is a directed acyclic graph – it does not require all nodes to know each event at all times.

2.1.2 BLOCKCHAIN

Bitcoin is a peer-to-peer electronic cash system, as proposed by Satoshi Nakamoto in 2009. It makes use of fundamental concepts within cryptography and peer-to-peer systems to achieve a distributed, decentralized, trustworthy infrastructure. In this context, a blockchain is a decentralized public ledger bearing records of transactions. This database is shared with the community; however, no one has the authority to control it, and only the miners can update records *by consensus*. If two users want to initiate a transaction, both of them must have a private key and a public key in order to have a digital signature, which is secure, agile, and yields a solid control of possession. Bearing a digital signature just plays the authentication part in the network, whereas the authorization is done by approving transactions that took place. A typical blockchain network is illustrated in Figure 2.1. As blockchain works as a distributed network, when someone wants to transact some Bitcoins, they have to broadcast the data, i.e., their public key, the public key of the receiver, and the amount transferred to the network. The details transferred to the network have to be verified by other nodes in the network (MacDonald, Allen, and Potts, 2016). A transaction is referred to as a transfer of amount between two individuals bearing Bitcoin wallets. These wallets have private keys that are used to digitally sign the transactions and act as proof that it belongs to the wallet's owner. After the issuance of a transaction, the digital signature helps to avoid any kind of alteration. Transactions, once broadcasted to the network, get confirmed in typically 10–20 minutes. After the verification of the transaction and labeling it to be a truthful transaction, it needs to be added to the blockchain as a newly created block. These blocks, which have been added to the chain, are labeled as confirmed, whereas the unconfirmed blocks, whose verification has been done but they have not yet been linked with the blockchain, are periodically broadcasted to the network (Garay, Kiayias, and Leonardos, 2015). The transactions residing in a block are considered to have occurred at almost the same time.

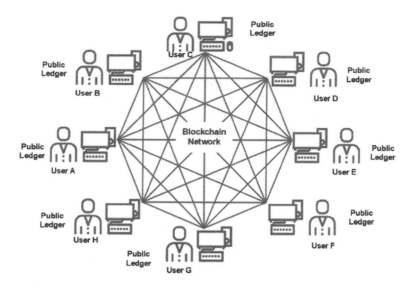

FIGURE 2.1   A typical blockchain network.

A block added to the blockchain has a link to the previous block, which forms an interlinked chain connected in a way that their order cannot be disturbed. A block comprises a digital signature, timestamp, and details of the transaction. Bitcoins are also divided into further units called *satoshis*. They have to be distinctive to have worth. For this, the miners in a network establish and update track of transactions for every Bitcoin ever used by solving extensive mathematical problems known as *proof of work*. The mining for Bitcoin software can be installed on any computer and typically requires a considerable amount of computing power to derive the calculations necessary for the transactions. Mining is done to establish consensus for approving pending transactions and adding them to the blockchain. The history of transaction is set in the chronological order to the first block ever mined. In order for the transactions to be confirmed, they have to be placed in a block; the built-in rules are there to verify the transactions placed, to prevent old blocks being modified or any other fraudulent activity, because by tampering any block, all the successive blocks will become invalid. Mining also prevents a member or a specific group from adding blocks easily without the consent of the majority of the population (Antonopoulos, n.d.). However, the process of verifying transactions could be personalized for any blockchain. Incentives and rules could be established or modified for the system's agility.

One of the most prominent characteristics of blockchain is that it is anonymous; i.e., transactions held between two parties are anonymous in such a way that neither the sender nor the receiver knows who the person at the other end is. Also, the transactions cannot be tracked back to any person, because the blockchain does not keep details of users or accounts, and hence, it preserves comprehensive segregation between the transaction performed and the identity of the user. Instead of the trace, if the user has ample number of Bitcoins to execute a transaction, blockchain uses referencing. When a user is sending Bitcoins to another user, it is called *output*, whereas the received amount is called *input*. Therefore, when a transaction takes place, blockchain refers to the inputs to validate if the user has enough amount received earlier. In order to avoid double spending, input needs to reference only once before it is tagged as spent.

2.2   DECENTRALIZED DISTRIBUTED SYSTEMS

A typical decentralized system is distributed, whereby multiple nodes are involved in the process of decision making; i.e., a transaction is not committed by a single machine, which prevents a single point of failure. Any decision (transaction commit) is made by individual nodes, and collectively, the system response is the aggregate of results of the participating nodes. However, a distributed system can also be centralized, as is the case with traditional systems such as grid and cloud computing, where various nodes share the processing of data, whereas the decision (commit) is centralized (Dolev and Strong, 1983). The major difference between the two is where and how the decision is made and the information is shared. A significant property is that no particular node will have comprehensive system information (Steen and Tanenbaum, 2007).

A technology that enables a system of nodes to manage and register transactions independently within a decentralized distributed system is called distributed ledger technology (DLT) (Wadsworth, 2018). It is considered a ledger of transactions retained in a decentralized form, which removes the involvement of any central body. Owing to the decentralized nature of the underlying system, *consensus* (agreement among nodes about adding transactions to blockchain) is fundamental to desired operation of such technologies. In this regard, DLTs such as blockchain and hashgraph use different algorithms to achieve consensus in a timely and efficient manner.

Blockchain, a DLT, conserves a stable record of transaction data, without manipulation. It works similar to the old manual ledgers used in earlier days, which had handwritten list of entries. A copy of the ledger is preserved on each node involved in the system to eliminate single point of failure, whereas the ledger keeps on updating the copies concurrently. In terms of consensus algorithm used, Bitcoin (a prominent example of blockchain) uses proof of work (Mingxiao et al., 2017) to achieve consensus, which also forms the basis of mining within this technology. Blockchain is being used for almost a decade now and has evolved continuously, particularly with respect to enhancing the security as well as scalability of the network operation.

Hashgraph uses gossip protocol to disseminate information and consensus algorithms to execute decentralized applications fast, securely, and fairly. It does not need proof of work to achieve consensus, like in blockchain technology. It is a consensus-achieving platform that is implemented in a private setting. It does not require the compute-intensive proof of work; instead, virtual voting is being performed to achieve consensus. It works on two techniques: gossip about gossip and virtual voting. Each node disseminates information by creating events on new transactions. They choose random nodes to spread whatever they know. The receiving nodes cumulate the events and create a new event out of it, which sends to other nodes (Leitão, Pereira, and Rodrigues, 2010). This process lasts until every other node in the network learns the information. Each node retains a graph of sender and witness nodes for all transactions. Finally, virtual voting takes place, and all nodes in the network decide if a particular transaction is valid, if it has been witnessed by more than two-third nodes. In hashgraph, convergence takes place pretty fast, due to which it is faster than the blockchain, handling more than 250,000 tps (Schueffel, 2017). It is Byzantine fault-tolerant and has complete certainty on the order of the events.

2.2.1 Significance of Consensus for Decentralized Distributed Systems

Decentralized distributed systems have substantial advantages in constructing a robust structure; however, consensus plays a profound role in attaining a final decision and therefore is significant for the correct operation of such systems. When a new transaction is broadcasted to the network, nodes decide whether to include that transaction to their copy of ledger or not. When the majority of the nodes reach on a single state, the consensus is attained. Achievement of the overall system reliability is one of the major problems in distributed computing, keeping in mind that a number of faulty processes are present, which often needs processes to settle on some data value that is required during computation (Coccoli, Bondavalli, and Simoncini, 2000). These processes are termed consensus, and they are the ones giving answers to the questions arising in case of a conflict, such as: *What happens when a node decides to not abide by the rules and to tamper with the state of the ledger? What happens when these nodes are a large part of the network, but not the majority?*

A malicious or malfunctioning element may demonstrate a sort of behavior that often goes unnoticed, sending contradictory data to parts of the system. The issue of handling this kind of failure is theoretically referred to as the Byzantine Generals Problem (Lamport, Shostak, and Pease, 1982). Before moving on to the Byzantine Generals Problem, let's first have a look at the Two Generals Problem published in 1975, which illustrates a scenario where two generals are attacking a common enemy. Suppose General 1 is the leader and the other followers. They will earn success only if they have a coordinated attack; thus, they need to cooperate and attack at the same time. In order to communicate and decide on a time, General 1 has to send a message to General 2. There are multiple possibilities that the message will not be delivered to General 2 or the messenger might get captured or killed. That will result in General 1 attacking, while General 2 retreats. Suppose if the General 2 receives the message, General 1 would still be unsure if General 2 has received the message or not; further, if General 1 received the acknowledgment, General 2 would be uncertain if General 1 has received the acknowledgment or not, and it goes on. Therefore, the agreement is not achieved, and it is proven to be unsolvable.

A comprehensive form of the Two Generals Problem is presented by (Lamport, Shostak, and Pease, 1982), which focuses on the same scenario as stated earlier, but instead of two generals, this problem works with more than two generals. In order to maintain the integrity of a particular system, not more than 33% of the total network population should be untrustworthy, which is referred to as the Byzantine Generals

Problem, to ensure that the Byzantine fault tolerance (BFT) is defined, which specifies the robustness of a system. Therefore, it sums up that the algorithm can reach consensus as long as the untrustworthy nodes are not more than one-third, and two-thirds of the members must be honest. The Byzantine Generals Problem can be put in a nutshell as how can we make sure that multiple entities, which are far apart from each other, are in full agreement (consensus) before an action is taken?

For instance, assuming there is a general in the Byzantine army who is planning an attack over an enemy city that is surrounded by several other lieutenants led by their own generals. The lieutenants are far apart in the distance from each other, and they need to have a coordinated attack in order to achieve success, as an uncoordinated attack will likely end in defeat. The general has decided to attack at dawn, but they need to be certain that all generals reach on the consensus and all attack at dawn. If they send messages to other generals through messengers, it might be possible that the messenger is captured and the message gets intercepted, or the enemy sends a fake reply, or the messenger gets killed and no reply is received, or the other side confirms to attack at dawn but they turn out to be untrustworthy. *How can the generals ever be certain that all lieutenants will reach consensus and attack concurrently?* If we map the explained example on computer systems, the lieutenants would be computers on a network and the generals would be computer programs running ledgers, which record transactions and events in the exact order that they happened, and they all are absolutely same for everyone, such that as soon as a change occurs on one of the copies of the ledger, all others are synchronized with it. In this way, consensus is achieved on an event, without the requirement of any third party as an intermediary for trust.

When the order of transactions is being calculated, there comes a time when consensus is reached ultimately, which is referred to as the *BFT*. It basically means:

We are going to come to consensus;
We will know when we've come to consensus; and
We're never wrong

It is mathematically assured that all other individuals will reach the same consensus. The BFT has two main categories: asynchronous byzantine (aBFT) and partially asynchronous byzantine. The difference is the level of system's presumptions. An aBFT assumes the practical scenario; that is, untrustworthy nodes are always present in the systems. Conversely, partial asynchronous BFT works on a false approach or an ideal-world assumption that evil characters don't exist in any system.

2.3 GOSSIP PROTOCOL – BUILDING BLOCK OF HASHGRAPH

Gossip in real life implies spreading information/rumor. It could be referred to as epidemics, because epidemic diseases are spread by infecting some people and from them to the others. The expression epidemic protocol is usually used as an alternate term for a gossip protocol, as it spreads data in a manner similar to the spread of an infection in a natural network (Demers et al., 1987). Similarly, in a distributed system, information disseminates by a member randomly choosing another one and sharing the information it knows. For wide-scaled distributed systems, gossip protocols were introduced for spreading information in a reliable way. However, the alluring properties help it to be used in a lot of different environments (Voulgaris, Jelasity, and Steen, 2003). The simplicity and flexibility in gossiping enhance its horizon to data aggregation and resource allocation. It could be explained in two phases: first is the random selection of a peer to send information, while the other is the repetition of sending data to different peers. Figure 2.2 illustrates the gossip simulation, with 40 nodes in total disseminating information to others and number of rounds it takes to complete (Gossip Protocols Simulator, n.d.). The gossip fan-out controls how many nodes we gossip with, considering the fan-out nodes as constant in the following example. Table 2.1 depicts the scalability characteristic of gossip protocol.

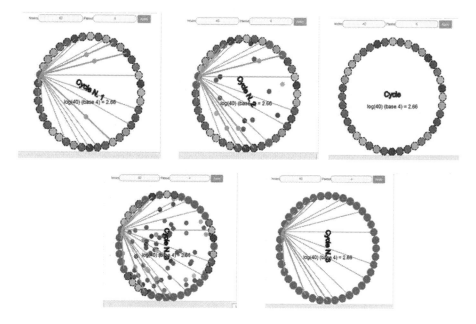

FIGURE 2.2   Sample simulation of the gossip protocol.

TABLE 2.1
The Scalability Characteristic of the Gossip Protocol

Nodes	Number of Cycles
10	2
20	3
40	4
80	5
200	6
500	7
1000	7

Gossiping can be classified into four different methods for implementation:

1. *Eager push methods*: Whenever the nodes receive messages, they send them quickly to randomly selected nodes.
2. *Pull methods*: Nodes enquire about recent messages from other randomly selected nodes. On receiving information about any such message that hasn't been received earlier, a request is sent for the new message.
3. *Lazy push methods*: Nodes on receiving any new message, gossips just the message identifier (i.e., hash of the message) to the other nodes. If the received identifier's message is required by some node it then sends a pull request.
4. *Hybrid methods*: Gossip is performed in two separate phases. A push message is used in the first phase to spread a message in the finest possible way. The second phase of pull gossip is used to recover from the errors produced in the first phase.

Eager push strategies achieve lower latency but generate more redundant traffic than pull strategies, as pull strategies have to go through two rounds in order to complete the process. Lazy push and pull gossip is somewhat similar, as both require two phases to complete message delivery. The difference is in the dissemination process: in lazy push, sender initiates it, whereas in pull gossip, receiver starts the process. In pull and lazy push gossip, copies of delivered messages are to be maintained for retransmission, if required, but in eager push gossip, retention is not needed. Therefore, it can be concluded that lazy push and pull gossip is more demanding, owing to the memory usage requirement.

2.3.1 Using Gossip Protocol to Achieve Consensus for Hashgraph

By analyzing hashgraphs, we identified some of the inherent assumptions that are made; i.e., gossip protocol is absolutely asynchronous, and any assumption about the progress rate or speed or the timeouts is not mentioned. It is presumed to make sure that when one node sends events to another, the receiving node will accept only the events with a valid signature and hashes. Every node is equal in the network, and honest nodes will eventually learn about the events that the other set of nodes know. The amount of time required cannot be anticipated (Gupta, Kermarrec, and Ganesh, 2006). The confirmation indicates the Byzantine assembly when more than $2^{n/3}$ of the nodes are straightforward; however, in order to achieve consensus, not more than one-third of the nodes could be dishonest in the network. Gossip protocol assumed that if honest members try to sync, they will eventually succeed if they keep on trying to send messages, even if attackers who try to control the network will ultimately allow any two honest members to communicate. The protocol makes sure that when one node sends events to another, the receiving node will only accept the events with a valid signature and hashes. Neither the signatures can be forged, nor the signed messages can be tempered. Even if they do, they are detected because cryptographic hashes and digital signatures ought to be secure. Consensus could be accomplished, regardless of whether malignant characters can control the system and erase or moderate down messages based on their personal preference. The main presumptions made are that more than two-thirds are following the convention effectively and that if messages are sent more than once, starting with one node, then onto the next over the web, inevitably, one will get past, and afterward, in the end, another will, and the decision will be labeled as fair when each and every transaction reaches a majority of the network (Eugster et al., 2004).

2.3.1.1 Gossip Protocol to Achieve Consensus for Decentralized Distributed Systems

A typical DLT runs a gossip protocol, meaning that each member repeatedly calls on others to synchronize with them. In this way, information is spread by each node recurrently picking another node arbitrarily and sending them whatever they have learned. We will discuss one of the DLTs, i.e., hashgraph. In this algorithm, each member creates an event, which is a small data structure containing timestamp (when he created the event), transactions, and hashes of the last two recent events, and is digitally signed by the creator. The motive of the underlined algorithm is to achieve consensus on the order of the events and the agreed timestamp for each of them. Suppose four nodes are present in system: A, B, C, D. B randomly chooses to call D and send all the events he knew that D doesn't know. Let's consider it to be the start of a gossip. Therefore, B only had one event initially. D therefore records the call in a new event, which comprises a timestamp, transaction, and hashes of the two events below itself (one is labeled as the self-parent and the second is the other parent). D then sends all his events to A, and A in return creates a new event recording, including the hashes of the latest event by himself and by D. After that, A sends all his events to C; consequently, C creates a new event, and this graph keeps on increasing. As it is connected by cryptographic hashes, it is labeled as hashgraph. Gossiping a hashgraph gives the nodes ample details; therefore, whenever a new transaction is added, it rapidly spreads to all other nodes. However, as the hashgraph grows, it might be possible at some point in time that some nodes have marginally different data of the newly created events, but they will converge quickly to sync with each other (Schueffel, 2017).

Consensus achievement is yet another process that makes use of virtual voting; i.e., each node of the network has a duplicate of the hashgraph. Therefore, nodes will compute for themselves what poll certain other nodes would have sent in case an agreement protocol is running by simply consulting the hashgraph (Allavena, 2006). So, consensus is achieved without using any bandwidth. This also helps in the integrity of the protocol, as the nodes will calculate the votes abiding with the rules. Even if a malicious node tries to attack, he could not post votes for the other nodes to calculate, because all of the nodes are calculating for themselves, assuming the virtual votes casted by the virtual version of the members.

In order to calculate the order of the occurred events, node A will conduct elections several times for itself, in which some of the events in A will be casting a vote and others will be polling in different elections. If it was node D's event, node A would calculate the votes of D, but node D itself would not be involved in the process. Node A would be performing these calculations locally, considering D to be virtually sending votes. As in other ledger technologies such as blockchain, hash-graph also has forking attacks; that is, if a malicious node creates an event x considering the self-parent to be ancestor z after which it creates another event and again gives the self-parent hash of z instead of x, then the node has created by forking. In order to avoid such attacks, hashgraph makes use of two major concepts: a state seeing another state and a state strongly seeing another. The yellow event is seeing the red event, which means that it has an entirely downward path to the red event; however, in order to strongly see another event, multiple directed paths should be there, passing through enough members. Figure 2.3 depicts that the yellow event can strongly see five nodes in the network; so, in order to achieve the supermajority, four of them should strongly see the bottom event; i.e., four will be greater than $2^{n/3}$. Thus, if an attacker tries to violate the hashgraph by forking, it won't be able to violate the consensus process.

Hashgraph works in the following manner: there are four nodes in a network: A, B, C, and D. To start a gossip, B randomly chooses to gossip with D. Therefore, B sent all his events that D did not know. After this, D creates another event and records his events along with the ones that B has shared; this signifies that the sync between the two took place. The new event is connected directly to D's previous event and B's last event, developing a graph of the order in which the nodes communicated. An event comprises of two hashes, self-parent and the other-parent, which means transactions and timestamp on which the event has been created. The node digitally signs the event it created before sending it. Node D sends all his events to A, and as a result, A creates an event recording the sync. A then gossips to C and sends all his events. C creates a fresh event recording the events, and this goes on until the information is disseminated in the whole network. Each event has the hashes of the events before it, and all are digitally signed by their creator. Therefore, it is said to be cryptographically secure. The round created for an event is N or N + 1, where N is the maximum of its parents-created rounds. The first event of each round is called a witness, but it's not necessary for each node to have a witness. Further, after determining the witness, we need to find out the famous witness. It is defined by considering the next round's witnesses. A node is said to be famous if the majority of the witnesses are seeing it in the next round. After their consent, an election is conducted, the result of which will specify if the witnesses are famous. The witness can see a specific event if it

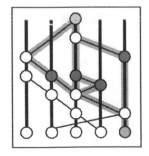

FIGURE 2.3   Sample hashgraph.

has a direct downward link from it. For example, we mark all events in each round by their round number D1, D2, D3, etc. If we want to check whether D2 is famous or not, we will see round 3 participants to check for D2's status. Let's check if in round 3 all the four nodes have a direct link to D2 – if all the nodes or the supermajority votes 'YES', the node is referred to as famous.

However, the votes are being counted by the nodes in the next round; for instance, here, in order to check if D2 is famous, B4 (it could be any other node as well) from the fourth round will collect the votes from each witness of the third round that it can see strongly. Strongly seeing a witness means there need to be multiple different downward links to the witness crossing through the supermajority of the nodes. Any constant that is more than 2/3 of the total nodes will be supermajority. If B4 can strongly see C3, it means that it has multiple direct links to C3, which passes from the majority of the nodes. In this case, more than 2/3 will be 3; therefore, if the links are passing through three of the four nodes to reach C3, then it is said to be strongly seen by B4 and hence it will collect C3's vote. In this way, B4 will also check for all other nodes, which are A3, B3, and D3, and whoever it could strongly see, it collects its vote. After collecting all the votes, if the supermajority of the network nodes has voted YES, then D2 is declared to be famous. Rounds are described as, if an event can strongly see supermajority witnesses from its own round, then that event is shifted to the next round. This voting will keep on going until a decision is made from the elections held. If it gets to the ninth round and still the decision is not made, then the tenth round is called the coin round, in which the supermajority and non-supermajority vote by selecting a middle bit of its signature as the vote.

Distributed consensus has been used since very long, but the hashgraph along with the consensus algorithm by Leemon Baird offered a new platform for it. The distributed consensus algorithm is said to permit a population to reach an agreement on transactional order generated by individuals from the community, keeping in mind that nobody trusts any individual; it turns out to be a system of developing trust. Any individual in a network cannot temper with the order of the transactions in a hashgraph. For instance, both A and B are buying the only headphones that were available at an online store at the same time. If we consider this scenario in blockchain, both the transactions could be placed in a single block by the miner, who has the entire authority to choose the order in which the transactions occur. In another case, A's transaction might get included in the block, and B's might get delayed. In the same scenario when plotted in hashgraph, no one can disturb the consensus order of transactions. Another way to justify the fairness of hashgraph is that none of the nodes have the authority to not let transactions enter the network or to delay them. Whereas in blockchain, the transactions can only be delayed by two or less mining periods. In hashgraph, manipulators cannot stop anyone to record a transaction; the only way that one can do that is by disconnecting the user from the network. Therefore, hashgraph is considered to be fair.

In hashgraph, speed depends on the bandwidth. The number of transactions an individual can download per second is the number of transactions a system can bear. If every individual has sufficient bandwidth for downloading 4500 tps, then it appears to be fast enough to grasp the whole transaction volume of VISA. Whereas the Bitcoin can handle 7 tps, which are very less as compared with hashgraph. Improving the speed may worsen the fairness of blockchain. The property of hashgraph, being provable, is as important as others. When an event takes place in a network, all other individuals in the network come to know quickly about its existence and the order where it needs to be placed. Every individual in the network is certain that all others know about the event. Therefore, if we consider it in a cryptocurrency, every individual just has to save the present balance of all wallets that are not void. Any transactions or blocks are not to be remembered, which makes the current size of Bitcoin storage from 60 gigabytes to barely some gigabytes.

The BFT is a property of hashgraph that makes it superior. An individual cannot stop a system from attaining consensus, neither they have the ability to change the consensus. There is a point in time when we reach consensus and we know that we have reached, and every other individual will have the same consensus. Whereas in blockchain, Byzantine is not guaranteed, as an individual is never certain that they have reached consensus. It is also considered to reach Byzantine agreement, because it is unable to handle network barriers. Miners getting isolated from the network give birth to forking, because multiple chains are created.

Hashgraph is being used as a distributed database and hence is Atomicity, Consistency, Isolation, Durability (ACID) compliant. Individuals in a network make use of this property to reach an agreement on the order of transactions. After consensus is attained, every individual inputs the transactions to its local copy of the DB by order of consensus. If the local DB is ACID compliant, then the entire system will have the same characteristics. Whereas in blockchain, there is no point in time when we are certain that consensus has been achieved. In order to attain ACID compliance as hashgraph, six confirmations could be considered as certain.

Efficiency in the blockchain is not 100%, as the block that has been mined may at times be marked as stale; therefore, the mining gets wasted. Whereas in hashgraph, there's no concept of stale; hence, it is considered to be 100% efficient. In Bitcoin, a lot of time, effort, and power are wasted in calculations (proof of work), which also have to make the speed of mining blocks slower. Expensive hardware needs to be used in order to drive the mining. Whereas in hashgraph, no such mechanism is used; therefore, it is inexpensive.

In hashgraph, each individual is assigned a time for consensus, and it is the average time at which every individual first received it. Hence, it is said to be timestamped. The timestamp is said to be honest and reliable automatically if the supermajority population is truthful and their clocks are trustworthy. It is considered to be a part of consensus; therefore, it assures to be Byzantine and provable. The timestamp is beneficial for smart contracts, as the consensus will be on if the event occurred in a given time. Whereas in blockchain, every block has a timestamp, but it only redirects to the miner's clock who mined the block.

The DoS resistance is found in both hashgraph and blockchain. An enemy might cease a miner's bandwidth by sending packets and cut them off from the rest of the network for a while, but the network keeps on working normally. If an enemy needs to attack the entire network, then it will require him to send unwanted packets to a larger population. A lot of blockchain variants have been suggested to evade proof of work. Nonetheless, they are not DOS resilient. If the current leader is being attacked by an intruder and he quickly attacks the new leader, the whole system will be halted in this way. Whereas, hashgraph without using proof of work prevents this issue from occurring.

Hashgraph comprises the above-mentioned characteristics, since it acts as a tree that is interweaved together to form a single shade and doesn't need to be trimmed. In hashgraph as well as blockchain, an individual can initiate a transaction that is placed in a container and gets disseminated in the network. In blockchain, the containers are implied to construct a long chain, whereas in the case that more than one miner construct multiple blocks, one of them will be selected by the network and others will be discarded. It also acts as a tree, but it needs to be pruned every now and then.

In hashgraph, nothing is discarded; therefore, all the branches always exist in the system and ultimately breed together into a whole, which sounds efficient than the blockchain. Blockchain does not succeed if fresh block arrives excessively fast, since the fresh branches would be growing speedily than they could be trimmed; therefore, proof of work is required in order to slow the process. However, hashgraph doesn't need to slow down any process. Each individual can initiate transactions at whichever time they feel like and at any speed.

2.3.2 SHORTCOMINGS OF GOSSIP PROTOCOL IN HASHGRAPH

Gossip protocol has two essential parameters referred to as fan-out and maximum rounds.

2.3.2.1 Fan-out

It is the term used for the number of gossip targets randomly nominated by a member in a network for a certain instance. It is one of the most important parameters on which latency of message dissemination is based. Large fan-out values assure higher fault tolerance with the cost of increased redundant network traffic. In the design of the gossip protocol, it is a critical parameter that can guarantee a more liable performance.

2.3.2.2 Maximum Rounds

The value of maximum rounds is defined as the number of times a gossip message is retransmitted. The value starts with zero and is increased at each gossip retransmission. It will be retransmitted till the value of its rounds be smaller than the value of maximum rounds. Based on the maximum round parameter, the gossip protocol can work in two different modes: one in which there is no threshold to the number of retransmissions of a message, whereas in the other, maximum round value is set to any number greater than zero. It basically limits the maximum retransmission of gossip messages. The rate at which new events enter the system can be raised up to a certain level, after which it needs to be reduced in order prevent the system from exhausting.

2.3.2.3 Built-in Redundancy of the Protocol

Where redundancy makes gossip protocol innately fault-tolerant and robust, it also creates needless transmission overheads. It produces more system traffic, which may drain the system capacity, making it difficult to communicate. Gossip protocols are less proficient in some instances than different methodologies that depend on a type of organized overlay to spread data (Leitão, Pereira, and Rodrigues, 2010). Since messages have a fixed maximum size, therefore, if the size of information increases from the threshold, then the fan-out value will decline, since the nodes will no more be able to share the complete information within the designated rounds. It could be concluded that a gradually growing rate of events exhausts the volume of the channel, and it may create glitches. This could depend on a lot of factors such as the rate at which events input, fan-out, message size, etc. The nature of the gossip protocol also has an effect; aggregation might be resistant to it, but dissemination of events will have a close impact (Birman, 2007).

2.3.2.4 High Latency of Message Delivery

Arbitrary delay increment impacts the latency of gossip dissemination. The rate by which the data is entering the system has a significant impact on the dissemination delays. If the rate surpasses the threshold of gossip, then there must be high latency of message delivery. If latencies jump unboundedly, even a slight increase in the message rate is enough to overflow buffers and at times overloads the system itself (Alvisi et al., 2007).

2.3.2.5 Message Exchange Is Done Periodically

Slow periodic exchange extremely creates abound to the data bandwidth of the protocol. In this way, the available capacity for the new events will be narrowed, as the carrying capacity will be bounded. Let's say that a certain number of messages entered the system and stayed for about $O(\log(n))$ time. In the meantime, it keeps on passing information to other nodes. Therefore, the meantime at which new gossip can be disseminated in the system will be the inverse of the stayed time, i.e., $1/\log(n)$. So, a fairly low rate of gossip turns out to be a hindrance. Speeding up the dissemination of data by reducing the periodicity will benefit but at the price of overloading the entire event dissemination system, which in return can cause the protocol to behave adversely due to high resource contention, voiding the features of gossip. Delays related to the periodicity of gossip rounds guarantee that it makes no difference – even if we run the gossip protocol fast enough, it will not be able to perform constructively until latency and reliable multicasting is compared (Birman, 2007).

2.3.3 Reflective Insight into the Limitations and Advantages

Blockchain can process 3–7 tps, which is way slower than the other TPNs such as VISA, which processes 56,000 tps, or Hyperledger, which processes 10,000 tps, creating scalability issues. In order to attain productivity, blockchain takes a lot of time to complete one block of transactions nearly 10 minutes in a Bitcoin system. Security is the major goal, as double-spending problems do occur in the network; each transaction needs to be verified to make sure the inputs are unique (Conti et al., 2018). The throughput is significantly low as compared with other systems. If it grows at some point in time, let's say, equivalent to VISA, then the size of the blockchain will proportionally grow, which is 197 GB as of 2019 for Bitcoin and 180 GB for Ethereum (Yli-Huumo et al., 2016). The issue of storage surfaces will be growing on daily basis. Hence, personal computers or storage devices won't be able to afford it. Blockchain has a drawback of a 51% attack. It is defined as an individual having complete control of the majority of the hash power, and it can temper the blockchain. This issue is more common among the chains having a smaller number of nodes. Massive amounts of energy are wasted in the mining process; however, an incentive is given to the miners for now, but as the Bitcoins are increasing, the amount will be decreasing, and there will come a time when there will be no more incentives given to miners. Further, regulatory jurisdiction in the financial sector is also a challenge for the implementation of blockchain. Considering the fact that blockchain incentivizes by giving away Bitcoins as rewards to the miners, which prevents them from manipulation, in hashgraph, no such perks are there, so it could be a podium for malevolent activities (Androulaki and Karame, 2014).

Blockchain allows sharing of computing power, and thus, an extensive range of computers could contribute to the network. As compared with the private computing power like Amazon maintains, Ethereum lets a wide variety of computers to take part in their network, all they need to do is install the software. It could help in the reduction of risks; that is, when a large number of nodes are involved in the system, it will be difficult to bring the network down by any means of malicious action. As the blockchain is a distributed ledger, everyone has a copy of the data and is easily accessible; therefore, any change or update of records is seen by every node claiming the transparency of the protocol. The documentation of transactions can be updated only by consensus of majority of nodes, and once it is approved, it is encrypted, and the chain is updated with the new record. Therefore, it is not possible for a single individual to alter the contents. As all transactions are recorded for lifetime, the audit trail could be seen to learn the origin of a particular asset, ensuring the auditability and traceability. The copy of the ledger being distributed to many nodes and synchronized by consensus develops trust and belief that the transactions are real. This helps a large range of transactions that otherwise won't be possible.

Hashgraph is fast, as it uses the gossip protocol to spread messages to the network and also performs some optimization of the gossiped messages to reduce the communication overhead. The gossip-about-gossip also yields a consensus protocol. However, there is another reason why Hashgraph is fast: it currently works in a permissioned setting. Even if a malicious node tries to shoot a malicious timestamp, other members that received the gossip generate the true time by consensus. Hashgraph is an asynchronous BFT system and is non-deterministic. It is ACID compliant; i.e., it ensures atomicity, consistency, isolation, and durability. In hashgraph, nodes use it to attain consensus on transactions, after which the transactions are updated to the local copies of the nodes. Whereas in blockchain, we cannot assure at any point in time that consensus has been reached. Hashgraph is distributed denial-of-service (DDOS) resilient; i.e., an attacker might overflow an individual with data in order to exhaust its power, but the network will be running as if nothing has happened.

Both blockchain and hashgraph allow any node to conduct transactions and to be placed in a container, after which they will be disseminated in the network. In blockchain, these blocks (container) ought to form an extended chain. If two or more nodes generate multiple blocks simultaneously, then the network nodes will perform consensus to select one and dispose the others. A blockchain is like a tree that is continuously pruned as it grows – this pruning is necessary to keep the branches of blocks from growing out of control and to ensure the ledger consists of just one chain of blocks. However, in hashgraph, each of the containers is utilized and nothing is disposed of. All branches of the tree exist, and they grow back together into a single piece. Thus, we find it more efficient. In blockchain, if the new container is initiated fast, it won't be able to process, as the branches of a tree grow faster than they could be trimmed. For this purpose, proof of work slows down the growth process. In hashgraph, no pruning is required, and it doesn't matter how fast the branches are growing. The transaction could be created and placed; therefore, it ensures more potential mathematical proof, ie, Byzantine and fairness. The hashgraph algorithm ensures fairness, Byzantine, ACID compliance, efficiency, inexpensiveness, fast, and DoS resilience.

2.4 PERFORMANCE EVALUATION

We have worked on both technologies in order to evaluate certain parameters that provide a comparison between the performance characteristics. Our main technical insight is to investigate core parameters behind blockchain and hashgraph in private and public settings in order to analyze the two different DLTs. We analyzed both technologies against major performance parameters, including the identification of latency, throughput, propagation time, and size. We opt for a quantitative approach analyzing the parameters with respect to both technologies, involving random selection and making statistical inferences. The analysis was done on different platforms, as both technologies work in different settings. For blockchain, we calculated the latency, throughput, propagation time, and size of the chain in different scenarios and different sizes of chains. Hashgraph is patented and runs in a private setting, and thus, we had limited scenarios to work on.

Latency in processing transactions is a major characteristic that differs blockchain from hashgraph. Latency turns out to be the leading factor in increasing the overall time for completing a task. In blockchain, the time required to process a block is at least 10 minutes, whereas considering the wise transaction calculation, it processes only 3 to 7 tps even if more new transactions enter the system.

The proof of work is continuously becoming more complex with the passage of time and hence results in more time consumption. Bitcoin has a major problem of throughput, as it can process 7 tps, which is slower than the VISA network, which processes 2,000 to 10,000 tps. It is claimed that the throughput may be increased at the cost of increasing the size of each block, which may, in turn, induce security risk by declining actual honest hash power. In blockchain, the longest chain is always known as the main chain, and successful blocks are attached over it. Therefore, if the malicious member has to pay someone, he might mine a malicious chain not including the legitimate payment transaction in it, and the community will be tricked to consider it as the main chain, thereby deleting the transaction from the ledger. However, practically, it is extremely challenging for an attacker to successfully create such a scenario.

The block size closely relates to the propagation time required by a fresh block to be visible to all the network population. Currently, the block size is 1 MB, and it takes 12.6 seconds on average for a node to see the fresh block. Amid this time, in most cases, a node broadcasts its freshly created node to the network, whereas another node, irrespective of the distance, also broadcasts its fresh block. Ultimately, one of the two blocks has to get dropped, because only one chain will be longest. However, the stale block (the one that has been dropped) might have verified some legitimate transactions. Therefore, in small blocks, the number of transactions dropped will be much lower than the larger blocks.

Dropping the blocks in order to continue with the longest chain is called chain reorganization. Moreover, in mining a large stale block, the hash rate consumed will be greater than the smaller ones, which increases the incompetence of the network. In a slightly different aspect, the hash rate involved in mining large blocks, taking a greater propagation time, is not being used for the security of the network; instead, more of the legitimate transactions are getting dropped, resulting in inefficiencies. Furthermore, if we try to increase the block size by decreasing the time to mine the block, in order to achieve an enhanced throughput, the chain will no longer be significant, as it might start to propagate on stale blocks. Propagation time needs to be small as compared with the mining time, because reducing the mining time reduces security. For example, if we decrease the mining time to a second and as defined previously, the propagation time will roughly be 12 seconds, then the nodes will start to mine upon the stale blocks, as the new blocks will still not be visible, wasting the hash rate of the system. It will also be expensive to function the complete nodes if the blocks will be large, as this affects the number of hashes operating complete nodes.

Collectively, it affects the decentralized nature of the Bitcoin with powerful mining pools operated by the attacker, hence increasing the chances of 51% attack.

Double spending is a major security issue. The main reason could be that if the mining entities get hold of the majority of the transaction recording in the blockchain and double spend the Bitcoins into their own wallets, masquerading could be done to make users resend transactions.

The size of Bitcoin blockchain is 197 GB. As of 2019, it grew by 49 GB in the previous year, and it keeps on growing at a greater pace each year. This is known as blockchain bloat. The solution that instantly comes to mind is to make the blockchain smaller, but that's in order to accommodate the conventional use of blockchain; it has to be big instead. This gives rise to centralization, because it would be difficult to accommodate such a huge amount of data with decreasing number of the servers running full nodes globally. Although in this age of big data, where tetra bytes of data have become the standard and solutions are pouring in to handle that, why can't we handle the huge size of blockchain? The data can be compressed, but the blockchain can't be – compressing it has an impact on the security and accessing of blockchain. Bloating might be reduced if some innovative compression algorithms facilitate in such a way that security, accessibility, and storage of blockchain remain integrated.

Hashgraph can also provide high performance in low expenses, without the issue of centralization, which is a single point of failure. It eliminates the requirement for potential computation and power consumption and develops on the performance statistics of the Bitcoin network.

Hashgraph is no doubt amazingly faster than blockchain, but until now, it has been implemented in a private setting; i.e., it is patented. Therefore, it is still unknown if it is going to face the same challenges as blockchain or other DLTs. It may show a positive behavior, remaining intact with all its promises, or enhance the limitations, degrading its performance. Talking about security and efficiency and claiming that it will demonstrate the same behavior when setting up as a public ledger is something that cannot be predicted beforehand. If by any chance hashgraph gains importance over blockchain, it will still remain a significant choice because of decentralization and data immutability. In different scenarios where the above-mentioned issues are negligible, blockchain will be a possible choice as well.

The blockchain involves the consumption of a lot of effort, resources, and energy. When the complex computational tasks are carried out on high-processing machines, then increased electricity consumption is inevitable. The estimated data so far is 24 terawatt per year.

Hashgraph provides a fusion of speed, security, and scalability, which is significant to attain the highest level of security in the DLT. It has importance especially because of asynchronous BFT (Figures 2.4 through 2.19).

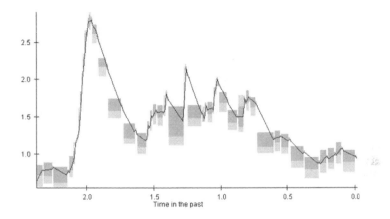

FIGURE 2.4 The graph depicts the number of transactions that are received from unique events per second: it goes from 100,000 (scaled to 1.0) to 250,000 (scaled to 2.5) transactions per second. Here, the light gray boxes show the lowest and highest values during that time period, whereas the dark gray box shows one standard deviation above and below the mean. It shows that the transaction per second goes to above 250,000 and at average remains near it.

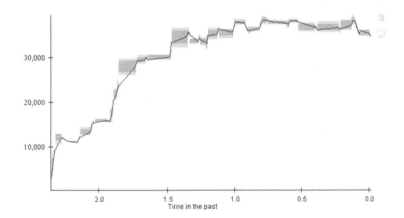

FIGURE 2.5 The graph depicts the average number of bytes transferred: it goes from 10,000 to above 30,000 bytes per second when sync occurs. Here, the light gray boxes show the lowest and highest values during that time period, whereas the dark gray box shows one standard deviation above and below the mean. We observed that the average bytes transferred are around 30,000, whereas it started off with approximately 5000 – as the system proliferates, the number gets increased and gets stable after touching the average position.

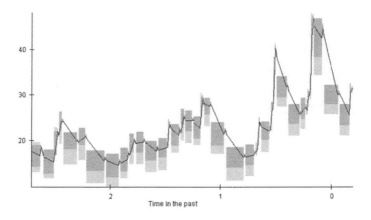

FIGURE 2.6   The graph depicts the number of bytes present in the transactions that are received per second. It goes from 20 to above 40 bytes per second when sync occurs. It is the graph derived for unique events, i.e., the events that are gossiped for the first time.

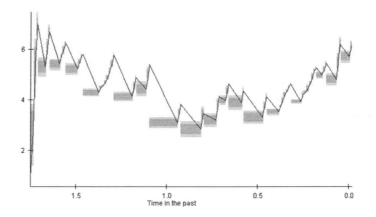

FIGURE 2.7   The graph depicts the number of events created by a particular node per second. It shows how the graph increases quickly, but then, to balance the bandwidth, it averages to around 5 events per second, keeping in mind that it's just for a single node. Therefore, imagine for around 100 nodes, we would be having 500 events per second in a small network.

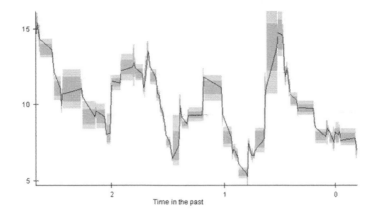

FIGURE 2.8 The graph depicts the number of events received that are already known; i.e., they have not gossiped earlier. It ranges from 6 to around 15, but it averages something between 7 and 13 per second by a particular node. As discussed in Figure 2.5, it is illustrated for a single node only.

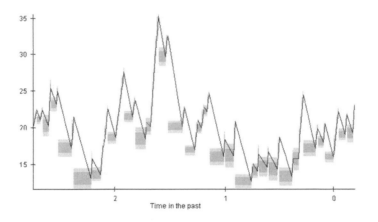

FIGURE 2.9 The graph depicts the number of unique events that are received per second by a single node. It ranges from 12 to around 35, but it averages something between 15 and 30 per second by a particular node.

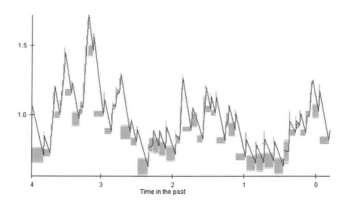

FIGURE 2.10 The graph depicts the average number of rounds initiated per second. We observed that around 1 to 2 rounds are created in a second under normal conditions.

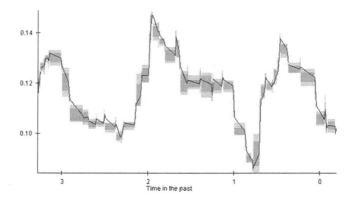

FIGURE 2.11 The graph depicts the average duration of successful sync between two nodes disseminating the data they know. It shows that the average duration is between 0.10 and 0.14 seconds.

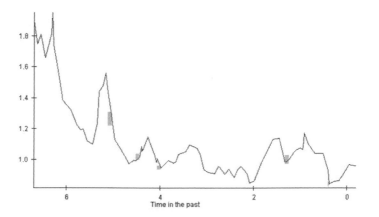

FIGURE 2.12 The graph depicts the average time it takes between creating an event to knowing its consensus. The average time ranges from 0.2 to 1.4 seconds.

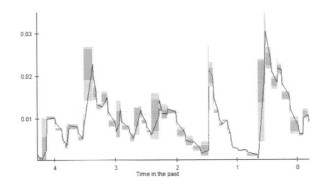

FIGURE 2.13 The graph illustrates the time after the achievement of consensus for a transaction to recording it. It requires minimal time; it goes from 0 to 0.03 seconds for a particular transaction.

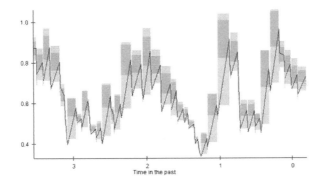

FIGURE 2.14 The graph illustrates the time duration of when a node has created an event and the other node has received that event and verified its signature. It ranges from 0.3 to 0.9 seconds. The round-trip time is observed from one node in a network to the other, creating an event and disseminating the details to the other nodes.

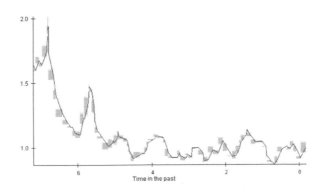

FIGURE 2.15 The graph depicts the time duration of when a node has created an event and the other node has received that event and also the consensus has been achieved. It ranges from 0.5 to 1.9 seconds, averaging to around 1 second. As observed in Figure 2.18, this round trip includes the consensus achievement of the event that has been created.

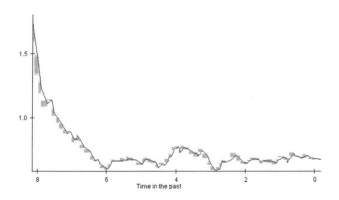

FIGURE 2.16   The graph depicts the time when a node received an event when it came to know the consensus has been reached. The range is between 0.1 and 0.7 seconds.

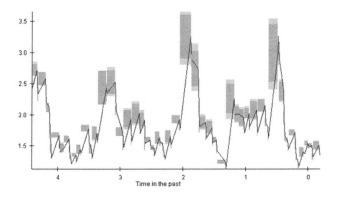

FIGURE 2.17   The graph depicts the time when the first event of a particular round is received to all the famous witnesses being known. Its range is from 1.0 and 3.2 seconds, but it averages around 1.2 to 2.2 seconds.

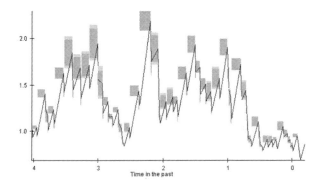

FIGURE 2.18   The graph depicts the time interval between the first event received in one round and the first event received in the next round. It ranges from 1.0 to 2.2 seconds, averaging to 1.2 to 1.9 seconds. A node is considered to be in another round if it can strongly see supermajority witnesses from its own round.

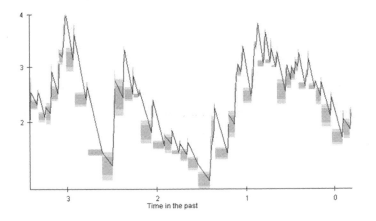

FIGURE 2.19   The graph depicts the number of syncs done per second, initiated by a particular node. It ranges from 1 to 4 syncs per second.

2.5   CONCLUSION

Blockchain technology has witnessed continuous evolution over the last few years, with a recent study by the World Economic Forum estimating that 10% of global GDP will be stored on blockchain by 2027. However, the technology has also witnessed limitations, especially in terms of scalability, which has affected its extensive adoption. For instance, a recent study by Deloitte says that 92% of the 26,000 blockchain-based projects initiated over the past 2 years are now dead (Trujillo, Fromhart, and Srinivas, 2017). Bitcoin is the most widespread implementation of blockchain but has also attracted controversy, as it supports to permit millions-of-dollar world wide market of unknown transactions, without any control by any government. Therefore, it has to undergo a lot of regulatory disputes, including governmental and financial ones.

Within this context, hashgraph technology has recently emerged as an alternative to blockchain, with the ability to address limitations of blockchain with respect to scalability. However, in order to address the challenge of scalability, a number of consensus paradigms have evolved other than proof of work, such as proof of stake, proof of authority or hybrids having less latency, better security, and demands of lower computational energy. Furthermore, blockchain cannot be considered obsolete by the emergence of hashgraph, as it has its merits and demerits. Moreover, blockchain is improving in performance by the enhancements that are being done; one of the latest is the Cryptographically secure Off-chain Multi-asset Instant Transaction (COMIT) network. COMIT is considered a super blockchain and claims to be resembling the Internet. It can link and interchange any digital assets with the same or other blockchains via the cross-chain routing protocol. It also claims to solve the double-spending issue in blockchain, without modifying the fundamental blockchains. Nevertheless, the fundamental features of blockchain, which are decentralization and data immutability, will carry the day.

One of the significant features of blockchain is its inherent decentralization. It abolishes the undesirable consequences of centralization. Such characteristics have enabled blockchain to be applied to a range of scenarios such as e-voting, security, and healthcare. However, in order to support wider application domains, further advancements to blockchain are required, especially with respect to scalability. Hashgraph attempts to address the scalability challenge of blockchain; however, as it is a patented technology, thorough analysis is limited. However, initial applications and experimentation with hashgraph technology have highlighted its potential for widespread adoption, which will require further efforts to realize this potential.

REFERENCES

Allavena, André. 2006. On the correctness of gossip-based membership protocols. Accessed 9 June 2019. https://morebooks.de/store/de/book/on-the-correctness-of-gossip-based-membership-protocols/isbn/978-3-639-43221-3.

Alvisi, Lorenzo, Jeroen Doumen, Rachid Guerraoui, Boris Koldehofe, Harry C. Li, Robbert van Renesse, and Gilles Trédan. 2007. "How robust are gossip-based communication protocols?" *Operating Systems Review* 41 (5): 14–18.

Androulaki, Elli, and Ghassan O. Karame. 2014. Hiding transaction amounts and balances in bitcoin. Accessed 9 June 2019. https://link.springer.com/chapter/10.1007/978-3-319-08593-7_11.

Antonopoulos, Andreas M. 2014. *Mastering Bitcoin: Unlocking Digital Cryptocurrencies.* O'Reilly Media, Inc. " USA, 2014.

Birman, Kenneth P. 2007. "The promise, and limitations, of gossip protocols." *Operating Systems Review* 41 (5): 8–13.

Coccoli, Andrea, Andrea Bondavalli, and Luca Simoncini. 2000. Consensus in asynchronous distributed systems. Accessed 9 June 2019. http://bonda.cnuce.cnr.it/documentation/reports/doc2000/pdf00/idpt2000.pdf.

Conti, Mauro, E. Sandeep Kumar, Chhagan Lal, and Sushmita Ruj. 2018. "A survey on security and privacy issues of bitcoin." *IEEE Communications Surveys and Tutorials* 20 (4): 3416–3452.

Crosby, Michael. 2016. "Blockchain technology: Beyond bitcoin." *Applied Innovation Review* 2 (6–10): 71.

Demers, Alan J., Daniel H. Greene, Carl H. Hauser, Wes Irish, John Larson, Scott Shenker, Howard E. Sturgis, Daniel C. Swinehart, and Douglas B. Terry. 1987. Epidemic algorithms for replicated database maintenance. Accessed 9 June 2019. http://textfiles.com/bitsavers/pdf/xerox/parc/techreports/csl-89-1_epidemic_algorithms_for_replicated_database_maintenance.pdf.

Dolev, Danny, and H. Raymond Strong. 1983. "Authenticated algorithms for byzantine agreement." *SIAM Journal on Computing* 12 (4): 656–666.

Eugster, Patrick, Rachid Guerraoui, Anne-Marie Kermarrec, and Laurent Massoulié. 2004. "Epidemic information dissemination in distributed systems." *IEEE Computer* 37 (5): 60–67.

Garay, Juan A., Aggelos Kiayias, and Nikos Leonardos. 2015. "The bitcoin backbone protocol: Analysis and applications." *IACR Cryptology ePrint Archive* 2014: 281–310.

Gossip Protocols Simulator. n.d. Accessed 3 May 2019. https://flopezluis.github.io/gossip-simulator/.

Gupta, Indranil, Anne-Marie Kermarrec, and Ayalvadi Ganesh. 2006. "Efficient and adaptive epidemic-style protocols for reliable and scalable multicast." *IEEE Transactions on Parallel and Distributed Systems* 17 (7): 593–605.

Khan, Kashif Mehboob, Junaid Arshad, and Muhammad Mubashir Khan. 2018. "Secure digital voting system based on blockchain technology." *International Journal of Electronic Government Research* 14 (1): 53–62.

Khan, Kashif Mehboob, Junaid Arshad, and Muhammad Mubashir Khan. 2019. A simulation and analysis of transaction malleability within blockchain based e-voting application. *Computers and Electrical Engineering.*

Lamport, Leslie, Robert Shostak, and Marshall Pease. 1982. "The byzantine generals problem." *ACM Transactions on Programming Languages and Systems* 4 (3).

Leitão, João, José Pereira, and Luís E. T. Rodrigues. 2010. Gossip-based broadcast. Accessed 9 June 2019. http://gsd.inesc-id.pt/~ler/reports/lpr_gossipbasedbroadcast.pdf.

MacDonald, Trent John, Darcy W. E. Allen, and Jason Potts. 2016. "Blockchains and the Boundaries of Self-Organized Economies: Predictions for the Future of Banking." *Social Science Research Network*, 1: 279–296.

Mingxiao, Du, Ma Xiaofeng, Zhang Zhe, Wang Xiangwei, and Chen Qijun. 2017. A review on consensus algorithm of blockchain. Accessed 9 June 2019. https://semanticscholar.org/paper/a-review-on-consensus-algorithm-of-blockchain-mingxiao-xiaofeng/0bf2cb4ae68275f4fd71a30f191dc95793a0d49e.

Nakamoto, Satoshi. 2009. Bitcoin: A peer-to-peer electronic cash system. Accessed 9 June 2019. http://bitcoin.org/bitcoin.pdf.

Nishara Nizamuddin, Khaled Salah, Muhammad Ajmal Azad, Junaid Arshad, and Muhammad Habib ur Rahman. 2019. "Decentralized document version control using ethereum blockchain and IPFS." *Computers & Electrical Engineering* 76: 183–197.

Schueffel, Patrick. 2017. Alternative distributed ledger technologies blockchain vs. tangle vs. hashgraph—A high-level overview and comparison. Accessed 9 June 2019. https://papers.ssrn.com/sol3/papers.cfm?abstract_id=3144241.

Steen, Maarten van, and Andrew S. Tanenbaum. 2007. *Distributed Systems: Principles and Paradigms*, Pearson Prentice Hall, Upper Saddle River, NJ.

Trujillo, Jesus Leal, Steve Fromhart, and Van Srinivas. 2017. Evolution of blockchain technology, deloitte. Accessed 8 June 2019. https://bit.ly/35zsLdT.

Voulgaris, Spyros, Márk Jelasity, and Maarten van Steen. 2003. "A robust and scalable peer-to-peer gossiping protocol." *Lecture Notes in Computer Science* 2872: 47–58.

Wadsworth, Amber. 2018. "Decrypting the role of distributed ledger technology in payments processes." *Reserve Bank of New Zealand Bulletin* 81 (5): 1–20.

Yli-Huumo, Jesse, Deokyoon Ko, Sujin Choi, Sooyong Park, and Kari Smolander. 2016. "Where is current research on blockchain technology? A systematic review." *PLoS One* 11 (10): 1–27.

3 Design Laboratory Exercises for Blockchain Technology

*Hongmei Chi, Bertony Bornelus,
and Angela R. Martin*

CONTENTS

3.1 INTRODUCTION

The application of blockchain has shown a promise to various areas such as security traceability, distributed data storage, and identity authentication. A new jobs report shows that software engineers with blockchain skills are in higher demand than at any time in the past, and the number of positions grew more than fivefold in 2018 [1]

Demand Growth for Engineering Roles

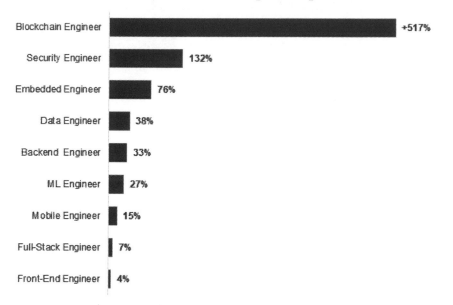

FIGURE 3.1   Demand for blockchain developers. (From Lucas Mearian, Demand for block-chain engineers is 'through the roof', https://www.computerworld.com/article/3345998/demand-for-blockchain-engineers-is-through-the-roof.html.)

(Figure 3.1). Currently, blockchain technology is safe, reliable, and secure technology. However, with many enthusiasts about the implementation for blockchain technology, many current or future IT professionals are unaware of blockchain and its use cases. In addition, there are few blockchain hands-on labs available. Thus, the objective of this paper is to set up a comprehensive practical laboratory that will improve the knowledge of IT professionals on block chains and block chain development.

Blockchain application has the potentiality to become a disruptive revolutionizing e-commerce technology to affect many industries such as financial and noncommercial, eliminating the need for third parties, reducing cyberattacks, and increasing transparency, where typical transactions yield high economic loss and negative sociotechnical impacts. Blockchain has multicontent to support student learning (Figure 3.2). There is a big learning curve for students to overcome. It is difficult for students to follow it in one course. Designing a set of practical laboratories to address these challenges one by one may be the appropriate solution [10].

Thus, this curriculum's modules and hands-on labs will describe the current blockchain application mechanism, platform, and development tools, specifically, the security behind blockchain to fully comprehend the use of this application. Developers must understand the moving parts, as well as the challenges of how current transactions are conducted and how to improve them using blockchain applications [6]. This chapter aims to provide an overview of blockchain technology and its applications for scientists to solve various problems in the real world. The labs would be built

FIGURE 3.2   Basic components in blockchain.

based on real-life scenarios, to enhance their ability to understand and solve real-life cybersecurity problems. This integrated approach would expose the students to the cost associated with the risk involved at each stage of the blockchain application [2].

The rest of this chapter is organized as follows. In Section 3.2, we present background materials and the motivation behind this work. In Section 3.3, we provide details of blockchain tools and software. Section 3.4 describes blockchain programming languages. In Section 3.5, we describe how to design curriculum modules and the laboratory setup. In Section 3.6, we describe, in detail, students' feedback. Finally, we provide concluding remarks and present directions to possible extensions to this work in Section 3.7.

3.2   BACKGROUND

There will be an exponential growth in the adoption of blockchain applications, with the most considerable increase in the financial services and significant growth in many other industries such as consumer products, technology, healthcare, and the public sector. Blockchain applications can influence many industries by improving transactions. Some sectors that have been affected by blockchain application are finance, Internet of Things (IoT), public and social services, security, and privacy. This chapter will examine the related works of each of these industries and the examination of how developing a novel hands-on laboratory exploration in academia will significantly enhance our undergraduate students' development. The need for blockchain application is to improve data security through linking transactions using cryptography, thus enhancing transparency and integrity. Typical operations are done using a centralized client-server infrastructure, where computers, commonly referred to as nodes, are connected to one central authority, whereas blockchain applications are a decentralized or distributed ledger with no single point of failure. There is no central authority and all nodes are connected, making it a secure form. This chapter will describe some of the current blockchain application mechanisms, platforms, and various use cases. Before diving into the apparatus, there must be an understanding of how blockchain functions. Developers must understand the moving parts such as cryptography, digital signatures, hash functions, and Merkle trees to fully comprehend the use of blockchain application. Also, there are numerous challenges with how current transactions are conducted and how to improve them using blockchain applications.

Blockchain application utilizes several data structure methods and a technique known as hashing, which takes an input of any length and creates a cryptographic fixed output using SHA-256. The hash function is a one-way function, meaning that the output is irreversible, which helps prevent hackers from reverse engineering the output into the original input. Any change to the input will alternately create a different output, and the original input will always get the same output, making it fast and efficient to verify that the message has not been tampered with through comparing the digest. Blockchain uses the hash to embody the current state of the blockchain. The input represents the entire sequence of events that have occurred in the blockchain ecosystem. Blockchain hashing is immutable, such that any change to any part of the input causes a considerable change to the output. This makes blockchain an accurate security application measure for preserving the authenticity of the data.

As seen in Figure 3.3, the blockchain uses a hash tree, also referred to as a Merkle tree, to record all transactions, which go through an algorithm to generate a hash. This provides a means of verifying the validity of the data based on the initial transaction. All blocks of transactions are not hashed at once, but rather, each transaction is hashed, with those transactions being linked and hashed together, ultimately creating one hash for the entire block. The hash of the Merkle root is typically contained in a block header along with the hash of the previous block, timestamp, nonce, and block version number. The Merkle trees and hashes are both significant components in allowing blockchain application to work while providing security, integrity, and immutability [3,4].

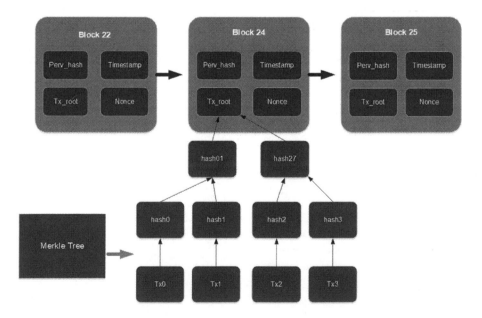

FIGURE 3.3   Blockchain Merkle tree.

In summary, blockchain applications have an enormous potentiality of affecting many industries in the years to come, including Finance, IoT, and the public sector. Financial services will see the most significant effect, with the demanding interest into Bitcoin and other Altcoins. Several banking systems have already adopted a quasi-centralized blockchain application system to enhance security and improve efficiency. The integration of blockchain applications and fog computing has a high chance of enhancing security for IoT device and ensuring data traceability. Lastly, the public sector, also, could see significant benefits from blockchain applications, allowing consumers higher confidences in services rendered, protecting consumers data, and decreasing operational cost.

3.3 BLOCKCHAIN TOOLS

There are several open-source blockchain application platforms and development tools. One of the most popular blockchain platforms is Ethereum, which serves as both a cryptocurrency and the development environment utilizing Ethereum Virtual Machine (EVM). Ethereum also provides a suite of utensils used to develop blockchain application using a smart contract and has formed its coding language known as Solidity [5]. This coding is influenced by other programming languages such as C++, Python, and Java. Ethereum provides a suite of tools for the development of blockchain application namely Remix IDE, Truffle, Boxes, and Ganache. This section will serve as a guideline on how the mechanism and platform are used to develop a blockchain application and its inner working [7] (Table 3.1).

3.3.1 HYPERLEDGER FABRIC

This blockchain framework, as seen in Table 3.1, is hosted by the Linux Foundation. The Ethereum foundation created a blockchain application using a modular architecture, allowing components, such as consensus and membership services, to plug and play. This framework is designed for a permission network, allowing known identities to participate in the system. Each user within the network should be authorized and have a fair amount of capital to be a part of this private blockchain.

3.3.2 R3 CORDA

In 2015, R3, a world's leading financial institution, built an open-source distributed ledger. Corda, governed by Hedera Hashgraph Council, allows institutions to transact directly to one another by using smart contract, eliminating third parties' cost and transaction fees, using the consensus algorithm, asynchronous Byzantine fault tolerance, as seen in Figure 3.1. This application does not have a cryptocurrency and is a permission blockchain, which allows only authorized users to gain access to data, enhancing privacy. Corda is applied to a variety of use cases such as government, supply chain, healthcare, and trade.

TABLE 3.1
Blockchain Development Platform

	Ethereum	Hyperledger Fabric	R3 Corda	Ripple	Quorum	Hyperledger Sawtooth
Industry focus	Cross-industry	Cross-industry	Financial services	Financial services	Cross-industry	Cross-industry
Ledger type	Permissionless	Permissioned	Permissioned	Permissioned	Permissioned	Permissioned
Consensus algorithm	Proof of work	Pluggable framework	Pluggable framework	Probabilistic voting	Majority voting	Pluggable framework
Smart contract functionality	Yes	Yes	Yes	No	No	Yes
Governance	Ethereum Developers	Linux Foundation	R3 Consortium	Ripple Labs	Ethereum Developers and JP Morgan Chase	Linux Foundation
Providers with experience (%)	93%	93%	60%	33%	27%	93%

3.3.3 RIPPLE

Founded in 2012, Ripple aims at financial institutions to provide payment to providers, digital asset exchanges, banks, and corporates by using a blockchain network, known as RippleNet, which does not use smart contract like other block-chains. Global payments are conducted through a digital asset known as XRP or Ripple, which is popular as Ether and Bitcoin. Ripple uses probabilistic voting to reach the consensus between nodes, allowing only authorized users to conduct transactions.

3.3.4 QUORUM

Ethereum-based distributed ledger, founder by J.P. Morgan, was developed to provide the financial services industry with a permission implementation of Ethereum. This platform is open source and free to use. Unlike Ethereum plat-forms, Quorum uses vote-based algorithms to process several hundred transactions per seconds.

3.3.5 HYPERLEDGER SAWTOOTH

Linux Foundation governs this platform, contributed by IBM and Digital Asset. Hyperledger Sawtooth is an enterprise-grade, modular platform that plugs and plays like Hyperledger Fabric and is used to create, deploy, and execute distributed ledgers. This allows digital records to be maintained without a central authority. Sawtooth's uses the proof of elapsed time to reach consensus, integrated with hardware security solutions, called trusted execution environments.

3.3.6 ETHEREUM

Founded in 2013, Ethereum is an open-source blockchain platform proposed by Vitalk Buterin. The Ethereum platform runs smart contracts on the EVM probabilistic. Each node within the network EVM is run as implemented. Ethereum is permissionless, which is open to the public (i.e., for anyone) to use. This platform uses the proof-of-work consensus algorithm, which is comparatively slower than other blockchains.

3.4 BLOCKCHAIN PROGRAMMING LANGUAGES

There are several programming languages used to program blockchain applications. This section will describe the different languages used by developers to develop block-chain applications, such as C++, Simplicity, JavaScript, Python, Rholang, and Solidity.

3.4.1 C++

Founded in 1985 by Mr. Bjarne Stroustrup, C++ was created as an extension of the C language. This object-oriented language maintained the flexibility, security, and efficiency of the original C language and is ideal for developing blockchain applications, due to the primitive control over memory's advanced multithreading capabilities, semantics, core object-oriented feature such as runtime polymorphism, and function overloading. Developers such as Bitcoin and Ripple use C++ because of the object-oriented features, giving them the ability to bind the data and the methods.

3.4.2 SIMPLICITY

Founded in November 2017 by Mr. Russell O'Connor, Simplicity is a new blockchain programming language. Its high-level coding language allows developers to write more human-readable smart contract intended to reduce sophisticated low-level understanding of the Bitcoin Script, the integrated smart contract language of the Bitcoin blockchain. This programming language makes it fast and easy to create smart contracts (Table 3.2).

3.4.3 JAVASCRIPT

Founded on 4 December 1995, by Netscape Communications Corporation, Mozilla Foundation, and Ecma International, and designed by Brendan Eich, this programming language is a loosely typed scripting programming language for the support of all major browsers and is primarily used for enhancing HTML and CSS web-pages into a fully-fledged user interface. Developers use JavaScript Node.js to build highly capable and innovating blockchain applications, which makes it easier for developers to use applications for wide use, not requiring developers to install new software.

3.4.4 PYTHON

Developed in 1990 by the Python Software Foundation and designed by Mr. Guido van Rossum, Python emphasizes code readability with syntax simplicity. A blockchain built using Python is usually slow because of the difficult cryptographic operations due to their interpreted nature. Python is widely used because of its massive opensource support, and you can find third-party python plugin and libraries when developing blockchain applications.

3.4.5 RHOLANG

This programming language is currently in development by RChain, a concurrent programming language specifically built for developing smart contracts. RChain runs on the Rho Virtual machine. Rather than using a variable to hold values and altering these values throughout the program's execution, the functional programming language is a series of mathematical functions to be performed consecutively. Rholang offers the same capabilities as Simplicity and Solidity.

TABLE 3.2
Blockchain Programming Languages

	C++	Simplicity	JavaScript	Python	Rholang	Solidity
Blockchain – focus	Universal	Specifically created for blockchain	Universal	Universal	Specifically created for blockchain	Specifically created for blockchain
Object – oriented	Yes	Higher-level programming language	Yes	Yes	Contract language	Higher-level programming language
Blockchain platform Programming language	Bitcoin Ripple Daemon	Bitcoin Script Ethereum EVM	Corda Hyperledger Quorum	Quorum	RChain	Ethereum EVM
Governance	ISO/IEC	Blockstream	Netscape Communications Corporation, Mozilla Foundation, Ecma International	Python Software Foundation License	RChain Cooperative	Ethereum EVM
Smart – contract oriented	Yes	Yes	Yes	No	Yes	Yes

3.4.6 SOLIDITY

Introduced in August 2014 by Gavin Wood and later developed by the Ethereum projects' Solidity team, headed by Christian Reitwiessner, this programming language was created for developers to write smart contracts on the Ethereum platform. Solidity's syntax is comparable to JavaScript, C++, and Python. This makes it easier for new developers to learn this programming language.

3.5 CURRICULUM MODULES

The application design is based on a combination of effortlessly researching blockchain applications, current use cases for blockchain technologies, and educational data mining and learning analytics to create a one-stop shop for educators and students and to learn about the various nuances of blockchain technology. It provides practical tools to educate cybersecurity professionals and to equip them to address the cybersecurity in the blockchain. Those hands-on labs developed will be a part of a new cybersecurity educational framework Web application available on personal computers and mobile devices. There will be a modularized approach to the lab development, to focus development on the skills for each aspect of blockchain and app. The labs will also include the integration of all elements of blockchain, along with its application. This section will show how this project will be designed and fit each student's demand, with experiential learning in mind. This section covers the concepts of blockchain education. As blockchain technology continues to grow and gain traction, many students are unaware of how blockchain works but are highly interested in its potentiality. The aim of this research is to develop an innovated application tool that can be used to introduce students to the nuances of blockchain development.

3.5.1 THE TRAINING MODEL

This application will cover several subject matters related to blockchain development: first, what is blockchain technology; second, understanding the computation behind blockchain: Merkle tree, Rivest Shamir Adleman (RSA) public-key exchange, some data structure methods (including hashing and pointers), and lastly, the differences between centralization, decentralization, and distributed network architectures. Third, we will examine how to implement blockchain using various programs such as sublime Integrated Development Environment (IDE) and bash command prompt. Furthermore, we will be exposing students to a new coding language created by Ethereum, known as, Solidity, a high-level smart contract-oriented language specifically used to create smart contacts.

Figure 3.4 shows an overview of the proposed framework, which consists of several components. The student's applications with the home page serving as the portal for the application are shown in the following example of the Figure 3.5.

The homepage for the new blockchain training model is shown in Figure 3.5. Students can view courses and recent publications related to the site, following

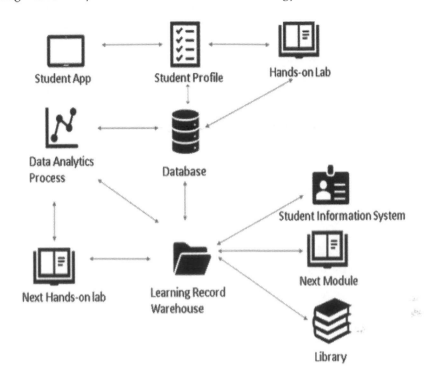

FIGURE 3.4 Block training model.

FIGURE 3.5 Homepage screenshot of our training model.

which students are able to register for courses and general use of the application. Lastly, if students have any issue, a help tab is available for access to the user's manual for the website. At the bottom of the homepage, students and site visitors can view the sitemap for a map of each webpage and a general overview of the website. Following this are the privacy policy and contact for more information about the site policy and contact information for the site creator [8].

As shown in Figure 3.6, when administrators log into the site, they will be able to view a report page containing the various courses and also each individual course and student's status. In the example of the Introduction to Blockchain, there are several tabs underneath the Introduction to Blockchain: assigned learners, completed learners, learners in progress, instructors, and training time. On the top right are content tabs to add and remove educational items. The tab 'USERS & PROGRESS' allows the administrators to view the various users and their progress. The 'FILES' tab allows the administrators to add and remove file for students to view. Last is the 'RULES & PATH' tab for courses.

At the bottom of the Administrator reporting page is progress overview of the course, broken down into day, month, and year to allow administrators to view completion of the course.

Our objective is to increase the future IT professionals' awareness and prepare them for the emergent of the blockchain revolution and Web 3.0. Students overwhelmingly expressed that they would like to learn more about blockchain technology to enhance their career prospect opportunities. Thus, creating a comprehensive hands-on lab will bridge the gaps between rapid advancement of technology and the classroom.

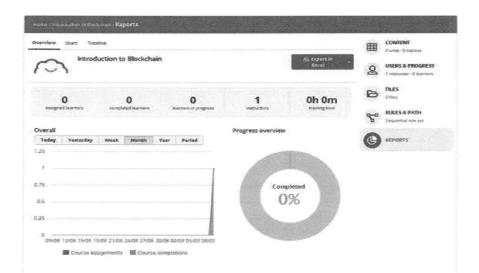

FIGURE 3.6   Example of site administrator reporting page.

3.5.2   CASE STUDIES

Designing specific hands-on labs application to help trainees understand the fundamental concepts of blockchain technology and implementation of the smart contract using the Ethereum platform, the labs would be built based on real-life scenarios to enhance their ability to understand and solve real-life cybersecurity problems. This integrated approach would expose those trainees to the cost to risk involved in each cycle of the application. Each course will be a mixture of content and process. Before trainees engage in a hand-on activity, they will be given a presentation to comprehend key concepts to better understand the lab at hand.

As shown in Figure 3.7, Contents Overview, we define to students various topics to help familiarize them with the nuances of blockchain technology and its application in the real world. Many students may or may not have taken a data structure course, which is the foundation of how blockchain technology is being implemented. Therefore, we give a brief overview of how all these method function and toil together. Sample questions about the Merkle tree, students are given examples throughout the lecture, following, students must apply the knowledge, by completing various questions to build comprehension.

Key objectives for this module are as follows:

- Enhancing students' understanding of how to apply abstract concepts to real-world applications
- Introducing study to innovated and new, emerging blockchain technology
- Preparing students for the current and emerging job market.

According to the survey questions answered by students, they are highly unaware of blockchain; however, they have heard about the prevalent blockchain application bitcoin. Therefore, we have introduced a course on cryptocurrency to reinforce how to successfully implement blockchain application.

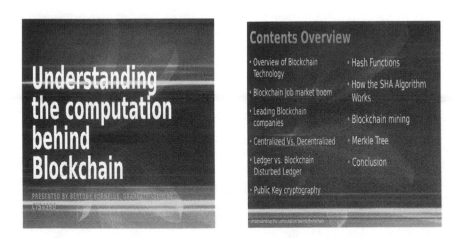

FIGURE 3.7   Sample module: Understanding the computation behind blockchain.

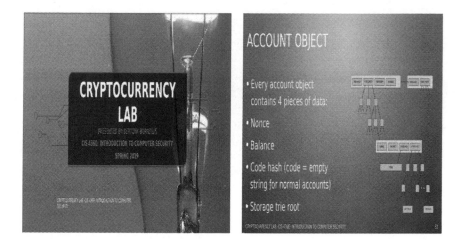

FIGURE 3.8   Sample lesson: Cryptocurrency lesson.

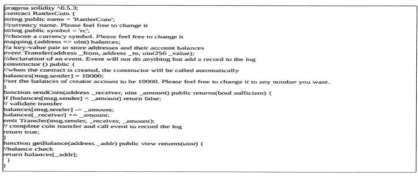

We just created some variables to record our currency's name and symbol - "RattlerCoin" and "rc". We use mapping to keep track of the balances of all addresses. In the constructor, it gives the initial creator 10,000 value of tokens. It's consistent with the basic definition of currency as I mentioned in the beginning——a

FIGURE 3.9   Sample hands-on lab: Cryptocurrency lab.

As seen in Figures 3.8 and 3.9, students will be introduced to new materials and they then must apply that understanding to the corresponding labs.

3.6   STUDENT FEEDBACKS

The goal is to develop a series of hands-on labs that would address every main application of blockchain, thus providing practical tools to train IT professionals and equip them to address the cybersecurity problem of blockchain. This approach will help students to learn and comprehend the fundamental concepts in the blockchain systematically. To facilitate active learning, each module is accompanied by lectures, video, student surveys, and one or more laboratory activities that reinforce the concepts that were taught in the lectures. A typically computer laboratory is augmented by new concepts or programming skills.

During Spring 2019, a joint survey was conducted at Florida A&M University, Introduction to Computer Security courses. During the study, students were asked a series of questions regarding blockchain, blockchain development platform, and interest in blockchain development. Sixty-two students responded to the questionnaire.

When students were asked 'Have you heard of blockchain?' 47% stated 'No' and 56% stated 'Yes'. Students who reported 'Yes' were also asked to describe blockchain.

An overwhelming number of students describe blockchain as an encrypted list of blocks, followed by cryptocurrencies and lastly a decentralized ledger. Next, we asked students if they had heard of Ethereum open-source blockchain platform and cryptocurrency.

A total of 66% of students stated that they have not heard of Ethereum, and 34% students stated that they have heard of Ethereum; descriptions from students who had heard of Ethereum may be seen in Figure 3.10.

A total of 31% responded 'Yes' to knowing about Ethereum; many described Ethereum as a cryptocurrency, followed by other, and lastly, a few referred to it as 'open source'. Students stated, overwhelmingly, that they have heard about blockchain and would like to learn more about blockchain technology.

Of the students who had not heard of blockchain, 31% indicated that they would like to learn more about blockchain technology, and 6% were not interested in learning about blockchain technology.

Lastly, students chose career opportunities as a reason for increased interest in blockchain technology at 47%, followed by 31% – cryptocurrencies, 13% – cryptography, 9% – mining, and none for d-Apps (decentralized Application web 3.0).

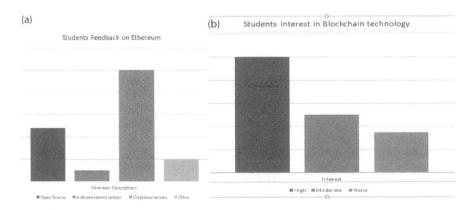

FIGURE 3.10 (a) Students' description of Ethereum. (b) Students' interest in blockchain technology.

In summary, students' feedback was positive, which means that they are interested in learning more and would love to work as blockchain developers. Access to proper training materials is critical to taking advantage of this trend.

3.7   CONCLUSION AND FUTURE WORK

The development of the hands-on exercises is based on the several curriculum modules described previously. Under our framework, we will develop various hands-on–related blockchains. Thus, Blocked U framework allows for the expansion of the framework into other disciplines of fields of study. We also described the laboratory structure and the associated hands-on exercises that are pertinent to each module. We believe that the real-world scenario-based approach to learning is enhanced by the carefully designed activities that accompany the lecture modules. This chapter covers the concepts of blockchain education. As blockchain technology continues to grow and gain traction, many IT professionals are unaware of how blockchain works but are highly interested in its potentiality. The aim of this chapter was to develop an innovated application tool that can be used to introduce any IT professional to the nuances of blockchain development.

As for future work, connected with these curriculum modules and activities are the following:

- The continuous evaluation of the effectiveness of the curriculum modules and laboratory exercises
- The enhancement of the hands-on exercises available online for academic and train more STEM majors
- The development of additional curriculum modules in the areas of IoT, healthcare, precision agriculture, precision fishing, public sector, and finance and banking [9]

ACKNOWLEDGMENTS

This work is supported in part by CyberFlorida for Capacity Building Award Program. Opinions expressed are those of the author and not necessarily of the granting agencies. The US Government is authorized to reproduce and distribute reprints notwithstanding any copyright notation herein.

REFERENCES

1. Lucas Mearian, Demand for blockchain engineers is 'through the roof'. Accessed 28 February 2019. https://www.computerworld.com/article/3345998/demand-for-blockchain-engineers-is-through-the-roof.html
2. Calvão, F. (2019). Cryptominers: Digital labor and the power of blockchain technology. *Economic Anthropology*, 6(1), 123–134.
3. Chi, H., Aderibigbe, T., & Kalaimannan, E. (2018). Design of cybersecurity hands-on laboratory exercises using secDLC framework. In *Proceedings of the ACMSE 2018 Conference* (p. 36). ACM.

4. Choi, B. G., Jeong, E., & Kim, S. W. (2019). Multiple security certification system between blockchain based terminal and internet of things device: Implication for open innovation. *Journal of Open Innovation: Technology, Market, and Complexity*, 5(4), 87.
5. Delmolino, K., Arnett, M., Kosba, A., Miller, A., & Shi, E. (2016). Step by step towards creating a safe smart contract: Lessons and insights from a cryptocurrency lab. In *International Conference on Financial Cryptography and Data Security* (pp. 79–94). Springer, Berlin, Germany.
6. Dillenberger, D., Novotny, P., Zhang, Q., et al. (2019). Blockchain analytics and artificial intelligence. *IBM Journal of Research and Development*, 63(2/3), 5.
7. Gaur, N., Desrosiers, L., Ramakrishna, V., Novotny, P., Baset, S. A., & O'Dowd, A. (2018). *Hands-On Blockchain with Hyperledger: Building Decentralized Applications with Hyperledger Fabric and Composer*. Packt Publishing Ltd, Birmingham.
8. Gill, S. S., Tuli, S., Xu, M., et al. (2019). Transformative effects of IoT, blockchain and artificial intelligence on cloud computing: Evolution, vision, trends and open challenges. *Internet of Things*, 8, 100118.
9. Mkrttchian, V., Gamidullaeva, L. A., Vertakova, Y., & Panasenko, S. (2019). New tools for cyber security using blockchain technology and avatar-based management technique. In *Machine Learning and Cognitive Science Applications in Cyber Security* (pp. 105–122). IGI Global.
10. Rao, A. R., & Dave, R. (2019, March). Developing hands-on laboratory exercises for teaching STEM students the internet-of-things, cloud computing and blockchain applications. In *2019 IEEE Integrated STEM Education Conference (ISEC)* (pp. 191–198). IEEE.

4 Blockchain Security and Potential Future Use Cases

Kevin Curran and Jack Curran

CONTENTS

4.1   INTRODUCTION

A blockchain is a distributed database that maintains an ever-growing list of data records secured from tampering or revision. It is not centralized, and that is impor tant, as there is no single point of failure. No single organization can claim owner- ship, but rather, the group works together to confirm legitimate new transactions. It is composed of data structure blocks, where each block holds batches of individual transactions and the results of any blockchain executables. All these blocks contain a timestamp and a link to a previous block. The blockchain ultimately serves as a public ledger of transactions that cannot be reversed (or without great difficulty or near-system failure). The nodes agree to validate new records being added to a database (the blockchain). The database is not stored in one single place but rather resides on many, if not all, nodes. Whenever a new insertion is to be made, which could be, say, an example of a sale of a bike from person X to person Y, then a new transaction record is created by person X, who adds the details of the ownership transfer and uploads it to the blockchain of nodes for them to add the new transac- tion to the blockchain. Should it be deemed a valid transaction (which is validated through clever quick computations) by most nodes, then the new record is added to the end of the blockchain and remains there forever. What is neat about this solution is the fact that no centralized authority is needed to approve the transaction but rather a majority consensus.

That is the blockchain in a nutshell, and at first glance, there is nothing revolutionary in that overview, yet it is revolutionary. Now, for the first time, we can have a system of barter, a system of storage, or even a lottery system that is run globally, with no central ownership, is semi-anonymous, and yet full of trustworthy transactions that cannot be cheated. That really does change things in many domains. Aside from the implementation of cryptocurrencies (which I will get to later), blockchain technology can also transform key aspects of society such as smart contracts to make micropayments more cost-effective or in the music industry to enable data sharing among the value chain from artist to final consumer realizing and releasing more value. Basically, here, we can track who owns the creative work (e.g., song) or who contributed to enforce an unambiguous ownership trail. A blockchain can also be used to store files in a decentralized manner, as opposed to a system such as Dropbox. StorJ is an example for blockchain-based file storage and retrieval (Blue et al., 2018).

Distributed ledger technology (aka blockchain) has been proposed as the solution for a multitude of use cases globally (Arora, H). Inevitably, those behind the suggestions have a blockchain product to vend or an initial coin offering, or simply do not understand the technology. A blockchain does possess unique properties and can allow individuals to exchange money and other assets with one another, without requiring an intermediary to do so. However, take a common blockchain example of deploying one in the supply chain, where information on goods such as clearance certificates, origin, proof of purchase, and a bill of lading, can be made part of a block and be easily accessible to suppliers, transporters, buyers, regulators, and auditors. Yes, one could argue that a properly implemented blockchain could lead to lower transaction, auditing, and accounting costs, and the addition of 'smart contracts' could automatically calculate new tariffs. The problem, however, is that such a system could not be a public-open blockchain. The 'writers' have to be vetted. One can also argue that existing cloud-based systems can equally deliver such a system – and more efficiently.

Many people are not aware that a major weakness of blockchain is that storing data or large files on the blockchain is a non-starter, as it can barely sustain small strings of text that simply record a balance transfer between two parties. Yes, there are new initiatives such as the InterPlanetary File System (IPFS) that could provide much of the infrastructure needed for content tracking and attribution, as it provides a permanent, decentralized Web, where links do not die and no single entity controls the data. However, there is little real-world uptake in IPFS to date. There is also the immutability of the blockchain, which can be an issue when we later discover that a transaction needs amending due to incorrect data. That is not a trivial problem.

There is also the overall security. For a blockchain to be secure, an adversary must not be able to overwhelm the consensus process. This means that an adversary cannot create a lot of 'mining' nodes and take over 50% or more of the new block creation. There have been mining pools that have reached this size, but the community responded, and these have shrunk. There are, of course, permissioned blockchains as well, which can avoid this problem. However, the '51% attack' remains a shadow on blockchain currencies. Large blockchains, especially those reliant on proof of work, can also struggle to process high transaction loads. There would also have to be agreement on the transparency model used, as not all suppliers will welcome a distributed ledger, which allows public viewing of goods. In summary, blockchain has the potential to bring efficiencies to many industries by reducing duplication and improving the ability to create, audit, track, and share data, but owing to the cooperation required to roll out such a technology, the likelihood of trouble-free implementations is quite low, and this could cause problems for anyone who implements one at this time.

This chapter looks at the aspects of blockchain security and some future trends in the blockchain.

4.2   BLOCKCHAIN SECURITY

The underlying advanced encryption standard is effectively unbreakable, but cybersecurity is always a game of cat and mouse, and there are always side-channel attacks on many technologies, not to mention the dangers associated with securing digital wallets (McCall, 2019).

Blockchain can be applied to securing the software supply chain. Hackers are endlessly finding new vectors of attack, as operating system giants and software companies take steps to patch known exploits. One such new mode of compromise is through the distribution of software libraries and programs containing exploits that trick unsuspecting users into installing. In 2017, the official repository for the widely used Python programming language was infected with modified code packages, which were uploaded to the Python Package Index. The packages contained the same code as the upstream libraries, but the hackers had also added an installation script, which was modified to include malicious code. This was a dangerous precedent. Source software packages are traditionally verified as authentic by running the file(s) through an MD5 hash check. This, however, has not gained wide use, and methods are known to bypass this mechanism. Blockchain provides an alternative for the verification of ownership. A blockchain, of course, is a distributed database that maintains an ever-growing list of data records secured from tampering or revision. It is not centralized, which is important, as there is no single point of failure and no individual or group can claim ownership, so the group works together to confirm legitimate new transactions. It is composed of data structure blocks, where each block holds batches of individual transactions and the results of any blockchain executables. All these blocks contain a timestamp and a link to a previous block. The blockchain can, therefore, serve as a public ledger of transactions that cannot be reversed at least without great difficulty or near-system failure.

There is active research in using Byzantine consensus protocols to leverage scalable collective signing to commit transactions irreversibly within seconds (Martino, 2016; Miller et al., 2016). SkipChains can be used to create a blockchain that is cryptographically traversable and efficiently verifiable both forward and backward in time (Malkhi et al., 2000; Malkhi and Reiter, 2013). Here, hashes can be used for backlinks and collective signatures for forwarding links. The offline and peer-to-peer (P2P) verifiability properties that SkipChains add will extend the applicability of future blockchain technology. It will also increase their robustness and resilience to communication failures and potentially provide hack-proof verification of software packages. In many ways, this is a core potential of blockchain for future security in that the combination of chained hashing and cryptography in a decentralized structure could make it more difficult for hackers to tamper with the data contained within (encrypted). This provides assurance about the data.

The blockchain can also play an important role in the security of the Internet of Things (IoT). There are inherent security risks in the IoT, such as disabling them should they become compromised and become parts of botnets, which has become a serious problem already. The security of IoT devices remains a challenge. Compromised IoT devices have been responsible for many large-scale botnets in recent times. Security standards are a key requirement that needs to be focused on before implementing for mass adoption in modern life, and this has more accountability for manufacturers with regard to roadmaps for updates for any devices they sell. However, the blockchain with its solid cryptographic foundation offers a decentralized solution that can help against data tampering. This, therefore, offers greater assurances for the legitimacy of the data. Blockchain technology could potentially allow billions of connected IoT devices to communicate in a secure yet decentralized ecosystem, which also allows consumer data to remain private. There are blockchain-based IoT frameworks such as ChainAnchor, which includes layers of access to keep out unauthorized devices from the network (Rizzo, 2016). IBM Watson IoT Platform enables IoT devices to send data to blockchain ledgers for inclusion in shared transactions with tamper-resistant records. It also validates the transaction through secure contracts. Another blockchain solution from Australian researchers uses a block miner to manage all local network transactions to control communication between home-based IoT devices and the outside world. It can authorize new IoT devices and cut off hacked devices. Telestra is using blockchain to secure smart home IoT ecosystems by storing biometric authentication data to verify the identity of people (Reichert, 2016). IBM's blockchain provides audit trails, accountability, new forms of contracts, and speed for IoT devices. They see the benefit of underpinning the IoT with blockchain as trust, cost reduction, and the acceleration of transactions.

Law enforcement and regulatory forces are for the foreseeable future facing a crisis in their investigations into virtual currency transactions. In addition, major problems such as the amount of energy now being used to mine coins may force national governments to step in. Of course, banning it would have to be a globally agreed solution, as Bitcoins cannot be easily traced to a geographical location. Bitcoin is arguably the most famous blockchain system, and with the use of the correct 'mixing' techniques, it can provide almost perfect anonymity. This has led to rise of ransomware, where hackers can demand payments in the given likelihood that they are untraceable. Existing non-block chain currency or payment technologies cannot offer such a solution. The reason for its popularity is due in no small way to the ingenuity of its underlying framework. It keeps a publicly accessible ledger of all transactions, where all transactions are confirmed and added to this ledger through the Bitcoin mining process. This public ledger prevents the dreaded 'double spend', which has afflicted many previous attempts at creating a usable virtual currency. What is clever, however, is that it can be difficult to associate an address with any other address in the Bitcoin network, so people can remain anonymous, provided they use adequate steps in using different Bitcoin addresses and 'mixing' technology. This separation of virtual currency accounts from real-world identities, along with the ability for an individual to create an arbitrary number of accounts, enables the development of novel, complex layering transaction patterns, and any Bitcoin user can create any number of addresses that they wish to. There is also a problem in the verification of blockchains. In Bitcoin, for instance, the incentive to validate the blockchain lies in the mining process, where miners compete to mine new coins. However, since that will end after 21 million are mined, it is hoped that the financial gains will then lie in the transaction fees, but incentivizing other blockchains may be a larger problem. There is also a potential issue in the governance of Bitcoin and other decentralized ledger technologies. They usually have a governance group of lead developers to implement the agreed changes, but there is nothing to stop a core of the blockchain from 'forking' off to a competing blockchain (Bowater, 2018).

4.3 BLOCKCHAIN USE CASES

Blockchain has already been used in a number of areas outside of cryptocurrencies. For instance, data centers are becoming the archive keepers of the world's information. The growth in data (160+ zettabytes by 2025) is one key factor driving the requirement for data centers to modernize, and like many other sectors, blockchain has become a key enabler to modernize. There are a number of ways in which blockchain is currently transforming the data center. The Ankr project (Song et al., 2019) is a decentralized cloud solution under development, with the aim of offering clients the infrastructure to run applications at lower prices compared with traditional cloud service providers (Figure 4.1). The Ankr Distributed Cloud Compute Network (DCCN) system is deployed over the computing resources managed by Kubernetes across a range of geographical locations.

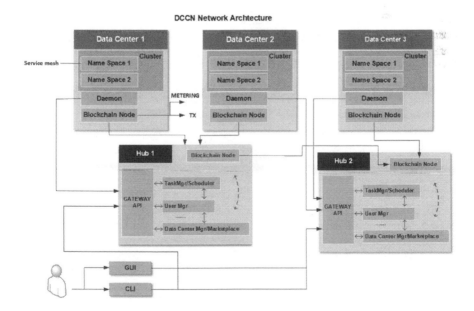

FIGURE 4.1   DCCN network architecture.

Other approaches to integrating blockchain into data centers include the following:

1. *Managing infrastructure*: Smart contracts in blockchains such as Ethereum would allow the automation of 'rules-based' operation and management functions in areas such as virtualization, asset management, capacity planning, and cooling.
2. *Managing uptime*: Even the best-designed data centers with multiple layers of redundancy have a latent centralized point of failure. Blockchain can potentially spread this risk among multiple devices but simultaneously maintain data currency, so that in case if failure, recovery is instant.
3. *Securing data center infrastructure management systems*: Blockchain can eliminate data loss and corruption by sharing data over its distributed ledger. Blockchain does not possess a central point of failure. Data integrity can be ensured through massive data replication.

There is also a valid argument for the adoption of blockchain for online identity. The world is becoming paperless through the move toward a cyberspace world; yet, when it comes to asserting who someone is with regard to banking, university accreditation, and so on, we end up having to fax, scan, or meet in person to assert our identities. There is simply no universally accepted virtual identifier that is accepted or trusted by all. The problem, of course, is non-trivial. Microsoft, however, is putting efforts into building an open, trustworthy, interoperable, and standards-based decentralized identity (DID) solution (Microsoft, 2019) (Figure 4.2). The open nature of the proposal is crucial. No one can 'own' this, and there are also a limited number of organizations that can make this happen – if ever – but Microsoft does have the potential.

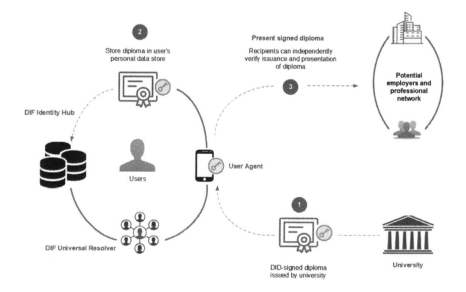

FIGURE 4.2 Example identity scenario. (From Microsoft, *Decentralized Identity*, Microsoft, https://query.prod.cms.rt.microsoft.com/cms/api/am/binary/RE2DjfY, 2019.)

The proposal for DID is not simplistic, with many elements in play, but the foundation is built on blockchain, which quite simply is the most appropriate technology to make it happen. The blockchain can cope with the myriad of untrusted parties while also asserting the identity of individuals with the highest assurance of truth. Of course, there remain the usual caveats about scalability and the consensus protocol, but here is a proposal that does make sense to implement via blockchain.

4.4 THE FUTURE OF BLOCKCHAIN

There are a number of potential use cases for blockchain such as a cryptocurrency based on an asset reserve, decentralized online identity, and electronic voting. We examine these scenarios here.

4.4.1 DIGITAL CURRENCIES

Libra is a digital currency built on the foundation of blockchain technology from Facebook and a number of other major technology companies. The mission for Libra is a global currency and financial infrastructure, which is composed of three parts. These parts are a secure, scalable, and reliable blockchain backed by a reserve of assets designed to give it an intrinsic value and governed by the independent Libra Association, tasked with evolving the ecosystem (Libra, 2019). The association is governed by the Libra Association Council, which is made up of one representative per validator node. This council makes decisions on the governance of the network and reserve. In the beginning, the group consists of the founding members: businesses, non-profit and multilateral organizations, and academic institutions from around the world. The target launch is 2020.

The security of the Libra Blockchain is built on correctly implementing aspects such as validators, Move programs, and the Move Virtual Machines (VM). They work to isolate aspects of code that contribute to a validator signing a block of transactions during consensus. They apply checks to increase assurance in the correctness of these components through formal specification and verification. They also claim that they will conduct code reviews, source control, and release management. This, of course, depends on the resources they actually allocate to it. There are additional security considerations that need to be given to blockchain applications such as capping the number of resources such as CPU, memory, and storage that can be given to nodes. This protects against denial of service to some degree. They also have verifiable random functions to protect against targeted denial-of-service attacks. It is difficult at this early stage to state how secure the Libra Blockchain is and whether the chain or the associated wallets can be hacked. At the start, the Libra Blockchain only grants votes to founding members, entities that meet predefined founding member eligibility criteria, so it is very unlikely that any of them will act maliciously.

They are working on validating the Libra protocol via an open-source libra core prototype implementation. This is written in Rust, primarily due to its focus on providing safe coding practices, systems programming support, and good performance.

They have also divided the internal components of the system for increased security, whereby the consensus safety component can run in a separate process. State machine replication protocols are also crucial, as they should guarantee that all honest nodes observe the same sequence of commits and that new commits are produced as long as valid commands are submitted.

4.4.2 E-Voting

The blockchain serves as a public ledger of transactions that cannot be reversed for future e-voting. The all-important consensus of the transaction (e.g., legitimate votes) is achieved through 'miners', all agreeing to validate new records being added to a database. Whenever a new insertion is to be made, e.g., a person votes, then a new transaction record is created by person A, who adds the details of his vote and uploads it to the blockchain of nodes for them to add the new transaction to the blockchain. Should it be deemed a valid transaction (which often is validated mathematically) by the majority of nodes, then the new vote is added to the end of the blockchain and remains there forever (Curran, 2018a). What is powerful about this solution is the fact that no centralized authority is needed to approve the votes but rather a majority consensus. Here, everyone agrees on the final tally, as they can count the votes themselves, and as a result of the blockchain audit trail, anyone can verify that no votes were tampered with and no illegitimate votes were inserted.

Of course, at this time, there are many who believe that a blockchain can be applied in most domains, while in reality, a blockchain only makes sense when multiple mutually mistrusting entities wish to interact and change the state of a system and are not able to agree on an online trusted third party. Some claim that the only true legitimate use case for a blockchain is cryptocurrencies; however, others think that the ledger's decentralized, tamper-proof nature makes it safe enough to allow fraud-free online elections. An interesting side effect of a blockchain is that it could allow for continuous voting, e.g., casting a vote every week or month. E-voting does bring some new problems such as ensuring privacy, especially in the case of public permissionless blockchains, but there are solutions for that. Other problems include the speed by which transactions can be verified. For instance, at this time, Bitcoin and Ethereum can only process less than 25 transactions per second, compared, for instance, with Visa or Mastercard, which can process thousands per second.

Some countries, however, have tried blockchain for voting. Some have also failed, such as the critical vulnerability found in the blockchain-based voting system that Russian officials planned to use in the 2019 Moscow City Duma election (Cimpanu, 2019). The Nasdaq also recently ruled the Estonia experiment safe enough to allow firms to start using blockchain for proxy voting. Blockchain may be championed as the solution to many problems in vain, but one domain where it might actually make sense is electronic voting. However, there are some who have grave concerns about using blockchain for voting within democracies (Lee, 2018).

4.5 CONCLUSION

Blockchains' most compelling use cases are in areas such as cryptocurrencies, e-voting, or harvesting unused computer processors, where all parties involved are untrusted and transactions must be immutable. Blockchain is an exciting viable technology that ushers in a new area of allowing untrusted global parties to transact with some assurance and transparency, but the use cases for this model remain finite. If you think blockchain is the answer to problem x......it more than likely is not.

REFERENCES

Blue, J., Furey, E., and Curran, K. (2018) An evaluation of secure storage of authentication data. *International Journal for Information Security Research (IJISR)*, 7(2):744–754.

Bowater, J. (2018) Bitcoin's anonymity: Clever or criminal? City A.M., 4 December 2018. www.cityam.com/bitcoins-anonymity-clever-criminal/

Cimpanu, C. (2019) Moscow's blockchain voting system cracked a month before election. ZDNet, 20 August 2019. www.zdnet.com/article/moscows-blockchain-voting-system-cracked-a-month-before-election/

Curran, K. (2018a) E-voting on the blockchain. *The Journal of the British Blockchain Association*, 1(2):1–6. doi:10.31585/jbba-1-2-(3)2018.

Curran, K. (2018b) Security and the internet of things. In *Cyber Security: Law & Guidance Handbook*, Bloomsbury Professional Ltd., London, UK, pp. 371–382.

Libra Association. (2019) *An Introduction to Libra*, Libra Association, May 2019. https://libra.org/en-US/wp-content/uploads/sites/23/2019/06/LibraWhitePaper_en_US.pdf

Lee, T. (2018) Blockchain-based elections would be a disaster for democracy. Ars Technica, 6 June 2018. https://arstechnica.com/tech-policy/2018/11/blockchain-based-elections-would-be-a-disaster-for-democracy/

Malkhi, D. and Reiter, M. (2013) Byzantine quorum systems. *Distributed Computing*, 11(4):203–213, 1998.

Malkhi, D., Reiter, M., and Wool, A. (2000) The load and availability of Byzantine quorum systems. *SIAM Journal on Computing*, 29(6):1889–1906.

Martino, W. (2016) Kadena—The first scalable, high performance private blockchain. Whitepaper, http://kadena.io/docs/Kadena-ConsensusWhitePaper-Aug2016.pdf

McCall, B. (2019) Blockchain: 5 things to know about the cryptocurrency technology. Irish Times, 25 April 2019. www.irishtimes.com/special-reports/blockchain-explored/blockchain-5-things-to-know-about-the-cyrptocurrency-technology-1.3863334

Microsoft (2019) *Decentralized Identity*, Microsoft, 2019 https://query.prod.cms.rt.microsoft.com/cms/api/am/binary/RE2DjfY

Miller, A., Xia, Y. Croman, K., Shi, E., and Song, D. (2016) The honey badger of BFT protocols. In *ACM SIGSAC Conference on Computer and Communications Security*, Vienna, Austria, pp. 31–42.

Reichert, C. (2016) Telstra explores blockchain, biometrics to secure smart home IoT devices. ZDNet, 22 September 2019. www.zdnet.com/article/telstra-explores-blockchain-biometrics-to-secure-smart-home-iot-devices/

Rizzo, P. (2016) MIT responds to bitcoin developer concerns over 'ChainAnchor'. Coindesk, 22 April 2016. www.coindesk.com/mit-dismisses-bitcoin-developer-criticism-project-proposal

Song, J., Wu, S., Liu, S., Fang, R., and Li, Q. (2019) ANKR—Build a faster, cheaper, securer cloud using idle processing power in data centers and edge devices. www.ankr.network/

5 Towards Secure Internet of Things
Blockchain Solutions, Challenges, and Open Issues

*Ranesh Kumar Naha, Sudheer Kumar Battula,
Khizar Hameed, K. C. Ujjwal, Md Anwarul Kaium
Patwary, Saurabh Garg, and Byeong Kang*

CONTENTS

5.1   INTRODUCTION

5.1.1   BACKGROUND

The shift of computing paradigm closer to the end devices has enabled Internet of Things (IoT) to create a wide-open network. This open network has enabled different time-sensitive applications such as smart cities (Awad et al. 2019), transportation (Battula et al. 2019), healthcare (Yang and Xu 2018), and disaster-related services (Ujjwal et al. 2019). This open network facilitates the addition of billions of devices into the information space, where the users not only consume the services but also contribute different kinds of resources for other applications. Moreover, the resources of IoT devices can currently be accessed by other devices as well. The current state of the art for the control of the IoT network is based on centralized principles, which are prone to cyberattacks (Abomhara 2015). The limited resources in IoT devices and highly distributed nature and heterogeneity of the devices further add constraints in securing the open IoT network. Given the rise of influence of IoT and its application in our daily lives, it is imperative to secure the network to prevent any security- and privacy-related attacks.

Few security architectures and solutions have been proposed to address the security and privacy issues according to each layer in the IoT paradigm. Khan and Salah (2018) proposed a taxonomy of IoT security solutions and also discussed various types of threats on the application, communication channel, and hardware related. Similarly, Arias et al. (2015), Malina et al. (2016), and Chen et al. (2017) proposed multiple types of security solutions to address the security and privacy challenges in IoT networks. However, most of the security frameworks are purely based on a centralized architecture, which is not suitable for a widely distributed and decentralized IoT environment. Moreover, conventional algorithms proposed for wireless sensor networks and other data communication protocols are not suitable for resource-constrained IoT environments, where IoT network demands scalable, distributed security, and lightweight protocols. As such, ensuring the high level of security in a wide-open network as IoT network is still an open challenge owing to various inherent features of IoT devices – limited resources, high distribution, and heterogeneity (Zhou et al. 2018).

Blockchain is a new technology entirely based on decentralization principles and secure cryptographic primitives. The secure cryptographic primitives allow the users to store the data on the immutable tamper-proof digital ledger of the blockchain, where it is nearly impossible or very difficult to alter the data. This tamper-proof ledger, coupled with the decentralization control mechanism, can leverage the current state of security of IoT network to make it more secure. Blockchain technology has high computational overhead, excessive bandwidth consumption, and computation delay (Dedeoglu et al. 2019). As such, the integration of blockchain technology to IoT network is not an easy task, as it comes with several challenges such as security, storage overhead, interoperability, scalability, data privacy, and legal issues (Reyna et al. 2018). Blockchain ensures a high level of security and robustness against privacy issues, but a suitable trade-off has to be carefully defined while integrating the technology in IoT network.

5.1.2 METHODOLOGY

This review focuses on the most recent solutions while presenting the overview of the existing solutions, including the blockchain-integrated ones. The study critically assesses the features and drawbacks along with associated challenges of the selected works. After the assessment, the study presents a comparative study of existing blockchain-based solutions categorized under different headings. The comparative analysis gives a comprehensive insight into the current state of the art of the existing blockchain solutions in IoT networks. Based on the knowledge of the current state, the review discusses open issues and future research directions in securing the sensitive IoT networks using decentralized and tamper-proof technology of blockchain in a balanced way.

5.1.3 CHAPTER ORGANIZATION

The rest of the chapter is organized as follows: Section 5.2 presents related reviews and surveys related to IoT security and blockchain. Section 5.3 discusses the existing challenges in IoT security, while Section 5.4 explains the existing solutions for secure IoT networks in detail. Section 5.5 describes the blockchain technology and solutions based on it for ensuring a high level of security in the IoT environment. Section 5.6 puts lights on the open issues and future research directions for integrating blockchain in the IoT network, while Section 5.7 concludes the chapter.

5.2 RELATED WORK

Lo et al. (2019) conducted a systematic review of the works to analyze the suitability of using blockchain-based platforms for IoT solutions from the perspectives of data and thing management. Hassija et al. (2019) published a work based on the survey of security-related challenges for IoT network and made a discussion on how the evolving technologies, such as machine learning, fog and edge computing, and blockchain technology, can be combined to tackle the issues. Sultan et al. (2019) in their review paper highlighted the issues existent in the IoT environment ever since the implementation of blockchain solutions in the IoT environment started.

Abdulghani et al. (2019) defined a comprehensive list of guidelines for IoT security and privacy at different levels for IoT architecture and discussed the challenges for such guidelines. Viriyasitavat et al. (2019) presented the business and research opportunities for integrating the blockchain technology in an IoT environment, along with analytical strength and weakness of such an integration. Wang et al. (2019) conducted a comprehensive survey of blockchain-based solutions in IoT applications and discussed the possible research discussion.

Given the current state of blockchain technology, there are a plenty of works that have explored the possibility of integrating the technology in an IoT environment with different motives. There are extensive surveys that have analyzed and assessed the suitability, challenges, and future research directions for such integration. However, defining a trade-off while integrating high-overhead blockchain-based solutions in time-sensitive IoT applications and networks has not been discussed in depth. The current state of knowledge in this regard has to be leveraged for more secure IoT networks dealing with sensitive data.

As such, this chapter reviews the current state-of-art solutions, including blockchain, in securing IoT applications. Besides, this work also discusses the challenges and open issues that need to be addressed to ensure a more secure IoT network. This chapter also discusses different factors that need to be considered while integrating blockchain technology into the open network in a balanced way.

5.3 EXISTING CHALLENGES IN IoT SECURITY

Given the participation of a large number of users and devices, security mechanism plays a vital role in the IoT applications. IoT system requires a twofold security scheme – physical device and software level security. Unlike other security mechanisms in any other system, the IoT environment also has three basic properties to maintain security: confidentiality, integrity, and availability. Security concern in the IoT environment has an impact on providing an effective IoT solution. Besides, IoT security needs to add an extra layer of security, as the IoT system is involved with vastly distributed autonomous physical devices and software applications.

The IoT devices may have different security issues because of the diverse nature of functionalities and services offered. The security challenges in IoT can be divided into two categories: technological challenges and security challenges. The technological challenges arise when the hardware and device architecture are not well-equipped with the security mechanism. The security challenges, on the other hand, arise when cryptographic mechanisms are not up to the mark to prevent the attacker. Despite many existing security mechanisms proposed to address the security issues in the IoT network, there are still many security issues in the network. Thus, ensuring a high level of security assurance in IoT networks is still an open challenge.

This section describes the current security challenges in the IoT environment, as illustrated in Figure 5.1. There are a lot of security concerns in IoT devices, concerning some well-known applications, which are described in the following subsections.

FIGURE 5.1   Security in IoT.

5.3.1 DEVICE IDENTIFICATION

Identifying a device correctly in IoT network is a fundamental issue, as the devices are growing at an unprecedented rate in the IoT environment (Li et al. 2017). Sending to and receiving messages from correct devices is the fundamental research problem, as each IoT platform has its identification format to maintain the communication between devices. It becomes more challenging to ensure secure communication in the IoT environment because of no existent standard identification methods. The diverse nature of the hardware architecture of different IoT devices makes it more complex. Several identification systems were proposed to ensure a robust IoT application in identifying the desired device. A device name system was proposed based on the resource requests. It works between heterogeneous IoT platforms. However, this system has limitations while ensuring the secured device identification in the cloud-based IoT environment (Koo et al. 2019).

A few researchers proposed methods to detect the faulty device in the IoT application to restrict to send the message to the wrong devices. The approach ensures the quality and service within the IoT network. A method called Detection and Identification Context Extraction (DICE) was proposed based on context extraction from the source device (Choi et al. 2018). DICE does not require any user's activity to detect the faulty device. The two-phase computation in DICE, including a real-time computation, helps in finding the faulty device. The proposed method improves the usability and feasibility. However, DICE does not address the issue regarding the threat by the malicious user from the service provider.

5.3.2 SECURE COMMUNICATION

Communication has a significant impact on any interconnected network. Especially in an IoT environment, where heterogeneous and different kinds of devices are connected, IoT devices do not use the encryption technique before transferring data. Thus, secure communication between devices in the IoT environment is a critical aspect to consider while building an IoT ecosystem. A few numbers of schemes have been proposed to ensure a secured communication channel between IoT devices. A digital certificate was proposed by Panwar and Kumar (2015) to provide secure communication on transport layer security. A digital certificate is necessary to be issued by a certificate authority to make secure communication more robust.

5.3.3 DATA SECURITY

Data security is a non-physical threat in IoT applications. Trusted data transfer between devices in the IoT environment is a key issue to provide a reliable IoT system. Owing to the heterogeneity characteristics of IoT applications, it is challenging to control and prevent anomalies and threats. There are a few desirable data security characteristics – confidentiality, integrity, and authentication to maintain data security. The features are explained in detail as follows.

5.3.3.1 Data Confidentiality

Data confidentiality keeps the data confidential in any data communication system. In the IoT environment, massive data exchange takes place between the devices for various applications such as banking transaction data, health fitness data, and many more. This data is very confidential and must be delivered to the desired devices; this confidential data can be vulnerable to unauthorized users within the IoT system (Ali and Ullah 2016).

5.3.3.2 Data Integrity

Data integrity plays a vital role in IoT security systems, as it is imperative to ensure that any unexpected sources have not tampered the data. Data tampering of any kind may cause severe damage to the security system. To avoid data manipulation and tampering from an outside attacker, a reliable data integrity scheme is necessary. Trustworthy data integrity needs to be established in the IoT environment to share trusted information between devices. An optimistic data integrity preservation technique was proposed (Bhattacharjee et al. 2017) to provide trustworthiness between devices. This preservation technique uses a Bayesian inference, which measures the trustworthiness by scoring data integrity from the collected data.

5.3.3.3 Data Authenticity

Data authenticity is another factor in the data security system in IoT system. Data authenticity can be ensured at the receiver side by an authentication algorithm for a reliable machine-to-machine communication. In an IoT application, sensing data are stored in a cloud environment, which is managed by a third-party organization. Thus, it becomes more insecure, and it may be attacked by outsiders and malicious cloud employees (Mahajan et al. 2011). The IoT network should ensure that the data has not been tampered or partially dropped by while it is transferred from one device to another. Li et al. (2017) proposed frameworks called dynamic tree chaining and geometric star chaining for authenticity and integrity for IoT data communication. The proposed work targets three entities in making a secured data communication channel. The three entities are sensing devices, cloud, and data applications.

5.3.4 ACCESS CONTROL

In an IoT network, devices are connected to exchanges messages and complete a job within the network. The IoT devices within the network are vulnerable to attack and being compromised by an attacker, which makes access control mechanism an important factor in the IoT network. Owing to a large number of devices and machine-to-machine communication, it is difficult to maintain a proper channel of communication and control access to the correct device. A reliable access control security solution can play a vital role in identifying a threat or a suspicious access. Several mechanisms have been proposed for IoT application to control intruder and unauthenticated access. Capability-based access control was proposed by Chen et al. (2015) for a distributed IoT network. It provides end-to-end security, which can be accessed by a group. In a multiagent system, different levels of access control are required, as different levels have different roles. As a result, it is not possible to control access by a single-level access control method. Multilevel access control was proposed by Rivera et al. (2015) to address this issue.

5.3.5 PRIVACY

Maintaining privacy in the IoT system has been one of the most critical areas to consider, particularly in a smart home application. The smart home application enables the users to monitor their home remotely, including fire alarms, thief, children, and pet behavior. Such features make life easier than before. However, this brings in various privacy issues. An intruder can illegitimately access the family activities, gather their data, and take control of the devices by a malicious user remotely. Furthermore, as a user, we accept the fact that the service provider can access our information to provide the desired services. A security mechanism was proposed by Santoso and Vun (2015) to preserve the privacy for smart homes based on the AllJoyn framework. It uses curve cryptography technique for the authentication process. Some existing solutions are playing a more significant role in securing the IoT system by addressing security issues. In the next section, some existing solutions are discussed based on the challenges presented earlier in this section.

5.4 EXISTING SOLUTIONS FOR IoT SECURITY

Various resource-limited sensors accompany IoT devices, and they exchange information through the cloud, fog, edge, and other mobile networks. An IoT device has limited resources in terms of device configuration and power. Hence, securing IoT devices and data throws a new challenge, which leads to numerous new requirements. These requirements include the need for securing devices, networks, data traveling through multiple hops, and preserving privacy. The IoT devices can be secured by authentication and authorization. On the other hand, for securing data, robust encryption processes are needed. Secure IoT protocols are required to secure the communication within the IoT networks. Besides, anonymization can help to

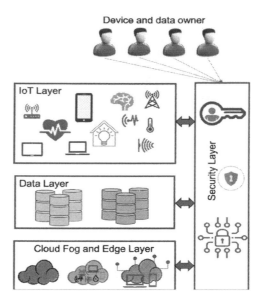

FIGURE 5.2   Architecture of IoT security.

preserve the privacy of sensitive data. Figure 5.2 shows a high-level architecture of IoT security. This section discusses some existing solutions for device security, network security, data security, and privacy preservation in the context of IoT. The features of all reviewed solutions are presented in Table 5.1.

5.4.1   IoT DEVICE SECURITY

Li et al. (2019a) proposed a statistical learning-based time series method for securing IoT devices. In their work, various statistical learning models such as linear regression, neural networks, and the recurrent neural network were employed to secure IoT devices. These statistical models were used to find the differences between prediction and observation to point out malicious activities in IoT network. For anomaly detection, local outlier factor, cumulative statistics thresholding, and adaptive online thresholding were considered. The authors used four different synthetic attacks (unauthorized access, port scan, virus attack, and network flood) to evaluate the robustness of the system. The proposed method identifies an attack on IoT devices with limited communication and computation resources to secure them.

Siboni et al. (2019) proposed a framework for security testing for IoT devices. Security testing is a complex task because of device quantity, type, connectivity, and heterogeneous nature of device hardware, software, and operating systems (OS). The IoT devices are used in different states and contexts, where security risk varies based on their usage. The framework can test devices with both open-source and proprietary OS. Besides, the framework measures the internal and external activity of the IoT devices for standard security testing and advanced monitoring.

TABLE 5.1
Features of Existing Solutions for IoT Security

Research Work	Device Security				Network Security		Data Security	Privacy Preservation
	Authentication	Authorization	Malicious Behavior	Security Testing	Protocol Security	Network Connectivity/ Communication	Encryption	Anonymization
Yeole, Kalbande, and Sharma (2019)	✓	✓			✓		✓	
Li, Shinde, et al. (2019)			✓					
Siboni et al. (2019)				✓				
Challa et al. (2017)	✓					✓		
Usman et al. (2017)							✓	
Maram et al. (2019)							✓	
Yin et al. (2019)								✓
Wu et al. (2017)	✓						✓	
Jayaraman et al. (2017)	✓	✓					✓	

5.4.2 IoT Network Security

IoT network protocol security needs to be ensured to avoid exposure of sensitive data to untrusted individuals. Yeole, Kalbande, and Sharma (2019) proposed a security protocol for IoT communication network by combining a three-level security check. In the first level, the sender and receiver authenticate each other by choosing a number from two different arrays of 50 and 5 elements. The elements of 50-digit array consist of 2 random-digit combinations, and 5-digit array consists of 5 single-digit numbers 0–5. Symmetric cipher encryption, which is the next security level in the protocol, sends the authentication request. Finally, integrity checksum checks if the key is tempered during communication.

Challa et al. (2017) proposed a signature-based authentication scheme to make IoT network communication more secure. Both the user device and information provider device should mutually authenticate each other to access the network information. A private session is established after that to make future communication secure. The method uses random numbers and timestamps to protect from a strong reply attack. However, the scheme requires the clock of all participant IoT devices to be synced.

5.4.3 Data Security in IoT Environment

Usman et al. (2017) proposed a lightweight encryption algorithm called Secure IoT (SIT) to secure data in an IoT environment. SIT used a 64-bit block cipher to encrypt data in the IoT environment. SIT algorithm is a composition of a uniform and Feistel substitution-permutation network. It can be implemented in a low-cost 8-bit microcontroller, which performs better when compared with many other recently proposed encryption methods. Data is dependent on the key for encryption and decryption. The encryption-and-decryption process is composed of five rounds, where one unique key is used in each round. Five different kinds of security analysis, namely linear and differential cryptanalysis, weak keys, related keys, interpolation attacks, and SQUARE attack, were done for the verification of the effectiveness of SIT algorithm. The algorithm was evaluated using six different evaluation metrics – key sensitivity, execution time, memory utilization, image histogram, image entropy, and correlation.

Maram et al. (2019) proposed an intelligent security algorithm for data security in the IoT environment. The algorithm employs an extend Substitution box (S-box) to work with UNICODE data privacy. The existing S-box was used with the American Standard Code for Information Interchange text only. S-box method is key-dependent and highly dynamic. The efficient data encryption method for UNICODE is important, because UNICODE supports over 150 languages. Security analysis and evaluation of the proposed intelligent security algorithm were done with the UNICODE of several languages. A data-anonymization technique for IoT environment was proposed by Yin et al. (2019) to secure private user data in healthcare. The anonymization in the proposed technique was achieved using the holomorphic method through identity-based encryption. The user could choose their anonymous parameters for anonymization for their healthcare data security.

The anonymization technique only works with the standalone healthcare system. Hence, further research is required to make it useful for cloud-based IoT solutions.

5.4.4 PRIVACY PRESERVATION IN IoT

Sensitive and private user information should not be revealed during their interaction with IoT devices and system actions. Yin et al. (2019) proposed a privacy preservation method for wearable IoT devices by using a mutual authentication scheme. Wearable devices are authenticated using a smartphone using a cloud server. Such a traditional way has various limitations such as inapplicability and desynchronization attacks. To mitigate these limitations, Wu et al. (2017) proposed an anonymous authentication method for a wearable device. The work can be further extended by adding group authentication.

Jayaraman et al. (2017) proposed a privacy preservation architecture for IoT to keep IoT devices private. In their architecture, sensed data is stored in Linked Sensor Middleware (LSM) by ingesting data through hashing. The data access scheme ensures privacy preservation by using the homomorphic properties of the Paillier cryptosystem. This property enables data retrieval without exposing data to the users or servers. The proposed method was evaluated in OpenIoT platform, and the overall performance of the algorithm was better in terms of query processing time.

Table 5.1 shows the different features of various works done so far in IoT security. From the table, it can be concluded that a combinational method, which can address device, network, and data security issues, as well as privacy preservation, is required for a secure IoT network.

5.5 BLOCKCHAIN SOLUTIONS IN IoT

The recent years have witnessed the adoption of blockchain technology in the IoT network. The adaptation has increased due to various secure features of blockchain, such as decentralization, distributed immutable ledger, transparency, tamperproofing, and auditability of data. These features have the potential to address the security and privacy vulnerabilities occurred with the massive number of smart devices in the IoT environment. Figure 5.3 shows the blockchain-based decentralized IoT architecture. The architecture consists of devices, miners, and shared immutable ledgers used to communicate among IoT devices securely. The immutable nature of a shared distributed ledger allows the storing of transactions on the blockchain in a more secure manner.

Indeed, security and privacy concerns have become a significant loophole in the IoT network. Such a loophole requires a demanding effort and attention from the developers and researcher communities to propose meaningful solutions to overcome it. The security challenges for the IoT network include confidentiality, integrity, availability, authentication, authorization, access control, and data sharing among the users and devices of the network. Moreover, the privacy challenge comprehends two types of privacy – identity privacy and transaction privacy. This section discusses and presents a detailed review of different blockchain-based IoT solutions designed to address the aforementioned security and privacy challenges in the IoT environment.

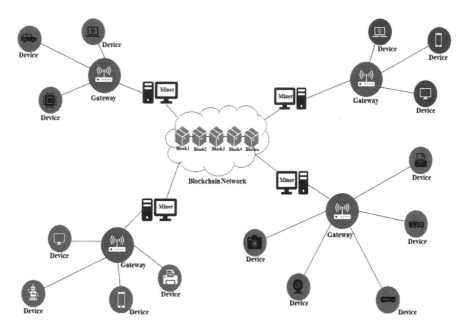

FIGURE 5.3   Blockchain-based IoT architecture.

5.5.1 SECURITY AND PRIVACY

Rahman et al. (2019) designed the blockchain-based decentralized security and privacy solution for devices, utilizing the smart contracts to enable and distribute the sharing economy among smart cities components in an efficient way. The proposed model allows the fog nodes to use the cognitive methods, such as machine learning and pattern recognition, to extract the data from the deployed mobile and IoT devices over the network. The model then performs the analytical process on data before storing it into the blockchain.

Xie et al. (2019) explored the trust management and user privacy challenges in the IoT-based vehicular network to support 5G services for vehicular ad hoc network operation under the concept of software-defined network (SDN). They designed a blockchain-based solution, backed by immutable ledgers, to support the trust management services among different vehicles. The proposed scheme also ensures the security of vehicles along with the user privacy by utilizing the inherent cryptographic primitives, such as digital signatures used in blockchain.

Another blockchain-based decentralized IoT network with SDN features was designed by Muthanna et al. (2019) to tackle the security and privacy challenges along with the availability and reliability concerns for the IoT network. The benefit of integrating the SDN with blockchain technology is that it can process and manage the various tasks locally at decentralized controllers in a trustful manner. In addition, the scheme also achieves greater reliability and efficiency in terms of resource computations, with the minimum possible delay between network components.

Dedeoglu et al. (2019) proposed a blockchain-based layered architecture to ensure the trustworthiness of data in a decentralized IoT environment. In the proposed architecture, each layer module is connected to establish the end-to-end trust between them. The data layer is liable for maintaining the trustworthiness of sensing data, while the blockchain layer is responsible for data verification. In addition, the gateway module is also implemented to compute the trusted reputation more securely.

With the advent of blockchain technology in industry 4.0, people are now adopting the blockchain solutions in businesses for establishing trust among different parties. However, the trust establishment among the industrial processes is a challenging task. Therefore, to address this challenge, Zhang et al. (2019) designed a blockchain-based decentralized model to ensure the security and trust factor among the industrial processes, with high-quality service. In addition to security, the model also ensures data provenance to facilitate and maintain the overall process activities in an efficient way.

Fan et al. (2018) proposed a blockchain-based decentralized IoT scheme with the public blockchain ledger to address the time-synchronization issues among the IoT devices. The ledger, which is used for storing the updated transactions, guarantees the synchronization among devices and protects devices from external attacks. In addition to the public ledger, the consensus algorithm, called Byzantine fault tolerance, was also utilized to maintain trusted and effective relationships among IoT devices.

Commercial applications based on IoT architecture are gradually increasing with the advancement of narrow-band concept designed for constrained IoT devices. A narrow-band IoT network is a low-power wide-area network designed to empower the services and features of low-range cellular devices to communicate remotely. However, there are still many security issues, including the authentication and privacy of data, which demand further effort from the researchers and academia to address them. One such effort was made by Hong, Hu, and Sun (2019), who proposed a blockchain-based decentralized IoT architecture for narrow-band devices. The architecture tried to achieve the authentication and accountability of data passed through different network layers and provides the guarantee of data protection during the validation process. Moreover, the security analysis also demonstrates the robustness of the scheme against various types of passive and active attacks on narrow-band IoT networks.

To achieve the confidentiality, integrity, and availability along with the anonymity challenges in IoT-based patient health systems, Dwivedi et al. (2019) proposed blockchain-based secure management and analysis system for the healthcare data. The proposed system considers the integration challenges, such as usage of extra bandwidth consumption and expensive protocols, during the implementation, which can incur extra computation overload on the IoT devices. Moreover, the security analysis is also performed to measure the system's accuracy against the deployment of malicious transactions.

With the invention of blockchain technology, the intrusion detection systems (IDSs) are the best way to prove the signatures in a peer-to-peer manner, which can greatly enhance the reliability and trust of devices on each other. Following this approach, Li et al. (2019b) proposed blockchain-based decentralized IDS to verify the signatures of IoT devices, without the need of a central third party between them. The proposed scheme achieved the robustness of the system against malicious scenarios and also increased the efficiency of the system.

5.5.2 PRIVACY PRESERVING

With the advancement of IoT networks and the successful provision of smart services to the users for the betterment of communities, the IoT devices have become a vital part of today's human lives. However, most of the IoT devices are not designed according to the proper security standards. Also, these IoT devices are not adequately receiving the security updates and patches from the company that designed and built them. As a result, these devices are prone to different types of security and privacy risks that need to be overcome. Zhao et al. (2019) proposed the blockchain-based scheme to securely deliver the software updates to IoT devices, with the guaranteed privacy to users. The proposed scheme utilizes the underlying cryptographic features such as hash and digital signatures available in blockchains to ensure the security properties such as availability, integrity, and privacy about data. In addition, a novel incentive mechanism called proof-of-delivery was also proposed for transmission nodes that are involved in the delivery of security patches and updates to IoT nodes. The transmission nodes utilized the attribute-based and double-authentication-preventing signatures to successfully verify the updates claims using the attributes of IoT devices. The security analysis of the scheme proves the robustness of the secure method against the privacy attacks on users.

Another blockchain-based decentralized scheme was designed by Shen et al. (2019) to preserve the privacy of IoT encrypted data over the network. In this scheme, support vector machine (SVM), in conjunction with different primitives such as polynomial multiplication and homomorphic encryption, is utilized to securely share the data among multiple providers. Each IoT device can save and share the encrypted data on an immutable distributed ledger. The security analysis of the system claims that it provides the confidentiality of sensing data while sharing it with different service providers.

5.5.3 DATA INTEGRITY

The development of the IoT network results in an increasing number of devices around the corner, which can transform and shape society for a new era. Traditionally, the existing IoT architectures entail the sensing devices to get data from the deployed environment and transmit to the centralized base stations. However, the centralized architecture endures from various types of challenges such as a single point of failure and security and privacy attacks, which pose data integrity at risk. To address these limitations in the IoT network, Hang and Kim (2019) proposed blockchain-based decentralized solutions for IoT devices. Such solutions confirm the protection of data integrity by using the cryptographic primitives, which include hash and digital signatures. The platform allows the IoT devices to store the real-time sensing data on the blockchain in an immutable way. Apart from that, the proposed architecture also allows to perform the control and management functions on IoT devices, which provide a secure and authentic way of the communication between IoT devices and users. The analysis result proves that the system is efficient and scalable to support a diverse range of IoT devices.

Malik et al. (2019) designed another approach to solving the traceability and integrity challenges in IoT-based supply management systems. The approach used the blockchain integrated reputation system to automate the supply management process, using the three-layer architecture approach. In this approach, the consortium blockchain is utilized to manage the trust reputation scores given by different participants to each product in the supply chain process. The computation results of the proposed scheme achieved the transparency, efficiency, and automation of trust scores, with minimal overhead and latency.

Chen et al. (2018) proposed a blockchain-based data integrity scheme to protect the data integrity in the decentralized IoT network. Existing data integrity solutions proposed for IoT environment were based on centralized architectures and hence suffer from the network bottleneck and single-point-of-failure issues. In the proposed solution, a stochastic technique is employed to overcome the limitations that occurred from the integration of IoT and blockchain network, such as resource consumption and limited computing power. Few IoT nodes called cooperative nodes are used to transmit the data in a random fashion, which increases the security level of the system by introducing uncertainty among them. In the proposed data integrity scheme, the lightweight miners are responsible for the data and block generation at edge level and also for broadcasting the same to other nodes in a secured fashion.

5.5.4 DATA SHARING

Traditional IoT security solutions mostly utilize third-party services, such as cloud, to process and store the user data with a minimal fee. The benefit of using these services is the convenience for the users to access their data. However, the limitation found in existing third-party solutions is that they mostly rely on centralized architectures. In such centralized architectures, the failure of a single node can create the risk of data loss and further disclose the personal information to others. Therefore, to tackle this challenge, Manzoor et al. (2019) implemented a blockchain-based decentralized solution, which facilitates the users to store the data safely on distributed databases. The proxy re-encryption method was utilized to encrypt the data while sharing it with cloud service providers. The smart contracts played a vital role in establishing the trusted relationship between sensor devices and cloud services. The benefit of the proxy re-encryption method in IoT network is that only the right person sees data in the network.

Agyekum et al. (2019) proposed another blockchain-based data-sharing scheme for IoT-based cloud networks, where a fine-grained access control mechanism was utilized to access the data from cloud computing. Traditional security mechanism design for cloud computing networks has proved inadequate to preserve the confidentiality of data shared with other parties (Pearson and Benameur 2010). Also, these mechanisms are prone to various types of security attacks, such as collusion attacks (Chow et al. 2010). Therefore, in this scheme, the proxy re-encryption scheme is utilized to provide a secure environment for decentralized IoT devices, using the inner-product encryption method with device attributes (Takashima and Okamoto 2014). The blockchain-based proxy server processes the data into different chunks and then initializes the proxy re-encryption method for generated IoT data.

With the distributed nature of devices and their generated streaming data, the secure management of IoT data is a crucial challenge for the IoT environment where trusted storage is required for maintaining the data and transactions at a safer place. Earlier, the single server was responsible for maintaining and handling the IoT generated data, which proved to be insufficient for the distributed IoT devices and their generated data. Therefore, to rectify these challenges, Nyamtiga et al. (2019) proposed a blockchain-based decentralized system for IoT devices. The potential solution first discovers the integration challenges of blockchain technology with IoT network and then addresses various security issues, including integrity, anonymity, and availability of IoT data stored at decentralized storage.

5.5.5 ACCESS CONTROL

Giving the right access to the right person in the right way is a very critical challenge in the intensive computing paradigm. Such a challenge requires demanding effort from the researcher and academia to solve it. In large-scale IoT networks, the access control mechanism is employed for giving access to IoT devices to specific users by using some intelligent techniques. However, existing access control mechanisms, designed for high-performance computing resources, are not directly applicable to the IoT networks, owing to a lack of intensive computations and being centralized in nature. Therefore, to address these issues, Ding et al. (2019) proposed a blockchain-based decentralized access control mechanism for constrained IoT devices. In this mechanism, the device attributes are utilized to maintain and control the access permission of IoT devices. The immutable feature of blockchain technology is utilized to securely store the attributes related to IoT devices on the distributed ledger. Moreover, the security analysis of the proposed scheme showed that the effective utilization of the qualities helped to protect against different types of security attacks, such as man-in-the-middle, replay, and impersonation attacks.

Ma, Shi, and Li (2019) proposed another blockchain-based access control mechanism to perform the distributed key management operations for a large number of IoT devices to reduce the delay from the cloud environment. In this mechanism, the fine-grained mechanism was employed to extend the behavior of devices for greater scalability in a decentralized network. The mechanism uses privacy-preserving principles to access IoT devices using advanced cryptographic protocols such as elliptic curve cryptography. The computational results and security analysis highlighted the significance of the proposed scheme and verified the greater scalability when compared with the network operation sizes.

The access control mechanisms with the combination of permission-based fine granularity methods, provides a secure way for IoT devices to use the network resources efficiently. To make such effort realistic, Ouaddah et al. (2016) proposed a blockchain-based decentralized access control and permission delegation method for IoT devices. In the method, the distributed ledger was used to store the events of the delegation in a secure form. Also, the query delegation method was proposed and tested on the proposed framework, which highlights the significance of access control policies for users and the IoT devices.

5.5.6 AUTHENTICATION

The IoT consists of a large number of devices involved in data capturing and transmission from one place to another, without the involvement of human beings in the whole process. However, the critical challenge faced by today's IoT network is the authentication and authorization of devices to transmit data in a secure and trusted manner. For the achievement of such challenges in IoT, Hammi et al. (2018) proposed the blockchain-based decentralized IoT authentication scheme to identify and authenticate the device by using the features of blockchain technology. The scheme works in the form of secure zones called bubbles, which are responsible for authenticating the IoT devices for secure communication among them. The smart contract features are utilized to assert the communication rules on miners to authenticate and register the IoT devices in a particular region.

The integration of blockchain technology into IoT has started to replace the existing centralized IoT solutions to overcome the various security and privacy issues. Not only decentralization but also other features, such as immutable ledger, transparency, and auditability, have the potentials to come up with new and significant solutions for IoT networks. Jiang et al. (2019) proposed a blockchain-based public key mechanism for thin clients as an example to make blockchain-integrated IoT network practicable. The thin clients behave as IoT devices and are capable of downloading a full copy of the distributed ledger into their storage. In addition, the proposed architecture also protects the privacy of thin IoT clients by using private information retrieval functions in the network. In this manner, the decentralized architecture can provide a secure environment to both thin and full nodes for securely exchanging their information.

With the increasing number of devices in the IoT network, the management of such devices is a very crucial task. Such a task demands potential efforts from the researcher communities to overcome this by proposing meaningful solutions. The integration of blockchain technology with IoT network brings new reforms in the maintenance of network operations by using the core features of blockchain. For example, the immutability feature in the blockchain allows the network administrator to manage and configure the devices by providing resistant against malicious modifications. To implement such an idea, Jiang et al. (2019) proposed a blockchain-based decentralized architecture, which manages and monitors the IoT devices by using a private blockchain. The architecture allows us to perform Create, Read, Update, and Delete operations with the utilization of advanced access control mechanisms. In the proposed architecture, an updated file related to the configuration for devices is stored at the immutable ledger. In case of any device failure, the file can easily be downloaded from the blockchain database. As a result, the data are updated and record on the database securely.

Table 5.2 shows the comparison between different blockchain-based security solutions specifically designed for resource-constrained IoT devices from different

TABLE 5.2
Comparison of Different Perspectives for Blockchain-Based IoT Security Solutions

References	Problems Addressed	Security Challenges Addressed	Techniques Used	Security Attacks Detected	Blockchain Network	Storage Used (On-Chain/Off-Chain)	Use Cases/Applications Studied	Implementation Setup
Rahman et al. (2019)	Security and privacy of data in the IoT environment	Security and Privacy	Artificial Intelligence Techniques	Not Defined	Private	Both	Smart City	Ethereum Blockchain
Xie et al. (2019)	The trustworthiness of IoT data	Data security User Privacy	Cryptographic primitives	Not Defined	Public	Both	SDN-enabled Vehicular Ad-hoc Network	Software-Defined Network
Manzoor et al. (2019)	Scalability and trust issues	Confidentiality Data Sharing	Proxy Re-Encryption	Not Defined	Private	Both	General	Ethereum Blockchain
Shen et al. (2019)	Secure and reliable data sharing	Privacy	Homomorphic cryptosystems PaillierSVM training algorithm	Data privacy attacks	Private	On-chain	Smart Cities	Not Defined
Zhang et al. (2019)	Trust among manufacturing processes	Security	Cryptographic Primitives	Not Defined	Private	On-chain	Smart Manufacturing System	Ethereum Blockchain
Hong, Hu, and Sun (2019)	Identity and privacy of IoT devices	Security and Privacy Authentication Accountability	Identity-based cryptography	Active and Passive attack	Private	On-chain	Narrowband IoT Network	Not Defined
Nyamtiga et al. (2019)	Secure management of IoT data and transaction	Anonymity Integrity	Data Off-loading scheme Open flow switches	Malicious attacks	Not Defined	Both	General	Ethereum Blockchain

(Continued)

TABLE 5.2 (*Continued*)
Comparison of Different Perspectives for Blockchain-based IoT Security Solutions

References	Problems Addressed	Security Challenges Addressed	Techniques Used	Security Attacks Detected	Blockchain Network	Storage Used (On-Chain/Off-Chain)	Use Cases/Applications Studied	Implementation Setup
Hang and Kim (2019)	Sensing data integrity issues	Security and privacy Integrity	Cryptographic primitives	Cyberattacks	Public	On-chain	General	Ethereum Blockchain
Malik et al. (2019)	Trusted related issues of data	Traceability Integrity	Reputation systems	Network attacks	Public	On-chain	Supply Chain	Ethereum Blockchain
Dedeoglu et al. (2019)	The trustworthiness of sensor data	Integrity	Cryptographic primitives	Collusion attack	Private	On-chain	Indoor target localization application	Not Defined
Ding et al. (2019)	Device access management issues	Access Control	Cryptographic primitives	Collusion attack Impersonation attack	Public	On-Chain	General	Not Defined
Dwivedi et al. (2019)	Security and privacy of patient data	Privacy	Cryptographic primitives	DoS attack Mining attack Storage attack Dropping attack Key Recovery attack	Private	On-chain	Healthcare	Ethereum Blockchain
Fan et al. (2018)	Time synchroniztion issues among IoT devices	Security	Cryptographic primitives	Cyberattacks	Public	On-chain	General	Not Defined
Hammi et al. (2018)	Authentication problem of IoT devices	Authentication Authorization Integrity	Cryptographic primitives	Sybil attack Spoofing attack	Public	On-Chain	General	Ethereum Blockchain

(Continued)

TABLE 5.2 (*Continued*)

Comparison of Different Perspectives for Blockchain-based IoT Security Solutions

References	Problems Addressed	Security Challenges Addressed	Techniques Used	Security Attacks Detected	Blockchain Network	Storage Used (On-Chain/ Off-Chain)	Use Cases/ Applications Studied	Implementation Setup
		Availability Non-Repudiation		Denial-of-service attack Message substitution attack Message replay attack				
Jiang et al. (2019)	Privacy and authentication of IoT devices	Privacy Authentication	Cryptographic primitives	51% attack	Public	On-chain	General	Not Defined
Košťál et al. (2019)	Management of IoT devices	Authentication Authorization Access Control	Cryptographic primitives	Not Defined	Private	On-chain	Enterprises Networks	Hyperledger Ethereum Blockchain
Li, Tug, et al. (2019)	Malicious signatures issues in Intrusion detection systems (IDSs)	Unforgeability	Cryptographic	Insider Attacks (Flooding and worm)	Consortium	Both	General	Not Defined
Ma, Shi, and Li (2019)	Key management issues in centralized architectures	Access Control Privacy	Cryptographic primitives	Not Defined	Private	Off-chain	General	Not Defined

(*Continued*)

TABLE 5.2 (Continued)
Comparison of Different Perspectives for Blockchain-based IoT Security Solutions

References	Problems Addressed	Security Challenges Addressed	Techniques Used	Security Attacks Detected	Blockchain Network	Storage Used (On-Chain/Off-Chain)	Use Cases/Applications Studied	Implementation Setup
Agyekum et al. (2019)	Data sharing problem in the IoT environment	Security and privacy Access control	Proxy Re-Encryption Scheme Inner-product encryption	Collusion attacks	Consortium	Both	General	Ethereum Blockchain
Zhao et al. (2019)	Secure delivery of software updates to IoT devices	Privacy (Users and Data)	Attributes-based signatures	DoS attack Chose message attack Selective attribute attack	Public	Both	General	Ethereum Blockchain
Ali et al. (2019)	Permission delegation issues in access control methods	Access Control	Process metadata language	DoS attack Sybil attack Eclipse attack Routing attack 51% attack Double spending Alternative history attack Race Attack Finney Attack	Public	On-chain	General	Ethereum Blockchain
Chen, Wang, and Wang (2018)	Data integrity issues of IoT data	Integrity Authentication	Cryptographic primitives	Centralized attack Link attack	Public	On-chain Off-chain	General	Not Defined

perspectives (such as problem addressed, security challenges, security techniques, attacks detected, blockchain network types, storage model [on-chain/off-chain], implementation set up, and use cases).

5.6 OPEN ISSUES AND FUTURE DIRECTIONS

This section discusses the open issues and research directions aimed at using the blockchain technology as a better solution to achieve a high level of security within the IoT network. Although the integration of blockchain into IoT offers a better solution for most of the security challenges stumbles, there are still a few security and privacy issues that usually come amid the integration.

5.6.1 IDENTITY MANAGEMENT

Similar to cloud, fog also provides a similar service to the end users for real-time operations over the network. Most of the services and applications build on IoT networks are time-sensitive, which require a quick decision on streaming data to perform legitimate actions. For example, blockchain-based authentication solutions can satisfy most of the security requirements for IoT applications. However, the decentralized authentication solutions may sometimes cause delays in providing the services, owing to the increase in authentication requests or failure of master authentication service. Such delays can lead to poor quality of service in the IoT network. Furthermore, authenticating the IoT device with user information can also affect the privacy of the user. Therefore, building an effective anonymous authentication scheme that minimizes the overhead of the process to support the requirements of delay-sensitive applications is still an open issue.

5.6.2 ACCESS CONTROL MANAGEMENT

Similar to identity management, authorization is also a most critical challenge in the IoT network to provide a secure environment for communication between users and devices. Owing to the decentralized untrusted IoT devices and poor control management services, the adversaries can easily get access to the IoT devices. Many blockchain-based authentication and authorization techniques have been proposed to provide decentralized management for a large number of IoT devices (Dukkipati et al. 2018, Novo 2018, Zhang et al. 2018). However, defining a similar rule for partially controlled heterogeneous devices is still an open challenge. Such a challenge requires significant solutions to overcome the limitations in the resource-constrained IoT environment. The future solutions should consider lightweight authentication and authorization protocols to save the processing time for sensitive applications.

5.6.3 TRUST MANAGEMENT

Blockchain-based authentication and authorization techniques are used to build a trust relationship among the devices in the IoT environment. However, these techniques authenticate the IoT device without considering the dynamic behavior of devices, to satisfy the requirements for basic IoT network. It is essential to propose a mechanism that can detect and prevent the underlying network from internal attacks to identify the trusted nodes and secure the relationship among them. Many blockchain-based techniques have been proposed to achieve trust management in the IoT environment (Chen et al. 2011, Bao and Chen 2012, Yan et al. 2014). These solutions lack standard and efficient protocols applicable to resource-constrained devices. Therefore, designing an efficient and trust management solution is still an open issue for an IoT environment.

5.6.4 INTRUSION DETECTION SYSTEM

Building an efficient IDS in an IoT environment, which is capable of detecting various types of security attacks such as port scanning, flooding, and few insider attacks on the network, is one of the most challenging tasks. To make this idea clearer and more understandable for the readers, Zarpelao et al. (2017) proposed a taxonomy consisting of different IDSs for IoT environment and also discussed various techniques used to enhance the IDS placement and detection methods along with the security threats and validation strategies. Many IDS models, such as network-based, distributed-based, host-based, and accelerating anomaly-based models, have been proposed to help the users detect and mitigate network attacks. However, most of the IDSs require some human intervention to define some rules for detecting and mitigating the attacks manually. Therefore, developing a fully automated IDS is still a complex task, owing to the limited computation capacity of IoT devices and the distributed nature of the network.

Graph-oriented applications are intrusion prone, especially dynamic graph-oriented IoT networks, in which devices grow over time (Patwary, Garg, and Kang 2019). As such, IoT network becomes vulnerable and intrusion friendly, because the devices may get disconnected and a new device may get connected. As a result, the security system becomes weak and attacker friendly. Therefore, an efficient IDS security network is necessary for the graph application to detect intrusion for the dynamically changing network.

5.6.5 HARDWARE SECURITY

Owing to the limited computational power and heterogeneous nature of the IoT nodes, developing secure and efficient algorithms for securing the hardware devices is a very intricate task. Also, a major challenge found in the hardware devices is the verification and refinement of the detected vulnerabilities in the IoT network. The other significant hardware issue is to update the security patches of the hardware devices against malicious and fraudulent behavior. Hence, designing the standard protocols or algorithms for the verification and delivery of security updates to the hardware devices is still an open design challenge for the IoT networks.

5.6.6 PRIVACY

In the IoT network, the role of the end devices is dual. They are deployed as the packet-forwarding nodes to broadcast the data to other nodes in the network as well as data storage and processing nodes to perform some useful computations on data. However, there are two major common issues found in the IoT devices that make them unsuitable for the deployment of critical operations. The first one is the privacy issue related to the user data where fake nodes can get access to user data to breach the privacy of users. The second is the privacy of the application data, where malicious applications running on the IoT nodes can perform unauthorized actions on the data. The associated overheads for various available cryptographic methods such as attribute-based encryption (Belguith et al. 2018) and cipher-text-based secure proxy (Yao et al. 2015) are bulky. Therefore, designing lightweight and efficient algorithms to preserve the privacy of the data is still an open issue in the IoT network.

5.6.7 PROTOCOLS AND STANDARDS

The IoT is a complex ecosystem that consists of a wide variety of different smart devices used in human life to make daily life tasks easier and more efficient. With the proliferation of IoT technologies such as wireless communication and embedded systems, various types of new IoT devices have come into the market, but they lack proper standardization. The verification of these devices in the real environment is very complex. The absence of proper standardization can further make such verification prone to various types of cyberattacks. Therefore, there is a need for proper protocols and standards for the end devices in the IoT network.

5.7   CONCLUSION

For the past few years, the progressive development in the IoT paradigm, along with fog computing, has seen an unprecedented surge in the number of end devices connected to the open IoT network. The trend is set to continue, with the addition of billions of devices into the information space, where the users not only consume the services but also contribute to other applications and services. The data generation and exchange within the network will be massive. This open network, coupled with tamper-prone centralized control architecture, has made the deployment of IoT applications vulnerable to security attacks and privacy issues. As such, this chapter highlighted the existing challenges in creating a secure IoT network in broad categories. The chapter presented an elaborated description of the basic principles of decentralization and tamper-proof digital ledgers in blockchain. The chapter then forwarded an explanation of how these components can provide better-than-existing solutions to create a secure open IoT network. The chapter also made a comprehensive comparison between various existing solutions, including blockchain solutions for a secure IoT network. The chapter leveraged the current state of blockchain solutions by critically analyzing the weak aspects of blockchain, which can degrade the performance of highly distributed and resource-constrained IoT environment. Such aspects include high overhead, computational delay, and excessive bandwidth consumption. Moreover, despite the progressing wave of adaptation of blockchain technology in IoT for a secure network, issues such as identity and access control management, trust management, intrusion detection, hardware security, and privacy are yet to be addressed to make the blockchain technology an efficient solution to vulnerable IoT network.

Given the level of security that the blockchain technology ensures, it is desirable to integrate the technology into the open IoT network to create a more secure network. However, the inherent features of end devices in the IoT network – limited resources and highly distributed nature – make the adaptation of the technology with high overheads and bandwidth requirements non-trivial. Nonetheless, the level of security assurance required in the network, the types of IoT applications, and the availability of resources should be considered carefully to define the trade-off for using the blockchain technology in the IoT environment to create a more secure network.

REFERENCES

Abdulghani, Hezam Akram, Niels Alexander Nijdam, Anastasija Collen, and Dimitri Konstantas. 2019. "A study on security and privacy guidelines, countermeasures, threats: IoT data at rest perspective." *Symmetry* 11 (6):774.

Abomhara, Mohamed. 2015. "Cyber security and the internet of things: Vulnerabilities, threats, intruders and attacks." *Journal of Cyber Security and Mobility* 4 (1):65–88.

Agyekum, Obour, Kwame Opuni-Boachie, Qi Xia, Emmanuel Boateng Sifah, Jianbin Gao, Hu Xia, Xiaojiang Du, and Moshen Guizani. 2019. "A secured proxy-based data sharing module in IoT environments using blockchain." *Sensors* 19 (5):1235.

Ali, Gauhar, Naveed Ahmad, Yue Cao, Muhammad Asif, Haitham Cruickshank, and Qazi Ejaz Ali. 2019. "Blockchain based Permission Delegation and Access Control in Internet of Things (BACI)." *Computers & Security* 86:318–334.

Ali, Inayat, and Zahid Ullah. 2016. "Internet of things security, device authentication and access control: A review." *International Journal of Computer Science and Information Security* 14 (8):456–465.

Arias, Orlando, Jacob Wurm, Khoa Hoang, and Yier Jin. 2015. "Privacy and security in internet of things and wearable devices." *IEEE Transactions on Multi-Scale Computing Systems* 1 (2):99–109.

Awad, Ali Ismail, Steven Furnell, Abbas M. Hassan, and Theo Tryfonas. 2019. "Special issue on security of IoT-enabled infrastructures in smart cities." *Ad hoc Networks* 92.

Bao, Fenye, and Ing-Ray Chen. 2012. "Dynamic trust management for internet of things applications." *Proceedings of the 2012 International Workshop on Self-Aware Internet of Things*, San Jose California, USA.

Battula, Sudheer Kumar, Saurabh Garg, Ranesh Kumar Naha, Parimala Thulasiraman, and Ruppa Thulasiram. 2019. "A micro-level compensation-based cost model for resource allocation in a fog environment." *Sensors* 19 (13):2954.

Belguith, Sana, Nesrine Kaaniche, Maryline Laurent, Abderrazak Jemai, and Rabah Attia. 2018. "Phoabe: Securely outsourcing multi-authority attribute based encryption with policy hidden for cloud assisted IoT." *Computer Networks* 133:141–156.

Bhattacharjee, Shameek, Mehrdad Salimitari, Mainak Chatterjee, Kevin Kwiat, and Charles Kamhoua. 2017. "Preserving data integrity in IoT networks under opportunistic data manipulation." *2017 IEEE 15th International Conference on Dependable, Autonomic and Secure Computing, 15th International Conference on Pervasive Intelligence and Computing, 3rd International Conference on Big Data Intelligence and Computing and Cyber Science and Technology Congress*, Fukuoka, Japan (DASC/PiCom/DataCom/CyberSciTech).

Challa, Sravani, Mohammad Wazid, Ashok Kumar Das, Neeraj Kumar, Alavalapati Goutham Reddy, Eun Jun Yoon, and Kee Young Yoo. 2017. "Secure signature-based authenticated key establishment scheme for future IoT applications." *IEEE Access* 5:3028–3043. doi:10.1109/ACCESS.2017.2676119.

Chen, Borting, Yu-Lun Huang, and Mesut Güneş. 2015. "S-CBAC: A Secure Access Control Model Supporting Group Access for internet of things." *2015 IEEE International Symposium on Software Reliability Engineering Workshops (ISSREW)*:67–67.

Chen, Dong, Guiran Chang, Dawei Sun, Jiajia Li, Jie Jia, and Xingwei Wang. 2011. "TRM-IoT: A trust management model based on fuzzy reputation for internet of things." *Computer Science and Information Systems* 8 (4):1207–1228.

Chen, Liang, Sarang Thombre, Kimmo Järvinen, Elena Simona Lohan, Anette Alén-Savikko, Helena Leppäkoski, M. Zahidul, H. Bhuiyan, Shakila Bu-Pasha, Giorgia Nunzia Ferrara, and Salomon Honkala. 2017. "Robustness, security and privacy in location-based services for future IoT: A survey." *IEEE Access* 5:8956–8977.

Chen, Yu-Jia, Li-Chun Wang, and Shu Wang. 2018. "Stochastic blockchain for IoT data integrity." *IEEE Transactions on Network Science and Engineering* 7 (1):373–384.

Choi, Jiwon, Hayoung Jeoung, Jihun Kim, Youngjoo Ko, Wonup Jung, Hanjun Kim and Jong Kim. 2018. "Detecting and identifying faulty IoT devices in smart home with context extraction." *2018 48th Annual IEEE/IFIP International Conference on Dependable Systems and Networks (DSN)*, 25–28 June 2018.

Chow, Sherman, Weng Jian, Yanjiang Yang, et al. 2010. "Efficient unidirectional proxy re-encryption." In: *International Conference on Cryptology in Africa*. Springer, Berlin, Heidelberg, pp. 316–332.

Dedeoglu, Volkan, Raja Jurdak, Guntur D. Putra, Ali Dorri, and Salil S. Kanhere. 2019. "A trust architecture for blockchain in IoT." *arXiv preprint arXiv:1906.11461*.

Ding, Sheng, Jin Cao, Chen Li, Kai Fan, and Hui Li. 2019. "A novel attribute-based access control scheme using blockchain for IoT." *IEEE Access* 7:38431–38441.

Dukkipati, Chethana, Yunpeng Zhang, and Liang Chieh Cheng. 2018. "Decentralized, blockchain based access control framework for the heterogeneous internet of things." *Eighth ACM Conference on Data and Application Security and Privacy*, Tempe, AZ, USA.

Dwivedi, Ashutosh Dhar, Gautam Srivastava, Shalini Dhar, and Rajani Singh. 2019. "A decentralized privacy-preserving healthcare blockchain for IoT." *Sensors* 19 (2):326.

Fan, Kai, Shangyang Wang, Yanhui Ren, Kan Yang, Zheng Yan, Hui Li, and Yintang Yang. 2018. "Blockchain-based secure time protection scheme in IoT." *IEEE Internet of Things Journal* 6 (3):4671–4679.

Hammi, Mohamed Tahar, Badis Hammi, Patrick Bellot, and Ahmed Serhrouchni. 2018. "Bubbles of trust: A decentralized blockchain-based authentication system for IoT." *Computers & Security* 78:126–142.

Hang, Lei, and Do-Hyeun Kim. 2019. "Design and implementation of an integrated IoT blockchain platform for sensing data integrity." *Sensors* 19 (10):2228.

Hassija, Vikas, Vinay Chamola, Vikas Saxena, Divyansh Jain, Pranav Goyal, and Biplab Sikdar. 2019. "A survey on IoT security: Application areas, security threats, and solution architectures." *IEEE Access* 7:82721–82743.

Hong, Hanshu, Bing Hu, and Zhixin Sun. 2019. "Toward secure and accountable data transmission in narrow band internet of things based on blockchain." *International Journal of Distributed Sensor Networks* 15 (4):1550147719842725.

Jayaraman, Prem Prakash, Xuechao Yang, Ali Yavari, Dimitrios Georgakopoulos, and Xun Yi. 2017. "Privacy preserving internet of things: From privacy techniques to a blueprint architecture and efficient implementation." *Future Generation Computer Systems* 76:540–549.

Jiang, Wenbo, Hongwei Li, Guowen Xu, Mi Wen, Guishan Dong, and Xiaodong Lin. 2019. "PTAS: Privacy-preserving thin-client authentication scheme in blockchain-based PKI." *Future Generation Computer Systems* 96:185–195.

Khan, Minhaj Ahmad, and Khaled Salah. 2018. "IoT security: Review, blockchain solutions, and open challenges." *Future Generation Computer Systems* 82:395–411.

Koo, Jahoon, Se-Ra Oh, and Young-Gab Kim. 2019. "Device identification interoperability in heterogeneous IoT platforms." *Sensors (Basel, Switzerland)* 19 (6):1433. doi:10.3390/s19061433.

Košťál, Kristián, Pavol Helebrandt, Matej Belluš, Michal Ries, and Ivan Kotuliak. 2019. "Management and monitoring of IoT devices using blockchain." *Sensors* 19 (4):856.

Li, Fangyu, Aditya Shinde, Yang Shi, Jin Ye, Xiang-Yang Li, and Wenzhan Song. 2019a. "System statistics learning-based IoT security: Feasibility and suitability." *IEEE Internet of Things Journal* 6 (4):6396–6403. doi:10.1109/jiot.2019.2897063.

Li, Wenjuan, Steven Tug, Weizhi Meng, and Yu Wang. 2019b. "Designing collaborative block-chained signature-based intrusion detection in IoT environments." *Future Generation Computer Systems* 96:481–489.

Li, Xin, Huazhe Wang, Ye Yu, and Chen Qian. 2017. "An IoT data communication framework for authenticity and integrity." *2017 IEEE/ACM Second International Conference on Internet-of-Things Design and Implementation (IoTDI)*.

Lo, Sin Kuang, Yue Liu, Su Yen Chia, Xiwei Xu, Qinghua Lu, Liming Zhu, and Huansheng Ning. 2019. "Analysis of blockchain solutions for IoT: A systematic literature review." *IEEE Access* 7:58822–58835.

Ma, Mingxin, Guozhen Shi, and Fenghua Li. 2019. "Privacy-oriented blockchain-based dis-tributed key management architecture for hierarchical access control in the IoT sce-nario." *IEEE Access* 7:34045–34059.

Mahajan, Prince, Srinath Setty, Sangmin Lee, Allen Clement, Lorenzo Alvisi, Mike Dahlin, and Michael Walfish. 2011. "Depot: Cloud storage with minimal trust." *ACM Transactions on Computer Systems (TOCS)* 29 (4):12.

Malik, Sidra, Volkan Dedeoglu, Salil S. Kanhere, and Raja Jurdak. 2019. "TrustChain: Trust management in blockchain and IoT supported supply chains." *arXiv preprint arXiv:1906.01831*.

Malina, Lukas, Jan Hajny, Radek Fujdiak, and Jiri Hosek. 2016. "On perspective of security and privacy-preserving solutions in the internet of things." *Computer Networks* 102:83–95.

Manzoor, Ahsan, Madhsanka Liyanage, An Braeke, Salil S. Kanhere, and Mika Ylianttila. 2019. "Blockchain based proxy re-encryption scheme for secure IoT data sharing." *2019 IEEE International Conference on Blockchain and Cryptocurrency (ICBC)*.

Maram, Balajee, J. M. Gnanasekar, Gunasekaran Manogaran, and Muthu Balaanand. 2019. "Intelligent security algorithm for UNICODE data privacy and security in IoT." *Service Oriented Computing and Applications* 13 (1):3–15.

Muthanna, Ammar, Abdelhamied, A. Ateya, Abdukodir Khakimov, Irina Gudkova, Abdelrahman Abuarqoub, Konstantin Samouylov, and Andrey Koucheryavy. 2019. "Secure and reliable IoT networks using fog computing with software-defined network-ing and blockchain." *Journal of Sensor and Actuator Networks* 8 (1):15.

Novo, Oscar. 2018. "Blockchain meets IoT: An architecture for scalable access management in IoT." *IEEE Internet of Things Journal* 5 (2):1184–1195.

Nyamtiga, Baraka William, Jose Costa Sapalo Sicato, Shailendra Rathore, Yunsick Sung, and Jong Hyuk Park. 2019. "Blockchain-based secure storage management with edge computing for IoT." *Electronics* 8 (8):828.

Ouaddah, Aafaf, Anas Abou Elkalam, and Abdellah Ait Ouahman. 2016. "FairAccess: A new blockchain-based access control framework for the Internet of Things. *Security and Communication Networks*, 9 (18): 5943–5964.

Panwar, Mukul, and Ajay Kumar. 2015. "Security for IoT: An effective DTLS with public certificates." *2015 International Conference on Advances in Computer Engineering and Applications*, Ghaziabad, India.

Patwary, Anwarul Kaium, Saurabh Garg, and Byeong Kang. 2019. "Window-based stream-ing graph partitioning algorithm." *Proceedings of the Australasian Computer Science Week Multiconference*, Sydney, NSW, Australia.

Pearson, Siani, and Azzedine Benameur. 2010. "Privacy, security and trust issues arising from cloud computing." *2010 IEEE Second International Conference on Cloud Computing Technology and Science.*

Rahman, Abdur, Mamunur Rashid, M. Shamim Hossain, Elham Hassanain, Mohammed F. Alhamid, and Mohsen Guizani. 2019. "Blockchain and IoT-based cognitive edge framework for sharing economy services in a smart city." *IEEE Access* 7:18611–18621.

Reyna, Ana, Cristian Martín, Jaime Chen, Enrique Soler, and Manuel Díaz. 2018. "On blockchain and its integration with IoT. Challenges and opportunities." *Future Generation Computer Systems* 88:173–190.

Rivera, Diego, Luis Cruz-Piris, German Lopez-Civera, Enrique de la Hoz and Ivan Marsa-Maestre. 2015. "Applying an unified access control for IoT-based intelligent agent systems." *2015 IEEE 8th International Conference on Service-Oriented Computing and Applications (SOCA), 19–21 October 2015.*

Santoso, Freddy K., and Nicholas C.H. Vun. 2015. "Securing IoT for smart home system." 2015 *International Symposium on Consumer Electronics (ISCE),* Madrid, Spain.

Shen, Meng, Xiangyun Tang, Liehuang Zhu, Xiaojiang Du, and Mohsen Guizani. 2019. "Privacy-preserving support vector machine training over blockchain-based encrypted IoT data in smart cities." *IEEE Internet of Things Journal* 6 (5):7702–7712.

Siboni, Shachar, Vinay Sachidananda, Yair Meidan, Michael Bohadana, Yael Mathov, Suhas Bhairav, Asaf Shabtai, and Yuval Elovici. 2019. "Security testbed for IoT devices." *IEEE Transactions on Reliability* 68 (1):23–44. doi:10.1109/TR.2018.2864536.

Sultan, Abid, Muhammad Azhar Mushtaq, and Muhammad Abubakar. 2019. "IoT security issues via blockchain: A review paper." *Proceedings of the 2019 International Conference on Blockchain Technology,* Honolulu, HI, USA.

Takashima, Katsuyuki, and Tatsuaki Okamoto. 2014. Cryptographic processing system, key generation device, encryption device, decryption device, signature processing system, signature device, and verification device. Google Patents.

Ujjwal, K.C., Saurabh Garg, James Hilton, Jagannath Aryal, and Nicholas Forbes-Smith. 2019. "Cloud computing in natural hazard modeling systems: Current research trends and future directions." *International Journal of Disaster Risk Reduction* 38:101188.

Usman, Muhammad, Irfan Ahmed, M. Imran, Shujaat Khan, and Usman Ali. 2017. "SIT: A lightweight encryption algorithm for secure internet of things." *International Journal of Advanced Computer Science and Applications* 8 (1):1–10. doi:10.14569/ijacsa.2017.080151.

Viriyasitavat, Wattana, Tharwon Anuphaptrirong, and Danupol Hoonsopon. 2019. "When blockchain meets internet of things: Characteristics, challenges, and business opportunities." *Journal of Industrial Information Integration* 15:21–28.

Wang, Xu, Xuan Zha, Wei Ni, Ren Ping Liu, Y Jay Guo, Xinxin Niu, and Kangfeng Zheng. 2019. "Survey on blockchain for internet of things." *Computer Communications* 136:10–29.

Wu, Fan, Xiong Li, Lili Xu, Saru Kumari, Marimuthu Karuppiah, and Jian Shen. 2017. "A lightweight and privacy-preserving mutual authentication scheme for wearable devices assisted by cloud server." *Computers & Electrical Engineering* 63:168–181.

Xie, Lixia, Ying Ding, Hongyu Yang, and Xinmu Wang. 2019. "Blockchain-based secure and trustworthy internet of things in SDN-enabled 5G-VANETs." *IEEE Access* 7:56656–56666.

Yan, Zheng, Peng Zhang, and Athanasios V. Vasilakos. 2014. "A survey on trust management for internet of things." *Journal of Network and Computer Applications* 42:120–134.

Yang, Po, and Lida Xu. 2018. "The Internet of Things (IoT): Informatics methods for IoT-enabled health care." *Journal of Biomedical Informatics.* 87:154–156.

Yao, Xuanxia, Zhi Chen, and Ye Tian. 2015. "A lightweight attribute-based encryption scheme for the internet of things." *Future Generation Computer Systems* 49:104–112.

Yeole, Anjali, D. R. Kalbande, and Avinash Sharma. 2019. "Security of 6LoWPAN IoT networks in hospitals for medical data exchange." *Procedia Computer Science* 152:212–221. doi:10.1016/j.procs.2019.05.045.

Yin, Xiao Chun, Zeng Guang Liu, Bruce Ndibanje, Lewis Nkenyereye, and S.M. Riazul Islam. 2019. "An IoT-based anonymous function for security and privacy in healthcare sensor networks." *Sensors* 19 (14):3146.

Zarpelao, Bruno Bogaz, Rodrigo Sanches Miani, Cláudio Toshio Kawakani, and Sean Carlisto de Alvarenga. 2017. "A survey of intrusion detection in internet of things." *Journal of Network and Computer Applications* 84:25–37.

Zhang, Yongping, Xiwei Xu, Ang Liu, Qinghua Lu, Lida Xu, and Fei Tao. 2019. "Blockchain-based trust mechanism for IoT-based smart manufacturing system." *IEEE Transactions on Computational Social Systems* 6 (6):1386–1394.

Zhang, Yuanyu, Shoji Kasahara, Yulong Shen, Xiaohong Jiang, and Jianxiong Wan. 2018. "Smart contract-based access control for the internet of things." *IEEE Internet of Things Journal* 6 (2):1594–1605.

Zhao, Yanqi, Yiming Liu, Aikui Tian, Yong Yu, and Xiaojiang Du. 2019. "Blockchain based privacy-preserving software updates with proof-of-delivery for internet of things." *Journal of Parallel and Distributed Computing.* 132:141–149.

Zhou, Wei, Yan Jia, Anni Peng, Yuqing Zhang, and Peng Liu. 2018. "The effect of IoT new features on security and privacy: New threats, existing solutions, and challenges yet to be solved." *IEEE Internet of Things Journal* 6 (2):1606–1616.

Section II

Blockchain for Cybersecurity and Privacy in IoT

6 Interchain
A Scalable Business-Oriented Framework for Internet of Things

Alireza Mokhtari Golpayegani,
Mani Zarei, and Alireza Souri

CONTENTS

6.1 INTRODUCTION

Over recent decades, the internet has faced lots of changes. From just being a network to facilitating e-commerce, from linked HTML contents to a wide range of multimedia feeds, the internet's growth and popularity are significant. These changes enabled standardized data formats to allow machines to process automatically and without human intervention. This fact, alongside the other technology progresses, made it possible to make machines interact with each other (Viriyasitavat, Da Xu, Bi, & Pungpapong, 2019). The vision of collaborating machines made researchers to create an automated interaction network called the Internet of Things (IoT), which is in use today and covers many innovative applications; however, it also creates many new challenges (Souri, Hussien, Hoseyninezhad, & Norouzi, 2019).

6.1.1 MOTIVATION

The IoT-based innovations will be helpful when they create new benefits that businesses would value; mainly, this is true for IoT technology. For us, it is essential to consider the current generation of the internet and, in effect, see it as of yesterday's 'future internet' while creating the newer generation. On the road to the next generation of the internet, we have considerable volumes of information about innovative technologies, statistics, and IoT challenges, to take advantage of them. Growing business interest and demand are also key reasons to move faster to create new technology generations. This speed demands stronger IoT industry business plans to address challenges such as lack of functional value, broken business models, high costs, and lack of privacy and to make solutions future-proof (Brody & Pureswaran, 2014).

6.1.2 OBJECTIVE

The goal of this work is to propose a new business-oriented solution for future internet based on blockchain technology (Lombardi, Aniello, De Angelis, Margheri, & Sassone, 2018). We propose a new scalable ecosystem to answer IoT business gaps by using blockchain and some other game-changing technologies. The proposed ecosystem that is based on Interchain is designed as an abstraction of a framework to work on making functional movements in implementation phases.

Collectively, the lack of satisfying business model within the IoT world is determined as a problem in which the following framework tries to answer it by using trustful social approach (Atzori, Iera, Morabito, & Nitti, 2012). In addition, this work examines the proficiency of the idea by implementing a generic application.

6.1.3 CONTRIBUTION

The core idea of the proposing framework is in line with IBM's idea of device democracy (Brody & Pureswaran, 2014), the social IoT (Atzori et al., 2012), and also special issue about engineering future interoperable and open IoT systems (Fortino, Di Fatta, Ochoa, & Palau, 2017). The special issue addresses the following five remarkable related works that shaped the fundamental ideas of proposing framework:

- The 'Plexi': Adaptive rescheduling web service of time-synchronized low-power wireless networks (Exarchakos, Oztelcan, Sarakiotis, & Liotta, 2017)
- Enabling IoT interoperability through opportunistic smartphone-based mobile gateways (Aloi et al., 2017)
- Making the system of systems interoperable (Varga et al., 2017)
- Enabling synergy in IoT (Andersen, Fierro, & Culler, 2017)
- Semantic interoperability in the IoT: An overview from the INTER-IoT perspective (Ganzha, Paprzycki, Pawłowski, Szmeja, & Wasielewska, 2017)

All these scalability methods, besides other studies that have targeted blockchain's horizontal and vertical scalability issues (Kim, Kwon, & Cho, 2018), seem perfect to help create an ideal solution for the IoT scalability, except that the business still demands to deliver more benefits.

It is worth mentioning that there is already a definition for the word 'Interchain', where it is used in terms of interconnected transactions between multiple blockchain (Spoke, 2017). This chapter also develops this concept to make IoT business scalable.

6.1.4 ORGANIZATION

This chapter is structured as follows: Section 6.2 presents several background topics. Section 6.3 covers works related to IoT business-oriented movements, IoT and blockchain integration potential possibilities, and finally the role of cloud-centric IoT in business models (Souri, Rahmani, Navimipour, & Rezaei, 2019). Section 6.4 presents the proposed framework architecture, and Section 6.5 discusses results. Section 6.6 covers the application scenarios, and Section 6.7 highlights future directions toward the full implementation of the proposed framework. Finally, Section 6.8 concludes the proposed architecture.

6.2 BACKGROUND

6.2.1 INTERNET OF THINGS

The IoT is expected to be the next big thing after the internet. Billions of things (e.g., sensors, mobile phones, vehicles, and smart devices) connect over the internet, and they generate and exchange many different types of data. In the IoT ecosystem, 'Things' refer to any types of object in the world that can communicate over the internet, whether wisely or not (Atzori, Iera, & Morabito, 2010).

In terms of functionality, there are six major blocks, as follows (Ray, 2018; Sebastian & Ray, 2015):

- *Device*: An IoT system that can have one or more data-involved capabilities and responsibilities, such as:
  - Data sensing, actuation, and control
  - Collect data from other devices
  - Exchange data with other connected devices
  - Send data to local or cloud-based repositories
  - Receive commands and perform I/O and processing tasks

- *Communication*: Where data transferring protocols are being defined and utilized within the link layer, network layer, transport layer, and application layer.
- *Services*: Objectives of an IoT system that are frequently device-oriented functions such as device modeling, control, and discovery.
- *Management*: Making the IoT system governable.
- *Security*: Securing an IoT system using authentication, authorization, privacy, and data security.
- *Application*: This section is known as the most crucial part, where interactions are getting available to users.

Having mentioned IoT functional blocks, it turns to investigate key IoT utilization factors given as follows (Ray, 2018):

1. *Dynamicity and self-adaption*: Address the ability of IoT devices to adapt their context dynamically according to the variations of the environment
2. *Self-configuring*: Refers to the potential of self-updating in association with infrastructure in order to set up collaboration with others
3. *Communication interoperability*: Checks out the communication support between several interoperable devices and with infrastructure
4. *Identity uniqueness*: Indicates a unique address, which is representing the device to be accessible for interactions
5. *Information network integration*: Enables dynamic discovery of IoT devices and allows them to exchange data with other devices and systems
6. *Context awareness*: Sensor devices can gain knowledge from their environmental parameters
7. *Intelligent decision-making capability*: Refers to the collaboration happening in a large area of IoT multi-hop network to make decisions about their missions

6.2.2   CLOUD COMPUTING

Cloud computing is a recent trend in information technology that takes computing from end-user devices to the World Wide Web (Ghobaei-Arani, Souri, Baker, & Hussien, 2019), while the maintenance and resource management are done centrally and are no longer a user's concern (Atzori et al., 2012).

The National Institute of Standard and Technology (NIST) has reported essential aspects of cloud computing as a model for enabling ubiquitous and on-demand network access to a shared pool of configurable resources (Mell & Grance, 2011). The report has enumerated networks, servers, storage, application, and services as a resource. It has also highlighted agile provisioning and minimal management effort of the solution.

In the cloud computing world, a smartphone can become an interface to a large data center. It presents ubiquitous access to all kinds of content, without any storage and computation consideration. A large amount of media content can be shared over the cloud too. Moreover, the cloud platform offers elastic scalability to meet the user's requirements.

6.2.3 Blockchain

The inspiration for blockchain started with Bitcoin's peer-to-peer transaction in 2009. The term refers to a shared and distributed ledger that enables the ability of a transaction's immutable recording. Each transaction may wrap an asset, whether it is tangible such as cash and house ownership or intangible such as patents or any other kind of intellectual property. All these transaction contents are valuable and can also be tracked or traded on a blockchain network.

Blockchain offers the following specifications:

- *Decentralization*: In centralized transaction systems, each transaction has to be validated using a trusted agency, which results in more cost and performance bottlenecks. In contrast with the centralized solutions, third parties are not required in the decentralized blockchain network.
- *Auditability*: Bitcoin blockchain stores data, and once the current transaction is recorded into the blockchain, the state of those referred unspent transactions switches from unspent to spend. Thus, transactions could be easily verified and tracked (Gupta, 2017).

6.3 RELATED WORKS

There are multiple existing business models for the IoT (Dijkman, Sprenkels, Peeters, & Janssen, 2015; Whitmore, Agarwal, & Da Xu, 2015), but it seems very clear now that the most successful IoT solutions must deliver compelling value propositions, simplicity, and reliability (Brody & Pureswaran, 2014). In contrast, the most successful IoT-based business models revolve around only selling data directly or indirectly. On the other hand, the number of connected devices is forecasted to grow to more than 25 billion in 2020 and then surge to 125 billion by 2030 (Howell, 2017). This growth demands more infrastructure, more efficient devices, and an easily scalable ecosystem to support such requirements.

The current proposing framework is structured based on the future internet and an IoT-based future business as well as on the blockchain system. The preliminary studies and practical findings are categorized in the following subsections.

6.3.1 IoT Business

The vast number of predicated connected IoT devices is enough to highlight challenges and potential opportunities ahead (Souri & Norouzi, 2019). This prediction makes it necessary to study the subject to determine how industries should change their infrastructures to adapt to the new emerging era. At this point, it is helpful to note the IoT business trends and industry coverage before addressing related works.

The hottest areas of IoT are shown in Figure 6.1. According to the Forrester forecast (Gillett, 2016), many challenges still exist. These categories are tightly coupled

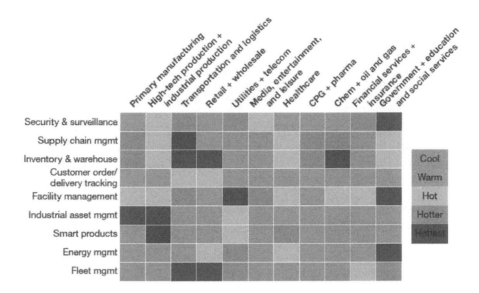

FIGURE 6.1   Heat diagram for key prospects of IoT contrasts by application and industry (Gillett, M. P. a. F. E., Forrester, courtesy of Cloudera, The IoT heatmap, 2016).

to one another. The critical differentiator for growth is the role of the business, because it attracts other interested audiences, topics, and a more comprehensive range of supplementary technologies. However, the platform fragmentation and lack of standards have surrounded the IoT ecosystem (Harald Bauer, 2015), and this has not been tackled because the business is also fragmented and lacks globalized plans to fund and support the need for scalability.

Next, for the IoT to gain higher acceptance levels among the wide-ranging populace, service providers, and others (which causes real scale), it must deliver applications (Evans, 2011).

Finally, two business-based works are investigated to make the subject clearer. However, they are not directly related to the majority of this work. The business of Things, which was covered by IBM in 2015, has declared three key insights to help IoT executives develop more competitive business models over the cognition market (Value, 2015):

- Things as agents
- Cooperating through complexity
- A new order of business

The business ecosystem is entirely described by the business model framework offered in (Dijkman et al., 2015), which enumerated value propositions as follows:

- Convenience/usability
- Getting the job done
- Performance

- Possibility of updates
- Comfort
- Accessibility
- Cost reduction
- Risk reduction
- Customization
- Design
- Price
- Newness
- Brand/status

It also covers crucial activities, partners, customer relationships, channels, revenue streams, essential resources, and cost structures, while the value proposition section is more related to the current work.

6.3.2 SCALABILITY

The primary focus of this work is scalability, which exists where a network of networks or a system of systems exists. However, the overall structure of the internet is also based on this perception. The concept of scalability in IoT can be discussed over many abstraction levels from the end thing's scalability potentials (Yin et al., 2018). Cellular network infrastructures (Jermyn, Jover, Murynets, Istomin, & Stolfo, 2015) and the edge parallel computing, both using gateways (Cañedo & Skjellum, 2016) or even modular and generic IoT management as a platform (M. Kim, Lee, & Park, 2016) or on the cloud (Douzis, Sotiriadis, Petrakis, & Amza, 2018). Nonetheless, these are not enough approaches to tackle the scalability issue. Another important approach of scalability studies over IoT is the distributed architecture (Reyna, Martín, Chen, Soler, & Díaz, 2018; Sarkar, Nambi, Prasad, & Rahim, 2014), which comes from interoperability issues.

Totally, there are limitations to the practical use of blockchain applications that concern scalability subjects, such as low transaction per second, block size issues, and increased chain size and electronic signature size. Answers to these issues include the following points of view (Kim et al., 2018):

- *On chain*: It refers to getting scalability through the changes of a single main blockchain.
- *Off chain*: It points to processing transactions outside the blockchain and then writing results to the main blockchain.
- *Side chain*: It refers to exchanging assets using other blockchain functions.
- *Child chain*: It has a hierarchical relationship, with the main blockchain as the root, where the parent stores the results after processing.
- *Interchain*: It enables communications between each blockchain.

6.3.3 BLOCKCHAIN AND IoT

Blockchain has its issues and challenges, like other technologies, but its concept has lots of potentials, whether being a platform for ownership transfer of money or being a parallel network of things in IoT. Both technologies can supplement each other in many ways (Swan, 2015) of interaction, using elements such as smart contracts (Christidis & Devetsikiotis, 2016). The consensus models of blockchain networks can be considered even at the consensus level of task allocation in IoT scenarios (Colistra, Pilloni, & Atzori, 2014). After composing, checking, and exploring ideas about the future of this paradigm, there are several solutions proposed regarding blockchain-based IoT architecture for smart homes (Dorri, Kanhere, & Jurdak, 2017). Connected Gateway for Bluetooth Low Energy (BLE)-based Devices (Cha, Chen, Su, & Yeh, 2018) and even commercial works such as the work done by Filament company where the distributed exchange is provided based on blockchain and the IoT (Company, 2016). It is also feasible that the elements in the IoT world can be shared using the blockchain to make an automatic payment, manage international travel, and manage digital rights (Huckle, Bhattacharya, White, & Beloff, 2016).

Blockchain also supports the provision of potential security solutions for the IoT security issues such as providing enough address space to cover 1.46×10^{48} IoT devices, managing identity of things, enabling data authentication and integrity, authorizing by smart contracts, and making secure connections (Khan & Salah, 2017).

6.3.4 INTERCONNECTED BLOCKCHAIN

Blockchain technology adaptations are gathering pace quickly, and this creates more solution possibilities of interest. After the creation of many opportunities in blockchain network itself, now the interoperability that is an open issue of the IoT is answered in blockchain network interactions. There are operational foundations that prove the ability such as AION (Spoke), Icon foundation ('ICON Foundation'), and Wanchain (Lu et al., 2017). Every one of these foundations is mostly related to financial scopes, but it is useful to address them directly (World, 2017).

6.4 FRAMEWORK ARCHITECTURE

Internet, as an interconnection of multiple networks, has generated many opportunities and challenges. It brought us the ability of e-commerce, the power of being informed, and the opportunity of being connected. After these capabilities, participants of the network can create their webpage to publish their content online. The segmentation of each hosting platform does not block the progress of the internet. The largest website visitors are humans, not machines, bearing in mind that visiting is not a valid action in the IoT world and direct interaction of humans is different in many ways. In contrast, in the IoT world, most of the interaction space is about machines.

The research investigates the capability of business interactions within the IoT ecosystem to bring dynamicity and scalability. This approach utilizes blockchain, cloud computing, and social IoT paradigm, as well as democracy factor, alongside the whole work. A general overview and components of the architecture are described as follows.

6.4.1 GENERAL OVERVIEW

The significant reasons for the design of the framework should be stated, based on the recent description and sections provided.

- Making a bigger IoT also needs business-oriented scalability.
- A scaled-up and healthy ecosystem comes from democracy, and it is in contrast with scattered and individually targeted business plans.
- The basic concept of the IoT concerns the transactional environment, where messaging matters. The centralized transactional services and centralized and exclusive brokers increase the vulnerabilities and require more secure third parties to prove trust.
- Consideration of blockchain as an answer to centralization issues is not enough to comply with democracy.
- Limiting the original infrastructures in every layer of operation to specific semi-centralized behavior is in contrast with democracy too. Thus, every human or machine should be able to participate in line with its abilities.

Regarding the reasons mentioned previously, democracy is considered a critical factor for scaling up and for support this argument. The proposal starts with the following principles:

- All IoT devices can participate in networks directly or by using a trusted party(s).
- People can participate in using their identities.
- Every connected entity has its valid identification in the network, without any requirement of centralized intermediary interference.
- There is no single centralized and exclusive subscription directory.
- Every node allocates its direct connections or public provisioning services.
- There is another primary definition of democracy, according to which there is no single force that controls what occurs and its outcome.

An Interchain-based ecosystem adopts business-oriented network in the IoT by using the following paradigms:

- Blockchain resulted in democracy to add scalability, where it means more trusted connections of nodes that can make smart contracts together.
- It utilizes cloud-based infrastructures to add scalability, where it brings throughput runtime.
- It uses social IoT to add scalability, where it provides more reliable and familiar connections to create business processes and cooperation between heterogeneous things.

Figure 6.2 shows the general view of connection within a simple blockchain network, while the simple structure of an interconnected blockchain network is displayed in Figure 6.3.

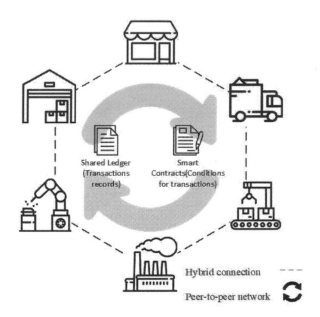

FIGURE 6.2 The simple view of a blockchain-based IoT network.

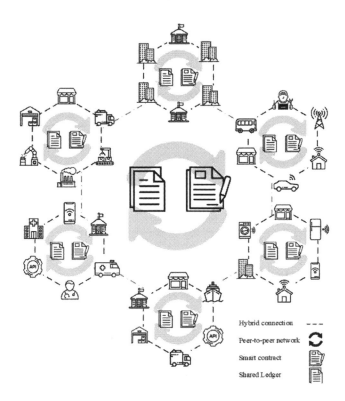

FIGURE 6.3 General view of the interconnected blockchain network.

6.4.2 COMPONENTS

A simple blockchain network builds trust through a shared ledger that replicates among the preselected participants. It prevents unauthorized access to the network by using permission-based identity management. The Interchain also utilizes the feature considering that the superblocks and brokers are the preselected participants to replicate the shared ledger among them. These three specific elements (shown in Figure 6.4) are aligned with the IoT paradigm, cloud computing capabilities, interconnected blockchain networks, and democracy principle.

6.4.2.1 Brokers

Major new elements must be introduced first to explore the framework architecture. The introduction of the framework starts with the definition of the broker's role and its functions and characteristics. A broker represents the capabilities of end nodes to make them work together beyond their current blockchain-based network. Brokers wire output of an end node to another one's input by using their business-specific mission. They know how to route between networks and keep ledgers up-to-date. The conditions of an end node are interpretable by a broker to make smart contracts, where it can be conducted through a model transformation that happens in a managed and configurable workflow (Cai et al., 2014).

According to the five kinds of relationships between IoT nodes (Atzori et al., 2012), brokers must define their mission scope; the mission can be defined as both geo-location based or working field related. Interchain offers the internal architecture of brokers, as shown in Figure 6.5.

Every mission-relevant participant must verify the validity of the transaction as the used ledger technology roles out. In addition, dynamic business rules may be built using smart contracts and workflow manager to support end-to-end business processes in an orchestrated and flexible manner.

A three-tier architectural model is presented to describe the proposed broker architecture. These tiers are the component layer, the communication layer, and the business layer.

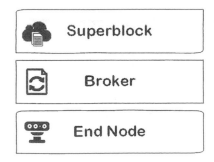

FIGURE 6.4   Major participant elements in Interchain.

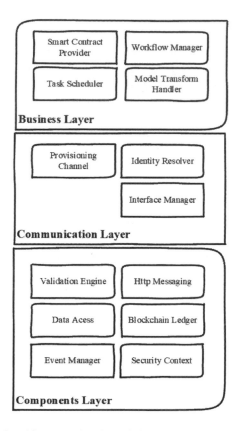

FIGURE 6.5 Internal architecture of an Interchain broker.

6.4.2.2 Component Layer

The layer is responsible for providing every required asset to make the element alive on the Interchain framework. This layer, as the lowest layer, provides necessary tools and utilities to serve the upper layers. It provides HTTP messaging component, where it is structured to make straightforward communications over Representational State Transfer (REST) (Belqasmi, Glitho, & Fu, 2011). The layer provides the specific blockchain network asset where the asset may comply with the Ethereum's ETH protocol (Viktor Trón, 2015), the Hyperledger Fabric (IBM Blockchain based on Hyperledger Fabric from the Linux Foundation, 2017), or the tangle-based IOTA (IOTA Developer Hub, 2018) infrastructures.

There is no exclusively chosen platform to serve the broker's ledger and consensus system for making the system flexible at this layer, and the strategy continues to cover the entire system. Therefore, the platform needs an interconnected blockchain network to manage the environment (this concept is covered in Section 6.4.2.1, where superblocks are defined). Validation is needed to verify the required argument of each device, where the argument refers to the values that a device may require when it accepts commands or makes smart contracts. Such a capable function needs a repository of data, whether it registers as local or anywhere else. Every broker-involved transaction generates an event to make the flow management easy and straightforward. Thus, an event manager is required at this level. It is also natural to satisfy security issues of the device itself, where administration or configuration is required, whether the action occurs by a human or automatically by a machine (Miloslavskaya & Tolstoy, 2019).

6.4.2.3   Communication Layer

A broker is a socially involved element, and social communication is one of the primary goals of the device. Thus, it needs to prove its identity itself, and it needs to verify the other related connection's identity too. Resolving identities is based on querying the local ledger and the parent superblock's ledger. Every other related node with the target node has to verify its identity, and the procedure comes from a consensus strategy of the existing distributed ledger technology. Provisioning across the whole of the framework is based on two states, where a node looks for service from other nodes or a node delivers a specific service for other nodes. There also needs to be an interface channel to broadcast the broker's state and understand other signals using standard protocols of network communication such as Bluetooth, ZigBee, and 6LoWPAN.

6.4.2.4   Business Layer

If the environment needs to support the growing underlying business, then it is clear that the business processes must be valid and thoroughly adapted to it. The layer offers a lightweight workflow activity manager to relate activities and their states to each other. The workflow management tool also contains the required assets to support multiple friendship selection logics (Militano, Nitti, Atzori, & Iera, 2016). The activities may be local and issued by the broker, or they may be available from other nodes. In the case of foreign activity, it would need to make a smart contract between another node(s) and broker, so the underlying distributed ledger technology must be able to accomplish this task. After the management of activities and deals between nodes, the ecosystem may need their tasks postponed, while the nodes may not have the ability to schedule themselves. In this case, a task scheduler is necessary at this point. As mentioned previously, in the validation engine description of the components layer section, every node accepts its specific arguments because of its business model limitations. Thus, a broker needs to understand each friend's business models, and it needs to know how to transform and correlate these models together to supply each one's input arguments. This important capability is made possible by adding the ability of information support base, both for data integration and intelligent interaction (Cai et al., 2014). Besides the internal architecture, brokers have the following key characteristics:

- According to the relationship types between the end nodes, an Interchain broker handles the relations where objects have co-location relationship and co-work relationship (Atzori et al., 2012).
- The broker may be a gateway (Morabito, Petrolo, Loscrí, & Mitton, 2016), which serves from the cloud's edge or a local station, but it still has its identity, which is issued by the corresponding superblock.

- Brokers can be searched from the superblocks directory or may be identified by a friend's relationships between the participants.
- Every broker must provide its coverage both under its proper context of missions and its geographical area of activity.
- Brokers could also be routers between multiple blockchain (Kan et al., 2018).

Also, the connection view of an Interchain-based network is displayed in Figure 6.6.
Every non-broker node in Figure 6.6 is considered an end node, where their interactions follow the hybrid model (Reyna et al., 2018).

6.4.2.5   Superblocks

Superblocks are the domain holders of end nodes and brokers. Each superblock has
a public ledger to keep tracking its dependent nodes (i.e., brokers or regular end
nodes). Every single node may work in a private blockchain-based network, and
then, it can be introduced to a superblock, or it could be added from the starting point
of its lifecycle. The end nodes and brokers need to initialize via superblock to utilize
the Interchain ecosystem.

Key specifications of a superblock are as follows:

- Superblocks provide and manage the identity of end nodes and brokers
  by using a distributed domain name system structure (Benshoof, Rosen,
  Bourgeois, & Harrison, 2016).
- Unlike the brokers, which are placed at the edge of the cloud, superblocks
  are inside the cloud to be more scalable at the infrastructure level.

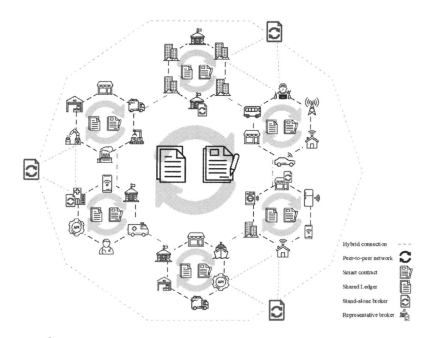

FIGURE 6.6   General view of Interchain participating brokers.

- Superblocks do not participate as an exclusive property, and every entity can run an instance of it.
- Superblocks, as the supervisors of the Interchain ecosystem, can operate geographically and be based on the working domains.
- Superblocks provide a public ledger that contains only a directory of authorized connected things to provide search capabilities for both regulators via an interface and objects via Application Programming Interface (API). Unlike the brokers where an end node may cooperate with more than one node, every end node just cooperates with a single superblock.
- Permission management is one of the primary responsibilities of superblocks, where they determine what kind of transactions and details should be transparent for every participant.
- Superblocks also provide cross-broker connections.
- Everyone can make and own a superblock.
- A superblock generates revenue via a pay-as-you-go transactional model. The transaction fee is based on several parameters such as the node's working domain, duration of being available in the system, and density of similar neighbor nodes.

6.4.2.6 End Nodes

The Interchain architecture includes end nodes as social members. Every node has a role in the framework to support minimum business flows within the ecosystem. Thus, the following three roles are considered in the framework, according to Figure 6.7:

- *Vendor node*: This node has certain business activities that result in serving particular services for other nodes and infrastructure. The services include tasks and digital or physical assets.
- *Requested node*: This type of node has its unique mission but requires some services now and then.
- *Intermediary node*: This node acts only as a relay to reach other nodes. This action may be upward or downward through the business flow.

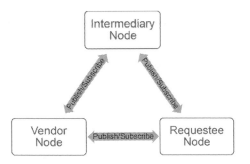

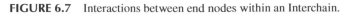

FIGURE 6.7   Interactions between end nodes within an Interchain.

Although there may be a direct channel to send a request and receive responses between nodes, they work asynchronously by using publish and subscribe method.

Every single and regular node of Interchain-based IoT environment corresponds to a virtual object (VO) (Farris et al., 2015). Nodes have reserved their own space at the edge of the cloud, no matter who prepared/runs the cloud-based Interchain service. Every node must be equipped with a specific distributed ledger technology and the ability of transaction handling over the environment. It must be able to report its states, both its mission states and its health states. The VO schema of an end node is defined as mentioned in Table 6.1. The VO is not a part of the superblock, and it could be located anywhere within the cloud.

TABLE 6.1
General Virtual Object Schema in an End Node

No.	Field Name	Access Level[a]	Description
1.	Owner	Public	Owner's identity (machine/human)
2.	Missions	Public	It is a list that is selectable from the parent superblock mission category
3.	Identity	Public	Valid and unique identity in the whole superblock
4.	Relationships	First friends	Hierarchy list of friends
5.	Address (IPV6/Any Valid Uri)	Private/partners	Valid network-level address to make working connections
6.	Ledger transactions	Private	A ledger to keep all transaction information from friendship requests or friends' states to partnership activity logs
7.	Mobility state	Friends	Determines whether the device moves or is fixed
8.	Geolocation	Public	Single-point longitude, latitude, and altitude of object's location, or if it is a moving object, the value contains the geo-fence
9.	Power mode	Friends	It may contain DC, AC, or both
10.	Latest states	Private/partner	The latest health states that are generated by the node to use in monitoring levels
11.	Superblock address	Public	Superblock's valid address (A valid http Uri)
12.	Update frequency	Public	The frequency of status update
13.	Uptime level	Public	Determines whether it is a full-time working object or works in specific periods

(Continued)

TABLE 6.1 (*Continued*)
General Virtual Object Schema in an End Node

No.	Field Name	Access Level[a]	Description
14.	Acquisition model	Private/partner	Determines whether it should be polled for data gathering or is an automated pushing node
15.	Accepting commands[b]	Private/partner	List of commands that can be requested from the node: each command contains name, description, output object schema, and argument object schema
16.	Activity context tags	Public	General tags list that made from its schema for further searchability and indexing
17.	Memory capacity	Public	Exposes the total memory that the device has
18.	Description	Public	Describes some comments and device descriptions

[a] It may be public for all, private for the object itself or the owner, or a specific level of friends (e.g., first friends, friend of friends, …). There is another level of access, where the related partners have enough rights to be informed.
[b] This field is being used at the activity management level of brokers.

6.5   RESULTS

Table 6.2 displays the support level of the IoT using the Interchain referred to in Figure 6.1 and the growing hot areas of the IoT. The data is provided through the adaptability check over 99 different scenarios. The proposed Interchain is supporting many of them, but several fields need a high level of participation to be supported by the Interchain. Several fields cannot be supported, considering their current IoT rate of usage.

6.6   APPLICATIONS

An Interchain environment, from a distance, might seem to be offering a dynamic and scalable ecosystem, but the ecosystem first needs to be built. To implement such a framework, it needs public participation to enhance real-world business, and also the project needs the support of the authorities, such as the regulators. To make sense of the implementation of the Interchain framework, we are using an example of a supply-chain system in a car factory and the related business model:

- The car manufacturer has its blockchain.
- Every node of the factory is connected through a trusted and preconfigured network.
- Identities are valid and resolvable via their domain.

TABLE 6.2
The Participation Support Level of Interchain Referring Hot Business Areas of IoT and Current Potentials

	Main Manufacturing	Industrial Production	Transportation and Logistics	Retail + Wholesale	Conveniences + Telecom	Media, Entertainment, and Leisure	Medical and Healthcare	CPG + Pharma	Oil and Gas	Financial Services + Insurance	Government + Education and Social Services
Security and safety	✓	✓	✓	✓	✓	✓	✓	×	✓	•	•
Supply chain management	✓	✓	✓	✓	✓	✓	✓	✓	✓	•	•
Account and warehouse	✓	✓	✓	✓	✓	✓	✓	✓	✓	•	•
User delivery and order tracking	✓	✓	✓	✓	✓	✓	✓	✓	✓	•	•
Competence management	✓	✓	✓	✓	✓	✓	✓	×	×	•	•
Industrial asset management	✓	✓	✓	✓	✓	✓	✓	✓	✓	•	•
Smart products	✓	✓	✓	✓	✓	✓	✓	×	×	•	•
Energy management	✓	✓	✓	✓	✓	✓	✓	✓	✓	•	•
Fleet management	✓	✓	✓	✓	✓	✓	✓	✓	✓	•	•

✓ Supported.
· Partly supported.
× Not supported.

A scenario happens like this:

1. An automated drilling machine needs a specific spare part (eg, drill bit).
2. The machine looks for a similar historical transaction. The transactions may contain the friendship list or ordering list.
   a. If the event has a history, then it follows the past transaction model.
   b. If the past transactions are not valid or do not exist, then the new transaction is required (step 3).
3. The machine publishes its requirement through the co-related brokers.
4. Brokers look for the most suitable supplier considering the geographical location, ranking among other suppliers, possible delivery mechanisms, and the price.
5. When the supplier is being selected, then the smart contract possibility is checked. If the result was true, then the contract endorsement will initiate, using the agreed consensus model. The contract is not finalized until this step; the payment and the delivery are completed to accomplish the step. Payment and delivery checks are not the direct facilities of the Interchain, so that they may involve other related nodes according to their contract and relationships.
6. If the supplier does not offer delivery options, the broker may also offer an automated delivery service using another end node or broker. It may reserve the most matching transport solution to provide delivery at the door of the factory.

In the above example scenario, maximum of two relationships have been exercised, but there could be many more. Consider that the first broker does not hold a link to the right broker, and it needs to provision the target service using its other relationships. The chain maybe longer, and the broker may call for a service using other brokers. Potential scenarios are limitless in different business fields.

6.7 FUTURE WORKS

Although the framework is a new definition to achieve business promotion and scalability within the IoT world, it needs a stable performance first.

The Interchain implementation can be studied in two dimensions: *framework development as a product* and *market integration*.

The major approach to continue the development and implementation of such a framework is to make the framework acceptable to ideally every business participant in the IoT world, or at least to a large-enough portion. It should be borne in mind that the IoT scalability volume is directly correlated to the accessibility of the ecosystem for the daily business of people. Now, Interchain offers a scalable mechanism through the business transformation of the IoT, and it seems the proposed framework provides the basic feeds to enhance the participation levels of the IoT in the real world. The framework is available for more autonomic networks of the IoT such as the internet of vehicles and vehicular ad hoc networks (VANETs) (Zarei, 2019), according to the provided multi-hop connectivity, cooperative information propagation, and decentralization (Zarei & Rahmani, 2016, 2017; Zarei, Rahmani, & Samimi, 2017).

Collectively, these are known open issues, and future directions are as follows:

- Blockchain interoperability solutions through Interchain
- Measuring latencies, energy, and data rates
- Studying round trips
- Detecting security challenges
- Machine-to-machine model transformation over blockchain
- Remote processing over cloud, considering the privacy
- Public catalogs of superblock and brokers
- Workflow management over brokers
- Application-centric scenarios
- Identity management over multidomain environments
- Studying possible commercial activities

6.8 CONCLUSION

This chapter explored the adaptability of the IoT to the interconnected blockchain networks, considering the scalability and business orientation parameters. Investigating the related works led to propose a novel framework, which we call the Interchain framework. The Interchain contains three significant roles for its participants: first, the end nodes that are considered regular social things in the IoT world, whether they are just a sensor, smart machine, or an integrated human node. Second, the brokers that are considered as social integrator entities for the blockchain-based network. Third, the superblocks that are the domain issuers and permission handlers of the participating business networks containing end nodes and brokers. Every node of the Interchain has its blockchain ledger and obeys the rules of its parent blockchain network. The Interchain is a blockchain technology agnostic, but it necessitates interconnection between blockchain networks. The approach of the Interchain is to prepare a higher and purer abstraction level of connectivity for the future internet; thus, the adaptability of the Interchain and the current IoT business fields are investigated. However, still, there is more work to be done and more open issues to study, such as:

- The implementation of such a framework needs to be measured by considering the available scenarios.
- The reflection of the business markets to such an ecosystem needs reviewing and evaluating.
- Social network optimizations may be studied over the Interchain to measure and enhance the rate of trust and velocity of networks.
- Maximum applicability rate of dynamic smart contracts needs to be studied, as the framework offers a dynamic partnership over social relationships, using business process management between nodes.

REFERENCES

Aloi, G., Caliciuri, G., Fortino, G., Gravina, R., Pace, P., Russo, W., & Savaglio, C. (2017). Enabling IoT interoperability through opportunistic smartphone-based mobile gateways. *Journal of Network and Computer Applications, 81*, 74–84.

Andersen, M. P., Fierro, G., & Culler, D. E. (2017). Enabling synergy in IoT: Platform to service and beyond. *Journal of Network and Computer Applications, 81*, 96–110.

Atzori, L., Iera, A., & Morabito, G. (2010). The internet of things: A survey. *Computer networks, 54*(15), 2787–2805.

Atzori, L., Iera, A., Morabito, G., & Nitti, M. (2012). The social internet of things (siot)–when social networks meet the internet of things: Concept, architecture and network characterization. *Computer networks, 56*(16), 3594–3608.

Belqasmi, F., Glitho, R., & Fu, C. (2011). RESTful web services for service provisioning in next-generation networks: A survey. *IEEE Communications Magazine, 49*(12), 66–73.

Benshoof, B., Rosen, A., Bourgeois, A. G., & Harrison, R. W. (2016). Distributed decentralized domain name service. Paper presented at the Parallel and Distributed Processing Symposium Workshops, 2016 IEEE International.

Brody, P., & Pureswaran, V. (2014). Device democracy: Saving the future of the internet of things. *IBM, 1*, 1–28

Cai, H., Da Xu, L., Xu, B., Xie, C., Qin, S., & Jiang, L. (2014). IoT-based configurable information service platform for product lifecycle management. *IEEE Transactions on Industrial Informatics, 10*(2), 1558–1567.

Cañedo, J., & Skjellum, A. (2016). Adding scalability to internet of things gateways using parallel computation of edge device data. Paper presented at the High Performance Extreme Computing Conference (HPEC), 2016 IEEE.

Cha, S.-C., Chen, J.-F., Su, C., & Yeh, K.-H. (2018). A blockchain connected gateway for BLE-based devices in the internet of things. *IEEE Access 6*, 24639–24649.

Christidis, K., & Devetsikiotis, M. (2016). Blockchains and smart contracts for the internet of things. *IEEE Access, 4*, 2292–2303.

Colistra, G., Pilloni, V., & Atzori, L. (2014). The problem of task allocation in the internet of things and the consensus-based approach. *Computer Networks, 73*, 98–111.

Company, F. (2016). Foundations for the next economic revolution: Distributed exchange and the Internet of Things. https://filament.com/assets/downloads/Filament%20Foundations.pdf.

Dijkman, R. M., Sprenkels, B., Peeters, T., & Janssen, A. (2015). Business models for the internet of things. *International Journal of Information Management, 35*(6), 672–678.

Dorri, A., Kanhere, S. S., & Jurdak, R. (2017). Towards an optimized blockchain for IoT. Paper presented at the *Proceedings of the Second International Conference on Internet-of-Things Design and Implementation*, IEEE/ACM, Pittsburgh, PA, USA.

Douzis, K., Sotiriadis, S., Petrakis, E. G., & Amza, C. (2018). Modular and generic IoT management on the cloud. *Future Generation Computer Systems, 78*, 369–378.

Evans, D. (2011). The internet of things: How the next evolution of the internet is changing everything. *CISCO White Paper, 1*(2011), 1–11.

Exarchakos, G., Oztelcan, I., Sarakiotis, D., & Liotta, A. (2017). Plexi: Adaptive re-scheduling web-service of time synchronized low-power wireless networks. *Journal of Network and Computer Applications, 81*, 62–73.

Farris, I., Girau, R., Militano, L., Nitti, M., Atzori, L., Iera, A., & Morabito, G. (2015). Social virtual objects in the edge cloud. *IEEE Cloud Computing, 2*(6), 20–28.

Fortino, G., Di Fatta, G., Ochoa, S. F., & Palau, C. E. (2017). Engineering future interoperable and open IoT systems. *Journal of Network and Computer Applications, 81*, 59–61.

Ganzha, M., Paprzycki, M., Pawłowski, W., Szmeja, P., & Wasielewska, K. (2017). Semantic interoperability in the internet of things: An overview from the INTER-IoT perspective. *Journal of Network and Computer Applications, 81*, 111–124.

Ghobaei-Arani, M., Souri, A., Baker, T., & Hussien, A. (2019). ControCity: An autonomous approach for controlling elasticity using buffer management in cloud computing environment. *IEEE Access, 7*, 106912–106924.

Gillett, M. P. a. F. E. (2016). Forrester, courtesy of Cloudera, The IoT heatmap. https://tdwi. org/whitepapers/2017/04/cloudera-forrester-the-iot-heat-map-2016.aspx. Accesses 12 May 2019.

Gupta, M. (2017). *Blockchain For Dummies, IBM Limited Edition*: John Wiley & Sons, Inc.

Harald Bauer, M. P., & Jan Veira. (2015). Internet of things: Opportunities and challenges for semiconductor companies By Harald Bauer, Mark Patel, and Jan Veira, USA. From www. mckinsey.com/industries/semiconductors/our-insights/internet-of-things-opportunities-and-challenges-for-semiconductor-companies

Howell, J. (2017). Number of connected IoT devices. From https://technology.ihs.com/596542/ number-of-connected-iot-devices-will-surge-to-125-billion-by-2030-ihs-markit-says

Huckle, S., Bhattacharya, R., White, M., & Beloff, N. (2016). Internet of things, blockchain and shared economy applications. *Procedia Computer Science, 98*, 461–466.

IBM Blockchain based on Hyperledger Fabric from the Linux Foundation. (2017). From www.ibm.com/blockchain/hyperledger.html

ICON Foundation. *ICON Whitepaper*. Zug, Switzerland.

IOTA Developer Hub. (2018). From https://dev.iota.org/

Jermyn, J., Jover, R. P., Murynets, I., Istomin, M., & Stolfo, S. (2015). Scalability of machine to machine systems and the internet of things on LTE mobile networks. Paper presented at the *World of Wireless, Mobile and Multimedia Networks (WoWMoM)*, 2015 IEEE 16th International Symposium on a.

Kan, L., Wei, Y., Muhammad, A. H., Siyuan, W., Linchao, G., & Kai, H. (2018). A multiple blockchains architecture on inter-blockchain communication. Paper presented at the *2018 IEEE International Conference on Software Quality, Reliability and Security Companion (QRS-C)*.

Khan, M. A., & Salah, K. (2017). IoT security: Review, blockchain solutions, and open challenges. *Future Generation Computer Systems 82*, 395–411.

Kim, M., Lee, N. Y., & Park, J. H. (2016). Study on the generic architecture design of IoT platforms. In: J. J. Park, Y. Pan, G. Yi, and V. Loia (Eds.), *Advances in Computer Science and Ubiquitous Computing*. Lecture Notes in Electrical Engineering book series (LNEE, Vol. 421 pp. 1039–1045). Bangkok, Thailand: Springer.

Kim, S., Kwon, Y., & Cho, S. (2018). A survey of scalability solutions on blockchain. Paper Presented at the *2018 International Conference on Information and Communication Technology Convergence (ICTC)*. Jeju, South Korea.

Lombardi, F., Aniello, L., De Angelis, S., Margheri, A., & Sassone, V. (2018). A blockchain-based infrastructure for reliable and cost-effective IoT-aided smart grids. *Living in the Internet of Things: Cybersecurity of the IoT Conference - 2018*, London, UK.

Lu, J., Yang, B., Liang, Z., Zhang, Y., Demmon, S., Swartz, E., & Lu, L. (2017). Building Super Financial Markets for the New Digital Economy. White paper. https://wanchain. org/files/Wanchain-Whitepaper-EN-version.pdf. Wanchan Foundation Ltd., Singapore.

Mell, P., & Grance, T. (2011). The NIST definition of cloud computing. Special Publication 800–145, National Institute of Standards and Technology Gaithersburg, MD.

Militano, L., Nitti, M., Atzori, L., & Iera, A. (2016). Enhancing the navigability in a social network of smart objects: A Shapley-value based approach. *Computer Networks, 103*, 1–14.

Miloslavskaya, N., & Tolstoy, A. (2019). Internet of things: Information security challenges and solutions. *Cluster Computing, 22*(1), 103–119. doi:10.1007/s10586-018-2823-6.

Morabito, R., Petrolo, R., Loscrí, V., & Mitton, N. (2016). Enabling a lightweight edge gate-way-as-a-service for the internet of things. Paper presented at the *Network of the Future (NOF), 2016 7th International Conference on the*, Buzios, Brazil

Ray, P. P. (2018). A survey on internet of things architectures. *Journal of King Saud University-Computer and Information Sciences, 30*(3), 291–319.

Reyna, A., Martín, C., Chen, J., Soler, E., & Díaz, M. (2018). On blockchain and its integration with IoT. Challenges and opportunities. *Future Generation Computer Systems*, *88*, 173–190.

Sarkar, C., Nambi, S. A. U., Prasad, R. V., & Rahim, A. (2014). A scalable distributed architecture towards unifying IoT applications. Paper presented at the *Internet of Things (WF-IoT)*, 2014 IEEE World Forum on.

Sebastian, S., & Ray, P. (2015). Development of IoT invasive architecture for complying with health of home. *Proceedings of I3CS, Shillong*, Lecture Notes in Networks and Systems, Series (Vol. 24, pp. 79–83).

Souri, A., Hussien, A., Hoseyninezhad, M., & Norouzi, M. (2019). A systematic review of IoT communication strategies for an efficient smart environment. *Transactions on Emerging Telecommunications Technologies*, (Special issue), e3736.

Souri, A., & Norouzi, M. (2019). A state-of-the-art survey on formal verification of the internet of things applications. *Journal of Service Science Research, 11*(1), 47–67.

Souri, A., Rahmani, A. M., Navimipour, N. J., & Rezaei, R. (2019). Formal modeling and verification of a service composition approach in the social customer relationship management system. *Information Technology & People*, 32(6), 1591–1607.

Spoke, M. (2017). Aion: The third-generation blockchain network. *Whitepaper, 2017.*

Swan, M. (2015). Blockchain thinking: The brain as a dac (decentralized autonomous organization). Paper Presented at the Texas Bitcoin Conference. *IEEE Technology and Society Magazine*, Vol. 15, pp. 41–52.

Value, I. I. f. B. (2015). The Business of Things. IBM Institute for Business Value. https://www.ibm.com/downloads/cas/WVNVNNMB.

Varga, P., Blomstedt, F., Ferreira, L. L., Eliasson, J., Johansson, M., Delsing, J., & de Soria, I. M. (2017). Making system of systems interoperable of the core components of the arrowhead framework. *Journal of Network and Computer Applications, 81*, 85–95.

Viktor Trón, F. L. (2015). Ethereum specification. From https://github.com/ethereum/go-ethereum/wiki/Ethereum-Specification

Viriyasitavat, W., Da Xu, L., Bi, Z., & Pungpapong, V. (2019). Blockchain and internet of things for modern business process in digital economy—The state of the art. *IEEE Transactions on Computational Social Systems*, 6(6), 1420–1432.

Whitmore, A., Agarwal, A., & Da Xu, L. (2015). The internet of things—A survey of topics and trends. *Information Systems Frontiers, 17*(2), 261–274.

World, H. I. (2017). Blockchain interoperability alliance: ICON x Aion x wanchain. From https://medium.com/helloiconworld/blockchain-interoperability-alliance-icon-x-aion-x-wanchain-8aeaafb3ebdd

Yin, H., Guo, D., Wang, K., Jiang, Z., Lyu, Y., & Xing, J. (2018). Hyperconnected network: A decentralized trusted computing and networking paradigm. *IEEE Network, 32*(1), 112–117.

Zarei, M. (2019). Traffic-centric mesoscopic analysis of connectivity in VANETs. *The Computer Journal*. doi:10.1093/comjnl/bxz094

Zarei, M., & Rahmani, A. M. (2016). Renewal process of information propagation in delay tolerant VANETs. *Wireless Personal Communications, 89*(4), 1045–1063.

Zarei, M., & Rahmani, A. M. (2017). Analysis of vehicular mobility in a dynamic free-flow highway. *Vehicular Communications, 7*, 51–57.

Zarei, M., Rahmani, A. M., & Samimi, H. (2017). Connectivity analysis for dynamic movement of vehicular ad hoc networks. *Wireless Networks, 23*(3), 843–858.

7 Blockchain-Based Trust and Security in Content-Centric Networking– Based Internet of Things

Mohamed Labbi, Yassine Chahid, Nabil Kannouf, and Mohammed Benabdellah

CONTENTS

7.1 BACKGROUND

This section includes some preliminary concepts to provide a clear description of this document. We briefly study the content-centric network architecture and the Internet of Things (IoT) and introduce blockchain technology.

7.1.1 CONTENT-CENTRIC NETWORKING

Content-centric networking (CCN) is an information-centric networking (ICN) (Mosko et al. 2016) instance that supports location independence by separating content from its source and reducing traffic through the caching feature. The exchanges on this architecture are based on the publish/subscribe model; the name of the object is published, and an object is requested by sending the Interest packet (Figure 7.1).

In CCN, data packets are sent in response to a request named Interest packet, and data fragments are cached along the path back to the requester. Instead of using the source and destination addresses of hosts, the CCN packets contain the name of the content object that the user wishes to access. It allows most users to have more bandwidth and less latency simultaneously and securely. The CCN promotes the use of multiple sources (Labbi et al. 2016) to retrieve the same content.

Table 7.1 contrasts the basic CCN concepts with those of Transmission Control Protocol/Internet Protocol Internet (TCP/IP). The key idea of CCN lies in using names rather than addresses to address and forward content on the network. They are used to identify the associated contents unambiguously. These names are also used in all network operations, such as announcing, requesting, and distributing content. Each content is divided into several parts; (MTU) was not specified, and there is some possibility that it may be larger than the MTU in IP networks. This structure allows a prefix-based lookup to be quick and efficient, similar to the current IP lookup. The form of the name is similar to Uniform Resource Locator (URL). It allows names to be context-dependent, i.e., */MyHome/Garage/Lights/ON/*. In the

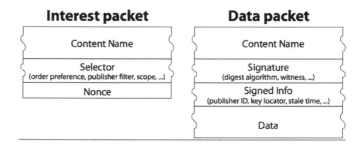

FIGURE 7.1   The CCN message formats.

TABLE 7.1
Comparison between CCN and TCP/IP

	CCN	TCP/IP
Routing	Location-independent	Using IP address
Security	Secures content itself	Secures the pipe
Naming	Addresses content by name instead of location	Related to host location
Caching	In any node of the network	In specific servers

following section, the authors explain how to take advantage of CCN naming to build name-based security mechanisms.

To manage packet transmission, three types of data structures are used at each node:

- *Content store*: It is similar to an IP router's buffer memory, but it also allows storage of data as long as possible for later reuse.
- *Pending interest table*: It is the table of pending Interest packet. It keeps track of Interest transmitted upstream to the source of the content. Each entry of the pending interest table contains the name of the requested content and the list of interfaces that have sent the corresponding Interest packet.
- *Forwarding information base*: It used to transmit Interest packets to the producers of the requested content. It contains the prefixes of the content names and the following interfaces to use to reach their destination.

7.1.2 INTERNET OF THINGS

The IoT reflects the extension of the Internet to things and places it in the real world. This has allowed all humanity to dive into the depths of the internet and research its mysteries to become one of the indispensable tools in our everyday life.

The IoT was formally introduced in the 2005 Internet Report of the International Telecommunications Union (ITU). The IoT has been fined as *'a global infrastructure for the information society, enabling advanced services by interconnecting (physical and virtual) things based on existing and evolving interoperable information and communication technologies'* (ITU Strategy and Policy Unit 2005). In fact, there is no standard definition for IoT.

The use of IoT has affected all aspects of everyday life. According to Gubbi et al. (2013), IoT applications can be found in many areas: (1) personal and home, (2) enterprise, (3) utilities, and (4) mobile. The IoT, which links billions of devices to the Internet, promises to create fantastic applications. The IoT offers unprecedented opportunities. However, security represents the biggest problem in deploying IoT. Thus, a proven and robust approach to deal with security issues is required (Balte et al. 2015). Sicari et al. (2015) described major security-related challenges while building IoT (Figure 7.2).

As computer technologies diversify, so do the possibilities of hacking. However, the IoT may not escape the rule. The dominant feeling is that the evolution of techniques is cumulative and that their power imposes a kind of forward flight whose constraint is, at the same time, anonymous and uncontrollable. When industrial actors and public authorities talk about gains in terms of growth and security, many public opinions point to risks and threats to people. In fact, deployments that do not start from scratch will certainly represent a brake. In our connected world, security is often compromised. The more objects we connect, the more value we will create from the generated data and the greater will be the risk of data theft and digital fraud. Subjects such as privacy and connectivity must be taken into consideration to ensure the possible success of the IoT. Moreover, connecting billions of various devices this

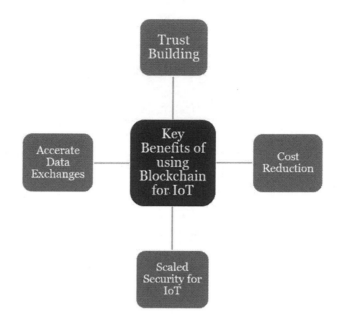

FIGURE 7.2   Major security issues in IoT.

way requires an equal amount of allocated IP addresses, which challenge the current state of the worldwide network. Even with the transition to IPv6, the design of new architectures allowing communication between connected objects and the routing of traffic generated by data growth remains a critical need.

7.1.3   BLOCKCHAIN TECHNOLOGY

Blockchain (Fernández-Caramés et al. 2018) is a technology that has been written about extensively, and many experts agree that it will profoundly change all sectors that rely on the transmission of information. It is a technology widely used in the context of the emission of cryptocurrencies such as Bitcoin (Nakamoto et al. 2008). However, by its very nature, blockchain can impact other sectors such as the IoT. With its decentralized data flow and storage model, its traceability and inviolability are envisaged for uses other than virtual currencies. It is undoubtedly a compelling method to require something digital and to publish information about that owned thing.

Using blockchain technology as the basis for IoT devices reduces the risk of hacking by reducing potential entry points. By giving up a central authority in the IoT networks, blockchain technology could allow these networks to protect themselves. The key benefits of using blockchain for IoT are shown in Figure 7.3.

The blockchain is made up of blocks (Figure 7.4), each containing the recording of all the exchanges made between its users at a given moment. These different

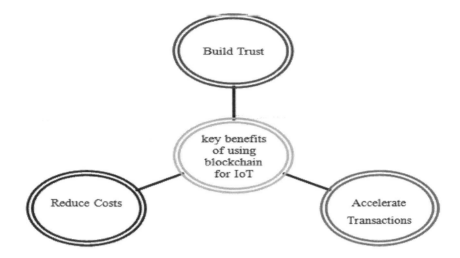

FIGURE 7.3 Benefits of using blockchain for IoT.

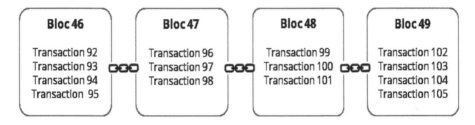

FIGURE 7.4 Blockchain.

blocks thus provide the history of all the transactions since its creation and allow each one to control the accuracy of the exchanged data. A block is only added to the database if it is validated by minors (network nodes). The average time required to accept a transaction into a mined block and add it to the ledger is 10 minutes (Figure 7.5).

A blockchain presents several major interests:

- *Transparency*: Although the exchanges remain anonymous, anyone can consult them.
- *Security*: Transactions are tamper-proof and secured by protocols based on asymmetric cryptography.
- *Decentralization*: Independent of any trusted third party, the entire network is responsible for authenticating transactions using cryptography.

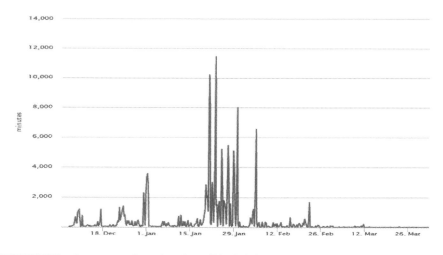

FIGURE 7.5   Average confirmation time. (Blockchain.com)

7.2   BLOCKCHAIN.COM

More specifically, all transactional can be put in a blockchain with the same principle – maintaining trust – on the one hand, by making transactions more efficient and faster, and, on the other hand, by significantly reducing their costs by removing the operational bottleneck known as a trusted third party. Indeed, blockchain technology could be a feasible tool to achieve the goal.

7.3   RELATED WORK

The IoT is an evolving field that changes rapidly and organically. New features are added, and new security vulnerabilities are discovered almost daily. The best practices and security guidelines of the IoT are still evolving, and many organizations around the world are applying them. At this fact, the establishment of security in IoT has been the subject of several studies in recent years (Elhoseny and Hassanien 2019a, 2019b; Elhoseny et al. 2016).

Only few studies have focused on the trust management, but the results are promising. Sicari et al. (2015) have made a state of the art on the work done about IoT in terms of security, privacy and trust. Through an in-depth literature review, the authors classified trust work into four categories: cooperative approach, fuzzy logic, social relations, and identity-based methods. Yan et al. (2014) carried out an analytical and critical study of the solutions proposed in the literature relating to the management of trust in IoT. This analysis showed that no solution takes into consideration a complete trust management that manages trust in each layer and interlayers of the architectural model defined for the IoT.

The paper by Nour et al. (2019) discusses security and privacy issues in information-centric wireless IoT networks and presents a comparison against the wireless IoT-based IP. The authors show that combining CCN and Wearable Internet-of-Things (WIoT) will significantly improve the performance and deal with most traditional host-centric security issues.

Saied et al. (2013) proposed a trust management system based on context knowledge, with the objective of avoiding selfish and malicious nodes that can launch internal attacks during collaboration such as data modification or bug injection, without them being identifiable. This solution allows remedying the energy constraint; however, it limits the scalability of the trust management system.

Gu et al. (2014) proposed a trust management mechanism based on IoT architecture modeling. This consists of decomposing the IoT into three layers, which are sensor layer, core layer, and application layer. Each layer is controlled by trust management. The scalability criterion is met as the proposed model is distributed. However, this layered model causes energy consumption due to overhead, and the man-in-the-middle attack can affect decision making.

Mahmoud et al. (2013) proposed a public-key infrastructure intended primarily for the smart grid, with a new format of certificates and a new system for their renewal. In the proposed scheme, the public-key infrastructure is hierarchical and fully connected; each certificate authority (CA) is responsible for managing certificates for a limited geographical area. To avoid the complexity of signature verification calculations in each certificate renewal, the authors proposed that the CA create a hash string for each certification, by iteratively hashing a secret random number n times to obtain the root hash value, which will be added to the data part and the signature part in the certificate. Using the hash chain when renewing certificates reduces energy consumption and increases resistance to attacks. However, objects often change privilege, and in this case, their certificates are revoked each time, which causes an increase in overhead.

Saied et al. (2014) proposed a lightweight collaborative key scheme that exploits the heterogeneity of objects to perform heavy cryptographic operations and ensure end-to-end security between pairs. To do this, the authors selected the two protocols, Internet Key Exchange and Transport Layer Security Handshake, as the most suitable protocols for IoT characteristics. The idea of this work consists in modifying the schematics of the two protocols to make them more adapted to IoT specifications. The solution proposed in this model exploits the heterogeneity of objects to establish a collaborative schema; in other words, to exploit the computing, storage, and energy resources of certain nodes to carry out costly services in terms of resources in place of the other nodes characterized by a strong constraint of resources, this approach is decentralized, which ensures scalability. However, the Diffie-Hellman key exchange scheme does not authenticate the participants in a key exchange; hence, it does not resist certain attacks such as the man-in-the-middle attack.

More recently, Farahat et al. (2019) proposed a system to protect citizen's personal data in smart cities. The proposed system protects information when transmitted wirelessly using the run-length encoding technique and then encrypt it with a rotated key using the Advanced Encryption Standard (AES) process.

To overcome the shortcomings of the studies outlined previously, we propose a hybrid solution based on the combination of blockchain technology and CCN-IoT.

7.4   INTRODUCTION

The Internet's open nature creates the opportunity to connect sensors, cars, smartphones, and other services to a scale that changes how we communicate with our environment and society. The immense potential offered by the IoT will make a difference to our world. The IoT's impact forecasts on the global economy are remarkable, with a growing increase in the number and use of IoT devices in a wide range of exciting new applications.

While 9 billion objects and sensors are already connected to the Internet, this number should be multiplied by five by 2020 (Dave 2011). Appliances, intelligent televisions, various sensors, and even power plants – more and more devices – are now connected to the Internet.

The IoT will offer wonderful possibilities. It will help us make better decisions in many aspects of our lives. At the same time, the IoT also presents significant challenges in terms of security. With the exponential development of connected objects, new vulnerabilities and threats are emerging. Today, security is the main obstacle to the explosion of the IoT. Not that the objects themselves are vulnerable; it is their connectivity and networking that weaken their security.

As the IoT develops and technology becomes increasingly inseparable from our society, we risk losing control. In the healthcare sector, we are rushing toward an environment where medical devices linked to the Internet track patients in real time. Soon, doctors will be able to make adjustments over the Internet, such as changing the settings of a pacemaker or insulin pump. With today's technology, we cannot prevent hackers from remotely administering a lethal dose of insulin to someone, nor can we prevent a person's pacemaker from being adjusted to cause death. The rise of this IoT is not without danger, especially since the risks, which were mainly virtual, extend to the physical domain.

Deployments of connected objects and sensors in all sectors will lead to a massive proliferation of data. Already, more than 2.5 quintillion bytes of data (https://www.domo.com/learn/data-never-sleeps-5?aid=ogsm072517_1&sf100871281=1) are generated every day, and this amount is growing exponentially. The application protocols of the Internet are not adapted, historically, to the very limited power of objects. However, the IoT can emerge only through the development of architectures integrating robust constraints of security, adaptability, and latency. Specific factors, such as data requirements, safety and power issues, and battery life, will determine which technology to use.

More recently, the CCN architecture (Jacobson et al. 2009) has attracted the attention of many researchers, owing to its several attractive advantages, such as security, energy efficiency, flexibility, and scalability, that fulfill the needs of the IoT. The CCN networks have been designed to meet the limitations of data access on the traditional Internet. The CCN networks are built to retrieve content or access resources using the resource name itself instead of the address of the node that hosts those resources.

The rise of the IoT, with its myriad of connected things, will open many security breaches. Object identity is recognized as a common security concern in the perception, application, and network layers. Moreover, in terms of computer identification, machine-to-machine interaction faces a more significant challenge. Security solutions should verify the veracity of device data, device integrity, and system identity while protecting data. Since CCN relies on basic materials for content integrity and authentication (public key infrastructure), effective authentication techniques should be employed for efficient and flexible trust management and secure communication.

An emerging solution is to use the blockchain technology as a distributed ledger of information to bring scalable, decentralized security and trust to IoT devices. Combining blockchain, CCN, and IoT seems like a potentially interesting approach. The combination between CCN and blockchain was also carried out by Conti et al. (2019), Labbi et al. (2018), and Zhu et al. (2018) In this chapter, we present a naming-based security model combined with blockchain technology that guarantees devices' identification and authentication, data integrity, name authenticity, and relevance.

The proposed method not only considers the IoT security issue but also accounts for introducing CCN as a potential networking architecture that addresses other IoT requirements. The combination of blockchain technology and CCN-IoT is an excellent solution to manage trust and key management and to avoid the dependency on a trusted third party.

This remaining chapter is organized as follows: Section 7.5 explores the feasibility and advantages of the CCN approach in the IoT. Section 7.6 introduces our approach base on the combination of CCN naming feature and blockchain technology. Section 7.7 introduces experimental results and their discussion. Finally, Section 7.8 concludes our work.

7.5 ADVANTAGES OF USING CCN FOR THE IoT

In recent years, the CCN approach has gained increasing attention and has emerged as a potential alternative networking solution to the IoT (Amadeo et al. 2014; Garcia-Luna-Aceves 2017; Labbi et al. 2018).

The CCN model improves the organization and retrieval of data and enhances network scalability, reliability, and security. It has the characteristic of dissociating information from its supplier, thus opening new horizons by natively supporting mobility and storage in the network. Owing to its intrinsic features, CCN allows a decentralized and intelligent data-delivery platform to serve today's heterogeneous IoT services that are hard to achieve over IP.

7.5.1 POWER CONSUMPTION

Connected objects use plenty of energy. How will the energy need of the 20 billion connected objects be met by 2050?

One of the most relevant features of CCN is the use of cache memory at the network level. It has a positive impact on energy aspects. It provides data for various applications, without having to request the content provider. In other word, sensors could sleep more (reduce energy consumption), while their data could still be available in cache nodes. In-network caching improves data gathering as well as delivery process. Experiments realized by Baccelli et al. (2014) have shown that energy savings can be accomplished through in-network caching.

7.5.2 Service Discovery

The IoT applications produce information using different vocabulary in various formats. As part of the Internet of the future, IoT intends to gather information and provide the right user with the right services, at the right time, in the right place, and on the right device, based on the context available.

Context awareness (Labbi, and Benabdellah 2019; Butt et al. 2013; Kim et al. 2016; Xiao et al. 2010) will play an essential role in determining the information to be processed and in reducing the number of services collected by returning only a subset of potentially relevant resources in conjunction with the scope of the request.

The CCN naming has a major impact on the functioning of the network. Each content is identified by a name – or prefix – that has a hierarchical structure, similar to URLs. This naming has the advantage of having a semantic meaning for users. The CCN prefixes are then presented as URLs in the following form:

/UMP/FSO/video/video.avi

This naming scheme offers a defining location identity for quick and accurate access to contents.

The CCN naming scheme provides a better abstraction to fit the problems for today's communication (Table 7.2). In IoT service discovery, the use of context is

TABLE 7.2

The CCN Hierarchical Naming for a Service Discovery Request to Get the Appropriate Service

CCN Name Queries for Appropriate Discovery	Matching Criteria
/MyHome/	Domain name
/MyHome/Garage/	Domain name, location
/MyHome/Garage/Lights/	Domain name, location, type based
/MyHome/Garage/Lights/ON/<signature>/	Domain name, location, type, action, and relevant information based

very relevant; it can play the role of a filtering mechanism that determines which data and services should be provided to the user, based on the context of the user.

7.6 BLOCK-BASED CCN-IoT ARCHITECTURE

The security risks inherent in connected objects are holding back some industrial deployments to date. To maintain information privacy, IoT devices and sensors must share such authentication materials. This requires a lightweight key management system to ensure trust between different things and to be able to distribute the keys that consume the devices' minimum capabilities.

The CCN employs a mechanism based essentially on the addition of digital signatures to content and the use of an understandable hierarchical naming system, ensuring producer identification and relevance. However, it requires the recovery of the producer's public key to ensure the authentication of the producer, the integrity of the data, and the authenticity of the names.

The integration of the blockchain in an IoT service thus appears as a solution to this problem. The blockchain, a transparent, secure information storage and transmission technology working without a central authority, could be a feasible tool to achieve the goal. This new model is beneficial to the security of connected objects, because it removes the restrictions imposed by the traditional model of trust in central authority that have made the IoT vulnerable.

Although our solution is intended to be used in a wide-ranging context, we consider in this section and as an illustrative example the case of a smart campus.

The campus is composed of several buildings; each building is composed of *K* floors and *N* rooms on each floor. Each room contains a number of connected objects (thermometer, light, camera,...).

7.6.1 TRUST ESTABLISHMENT

In this section, we explain the manner of adding devices to the blockchain. We propose the use of blockchain technology as a system for distributing and managing the public keys of the publisher to consumers.

Using blockchain as a trusted anchor for security has two key steps: registration and verification.

7.6.1.1 Registration and Publication

The registration process allows the blockchain to acquire the necessary information about IoT devices and a definition of the content that can be made available to customers. A content object is represented by a single and unique hierarchical name. It acts as a public identity, such as */comp.ump/building1floor2/Room4/thermometer/ timestamp* references a thermometer in Room 4 (Figure 7.6).

The name prefix in the namespace (*/comp.ump/*) will be used as an identity to retrieve content from the IoT devices.

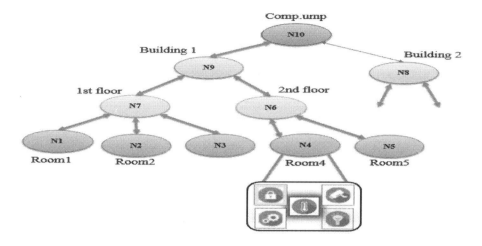

FIGURE 7.6   Hierarchical naming.

Algorithm 1 describes the registration of a new identity with a corresponding public key.

Before a content provider publishes contents, it registers an identity with a corresponding public key. Each new object registers by sending a register message to the blockchain. The register message contains the identity of the new object jointly with its public key, which will be used during verification operation. The public key depends on the namespace where this key is acceptable for verifying packets signatures. A rigid link between the keys and the namespaces is then established. Each node of the blockchain is notified and then iterates through the blockchain and checks if that identity has never been previously registered. In the case when the identity is already registered, the pair is rejected. Otherwise, it performs a publication action by storing the pair in the blockchain. Once an entity has been registered, its identity and public key pair become public.

Algorithm 1: Registration

1: The identity owner generates P_rK and P_uK
2: The identity owner posted (ID, P_uK) to the blockchain, where:
   - ID is the domain name (globally routable name segment)
   - P_uK is the public key
   If *ID is previously registered*, **then**
   | The pair is Rejected   . by the block miner
      else
   | add the pair

Algorithm 2 describes the operations performed by the consumer to register Name/Value pair in blockchain.

Algorithm 2: Steps of Name/Value pair registration in blockchain

1: Generates P_rK and P_uK
2: Hash $\rightarrow$ (Name, Content, SignInfo)
3: Encrypt the message digest
        $Value = $ (Name, Content, SignInfo)$_{PrK}$
4: Place Name/Value pair on the blockchain
5: The miners verify if the name is previously registered. If so, the pair will be
    rejected; if not, then it can be added.

To link the name to the content, a digital signature is embedded in each data packet. Indeed, this signature is calculated on the whole packet (Name, Content, SignInfo...) using the private key of the producer to ensure the provenance for that content. Its verification ensures that the data received has not been altered (data integrity) and that it corresponds to the name expressed in the Interest packet, since this name is the same as that of the data packet (authenticity of names). The verification of the signature of the data packet requires the public key of the producer. For that, after producing a digital signature for that content, Name/Value pair is posted on the blockchain, allowing applicants to decide whether a public key is acceptable and able to verify the signature of a data packet.

7.6.1.2   Verification

To ensure the validity and provenance of a content, an applicant must verify the signature of the received data packet. It is based on the information on this signature included in this packet, to retrieve the public key needed for its verification.

Algorithm 3 describes the lookup operation.

Lookup operation ensures that a given public key corresponds to a given identity. Thus, when a user wants to check whether a public key belongs to the identity, he crosses the blockchain and searches for the identity and public key pair of each transaction. In the case when the ID does not correspond to the public key, FALSE is returned to the object; otherwise, TRUE is returned.

Algorithm 3: Lookup operation

Input: ID, P_uK
Output: TRUE or FALSE
1: User performs a lookup of ID
2: **If** *P_uK correspond to ID,* **then**
3:   | return TRUE
4: **else**
5:   | return FALSE

7.6.1.3 Data Delivery

After registration, object and services are available for users and applications. When they want to retrieve a content, they send a request message (Interest packet) with the name of the data they want to the next hops. As data can be placed closer to the users (in-network caching), the response time to requests can be reduced, as well as the amount of traffic on the network. Moreover, in-network caching allows that the sensors go on sleep mode and thus reduce energy consumption. It is worth noting that the producers sign contents with their keys, which therefore must be available at the consumer or can be retrieved from the blockchain.

Before routing content to the requester, network nodes store a copy in their caches (in-network caching) to respond to subsequent requests. As soon as the consumer receives the data packet, it checks the status of the key (valid or not) by performing a query that includes the name of the content of the desired content or the identity of the content owner to the blockchain. If the key is valid, it calculates a hash of received data packet and compares it with the received hash. If the two hashes match, then the content is validated.

7.7 EXPERIMENT RESULT AND DISCUSSION

In this section, we evaluate the lookup operation that ensures that a given public key corresponds to a given identity. The experiment is performed using Intel Core i5 2.20 GHz processor, 1 TB HDD, 6 GB DDR3 memory, and Microsoft Windows 10.

We used the blockchain data structure proposed by https://medium.com/crypto-currently/lets-build-the-tiniest-Blockchain-e70965a248b, written in *Python*.

We made some modifications to adapt it to our approach. As one can see in Figure 7.7, the time taken by the lookup operation depends on the size of the block-chain. From a chain length greater than 500 blocks, the verification time becomes longer. For instance, for a chain with the length of around 950 blocks, lookup operation took approximately 11 seconds.

There is really no upper limit on the number of blocks; the blocks continue to be added at an average rate of 1 every 10 minutes at the end of the chain. This process will not stop because the huge number of connected devices will need blocks to store their daily transactions. In terms of number of transactions per block, the current average is actually close to 1500 and the current block size is 1 MB (1024 KB) (Blockchain.com).

However, we think that the use of a distributed hash table, where (identity, key) pairs are stored, can support fast lookup operation. Any node can efficiently retrieve the public key associated with a given identity, without traversing the entire blockchain.

Unlike common public key infrastructures (PKIs), access to information is not read or written by any central authority. Using blockchain removes reliance on a centralized authority and solves the problem of the single points of failure. Nonetheless, the characteristics of the blockchain are highly appropriate for storing and maintaining public keys and claiming ownership of something electronic that

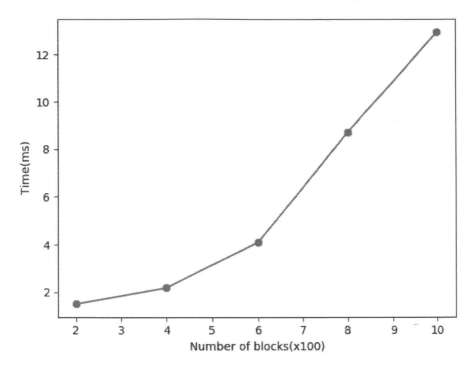

FIGURE 7.7 Lookup operation.

everyone knows about. Since each user has a copy of the blockchain, it is impossible to manipulate information and cover up users' tracks.

7.7.1 LIMITATION AND CHALLENGES

The design or adaptation of the blockchain technology in CCN faces several obstacles. Obviously, some issues arise from the nature of the blockchain technology. Some other challenges are presented in Ghandour et al. (2019), such as regulatory issues, standards challenges, and lack of knowledge.

Moreover, the exponential increase in the size of the blockchain will increase the lookup operation time, which requires a traversal of the entire blockchain. Larger blocks (Figure 7.8) create technical challenges. It also means more computing power required to mine that block onto the chain. The Ethereum ChainData volume with FAST Sync, for instance, exceeded 38.89 GB in December 2017 compared with 20.46 GB in September 2017 (https://etherscan.io/chart2/chaindatasizefast).

7.8 CONCLUSION AND FUTURE WORK

The IoT promises unprecedented comfort. However, for IoT to reach its full potential, it is essential to gain and maintain consumer confidence in privacy and security. In this chapter, we introduce a hybrid solution based on the combination of CCN

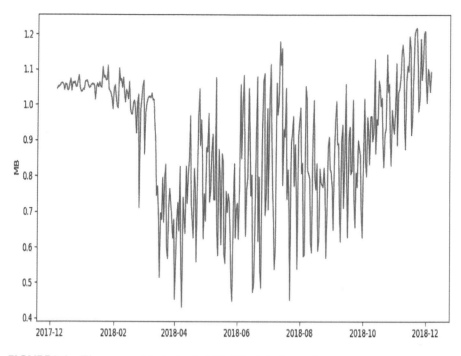

FIGURE 7.8 The average block size in MB. (Blockchain.com)

naming feature and blockchain technology to build trust between parties and devices and protect data in the IoT, while considering the resource constraints of many IoT devices.

Although the CCN approach represents a promising candidate for the IoT, it is still a very young field of research. Many problems are still open and remain without clear answers. The proposal of an appropriate naming system, ensuring the majority of security services, represents an unresolved issue.

For that, we aim to reinforce the security model adopted in CCN, by proposing an adequate naming system and by integrating cryptographic mechanisms in the content. Moreover, future work of this research may include using other systems, such as Certcoin, that use cryptographic accumulators to provide efficient support for key lookup.

REFERENCES

Amadeo, Marica, Claudia Campolo, Antonio Iera, and Antonella Molinaro. "Named data networking for IoT: An architectural perspective." In *2014 European Conference on Networks and Communications (EuCNC)*, 1–5. IEEE, 2014.

Baccelli, Emmanuel, Christian Mehlis, Oliver Hahm, Thomas C Schmidt, and Matthias Wählisch. "Information centric networking in the IoT: Experiments with NDN in the wild." In *Proceedings of the 1st ACM Conference on Information-Centric Networking*, 77–86. ACM, 2014.

Balte, Ashvini, Asmita Kashid, and Balaji Patil. "Security issues in Internet of things (IoT): A survey." *International Journal of Advanced Research in Computer Science and Software Engineering* 5, no. 4 (2015): 1–10.

Butt, Talal Ashraf, Iain Phillips, Lin Guan, and George Oikonomou. "Adaptive and context-aware service discovery for the internet of things." In *Internet of Things, Smart Spaces, and Next Generation Networking*, Part of the Lecture Notes in Computer Science book series (LNCS, vol. 8121), 36–47. Springer, Berlin, Germany, 2013.

Conti, Mauro, Muhammad Hassan, and Chhagan Lal. "BlockAuth: BlockChain based distributed producer authentication in ICN." *Computer Networks* 164 (2019): 106888.

Dave, Evans. "The internet of things: How the next evolution of the internet is changing everything." *CISCO White Paper* 1, no. 2011 (2011): 1–11.

Elhoseny, Mohamed, Hamdy Elminir, Alaa Riad, and Xiaohui Yuan. "A secure data routing schema for WSN using elliptic curve cryptography and homomorphic encryption." *Journal of King Saud University-Computer and Information Sciences* 28, no. 3 (2016): 262–275.

Elhoseny, Mohamed, and Aboul Ella Hassanien. "An encryption model for data processing in WSN." In *Dynamic Wireless Sensor Networks*, Part of the Studies in Systems, Decision and Control book series (SSDC, vol. 165), 145–169. Springer, Cham, Germany, 2019a.

Elhoseny, Mohamed, and Aboul Ella Hassanien. "Secure data transmission in WSN: An overview." In *Dynamic Wireless Sensor Networks*, Part of the Studies in Systems, Decision and Control book series (SSDC, vol. 165), Springer, 115–143. Springer, Cham, India, 2019b.

Farahat, I.S., A.S. Tolba, Mohamed Elhoseny, and Waleed Eladrosy. "Data security and challenges in smart cities." In *Security in Smart Cities: Models, Applications, and Challenges*, 117–142. Springer, Cham, Germany, 2019.

Fernández-Caramés, Tiago M., and Paula Fraga-Lamas. "A review on the use of blockchain for the internet of things." *IEEE Access* 6 (2018): 32979–33001.

Garcia-Luna-Aceves, José Joaquin. "ADN: An information-centric networking architecture for the internet of things." In *Proceedings of the Second International Conference on Internet-of-Things Design and Implementation*, 27–36. ACM, 2017.

Ghandour, Ahmed G., Mohamed Elhoseny, and Aboul Ella Hassanien. "Blockchains for smart cities: A survey." In *Security in Smart Cities: Models, Applications, and Challenges*, 193–210. Springer, Cham, Germany, 2019.

Gu, Lize, Jingpei Wang, and Bin Sun. "Trust management mechanism for Internet of Things." *China Communications* 11, no. 2 (2014): 148–156.

Gubbi, Jayavardhana, Rajkumar Buyya, Slaven Marusic, and Marimuthu Palaniswami. "Internet of things (IoT): A vision, architectural elements, and future directions." *Future Generation Computer Systems* 29, no. 7 (2013): 1645–1660.

ITU Strategy, and Policy Unit. "ITU internet reports 2005: The internet of things." *Geneva: International Telecommunication Union (ITU)* 1 (2005): 62.

Jacobson, Van, Diana K. Smetters, James D. Thornton, Michael F. Plass, Nicholas H. Briggs, and Rebecca L. Braynard. "Networking named content." In *Proceedings of the 5th International Conference on Emerging Networking Experiments and Technologies*, 1–12. ACM, 2009.

Kim, Hyunwook, Robiul M. Hoque, Seo Hyungyu, and Sung-Hyun Yang. "Development of middleware architecture to realize context-aware service in smart home environment." *Computer Science and Information Systems* 13, no. 2 (2016): 427–452.

Labbi, Mohamed, and Mohammed Benabdellah. "CCN context-naming for efficient context-aware service discovery in IoT." In *International Conference on Mobile, Secure, and Programmable Networking*, 37–50. Springer, 2019.

Labbi, Mohamed, Nabil BenSalah, Nabil Kannouf, Youssef Douzi, Mohamed Benabdellah, and Abdelmalek Azizi. "A game theoretic approach to multipath traffic control in content-centric networking." In *2016 International Conference on Advanced Communication Systems and Information Security (ACOSIS)*, 1–7. IEEE, 2016.

Labbi, Mohamed, Nabil Kannouf, and Mohammed Benabdellah. "IoT security based on content-centric networking architecture." In *Security and Privacy in Smart Sensor Networks*, 179–199. IGI Global, USA, 2018.

Mahmoud, Mohamed M.E.A., Jelena Misic, and Xuemin Shen. "A scalable public key infrastructure for smart grid communications." In *2013 IEEE Global Communications Conference (GLOBECOM)*, 784–789. IEEE, 2013.

Mosko, Marc, Ignacio Solis, and C. Wood. "CCNx semantics." *IRTF Draft, Palo Alto Research Center, Inc*, 2016.

Nakamoto, Satoshi, et al. *Bitcoin: A Peer-to-Peer Electronic Cash System*. 2008. https://bitcoin.org/bitcoin.pdf.

Nour, Boubakr, Kashif Sharif, Fan Li, and Yu Wang. "Security and privacy challenges in information centric wireless IoT networks," 2019. https://hal.archives-ouvertes.fr/hal-02189504/.

Saied, Yosra Ben, Alexis Olivereau, Djamal Zeghlache, and Maryline Laurent. "Lightweight collaborative key establishment scheme for the internet of things." *Computer Networks* 64 (2014): 273–295.

Saied, Yosra Ben, Alexis Olivereau, Djamal Zeghlache, and Maryline Laurent. "Trust management system design for the internet of things: A contextaware and multi-service approach." *Computers & Security* 39 (2013): 351–365.

Sicari, Sabrina, Alessandra Rizzardi, Luigi Alfredo Grieco, and Alberto Coen-Porisini. "Security, privacy and trust in internet of things: The road ahead." *Computer Networks* 76 (2015): 146–164.

Xiao, Hua, Ying Zou, Joanna Ng, and Leho Nigul. "An approach for contextaware service discovery and recommendation." In *2010 IEEE International Conference on Web Services*, 163–170. IEEE, 2010.

Yan, Zheng, Peng Zhang, and Athanasios V. Vasilakos. "A survey on trust management for internet of things." *Journal of Network and Computer Applications* 42 (2014): 120–134.

Zhu, Konglin, Zhicheng Chen, Wenke Yan, and Lin Zhang. "Security attacks in named data networking of things and a blockchain solution." *IEEE Internet of Things Journal* 6(3) (2018): 4733–4741.

8 Blockchain for Internet of Vehicles Security

Anis Herbadji, Hadjer Goumidi, Yasmine Harbi,
Khadidja Medani, and Zibouda Aliouat

CONTENTS

8.1   INTRODUCTION

According to the International Organization of Motor Vehicle Manufacturers (OICA[1]), over 70 million vehicles were produced in 2016. The number of vehicle sales grew up from 50 million in 2015 to 78 million in 2018. This number is still increasing, leading to a corresponding increase in the number of vehicles on roads. Therefore, roads' safety and efficiency, as well as passengers' entertainment, are becoming one of the significant interests for researchers and developers. With the advancement in communication technologies and vehicular industry, the paradigm of the intelligent transportation system (ITS) appeared, in which smart vehicles have been integrated with vehicle-to-vehicle/infrastructure-based vehicular ad hoc communications to exchange road information and critical events with one another.

Recently, the Internet of Things (IoT) has emerged as an underlying technology that allows real-time data sensing, processing, and convey among a variety of

---

[1] The International Organization of Motor Vehicle Manufacturers official website: http://www.oica.net.

intelligent/smart objects. The application of the IoT in the transportation domain reveals an essential development of the ITS. Thus, the interaction of vehicles as smart objects and IoT components has driven the evolution of classical vehicular ad hoc networks (VANETs) into the Internet of Vehicles (IoV), in which several communication types, such as vehicle-to-home, vehicle-to-pedestrian, and vehicle-to-Internet connections are provided. The IoV is an internet-enabled vehicles network that comprises connected vehicles services varying from traffic safety and efficiency to infotainment applications. This technology promises to facilitate and enhance vehicles mobility issues.

The IoV is characterized by disseminating critical data in open-related environments via unsecured communication channels. Hence, the transmitted data may face several security threats, such as fake information convey, tampering messages, and intercepting vehicles' personal information. Human safety and security remain the main issues that developers need to consider in IoV systems. For example, an attacker can join the network and broadcast fake messages to mislead the vehicles. In addition, hijackers could attack and get remote control over vehicles. Such attacks may cause target vehicles to change their route, leading to system efficiency diminution or worse to harm human lives by causing traffic jams and road accidents. Moreover, a replay attack may be triggered by an adversary vehicle, which is able to record, read, and modify data and resend a packet acting as the original sender. Hence, ensuring authentication, confidentiality, non-repudiation, data integrity, and privacy is pivotal.

Several works investigating security and privacy requirements can be found in the literature. Some solutions are proposed to grant the integrity of the exchanged messages. These solutions are based on public key infrastructures (PKIs) and digital signature mechanisms, thus ensuring the non-repudiation and integrity of exchanged messages. However, the storage of information and the reliability of vehicles are not resolved. In addition, dealing with data access without authentication is a challenging task, especially in decentralized architectures, as in the IoV. Nevertheless, depending on a third party to verify the vehicles' identity is not practical, particularly in critical events' dissemination. More in general, relying on a centralized solution with a single point of failure may hinder scalability and lead to higher latency, especially in end-to-end IoV communications. The blockchain technology has drawn a lot of attention in the last few years owing to its attractive benefits, including decentralization, immutability, integrity, authorization, and transparency. A blockchain is an open, distributed peer-to-peer (P2P) data storage mechanism that is designed to efficiently record transactions in a verifiable and permanent way (Iansiti and Lakhani 2017). Data are stored in a block that is timestamped and linked to previous blocks. This structure offers data immutability; once the data are added, they cannot be altered or deleted. In addition, the decentralization of the exchanged data over the whole network implies faster compromise between the different participating parties and establishes nodes' transparency, which minimize the chance of fraudulent entity. Moreover, data can be quickly backtracked in case of system failure. Thus, blockchain can achieve trust, data accuracy, fault tolerance, and reliability, which are significant issues in traditional security technologies.

Blockchain is largely studied in the context of ad hoc networks and IoT. However, the unique characteristics of vehicular communications, such as the environment, the mobility and the high requirements of securing these communications in decentralized and transparent manner, made the blockchain an excellent topic to discuss in the context of IoV applications. Nonetheless, few survey papers that investigate blockchain in the context of IoV can be found in the literature. The motivation of this chapter is to present an analytical study of IoV blockchain-based security solutions and to provide a comparison between classical and blockchain-based solutions. To do so, the contributions of the chapter are as follows:

- First, we give a summary of IoV security and privacy requirements and possible attacks. Also, a classification of a set of classical solutions concerning their security challenges is provided.
- Second, to highlight the usage of blockchain for securing IoV applications, we first present the key characteristics, the architecture, and the applications of blockchains. In light of the need for a decentralized, transparent, safe-storage, and fault-tolerant mechanism to secure the vehicular communications, blockchain-based solutions may improve the IoV security and privacy requirements. To highlight the feasibility of implementing the blockchains in IoV systems, we survey 14 research papers found in the specialized literature up to 2019. Also, we provide a comparative analysis of the classical and blockchain-based solutions. The comparison addresses the treated attack model, the security requirements, the used technique, and the cost and limitations of each surveyed solution.
- As IoV is a large network concerned with human life, the design of security solutions has to fulfill the requirements of scalability, latency, and privacy. These issues remain open topics to be addressed in the context of IoV blockchain-based solutions. In light of these requirements, we finally propose a new layered architecture and provide future works that could be a guidance for other researches.

The remainder of this chapter is organized as follows: Section 8.2 introduces the IoV's basic notions, architecture, applications, and challenges. Section 8.3 presents the security requirements and threats in the IoV and discusses classical security solutions. The IoV blockchain-based technology is presented in Section 8.4. Also, a comparative analysis of blockchain-based and classical security solutions is provided. Section 8.5 discusses the open issues related to the integration of blockchain in the IoV. Section 8.6 describes the proposed architecture and provides future work, before a conclusion is given in Section 8.7.

8.2   VEHICULAR COMMUNICATIONS

In this section, we present the basic concepts and definitions related to the vehicular communications, including smart vehicles, VANETs, vehicular cloud computing (VCC), and IoV. Then, we detail the architecture of the IoV, its applications, and its challenges.

8.2.1 Smart, Connected, and Automated Vehicles

Owing to the increasing development of transportation means, vehicles today are said smart vehicles. They advocate novel functionalities to the transportation systems, such as vehicles data collection and communication. They allow the driver to access different resources and services. The main purpose of smart vehicles is to address safety issues. Thus, it will be possible to assist drivers' decisions to prevent wrong behaviors. Furthermore, automated driving may be the result of combining different functionalities, such as control, communications, and computing capabilities (Varaiya 1993; Vegni, Mauro, and Roberto 2013).

Generally, a smart vehicle is equipped with sensing devices to collect the necessary data and measure various parameters, such as speed, acceleration, and distance from neighboring vehicles. In addition to Global Positioning System (GPS), the new cars are equipped with multiple sensors, including radio, radar, camera, speedometer, temperature, fuel gauge, rain, wheel rotation, and tachometer sensors. These different sensing devices permit events and environment data collecting. Besides, smart vehicles support multiple interfaces (e.g., Universal Mobile Telecommunications System (UMTS), Bluetooth, and IEEE 802.11.b) to be connected to smartphones, other vehicles, or the Internet. A central processing unit is also deployed to execute different applications and communication protocols. Therefore, an embedded operating system is needed to process status information and control all devices. Although major manufacturers (e.g., BMW, Toyota, and Volvo) and IT corporations (e.g., Google, Apple, and Huawei) have initiated their smart vehicle projects, a few numbers of vehicles in use today are equipped with intelligent systems. Therefore, the functionalities related to the ITS remain limited (Wu, Yang, and Li 2016), and a driver is still required behind the wheels.

8.2.2 Vehicular Ad Hoc Network

Yousefi et al. defined VANET as the *'computer network on wheels'* (Yousefi, Mousavi, and Fathy 2006). VANET is the network that provides data communication among vehicles. The connected nodes in VANET consist of vehicles on roads that are capable of data storage and processing. Usually, the vehicle can communicate in two different modes, infrastructure mode and ad hoc mode. In the infrastructure mode, data is spread up through vehicle-to-infrastructure communication (V2I). In turn, other vehicles get the information needed from the available roadside units (RSUs). In the ad hoc mode, the vehicles exchange data between them through vehicle-to-vehicle communication (V2V) in a multihop manner. To get better performances, hybrid communications use both V2I and V2V communications.

The primary aim of VANET is to improve driving safety and efficiency. The vehicles can exchange congestion information with their neighboring vehicles, helping them to select the appropriate route to reduce traffic jam. Moreover, the VANET applications may aid the end user to map for restaurants or petrol pumps, for example. In general, the VANET applications are oriented to safety issues, such as precrash sensing, cooperative forward collision and lane-change warning, alert messaging, road traffic optimization, and P2P audio and video streaming to improve the quality of the transportation (Hartenstein and Laberteaux 2010).

8.2.3   VEHICULAR CLOUD COMPUTING

The cloud computing is a model that allows access to several configurable computing resources, known as data centers, such as networks, servers, storage, applications, and services (Whaiduzzaman et al. 2014). These data centers can be delivered rapidly, with little arrangement potential or service provider interaction.

The fast development of the intelligent transportation system (ITS) and the integration of cloud computing for mobile networking create the new concept of VCC. The VCC provides traditional and emergent services to improve traffic management and real-time information distribution in vehicular environments. When network nodes store their data in the cloud to be used as input to various applications, the communication and the transfer of that information are carried out by the aid of V2V and V2I communications through cellular communication devices (i.e., WiFi, WAVE, Worldwide Interoperability for Microwave Access (WiMAx), 4G, and 5G). However, vehicles, such as ambulances, cars in garages, and fire trucks, can serve their resources to be used by the VCC as data centers or service providers.

The VCC provides potential services (Whaiduzzaman et al. 2014), including the following:

- *Network as a service (NaaS)*: The vehicles having Internet access facilities can provide Internet access to other vehicles while moving on the roads.
- *Storage as a service (STaaS)*: The vehicles having large storage capacity can provide a storage pool to other vehicles to allow them running their applications and services.
- *Cooperation as a service (CaaS)*: The vehicles having services subscribed provide necessary information to other vehicles, the drivers of which are interested in the same services. The CaaS allows drivers to evolve by the minimal infrastructure to obtain services.
- *Entertainment and information as a service (ENaaS/IaaS)*: The vehicles on the move provide information for safe driving, such as road conditions, warning, road crash, or any emergency event information. This service is known as information as a service (IaaS). In addition, entertainment as a service (ENaaS) allows many commercials to come to the car screen of the driver, such as advertisements and movie streaming.

8.2.4   INTERNET OF VEHICLES

The real-time connection of smart objects, such as vehicles, sensors, and smartphones among advanced wireless access technologies, has created a new paradigm called the IoT. The IoT is a social network where the entities are smart objects rather than human beings. It integrates smartness into the existing areas, such as healthcare and industry fields. In the transportation domain, it is referred to as the IoV.

The IoV is an emerging cyber-physical system that integrates VANET, IoT, and mobile cloud computing (Hossain, Hasan, and Zawoad 2017). Based on these three concepts, the IoV is defined as a large-scale distributed system for wireless communication and information exchange according to agreed communication protocols and

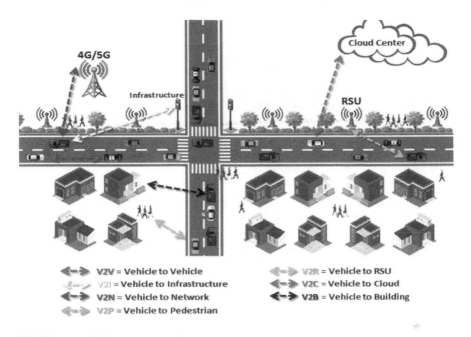

FIGURE 8.1 V2X communications.

data interaction standards (e.g., IEEE 802.11p, WAVE, 4G, and 5G). It demonstrates an exemplary implementation of the IoT technology in ITS, which allows intelligent traffic management, smart dynamic information service, and smart vehicle control.

As shown in Figure 8.1, the IoV evolves through vehicle-to-X (V2X) communications, where X may be another vehicle, sensor, pedestrian, cloud, RSU, or any other device, to increase the effectiveness, environmental performance, safety, resilience, and efficiency of the transportation ecosystems. In addition to smart safety management, the IoV offers smart commercial and infotainment applications to vehicular communications. It also provides reliable Internet service in vehicles owed to the inclusion of V2X communications. However, the interoperability of heterogeneity of devices is one of the main challenging tasks in IoV development. Existing computing and communication devices would be compatible with vehicular networks of the IoV. In addition, as vehicular communications will generate large amounts of real-time data, processing and decision-making capability must deal with the growth of vehicular networks and volume of data.

8.2.4.1 Layered Communication Architecture

Layered communication architecture is paramount to ensure reliable communication in the network. The latter designs important communication protocols and services, including physic, medium access control, network, application, and security. Providing a communication protocol stack to model the basic vehicular communication systems has been the concern of many academic researches (Wan et al. 2014; Jiacheng et al. 2016; Kaiwartya et al. 2016; Contreras-Castillo, Zeadally, and Guerrero Ibáñez 2017).

Juan et al. proposed a seven-layered architecture model that supports all communication types in the IoV (Contreras-Castillo, Zeadally, and Guerrero Ibáñez 2017). The seven layers, from bottom to top, are user interaction, acquisition, preprocessing, communication, management, business, and security layers. The user interaction layer provides a user-vehicle interface to manage notifications and interactions between the driver and the vehicle to reduce the driver's distractions. The data acquisition layer aims to gather data relevant to safety, traffic information, and infotainment from all sources located on the vehicle, on the street, or on the highway. In this context, several data collection schemes have been proposed (Bali and Kumar 2016; Aadil et al. 2018; Zhou et al. 2018; Senouci, Aliouat, and Harous 2019; Senouci, Harous, and Aliouat 2019; Wang et al. 2019). The data-filtering and preprocessing layer analyzes the collected data and performs filtering to avoid the dissemination of irrelevant data and then reduce the network traffic. The communication layer is responsible for intelligently selecting the appropriate network to send the information to provide heterogeneous and full connectivity, with an optimal quality to the user. The control and management layer is a global coordinator that aims to manage different network service providers. The functions of the business layer include storing, processing, and analyzing all the information received from the other layers. Thus, a decision can be taken to choose the best strategy of applying the business model in order to improve different data services or to develop new applications. Finally, the security layer communicates with all other layers to provide security functions, including authentication, integrity, non-repudiation, confidentiality, availability, and so on. The protocols of this layer should be implemented to mitigate various types of security attacks in IoV, such as denial-of-service (DoS) and Sybil attacks.

We provide in Figure 8.2 the protocol stack of current vehicular network protocols in different layers of the proposed architecture model.

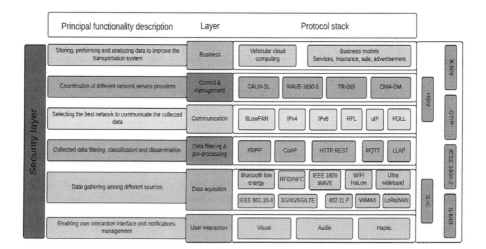

FIGURE 8.2 IoV layered communication architecture and protocol stack.

8.2.4.2 IoV Applications

The main motive behind vehicular communication is to increase driving safety and efficiency. Owed to the facilities offered by the integration of VANET, VCC, and IoT in the context of IoV, the latter provides a large scale of applications and services to the end user. The IoV applications can be divided into three main categories: safety-based, efficiency-based, and infotainment-based applications (Figure 8.3).

Safety-based applications mainly include precrash sensing and cooperative collision warning messaging. A vehicle that detects a collision or an imminent crash has to take the appropriate decision. The system may provide a warning to the driver. This latter initiates an alert message broadcasting to alert the surrounding vehicles of the upcoming collision. Warning systems can be deployed to avoid accidents (e.g., work-zone warning, stopped-vehicle warning, and low-bridge warning

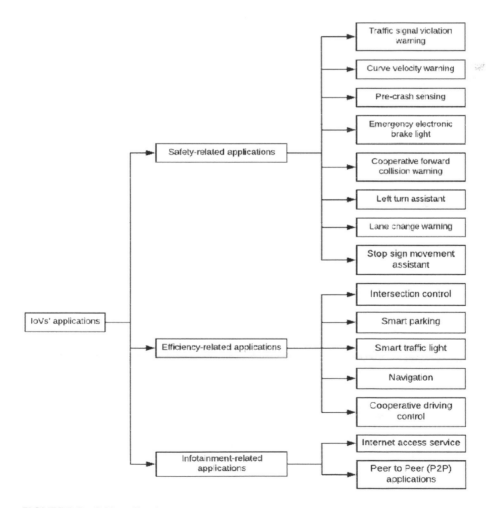

FIGURE 8.3 IoV applications.

for trucks). Such applications may also manage traffic flows and identify alternative routes. In this context, reliability and latency are significant concerns. With
automated vehicles, emergency electronic brake light applications can take place.
According to the Vehicle Safety Communication consortium, the safety applications include eight high-potential applications: traffic signal violation warning,
curve velocity warning to guide the driver about speed limit and avoid collisions,
pre-crash sensing, emergency electronic brake light for crash prevention, cooperative forward-collision warning, left-turn assistant (i.e., a driver getting ready to
make a left turn might easily overlook a pedestrian crossing on the right side of the
street) Lane Change Warning and Stop Sign Movement Assistance. Therefore, the
number of accidents can also be reduced with the help of early-warning system,
lane-change warning, and stop-sign movement assistant. As a way of illustration,
SCOOP[2] is a cooperative ITS project that seeks to link approximately 3000 vehicles with 2000 kilometers of roads. Vehicles are equipped with sensors to detect
events, such as slippery road and emergency brake, and to transmit the information to neighboring vehicles (V2V) or road operator (V2I) through onboard units.
The road operator can also transmit information to the vehicles (I2V) through their
onboard units. The main objective is to enhance driving safety and efficiency.

Efficiency-based applications aim to provide real-time information to minimize
congestion and fuel consumption. Traffic information can help the drivers to find
the best route to their destination when it relates to the immediate area. In general,
efficiency-based applications are concerned with transportation management, such
as intersection control, smart parking, smart traffic light, navigation, and cooperative driving applications. For example, high-precision positioning for cooperative
ITS (HIGHTS[3]) is a European research project, supported by the European Union,
that focuses mainly on smart, green, and integrated transport for the cooperative
ITS. This project integrates traditional satellite systems with the innovative use of
onboard sensing and infrastructure-based wireless communication technologies
(e.g., Wi-Fi, ITS-G5, UWB tracking, Zigbee, Bluetooth, and LTE) to produce highly
accurate positioning of vehicles. The goal of the HIGHTS project is to achieve a
high-precision positioning system with an accuracy of 25 cm.

Infotainment-based applications and diversity offer value-added services that
increase market penetration. They mainly include Internet access services and P2P
applications. Passengers in their vehicles could download music, movies, and games
and connect to home computers. Moreover, in the absence of fixed Internet connectivity, vehicles can provide Internet access to other vehicles. P2P applications are
also of vital interest; they enable data sharing among the moving vehicles, such as
sharing music, games, videos, and chatting.

8.2.4.3 IoV Challenges

Despite the different applications of the IoV, following important research issues are
challenging and need to be addressed for IoV applications:

---

[2] http://www.scoop.developpementdurable.gouv.fr/en/
[3] http://hights.eu

- *Topology change*: The velocity of the moving vehicles may cause a frequent change in the network topology. Therefore, a high rate of arrival and departure of nodes can be affected. Dealing with such a limitation drains an important communication overhead. Researchers should consider this constraining feature while developing IoV solutions.
- *Road traffic*: Depending on the traffic, the density of nodes in vehicular environments may change. In high traffic, the collision caused by the communication in progress increases the message latency. Moreover, the nature of traffic makes some isolated vehicles on the roads. The usage of short communication range palliates the interference issue.
- *Road infrastructure*: High building and the intersections may affect traffic jams and fade. In addition to the interference, the hidden node problem is pointed out as a significant limitation. The design of vehicular communications in these features is more challenging. Thus, the control algorithm should consider the change in the mobility pattern.
- *Energy and storage capabilities*: The nodes in vehicular networks have ample energy and computing power, including both storage and processing, because they are not small handheld devices.
- *Scalability*: Some IoV applications, such as safety-based applications, require the correct behavior in a sparse network as well as in traffic jam scenarios. However, the design of the system has to cope with any increase in traffic density.
- *Latency*: The nature of vehicular communication requires the immediate relaying of information, without the introduction of any delay, which can be caused by different reasons, such as high traffic and network collisions.
- *Reliability*: Failures can independently appear at any time. Reliability is referred to as the possibility of continuous running, with and without failures.
- *Availability*: The availability is defined as the probability that the system is available at any time. The mean time between failures (MTBF) should be as short as possible. With the shortest MTBF, the best maintainability is offered.
- *Safety*: It reflects the system capacity to operate, naturally or unnaturally, without the jeopardy of having damaging or mortal results on the human body and without damaging the environment. The importance of safety requirements is owed to the ability to exclude undesirable situations.
- *Quality of services (QoS)*: Real-time IoV systems must consider several metrics, such as transmission delay, latency, availability, and specific quality requirements of the application. To address this diversified problem, QoS requirements have to manage the network resources to provide the QoS guarantees in IoV.
- *Security*: It reflects the ability of the system to protect itself from accidental or intentional attacks. The system security is an essential prerequisite to ensure its availability, reliability, and safety.

8.3   IoV SECURITY AND PRIVACY

Security is one of the most challenging issues in IoV. To exchange messages safely and to ensure that critical data are not tampered or intercepted by attackers, the security of the IoV system must be addressed. In this section, we present the security issues of IoV. First, we highlight the security requirements that must be considered. Then, we discuss IoV security challenges and attacks and present classical solutions. Finally, we provide a classification of the classical security solutions according to the IoV security challenges.

8.3.1   SECURITY REQUIREMENTS

8.3.1.1   Authentication

The critical nature of messages requires authentication to ensure that the message is generated by a legitimate user. Due to the high mobility of vehicles and the fast changing of vehicles' location, providing vehicles' authentication is highly required in IoV. Each new vehicle that joins the network should be authenticated before exchanging data (Harbi et al. 2019). Vehicles can ensure the authentication by associating each message to their private key along with their certificate or by using pseudonyms.

8.3.1.2   Confidentiality

Sensitive data should not be accessed by unauthorized users. The information must be protected, and access to specific resources must be restricted. To ensure the confidentiality of messages, the signature alone is not sufficient, it is necessary to sign and encrypt the messages.

8.3.1.3   Non-repudiation

Non-repudiation provides the proof that the information is originated from an entity. It ensures that an entity cannot deny sending or receiving a message. Digital signatures can be used to provide non-repudiation. This security requirement can facilitate the identification of attackers even after the attack happens via a tamper-proof device (Mejri, Ben-Othman, and Hamdi 2014).

8.3.1.4   Integrity

The data must not be altered or tampered during the transmission process. ElGamal signature is a method used to ensure the integrity of messages and the security of communication between vehicles (ElGamal 1985).

8.3.1.5   Availability

The data should be available to legitimate entities in real-time, especially in safety-based applications, because any delay, even if it takes milliseconds, will make the message meaningless, and the result might be devastating. We ensure the information availability by resisting attackers that try to take down the system and make it unavailable.

8.3.2 IoV Attacks

The dynamic nature of vehicles and the usage of wireless channels to exchange messages affect the security requirements and make the network vulnerable to various types of attacks.

8.3.2.1 Definition and Classification of Attackers

An attack can be defined as any abnormal behavior that comes from an entity with bad intentions, which is called an attacker.

An attacker is an entity that tries to lunch the attack on the network, aiming to steal or tamper information or to destroy or take down the network. Based on capability, the attackers can be classified into four types (La Vinh and Cavalli 2014; Hasrouny et al. 2017):

- *Insider vs. outsider*: The insider attacker represents the authenticated user to communicate with other members on the network. The outsider is the intruder with limited capacity to attack.
- *Malicious vs. rational*: The malicious attacker tries to harm the network without looking for benefit, whereas the rational attacker anticipates its own advantages from the attacks.
- *Active vs. passive*: An active attacker can generate new packets and signals to damage the network. A passive attacker can only sense the network, but it cannot generate new packets.
- *Local vs. extended*: A local attacker can manipulate limited entities. An extended attacker can control several entities distributed across the network.

8.3.2.2 Types of Attack

Vehicles' communications can be threatened by several types of attacks. Table 8.1 summarizes the IoV attacks.

- *DoS*: The attacker tries to bring down the network by sending a large number of dummy messages to jam the channel and make the services unavailable to the users. Distributed denial-of-service (DDoS) is a DoS from different locations.
- *Sybil attack*: An attacker creates multiple fake identities for confounding other vehicles by sending wrong messages to gain significant influence. This type of attack is difficult to detect and even more challenging to correct, especially when the victim node is isolated.
- *Man-in-the-middle (MiM) attack*: A malicious node intercepts the communication established between vehicles and sends back false messages. It is necessary to ensure a confidential solution by using powerful cryptographic algorithms with secure authentication and data integrity to deal with the MiM attacks.
- *Spamming*: An attacker transmits spam messages in the network to drain the network bandwidth and increase the transmission latency. Spamming is more challenging to control and manage because of the absence of centralized administration.

- *Black-hole and gray-hole attacks*: In a black-hole attack, a malicious node claims to be in the shortest path to the destination node. It arises when participating nodes refuse to participate in the network, or there is no node in that area. When the false route is successfully established, the malicious node drops or forwards the packet. It is more difficult to detect a gray-hole attack because the attackers behave normally first but drop messages any time, without specific objectives.
- *Eavesdropping attack*: It aims at extracting confidential information from the protected data transmitted over the network; it takes the advantage of unsecured network communications. An active form of eavesdropping is an MIM attack.
- *Bogus information attack*: The idea is to inject incorrect or bogus information in the network for personal advantage.
- *Message alteration or suppression attack*: The attacker alters some part of the transmitting message or drop packet from the network.
- *Illusion attack*: The attacker intentionally misleads the sensors on the vehicle to produce the wrong data.

8.3.3 CLASSICAL SECURITY SOLUTIONS FOR IoV

In this section, we discuss several IoV security challenges and present classical solutions available in the literature. A classification of these solutions is provided in Table 8.2.

Owing to the high mobility of vehicles and the fast changing of vehicles' positions, the IoV systems require an efficient execution time. For this, a fast cryptographic

TABLE 8.1
IoV Attacks

Attacks	Threaten Service	Attacker's Type	Solutions
Denial of service	Availability	I/O, A, M, L/E	Digital signature, routing protocols, or trustworthiness of a node
Sybil attack	Authentication Availability	I, A, R/M, L/E	Central validation authority (VA), PKI for key distribution/revocation
MiM	Confidentiality Authenticity Integrity Non-repudiation	I, A/P, M/R, L	Strong authentication methods, powerful cryptography
Spamming	Availability Confidentiality	I, A, M, L/E	Digital signature of software and sensors
Eavesdropping	Confidentiality	I, P, R, L	Symmetric/asymmetric encryption of secure messages
Message tampering	Integrity Authenticity	I/O, A, R/M, L	Similarity algorithm, trust and reputation management system
Tracking	Privacy	I/O, A/P, R, L	Set of anonymous key changes, group signatures

TABLE 8.2
Classification of Classical Security Solutions for IoV

Solution	Technique Used	Description	Security Challenge
Gazdar, et al. (2012)	Trust model based on the Markov chain	Acting as a monitor and updating the trust metric of the vehicle's neighbors	Privacy
Yan, et al. (2013)	VM division algorithm	VM divided into sub-VM when the number of vehicles increases	The network size, the high mobility
Hussain and Oh (2014)	Modify the location information	Leveraging the modified location-based encryption	Secure location
Hussain, et al. (2015)	Cloud-based secure and privacy-aware traffic dissemination services	Using GPS-based location encryption schemes to preserve private information	Secure location
Liu, et al. (2016)	CP-ABE algorithm	Only vehicles that satisfied the access stricture can access the messages	Secure communication
Jenefa and Anita (2018)	Pseudo-ID	Encrypting the vehicle's real ID using its private key and uses it instead of the real ID	Privacy
Wan and Zhang (2018)	Efficient identity-based data transmission	Encrypting the real identity using an algebraic signature and IBS algorithm	Privacy
	Lagrange interpolation method	Lagrange method is used instead of a mapping scheme for integrity and confidentiality protection with low computation tasks	Secure communication
Nkenyereye, Park, and Rhee (2018)	Pseudonym technique	TA generates the corresponding pseudoidentity for vehicle communications	Privacy
Limbasiya and Das (2018)	Secure Message confirmation based on batch verification	Practicing varied private keys for different vehicle users and including the time-stamp in the computation of different credentials	Secure communication
Feng and Wang (2019)	PAU scheme	Evaluating the privacy protection of vehicles by analyzing the user's historical behavior	Privacy
SathyaNarayanan (2019)	WAVE protocol and Blowfish algorithm	Improve the communication efficiency by avoiding the information tracing by other vehicles from the cloud storage	Secure communication

algorithm must be used. The security schemes in IoV must be scalable to handle the regular and special traffic such as the large volume of traffic caused by special events. The method presented in Yan et al. (2013) can improve the scalability of security schemes by using a virtual machine division algorithm. In this scheme, the virtual machine is divided into subvirtual machines when the number of vehicles increases.

Private information in IoV, such as vehicle identification, location, or sensitive data, must be kept secret. The authors in Jenefa and Anita (2018) presented a secure vehicular communication using identity-based signature. In this scheme, the real identifier of the vehicle is encrypted using the vehicle's private key to generate a pseudoidentity. This pseudoidentity is used to ensure vehicle's privacy. In Gazdar et al. (2012), the authors proposed a trust model based on the Markov chain, in which each vehicle can act as a monitor and update the trust metric of its neighbors according to their behavior.

In Nkenyereye, Park, and Rhee (2018), the authors ensured vehicle privacy using a pseudonym technique, in which each vehicle provides its real identifier to a trusted authority (TA). The TA generates the corresponding pseudoidentity, which is used later by the vehicles in the anonymous credential request. In Feng and Wang (2019), the authors proposed a privacy assessment method with uncertainty consideration (PAU) to address the privacy issue. In this scheme, the authors focused on evaluating the privacy protection of vehicles by analyzing the user's historical behavior. The PAU expands the subjective logic of uncertainty for measuring the records in the user's historical behavior. Thereby, using the vehicle's real-time communication observations, the real-time privacy capability of a vehicle is calculated. The privacy aggregation algorithm is used to improve the accuracy of privacy assessment by combining the vehicle's real-time and offline communication. The authors in Wan and Zhang (2018) encrypted the real identity of vehicles by using an algebraic signature and the Identity based System (IBS) algorithm to ensure the vehicle's privacy and to minimize the complication pseudonym management.

It is indispensable to provide secure communication between vehicles to ensure efficient and safe driving. In Liu et al. (2016), the authors presented secure message dissemination with policy enforcement in VANET. A sensor-enabled secure vehicular communication for emergency messages dissemination using cloud services (SSVC) scheme is proposed in SathyaNarayanan (2019). The SSVC improves communication efficiency and reduces the delay using the WAVE protocol. It uses the Blowfish algorithm (Schneier 2008) to avoid information tracing by other vehicles from the cloud storage. In Wan and Zhang (2018), the authors presented an efficient identity-based data transmission (EIBDT) for VANET. The EIBDT scheme ensures secure communication and data transmission by using the Lagrange interpolation method, instead of using a mapping scheme for integrity and confidentiality protection with low computation cost.

The vehicle's identification must be verified before access to the resources, in which all vehicles perform their work according to the privileges of the rules. Huang and Verma (2009) introduced the first Ciphertext-Policy Attribute-Based Encryption (CP-ABE) algorithm in VANET, where each vehicle has its own access rights and capabilities according to its attributes. The vehicles that have certain attributes, which satisfy the access policy, can access the broadcasted message and decrypt it. The authors in Liu et al. (2016) presented a CP-ABE scheme to provide differentiated access-control services, in which the vehicles authorize most of the decryption computation to the nearest RSU to minimize the computation cost. In Limbasiya and Das (2018), a secure message confirmation scheme based on batch verification for VCC is proposed. It is based on four phases: pseudonym, key generation, message signing, and verification phases. It ensures secure, authenticated, integrated, confidential, and available messages in VCC.

In IoV, the vehicles' position or location plays an important role to exchange data between vehicles. Most applications in vehicular systems such as emergency alerts, collision avoidance, and traffic reports rely on location information. The authors in Hussain and Oh (2014) preserved the privacy of vehicle location by leveraging the modified location-based encryption. The method presented in Hussain et al. (2015) preserves the users' authentication, confidentiality, and private information by using GPS-based location encryption.

One of the recent techniques used to solve the IoV security issues is the blockchain technology introduced by Nakamoto et al. (2008). In the next section, we introduce the concept of blockchain and present its key characteristics, architecture, and applications.

8.4 BLOCKCHAIN FOR IoV SECURITY

The emerging blockchain technology, for the cryptocurrencies, has revolutionized the cybersecurity domain with more securely distributed access and management. This is principally owed to the key advantages it offers, such as immutability and transparency. The blockchain allows for securing transactions/communications, without having to be dependent on a third party. Moreover, once the data are added to the chain, they cannot be altered or deleted. The blockchain can achieve trust, data accuracy, and reliability, which are significant issues in traditional security technologies.

In light of the requirement of security and reliability in vehicular communications, the integration of blockchain in IoV systems has drawn increasing attention in the last few years. This is founded on the P2P nature of both IoV and blockchain-based architectures. Blockchain-based solutions have been used to build trustworthiness and reliability in the vehicular environments with similar properties of P2P networks, such as the decentralization and untrustworthiness of vehicles (peers), the need for a safe storage system, public auditability, and transparency. In addition, blockchain-based IoV solutions may improve the fault tolerance of V2X communications by preventing a third party to control the system.

In this section, we discuss the key characteristics of the blockchain and provide a technical explanation of its architecture. Then, the most known consensus protocols are presented and some real-life use cases of the blockchain technology are cited. Finally, we highlight the feasibility of implementing blockchain in IoV systems security by presenting the available blockchain-based solutions in the literature and comparing them with the classical security solutions.

8.4.1 DEFINITION

Blockchain is a combination of technologies that have existed for a long time. It can be referred to as decentralized ledgers that store records of transactions across the P2P network.

Bitcoin is the first and the most popular implementation of blockchain, and it was the first asset to be recorded as a transaction on a blockchain ledger. The term blockchain has not been mentioned at all in Nakamoto's Bitcoin whitepaper, and thus, it has no standard definition. The name blockchain is inspired by its technical structure of a chain of blocks. Each block is linked to the previous block (parent block) with a cryptographic hash, to ensure that the data are tamper-proof and unforgeable (i.e., ensuring the immutability of records).

A block is a data structure that allows the storage of a list of transactions. Peers create these transactions and exchange them in the blockchain network, resulting in the modification of the state of the blockchain. As a distributed network, there is no trust between peers, and thus, a consensus protocol is established to agree on a single copy of the ledger.

8.4.2　Key Characteristics

The blockchain technology is a collection of different core technologies, such as cryptographic hash, digital signatures, and distributed consensus. It has several key characteristics, including decentralization, immutability, transparency, and auditability.

8.4.2.1　Decentralization

In a centralized system, each information or transaction is stored in a central entity. The transaction needs to be validated through the central trusted entity. The latter can be targeted by attackers and lead to a failure point.

In a decentralized system, each entity in the network owns the information, so it is replicated over the network. A transaction in the blockchain network is done directly between the peers, without depending on a central entity. In this manner, blockchain can enhance the performance of the network by replicating the information over the network peers, canceling the failure point problem, and eliminating the role of a third party.

8.4.2.2　Immutability

All centralized databases can be corrupted and require trust in a third party to ensure information integrity. In the blockchain, each transaction circulating within the network needs to be confirmed and recorded in the distributed blocks. Adding the transactions into the block using a consensus algorithm makes it impossible to tamper. It means that, once something has been added to the blockchain, it cannot be modified, even if it is a mistaken error. To correct the error, a new transaction must be added.

8.4.2.3　Transparency

In a blockchain system, all transactions are transparent and done using public addresses, while the real identity is secure.

8.4.2.4　Auditability

The blockchain is auditable because each transaction is viewable for public verifiability. Users can easily access the blockchain and verify all the transactions. However, the degree of auditability can differ according to the application and the type of the blockchain.

8.4.3　Blockchain Types

Blockchains are classified in terms of permission into two major classes, namely public and private blockchains.

8.4.3.1   Public Blockchain

Public blockchain or permissionless blockchain is open and decentralized. Any peer that joins the network can read, send, or receive transactions. Moreover, the peer can participate in the consensus process. There is no central authority to manage membership. Bitcoin is an example of a public blockchain.

8.4.3.2   Private Blockchain

Private blockchain or permissioned blockchain has restrictions on joining the network, reading or writing transactions, or participating to create blocks (mining). In this system, a central authority manages the membership and attributes the rights to the peers. This management ensures the trustworthiness of the participant peers. Hyperledger is the most known permissioned blockchain.

8.4.3.3   Consortium Blockchain

Another type is the consortium blockchain, which is a hybrid blockchain (i.e., the network includes public and private blockchains). This type is required when different companies operate a blockchain together; these companies are equally involved in the consensus protocol. Quorum is a solution to develop consortium blockchains.

8.4.4   ARCHITECTURE

8.4.4.1   Transaction

Transactions are the fundamental units of a blockchain (Antonopoulos 2014). Transactions are data structures that can represent various actions. In cryptocurrency, it represents the transfer of value between participants. The transaction lifecycle is introduced as follows (Bashir 2018; Bikramaditya, Gautam, and Priyansu Sekhar 2018):

- A transaction's lifecycle starts with the transaction's creation.
- The transaction is then broadcasted on the blockchain network.
- Each node validates and broadcasts the transaction, until it reaches almost every node in the network.
- The transaction is verified and included in a block of transactions.
- The block is broadcasted and recorded on the blockchain.

Once a transaction is confirmed and recorded in the blockchain, it cannot be edited or removed. The structure of a transaction is dependent on the application, but at the minimum, it requires a value, a hash, identity information, and timestamp information.

8.4.4.2   Block

A block is a container data structure that groups valid transactions for inclusion in the blockchain. The block is made of a header, containing metadata, followed by a body that contains a long list of transactions (Antonopoulos 2014). The block header of the Bitcoin contains the following information:

- *Block version*: The version of the block that describes the structure of the data and indicates which set of block validation rules to follow.

- *Parent block hash*: A hash value that references to the previous (parent) block in the chain.
- *Merkle tree root hash*: The hash value of the root of the Merkle tree of all transactions in the block.
- *Timestamp*: The current time when the block is created.
- *nBits*: A shortened version of the target.
- *Nonce*: A field used by miners in the consensus algorithm.

A block is identified by hashing the block header by using a hash algorithm. The resulting hash is called the block header hash. The block hash is not recorded in the block itself; it is computed by each node when the block is received. Another way to index a block is by its position in the chain; it is called block height. The first block (genesis block) is at block height 0. Each newly added block will have a higher height than the previous one. Therefore, we have two ways to identify the block, either with the block hash or with the block height.

8.4.4.3 Chain of Blocks

Nodes maintain a copy of the blockchain, starting with the genesis block. When a new block is generated, the chain is extended and updated constantly. When a node receives blocks, it validates these blocks and links them to the existing blockchain by using the previous block hash field.

Any attempt in changing the header or block content breaks the entire chain. Assume that an adversary changed the data in block i, as shown in Figure 8.4. The hash stored in the block header of block i + 1 would not match with the new hash. Let's say that the adversary also changed the hash stored in the block header of block i + 1, so that it matches the hash of the altered data. By doing that, the hash of the block i + 1 will change, and it will not match with the one stored in the header of block i + 2 and so on. The adversary has to keep doing this until the final or the most recent block. Because many peers in the network have a copy of the blockchain along with the most recent block hash, there is no way to change all the hashes. This makes it tamper-proof, and this is how immutability is guaranteed in the blockchain.

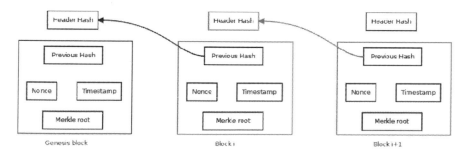

FIGURE 8.4 Non-valid blockchain.

8.4.4.4 Merkle Tree

Each block in the Bitcoin blockchain contains a summary of all the transactions in the block using the Merkle tree. The Merkle tree, also known as the binary tree, is named after Ralph Merkle, who proposed his idea in 1980 paper. It is a data structure used for efficiently storing and verifying the integrity of a large set of data (Antonopoulos 2014). It constructs recursively the data hashes; then, the hashes are hashed again and merged until the Merkle tree is merged into a single hash. The last hash is also called the root hash (the root of the tree). It contains the information of its leaves (individual transactions) and branches (hashes of the leaves) in a short string. It provides a very efficient way to verify the existence of a transaction in a block.

The verification procedure is provided through the Merkle path or the authentication path. Here, we illustrate the application of the power of Merkle tree through a simple example. As shown in Figure 8.5, to prove that the transaction Tx4 (noted in red) is included in the block, we need a Merkle path, which consist of only three hashes (noted in blue): H3, H12, and H5678. With these provided hashes, a node can prove the existence of Tx4 in the block and a part of the Merkle root, by computing the three hashes H34, H1234, and the root H12345678.

As a binary tree, the Merkle tree needs an even number of transactions. In case of an odd number, the last transaction is duplicated. The same process of construction can be generalized to construct trees of any size.

8.4.5 Consensus Algorithms

The consensus is a process of agreement between unreliable nodes on a final state of data. To achieve consensus, different algorithms can be used. It is simple to provide an agreement between two nodes (e.g., in client-server systems). However, when multiple nodes are participating in a distributed system and they need to agree on a single value, it becomes very difficult to achieve consensus.

Distributed consensus has been used in blockchain to reach consensus among the untrustworthy nodes, in order to agree on a single version of truth between peers. The most used blockchain consensus algorithms are detailed as in the following subsections.

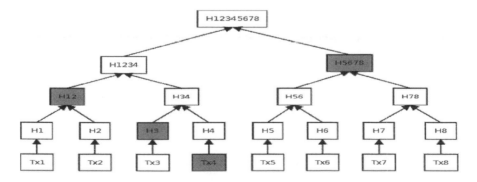

FIGURE 8.5   The Merkle tree.

8.4.5.1   Proof of Work

The proof-of-work (PoW) algorithm means that certain work is done for a block of transactions before it gets proposed to the whole network. An example of old usage of this algorithm to reduce spam emails is the proof that enough computational resources have been done before sending spam emails and therefore reducing the transmission of spam emails. In a blockchain network, if a node wants to publish a block of transactions, a work has to be done to prove that the node is not likely to attack the network (Bikramaditya, Gautam, and Priyansu Sekhar 2018).

In PoW, each node of the network is calculating a hash value of the block header. The block header contains a nonce, and miners change the nonce frequently to get different hash values. The consensus requires that the calculated value must be equal to or smaller than a given value. When one node reaches the target value, it would broadcast the block to other nodes that confirm the correctness of the hash value. If the block is validated, other miners would append this new block to their own blockchains.

Nodes that calculate the hash values are called miners, and the PoW process is called mining. It is used in Bitcoin and other cryptocurrencies. The main problem of this algorithm is the huge consumption of energy.

8.4.5.2   Proof of Stake

The proof-of-stake (PoS) algorithm works where nodes or users have enough stakes (economic stake) in the system. It is not about mining but about validating blocks of transactions. In PoS systems, the validators have to prove the ownership of the amount of currency to be able to participate in validating the transactions, because it is believed that people with more currencies would be less likely to attack the network (Zibin et al. 2018). The probability of a validator to produce a block is proportional to its stakes; the more the number of stakes, the greater is its chance to validate a new block of transactions.

Because the creator of a block in a PoS system is deterministic based on the economic stake, the PoS requires less energy, and it works much faster compared with PoW systems. However, it also suffers from the problem that the rich become richer (Bikramaditya, Gautam, and Priyansu Sekhar 2018).

8.4.5.3   Practical Byzantine Fault Tolerance

Practical Byzantine fault tolerance (PBFT) achieves state machine replication, which provides tolerance against Byzantine nodes. Many blockchain initiatives, such as Hyperledger, Stellar, and Ripple are using the PBFT consensus. The algorithm is derived from the Byzantine generals' problem. All nodes within the system communicate with each other, and the majority of honest nodes have to agree on the state of the system. The most important factor of this algorithm is the communication level, which is very high, because it needs to verify all the information found on the network (Zibin et al. 2018).

8.4.6   Blockchain Applications

8.4.6.1   Supply Chain Management

In supply chain, the links of materials and services required for manufacturing a given product are complex. It includes various intermediate cycles and many involved entities until the final step, which is the delivery of the product. This complexity is costly in terms of time and resources. Employing blockchain creates a global tamperproof system for digitizing trade workflow, tracking shipments, and eliminating the costly communications between parties.

In a recent test by Maersk, transporting a single container of flowers from Kenya to the port of Rotterdam required about 200 communications. The blockchain has been implemented to provide trust and security and improve the efficiency of global supply chains.

Food origin is another concern. It is hard to pinpoint the food's origin. The old paper system implies that a global view of the product's cycle is impossible. In addition, a customer wants to know how the product is produced. Blockchain provides an easy way to certify the stories of the products.

8.4.6.2   Finance

Currently, finance offers the strongest use cases for blockchain technology. The emergence of blockchain systems, such as Bitcoin and Hyperledger, has brought a huge impact on traditional financial and business services. Blockchain technology could be applied to many financial areas. The global payments sector is sensitive, costly, and open to money laundering. It takes days for money to cross the world. Countries can collaborate in designing their blockchains for interbank payments, and they can allow interaction between chains.

The insurance industry, which spends large sums of money each year on processing claims and loses millions of dollars to fraudulent claims, the blockchain can be the best-fit solution to this kind of problem.

Cryptocurrency or digital coins are the coins that are passed through an electronic network. The idea is to create a huge network of distributed nodes that are not given any special privileges. There is no centralized entity, nor is there any hierarchy. A currency system is a decentralized architecture, where everyone is treated as an equal and there is no governing body, which can determine the value of the currency (e.g., Bitcoin and Ethereum).

8.4.6.3   Protection of Intellectual Property

The Internet facilitated content reproduction for web users, whereas copyright holders were losing control of their intellectual property, which led to financial problems. The blockchain can protect copyrights by creating a decentralized database of copyrights. If the creator of some digital object wants to prove ownership at a later time, he/she can use a public blockchain as a time-stamping service by committing to the digital object, together with his identity, and publishing this commitment on the blockchain. This allows proving later that the object existed at that time and was associated with the respective identity (Karl and Arthur 2018).

8.4.6.4   E-Voting

e-Voting system is just like the old paper system, which is easy to be compromised and has many problems. As votes should be anonymous, privacy is the main requirement. In addition, vote should be publicly verifiable to avoid the manager of the e-voting system to compromise the votes. It was revealed that a major US voting machine manufacturer had installed remote-access software on some systems. This software allowed for the alteration of votes when counting the total.

In e-voting, many untrusted parties are involved. The blockchain technology can be used to solve this issue by providing a distributed ledger and ensure that the vote is counted as transparent as possible (Karl and Arthur 2018).

8.4.6.5 Healthcare

The healthcare field is a sensitive sector where privacy preserving of medical data is a major issue. The blockchain can provide a secure environment for storing and sharing data between providers, payers, and patients in the healthcare systems. The blockchain can be used for healthcare management, such as supervising drugs, regulation compliance, testing results, and pharma supplies.

8.4.6.6 Smart Cities

Smart cities are addressing urbanization problems by integrating new technologies. Many projects have been implemented using the blockchain in smart cities, such as the Smart Dubai 2021. This project aims to move all government operations and records on the blockchain by the year of 2021; the goal of this project is to provide better services to citizens. Many applications are attached to this project; one, for example, is the smart mobility objective, which includes automated traffic signals and autonomous cars as a transportation alternative.

With these kinds of applications, smart cities are tending to be better in terms of efficiency and transparency, which would improve the life of residents of these cities.

8.4.7 BLOCKCHAIN-BASED SOLUTIONS

The authors in Busygin et al. (2018) introduced a floating genesis block as an attempt to deal with the blockchain size growth. The main idea is to include not only the hash of the current block (state update) but also the hash of all the system state (blockchain). As the next chain state could be computed from the previous one by applying the state update, only a single state could be stored. Thus, all previous data except block headers could be deleted.

In order to avoid a secret chain attack, the authors in Bruce (2017) suggested newly arrived node to download the system state from a trusted source. However, this solution could only be applied with transactions of a limited lifetime. This may conflict with the traceability requirements, such as routing and authentication of transactions.

Sharma and Park (2018) introduced novel hybrid network architecture for smart cities. The proposed architecture takes the advantages of both software-defined service and blockchain technologies to deal with high latency, bandwidth, and scalability requirements. In addition, a memory-hardened PoW scheme is implemented to ensure security and privacy. The memory-hardened PoW consists of disk encryption and instantiation parameters for cryptocurrency applications (Coelho, Larroche, and Colin 2017). For an attacker, it is very laborious to elucidate knowledge of the proper chain elements with their correct path in the Merkle tree.

In Hossain, Hasan, and Zawoad (2017), the authors proposed a digital forensic framework that investigates criminal cases in IoV systems. The main purpose is to collect evidence and store them into an external service that maintains a secure provenance. Evidence is signed and stored in a secure blockchain, where each block contains a set of proof of past stories (PPS) as evidence. This ensures the integrity of the stored evidence and allows investigators to verify the integrity of the evidence and to prevent attackers from manipulating outcomes of an investigation. As PPS does not contain any information related to nodes' real identities and interactions, it is published on the Internet, and privacy cannot be violated.

The authors in van der Heijden et al. (2017) proposed a blockchain-based solution that provides the accountability of messages and revocations through a distributed ledger called event data record. It allows a collaborative and transparent decision through this ledger, without requiring trust in any centralized third party. Scalability is ensured using a hierarchical consensus by creating clusters formed by vehicles. The authors employed a permissioned blockchain that backups the transactions. The cars form clusters and propagate the agreed state to the RSUs, which in turn publish their results to misbehavior authorities. These transactions are published to a permissionless public blockchain for public verifiability and to provide global revocation of misbehaving vehicles. Vehicles participate in clustered communications (permissioned blockchain) to agree on a common state and decide to revoke the corresponding vehicle. The clusters reduce the state updates and eliminate the vehicles from mining into the public blockchain. Hence, the size and frequency of updates from vehicles are reduced. Moreover, the authors provided the algorithm's scalability by using a hierarchical consensus; the authentication is ensured by revoking misbehaving vehicles.

Singh and Shiho (2018) proposed a branch-based blockchain solution for securing intelligent vehicles' communications. The proposed method includes two blockchains and uses a secure unique cryptoidentity called intelligent vehicle trust point (IVTP) to enable trustworthiness among vehicles. The vehicle that has more IVTPs seems to be trustworthy. The local dynamic blockchain (LDB) stores data temporally according to its size. The main blockchain (MB) stores permanently unusual data forwarded by LDB. The MB uses the Merkle tree to keep track of the IVTP between vehicles, which use and verify the IVTP with the LDB to communicate with each other. The authors introduced the LDB branching to split the blockchain into multiple parallel chains, each chain covers a distinct geographical region.

In Sharma (2019), the authors proposed an energy-efficient model for blockchain-enabled IoV by controlling the number of transactions required to update ledgers through a distributed cluster. The excessive transactions and energy consumption for ledger updates are the main concern in this study. The proposed solution uses distributed clustering based on the stochastic volatility model. The solution of energy-efficient transition was attained by performing optimal offloading and selecting new Cluster Head (CHs), whenever the network's energy consumption goes beyond the set limits.

Authors in Li et al. (2018) proposed a privacy-preserving blockchain-based incentive announcement network for communications of smart vehicles by using CreditCoin. The algorithm is used to address the lack of motivation of users and to forward announcements without revealing users' identities. The proposed scheme is based on two phases: announcement and incentive mechanisms. The announcement protocol namely echo-announcement provides threshold authentication and a certain privacy level to guarantee that anonymous announcements are reliable in CreditCoin. The incentive mechanism works together with the echo-announcement in which every user in CreditCoin owns a credit account at several addresses. The account contains reputation points called the coins. Users reward traffic announcements from a certain area by paying some coins as incentives. The authors prevented the MiM attack by using consensus algorithm (i.e., if an attacker modifies any contents of the transaction, such as the values of coins or addresses, the transaction will be rejected by users through the verification of the consensus phase). The proposed method also resists DoS, message tampering, and Sybil attacks.

The authors in Kchaou, Abassi, and Guemara (2018) proposed a distributed trust management scheme for cluster-based VANET to verify the correctness of messages based on the vehicle's behavior and the credibility of the message. The proposed scheme is based on transmission of messages, in which the miner verifies if the message is correct or not based on the control of the vehicle's behavior and the reception of the credibility of the message by the CH. A block contains several validated messages. In this scheme, the DoS attack can be prevented using a reputation value (i.e., if the reputation value of a vehicle reaches the minimum value, then it is considered as dishonest vehicle and added to the blacklist).

In Zhang and Chen (2019), the authors proposed a data security sharing and storage system based on the consortium blockchain (DSSCB). They employed digital signature technique based on bilinear pairing for elliptic curves to ensure reliability and integrity. The emerging consortium blockchain technology is used to provide a decentralized, secure, and reliable database, which is maintained by the entire network. The DSSCB uses smart contract to limit the triggering conditions for preselected nodes when storing, transmitting, and allocating data coins to vehicles that participate in the contribution of data.

Arora and Kumar (2018) introduced an authenticated and secure data transfer algorithm using the blockchain technology to ensure true information communication between the IoV nodes. They used two chains of blocks, one for the authentication and the other one for the communications. Their method ensures security through two steps. In the authentication phase, every vehicle needs to register with the register authority. This phase aims to authenticate the vehicles and prevent any malicious node from joining the network. In the communication phase, the authenticated vehicles can exchange data with each other, using digital signature and group key to secure the communications. Security is granted by enabling only authenticated vehicles to participate in the network. These vehicles are provided with a shared symmetric group key to encrypt the transferred messages, thus protecting the confidentiality of data.

Zhaojun et al. (2018) proposed a blockchain-based reputation system to establish trust and preserve privacy in VANET. They used two major authorities: a local enforcement authority (LEA) that manages the whole system and stores the pair of identity and public key and a certificate authority that issues the certificate for vehicles and revokes the misbehaving ones. They employed three blockchains: a chain for recording the exchanged messages as persistence evidence and two others for the issued certificates and the revoked keys. The basic security requirements are granted with PKI, and public keys are used as pseudonyms in communications, without exposing any information about real identities. The authentication mechanism is based on certificates and PKI, which protect against outsiders' attackers and identify the connected vehicles. To establish trust among vehicles, a reputation system is presented to prevent the distribution of forged messages. It evaluates the score of the vehicle that broadcasts the message and decides to accept or ignore the message based on its score. The reputation algorithm consists of a reward mechanism, and the score of a vehicle is increased or decreased depending on the vehicle behavior.

Shrestha et al. (2019) proposed a blockchain-based scheme to secure critical event messages distribution in VANET. They used a public blockchain to store trustworthy vehicles and messages exchanged in a particular geographical location (i.e., local blockchain for each country). First, the vehicle sends an initiation message containing its public key to the RSU. The latter sends a session identity to the vehicle, which sends back the signed session identity. The RSU authenticates the vehicle and publishes the location certificate signed by its private key. Then, the legitimate RSU creates a genesis block (i.e., first block of the blockchain), and all vehicles download the blockchain. The new blocks are mined by vehicles that have high trust level and computing power. When receiving an event message, each vehicle independently checks the message and stores it in its message pool if it is trustworthy. Then, the event message is broadcasted within the network. The miner vehicle creates a new block for trustworthy event message using the PoW algorithm. Each vehicle updates the public blockchain by adding the new block. To reduce delay of block generation and propagation, the authors presented a new architecture using edge cloud computing.

To secure announcement messages in the IoV, the authors in Zhang et al. (2019) proposed a blockchain-based scheme. They used parent blockchain and auxiliary blockchain for each region (country). The vehicle generates an asymmetric key pair and sends its public key with its identity to the traffic management authority. The latter stores the public key in the parent blockchain. Moreover, the vehicle generates a pool of short-term asymmetric key pairs, blinds the short-term public keys by using fair blind signature scheme, and signs the blinded short-term public keys. These are sent to the issuer that verifies the signature and generates a session identity to trace the real identity of the vehicle. The public key and the session identity are stored in the auxiliary blockchain. Each vehicle signs the announcement message by using its short-term private keys based on multisignature scheme, and then, it broadcasts the signed message within the network. If the signed message is trustworthy, it will be stored in the auxiliary blockchain of the region and the vehicle will be rewarded using Vcoin. Otherwise, the vehicle will be traced to pay a penalty using Vcoin, and its public key will be blacklisted. The proposed scheme achieves message authenticity, vehicle privacy, and reliable message distribution.

In Kang et al. (2019), the authors used blockchain technology to provide secure data sharing in the IoV. They proposed an enhanced Delegated Proof of Stake (DPoS) scheme with secure miner selection and block verification to address collision attacks in the IoV. The miners are selected using reputation-based voting. They participate in block verification by using contract theory to prevent internal collisions. The proposed scheme improves the detection rate of malicious miners and decreases miners' collisions. Table 8.3 depicts the classification of these 14 blockchain-based solutions.

8.4.8 Classical Solutions vs. Blockchain-Based Solutions

In this subsection, we classify and address the cost and limitations of the classical and blockchain-based solutions that have been proposed to secure the IoV. This classification, according to types of attack, security requirements, and mechanisms used, is illustrated in Table 8.4.

TABLE 8.3

Classification of Blockchain-Based Solutions

References	Communication Types	Blockchain Content	Blockchain Type	Consensus Algorithm	Participant	Applications
Hossain, Hasan, and Zawoad (2017)	V2X	Story of occurred events	Public	–	LEA and investigator	Investigation
van der Heijden, et al. (2017)	V2X	Messages, revocations	Private	–	Cluster of vehicles and RSUs MAs	Cross-border vehicular networks
Busygin, et al. (2018)	V2V	Nodes' messages	Public	PoW	–	Routing
Sharma and Park (2018)	V2X	IoT services requests	Public	Memory-hardened PoW	Controller nodes, specific vehicles	Free application
Singh and Shiho (2018)	V2X	Local blockchain: messages, misbehavior; Main blockchain: IVTP, transactions	– –	– PoW	Vehicles Vehicles	Intersection deadlock
Arora and Sumit Kumar (2018)	V2X	Authentication information; Messages	Private –	– –	RA Sn	Free application
Zhaojun, et al. (2018)	V2V V2I	Certificate; Revoked keys; Messages	Private Private Private	PoW PoW PoW	CA, vehicles; CA, vehicles; Vehicles	Free application
Li, et al. (2018)	V2X	Vehicles' announcement, vehicles' coins	Public	PBFT	RSUs, official public vehicles	Motivating vehicles to forward announcement.

(Continued)

TABLE 8.3 (*Continued*)
Classification of Blockchain-Based Solutions

References	Communication Types	Blockchain Content	Blockchain Type	Consensus Algorithm	Participant	Applications
Kchaou, Abassi, and Guemara (2018)	V2V V2R	Validated messages	Public	PoW	RSUs	Calculating vehicles' reputation
Sharma (2019)	V2X C2C	Local Global	–	PoW	Vehicles	Free application
Zhang and Chen (2019)	V2V V2R R2R	Messages	Public	PoW PBFT	– RSUs	Safety warning
Shrestha, et al. (2019)	V2V V2I V2X	Public	Node trustworthiness, message trustworthiness	PoW	Full vehicles (with high trust and computing power)	Critical events (e.g., traffic jam, accident)
Zhang, et al. (2019)	V2V V2I	–	Parent BC: identities, public keys; Auxiliary BC: session identities, public keys, signed message (local)	PBFT	RSUs	Announcement messages (e.g., icy road, flooding)
Kang, et al. (2019)	V2V V2I	Public	Data-sharing records, reputation opinions	DPoS	Reputation-based voting (RSUs)	Intelligent transportation system

TABLE 8.4

Classical vs. Blockchain-Based Security Solutions

References	Blockchain-Based	Attack Model	Security Requirement	Mechanism Used	Cost	Limitations
Liu, et al. (2016)	No	MiM attack Eavesdropping	Confidentiality Integrity	Access policy	High computation, low storage	Lack of privacy and vehicles authentication
Hossain, Hasan, and Zawoad (2017)	Yes	Malware infection DoS attack Message tampering	Authentication	Evidence collection and verification	Low communication, high latency	Lack of privacy
van der Heijden, et al. (2017)	Yes	Bad mouthing attack Sybil attack	Availability Authentication	Misbehavior detection algorithms Use at most two pseudonyms	Optimized with clusters and local blockchain	Stability of clusters to provide consensus
Busygin, et al. (2018)	Yes	–	Integrity	Deleting outdating information by hashing the whole chain to deal with the growth of data size	Medium bandwidth, optimized latency	DoS and Sybil attack possibility
Sharma and Park (2018)	Yes	Message tampering	Integrity	Digital signature to ensure data integrity	Optimized bandwidth usage, optimized latency	Lack of privacy
Li, et al. (2018)	Yes	MiM attack DoS attack Message tampering Sybil attack	Confidentiality Authenticity Integrity Non-repudiation Availability	Consensus algorithm, Credit network, Hash chain, Unlocking script	High latency	High computation time and storage capacity
Kchaou, Abassi, and Guemara (2018)	Yes	DoS attack	Availability	Reputation value	High latency	High computation time and storage capacity

(Continued)

TABLE 8.4 (Continued)
Classical vs. Blockchain-Based Security Solutions

References	Blockchain-Based	Attack Model	Security Requirement	Mechanism Used	Cost	Limitations
Singh and Shiho (2018)	Yes	Blackhole, Bogus attack, Illusion attack, Tracking attack, Sybil attack, Impersonation	Trust, Privacy, Authentication, Availability	IVTPs, Branching algorithm	Low latency	Trustworthiness of vehicles just by mining blocks and earning IVTP; Test in one use case intersection deadlock
Jenefa and Anita (2018)	No	Sybil Attack	Authentication, Availability	Offline signature	Low latency	Communication not secured
Wan and Zhang (2018)	No	MiM attack, Eavesdropping, Tracking attack	Confidentiality, Integrity, Privacy	Lagrange interpolation method, Algebraic and IBS signatures	Low computation, medium storage	Insecure privet key distribution
Limbasiya and Das (2018)	No	MiM attack, Sybil attack	Confidentiality, Availability, Authentication	Practicing varied private keys for different vehicle users, Including the time stamp in the computation of different credentials	Low latency, low storage, medium computation, reduce energy computation power	Lack of privacy
Arora and Sumit Kumar (2018)	Yes	Tracking attack, Sybil attack	Privacy, Authentication	Pseudoidentity (PIDi), Identification public ledger (B)	Fast encryption and decryption with symmetric group key	Confidentiality of PIDi, Distribution of the group key, Multiple group key problem
Zhaojun, et al. (2018)	Yes	Tracking attack, Sybil attack, Blackhole Bogus attack, Illusion attack	Privacy, Authentication, Trust	Public keys as identity, Certificates, Reputation management algorithm	High latency of certificate	Certificate update, Reputation score update

(Continued)

TABLE 8.4 (*Continued*)
Classical vs. Blockchain-Based Security Solutions

References	Blockchain-Based	Attack Model	Security Requirement	Mechanism Used	Cost	Limitations
Sharma (2019)	Yes	Flooding attack	Availability	Distributed clustering (performing optimal offloading and selecting new CHs whenever the energy demand of the network increases)	Reduced number of updated through distributed clusters and local blockchain	Principals of blockchain security are not considered
Feng and Wang (2019)	No	Sybil attack	Authentication Availability	Historical data accumulated in the cloud	High latency, high storage	Required to improve efficiency and reduce complexity
SathyaNarayanan (2019)	No	MiM attack Eavesdropping Sybil attack	Confidentiality Integrity Authentication	Blowfish method Access navigation servers	Low latency	Lack of privacy
Zhang and Chen (2019)	Yes	–	Non-repudiation Integrity	Digital signature	Low overhead, low storage	High computation, High latency
Shrestha, et al. (2019)	Yes	Impersonation Replay, Spamming, DoS, Double-spending attacks	Authentication Trust	Public-key cryptography Location certificate	High computation, medium communication, Low storage	High delay
Zhang, et al. (2019)	Yes	Modification attack Rogue key attack	Authentication Non-repudiation Authenticity Privacy-preserving Authorization Identity management	Fair blind signature Threshold secret sharing Multi-signature and threshold	High storage	Low throughput
Kang, et al. (2019)	Yes	Collusion attack Compromised block manager	Authentication Privacy	Elliptic curve Digital signature Asymmetric cryptography	Medium computation	Uncertainty of reputation opinion

8.5 OPEN ISSUES

The implementation of blockchain in various IoV applications faces several challenges and issues. In this section, we discuss the open issues related to blockchain-based IoV security.

8.5.1 SCALABILITY

The implementation of blockchain-based IoV solutions relies on the fact that the communication overhead generated to maintain the chain can increase with the growth in the size of the network. Hence, the security schemes for IoV must be scalable, owing to the dynamic environment of vehicles. Because the IoV is inherently scalable, the blockchain grows with the growth of the network. Each vehicle needs large resources to store the blockchain data. The unlimited growth of blockchain data may lead to node's local data store starvation. One solution consists of deleting the outdating data by including the hash value of the whole chain in the block header (Busygin et al. 2018). Another one is to develop blockchain compression techniques (Fernandez-Carames and Fraga-Lamas 2018). The authors in Dorri et al. (2017) proposed to use a periodic backup of the in-vehicle data to external backup storage. The data storage issue can be also mitigated by using clustering mechanisms such as in Sharma (2019) and van der Heijden et al. (2017).

8.5.2 DELAY AND LATENCY

Ensuring the security of real-time blockchain (BC)-based IoV applications is still challenging. The messages shared between vehicles, such as alert messages in case of accidents or abnormal deceleration, are processed and added sequentially to the distributed chain. The high computations of consensus algorithm for block generation and propagation increase delay and latency rates, because the execution of the blockchain consensus algorithm (mining) is a power-hungry process. Therefore, the choice of the consensus mechanism, as well as the participant nodes, can significantly affect the computation time of the proposed blockchain-based solution. The authors in Dziembowski et al. (2015) presented an alternative to the PoW algorithm. In Luu et al. (2016), the authors proposed the use of sharding blockchain to process transactions in parallel to reducing the delay and latency rates. Whereas the authors in Li et al. (2018), Zhang and Chen (2019), and Kang et al. (2019) used the RSUs as miners or LEA as competent entities to minimize the computation cost of the consensus process. To provide energy efficiency, the authors in Durnev et al. (2018) proposed the use of power consumed in the mining process in something useful.

8.5.3 PRIVACY

In a blockchain-based IoV system, an adversary can eavesdrop on the data circulated within the network. Moreover, user information can be stored in the blockchain in plaintext. Owing to the transparent nature of the BC, the anonymity is not guaranteed. Hence, privacy preserving is still challenging in BC systems (Feng et al. 2018). Several privacy-preserving schemes for blockchain have been introduced (Axon,

Goldsmith, and Creese 2018). Private blockchains or acting pseudonymously techniques are mostly used to palliate this limitation. However, it is still possible to link
addresses to users' real identity, as many users make transactions with the same
address frequently. Authors in Li et al. (2018) proposed a vehicular announcement
protocol, which achieves efficiency, privacy preserving, and anonymity. Mixing service is a kind of service that provides anonymity. It transfers funds from multiple
input addresses to multiple output addresses (Moser 2013).

8.6   THE PROPOSED ARCHITECTURE AND FUTURE WORK

The ultimate goal of ITS is to enhance driving safety by sharing critical messages,
such as alert messages in case of abnormal deceleration. These massages require a
real-time transmission; the transmission of safety message after the required time
makes it inutile and can result in huge damages.

To reduce delay and latency rates and provide scalability in critical blockchain-based
IoV applications, we propose using fog computing at the edge of the network. This paradigm extends the resources of cloud computing to the network's edge and consists of fog
nodes (e.g., smart gateways) that are connected to the edge devices of the IoV.

The proposed architecture allows the vehicle to distribute alert messages in real
time with low delay and latency. In our system, we have a global blockchain and
many local blockchains related to the fog nodes' number. The global blockchain
resides in a data center or cloud server and contains all transactions. The local ones
are deployed on each fog node and contain last transactions. Our architecture consists of four main layers as shown in Figure 8.6.

8.6.1   ONBOARD LAYER

It includes vehicles equipped with a computer, storage unit, and an onboard unit that
has broadband wireless communication to send data using Wi-Fi, WiMax, 3G, or
4G. The vehicles broadcast critical messages through V2V or V2I communications.

8.6.2   INFRASTRUCTURE LAYER

It includes RSUs that receive the vehicles' messages and record the trustworthy ones
in a pool. When the pool size is equal to the block size, it sends the pool to the nearest fog node.

8.6.3   FOG LAYER

It ensures the connection between the infrastructure and the cloud layer. Fog nodes
reside as close as possible to the RSUs and provide efficient data processing and
storage. When the fog node receives the messages from the RSU, it broadcasts them
to all fog nodes to obtain a consistency agreement, using the consensus algorithm.
After verification of the data block, the block generation solution is broadcasted, and
the block is recorded in the auxiliary blockchains. These latter are public and can be
accessed by vehicles to verify the validity of messages.

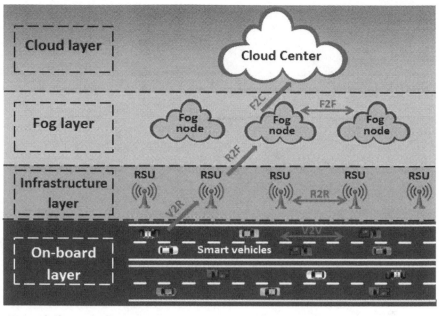

V2V = Vehicle to vehicle communication   V2R = Vehicle to RSU communication
R2R = RSU to RSU communication   R2F = RSU to Fog communication
F2F = Fog to Fog communication   F2C = Fog to Cloud communication

FIGURE 8.6   Proposed architecture.

8.6.4   CLOUD LAYER

It is used to store the blocks that can be used only for messages traceability. The emergency messages require a predefined time; after expiration, the old messages are stored in the MB deployed in the cloud. The fresh or recent messages are stored in the auxiliary blockchains deployed on fog nodes.

The integration of the fog computing paradigm reduces the delay of the block generation because the data are analyzed locally. However, the choice of consensus algorithm has not been studied. Designing specific consensus protocols for critical blockchain-based IoV applications would be beneficial. We proposed to delete old block from the chain even if it contradicts the characteristic of immutability of blockchain, to provide IoV scalability. Therefore, editable blockchains are highly required. Moreover, in a fog-based network, trust management between fog nodes is an issue that needs to be addressed.

8.7   CONCLUSION

In this chapter, we provided an overview of the vehicular communications and detailed the IoV architecture, applications, and challenges. We discussed the IoV security and privacy and the potential attacks and classified the classical security solutions according to the IoV challenges. Moreover, we presented the basic concepts of the blockchain, its architecture, and its applications. We surveyed the state of the art of the existing blockchain-based schemes designed for the IoV security and classified according to the blockchain concepts and applications. A classification of classical and blockchain-based solutions is provided based on attacks model, security requirements, costs, and limitations. Finally, we discussed open issues related to the integration of the blockchain to secure the IoV and presented a new architecture to overcome the scalability, delay, and latency issues.

REFERENCES

Aadil, Farhan, Waleed Ahsan, Zahoor Ur Rehman, Peer Azmat Shah, Seungmin Rho, and Irfan Mehmood. "Clustering algorithm for internet of vehicles (IoV) based on dragonfly optimizer (CAVDO)." *Journal of Supercomputing*, 74 (2018): 4542–4567.

Antonopoulos, Andreas M. *Mastering Bitcoin: Unlocking Digital Cryptocurrencies.* O'Reilly Media, Inc, USA, 2014.

Arora, Arushi and Yadav, Sumit Kumar, "Block chain based security mechanism for Internet of Vehicles (IoV). *Proceedings of 3rd International Conference on Internet of Things and Connected Technologies (ICIoTCT)*, Jaipur, India, 2018.

Axon, Louise, Michael Goldsmith, and Sadie Creese. "Privacy requirements in cybersecurity applications of blockchain." In *Advances in Computers*, Vol. 111, pp. 229–278. Elsevier, 2018.

Bali, Rasmeet S., and Neeraj Kumar. "Secure clustering for efficient data dissemination in vehicular cyber-physical systems." *Future Generation Computer Systems*, 56 (2016): 476–492.

Bashir, Imran. *Mastering Blockchain: Distributed Ledger Technology, Decentralization, and Smart Contracts Explained.* Packt Publishing Ltd, Birmingham, UK, 2018.

Bikramaditya, Singhal, Dhameja Gautam, and Panda Priyansu Sekhar. *Beginning Blockchain: A Beginner's Guide to Building Blockchain Solutions.* Apress, Berkeley, CA, USA, 2018.

Bruce, J.D. "The mini-blockchain scheme." *Whitepaper*, http://cryptochainuni.com/wp-content/uploads/The-Mini-Blockchain-Scheme.pdf, Crypto Chain University, New York. 2017.

Busygin, Alexey, Artem Konoplev, Maxim Kalinin, and Dmitry Zegzhda. "Floating genesis block enhancement for blockchain based routing between connected vehicles and software-defined VANET security services." *Proceedings of the 11th International Conference on Security of Information and Networks.* ACM, 2018. 1–2.

Coelho, Fabien, Arnaud Larroche, and Baptiste Colin. *Itsuku: A Memory-Hardened Proof-of-Work Scheme.* Doctoral dissertation, MINES ParisTech-PSL Research University, 2017.

Contreras-Castillo, Juan, Sherali Zeadally, and Juan Antonio Guerrero Ibáñez. "A seven-layered model architecture for internet of vehicles." *Journal of Information and Telecommunication*, 1 (2017): 4–22.

Dorri, Ali, Marco Steger, Salil S. Kanhere, and Raja Jurdak. "Blockchain: A distributed solution to automotive security and privacy." *IEEE Communications Magazine* (IEEE) 55, no. 12 (2017): 119–125.

Durnev, Valery G., D. M. Murin, Valery A. Sokolov, and D. J. Chalyy, "On some approaches to the solution of the 'Useful Proof-of-Work for Blockchains' task." *Automatic Control and Computer Sciences*, 52, no. 7 (2018): 880–884.

Dziembowski, Stefan, Sebastian Faust, Vladimir Kolmogorov, and Krzysztof Pietrzak. "Proofs of space." *Annual Cryptology Conference.* Springer, 2015. 585–605.

ElGamal, Taher. "A public key cryptosystem and a signature scheme based on discrete logarithms." *IEEE Transactions on Information Theory* (IEEE), 31, no. 4 (1985): 469–472.

Feng, Qi, Debiao He, Sherali Zeadally, Muhammad Khurram Khan, and Neeraj Kumar. "A survey on privacy protection in blockchain system." *Journal of Network and Computer Applications* (Elsevier), 126 (2018): 45–58.

Feng, Xia, and Liangmin Wang. "P: Privacy assessment method with uncertainty consideration for cloud based vehicular networks." *Future Generation Computer Systems*, 96 (2019): 368–375.

Fernandez-Carames, Tiago M., and Paula Fraga-Lamas. "A review on the use of blockchain for the internet of things." *IEEE Access* (IEEE), 8 (2018): 32979–33001.

Gazdar, Tahani, Abderrezak Rachedi, Abderrahim Benslimane, and Abdelfettah Belghith. "A distributed advanced analytical trust model for vanets." *Global Communications Conference (GLOBECOM) IEEE*, 2012. 201–206.

Harbi, Yasmine, Zibouda Aliouat, Saad Harous, Abdelhak Bentaleb, and Allaoua Refoufi. "A review of security in internet of things." *Wireless Personal Communications* (Springer), 108 (2019): 1–20.

Hartenstein, Hannes, and Kenneth Laberteaux. *VANET: Vehicular Applications and Inter-Networking*. Wiley Online Library, New Jersey, USA, 2010.

Hasrouny, Hamssa, Abed Ellatif Samhat, Carole a Bassil, and Anis Laouiti. "VANET security challenges and solutions: A survey." *Vehicular Communications* (Elsevier) 7 (2017): 7–20.

Hossain, Md Mahmud, Ragib Hasan, and Shams Zawad. "Trust-IoV: A trustworthy forensic investigation framework for the internet of vehicles (IoV)." *Proceedings—2017 IEEE 2nd International Congress on Internet of Things, ICIOT 2017*. 2017. 25–32.

Huang, Dijiang, and Mayank Verma. "ASPE: Attribute-based secure policy enforcement in vehicular ad hoc networks." *Ad Hoc Networks* (Elsevier), 7, no. 8 (2009): 1526–1535.

Hussain, Rasheed, and Heekuck Oh. "Cooperation-aware vanet clouds: Providing secure cloud services to vehicular ad hoc networks." *Journal of Indian Prosthodontic Society*, 10, no. 1 (2014): 103–118.

Hussain, Rasheed, Zeinab Rezaeifar, Yong-Hwan Lee, and Heekuck Oh. "Secure and privacy-aware traffic information as a service in vanet-based clouds." *Pervasive and Mobile Computing*, 24 (2015): 194–209.

Iansiti, Marco, and Karim R. Lakhani. "The truth about blockchain-Harvard business review." *Harvard Business Review*, 2 (2017): 118–127.

Jenefa, J. and E.A. Mary Anita. "Secure vehicular communication using id based signature scheme." *Wireless Personal Communications*, 98, no. 1 (2018): 1383–1411.

Jiacheng, Chen, Zhou Haibo, Zhang Ning, Yang Peng, Gui Lin, and Shen Xuemin. "Software defined Internet of vehicles: Architecture, challenges and solutions." *Journal of Communications and Information Networks*, 1 (2016): 14–26.

Kaiwartya, Omprakash, et al. "Internet of vehicles: Motivation, layered architecture, network model, challenges, and future aspects." *IEEE Access*, 4 (2016): 5356–5373.

Kang, Jiawen, Zehui Xiong, Dusit and Ye, Dongdong Niyato, Dong In Kim, and Jun Zhao. "Towards Secure Blockchain-enabled Internet of Vehicles: Optimizing Consensus Management Using Reputation and Contract Theory." *IEEE Transactions on Vehicular Technology* (IEEE), 68, no. 3 (2019): 2906–2920.

Karl, Wust, and Gervais Arthur. "Do you need a blockchain?" *2018 Crypto Valley Conference on Blockchain Technology (CVCBT)*. IEEE, 2018. 45–54.

Kchaou, Amira, Ryma Abassi, and Sihem Guemara. "Toward a distributed trust management scheme for vanet." *Proceedings of the 13th International Conference on Availability, Reliability and Security*. Hamburg, Germany: ACM, 2018. 1–6.

La Vinh, Hoa, and Ana Rosa Cavalli. "Security attacks and solutions in vehicular ad hoc networks: A survey." *International Journal on AdHoc Networking Systems (IJANS)*, 4, no. 2 (2014): 1–20.

Li, Lun, et al. "CreditCoin: A privacy-preserving blockchain-based incentive announcement network for communications of smart vehicles." *IEEE Transactions on Intelligent Transportation Systems*, 19, no. 7 (2018): 2204–2220.

Limbasiya, Trupil, and Debasis Das. "Secure message confirmation scheme based on batch verification in vehicular cloud computing." *Physical Communication*, 2018.

Liu, Xuejiao, Yingjie Xia, Wenzhi Chen, Yang Xiang, Mohammad Mehedi Hassan, and Abdulhameed Alelaiwi. "SEMD: Secure and efficient message dissemination with policy enforcement invanet." *Journal of Computer and System Sciences*, 82, no. 8 (2016): 1316–1328.

Luu, Loi, Viswesh Narayanan, Chaodong Zheng, Kunal Baweja, Seth Gilbert, and Prateek Saxena. "A secure sharding protocol for open blockchains." *Proceedings of the 2016 ACM SIGSAC Conference on Computer and Communications Security*. ACM, 2016. 17–30.

Mejri, Mohamed Nidhal, Jalel Ben-Othman, and Mohamed Hamdi. "Survey on VANET security challenges and possible cryptographic solutions." *Vehicular Communications* (Elsevier), 1, no. 2 (2014): 53–66.

Moser, Malte. "Anonymity of bitcoin transactions: An analysis of mixing services." *Proceedings of Münster Bitcoin Conference*. Münster, Germany, 2013. 17–18.

Nakamoto, Satoshi, et al. *Bitcoin: A Peer-to-Peer Electronic Cash System*. Working Paper, 2008.

Nkenyereye, Lewis, Youngho Park, and Kyung-Hyune Rhee. "Secure vehicle traffic data dissemination and analysis protocol in vehicular cloud computing." *The Journal of Supercomputing*, 74, no. 3 (2018): 1024–1044.

Sathya Narayanan, P. S. V. "A sensor enabled secure vehicular communication for emergency message e dissemination using cloud services." *Digital Signal Processing*, 85 (2019): 10–16.

Schneier, Bruce. "The blowfish encryption algorithm retrieved." 2008. http://www.schneier.com/blowfish.html.

Senouci, Oussama, Saad Harous, and Zibouda Aliouat. "A new heuristic clustering algorithm based on RSU for internet of vehicles." *Arabian Journal for Science and Engineering*, 44 (2019): 1–19.

Senouci, Oussama, Zibouda Aliouat, and Saad Harous. "MCA-V2I: A multi-hop clustering approach over vehicle-to-internet communication for improving VANETs performances." *Future Generation Computer Systems*, 96 (2019): 309–323.

Sharma, Pradip Kumar, and Jong Hyuk Park. "Blockchain based hybrid network architecture for the smart city." *Future Generation Computer Systems*, 86 (2018): 650–655.

Sharma, Vishal. "An energy-efficient transaction model for the blockchain-enabled internet of vehicles (IoV)." *IEEE Communications Letters*, 23, no. 2 (2019): 246–249.

Shrestha, Rakesh, Rojeena Bajracharya, Anish P. Shrestha, and Seung Yeob Nam. "A new-type of blockchain for secure message exchange in VANET." *Digital Communications and Networks* (ELSEVIER), 2019, in press.

Singh, Madhusudan, and Kim Shiho. "Branch based blockchain technology in intelligent vehicle." *Computer Networks*, 145 (2018): 231–219.

van der Heijden, Rens W., Engelmann Felix, Mödinger David, Schönig Franziska, and Karg Frank. "Blackchain: Scalability for resource-constrained accountable vehicle-to-x communication." Edited by ACM. *The 1st Workshop on Scalable and Resilient Infrastructures for Distributed Ledgers*. Las Vegas, NV: ACM, 2017. 4.

Varaiya, Pravin. "Smart cars on smart roads: Problems of control." *IEEE Transactions on Automatic Control*, 38, no. 2 (1993): 195–207.

Vegni, Anna Maria, Biagi Mauro, and Cusani Roberto. "Smart vehicles, technologies and main applications in vehicular ad hoc networks." In *Vehicular Technologies-Deployment and Applications*, 3–20. InTech, Rijeka, Croatia, 2013.

Wan, Changsheng, and Juan Zhang. "Efficient identity-based data transmission for vanet." *Journal of Ambient Intelligence and Humanized Computing*, 9, no. 6 (2018): 1861–1871.

Wan, Jiafu, Daqiang Zhang, Shengjie Zhao, Laurence T. Yang, and Jaime Lloret. "Context-aware vehicular cyber-physical systems with cloud support: Architecture, challenges, and solutions." *IEEE Communications Magazine*, 52, no. 8 (2014): 106–113.

Wang, Xiaojie, et al. "Optimizing content dissemination for real-time traffic management in large-scale internet of vehicle systems." *IEEE Transactions on Vehicular Technology*, 68, no. 2 (2019): 1093–1105.

Whaiduzzaman, Md, Mehdi Sookhak, Abdullah Gani, and Rajkumar Buyya. "A survey on vehicular cloud computing." *Journal of Network and Computer Applications*, 40 (2014): 325–344.

Wu, W., Z. Yang, and K. Li. "Internet of vehicles and applications." In *Internet of Things*, vol. 1, pp. 299–317. Elsevier, 2016. Ch. 16.

Yan, Gongjun, Ding Wen, Stephan Olariu, and Michele C. Weigle. "Security challenges in vehicular cloud computing." *IEEE Transactions on Intelligent Transportation Systems* (IEEE), 14, no. 1 (2013): 284–294.

Yousefi, Saleh, Mahmoud Siadat Mousavi, and Mahmood Fathy. "Vehicular ad hoc networks (VANETs): Challenges and perspectives." *2006 6th International Conference on ITS Telecommunications*. IEEE, 2006. 761–766.

Zhang, Lei, Mingxing Luo, Jiangtao Li, Man Ho Au, Kim-Kwang Raymond Choo, and Tong and Tian, Shengwei Chen. "Blockchain based secure data sharing system for internet of vehicles: A position paper." *Vehicular Communications* (Elsevier), 16 (2019): 85–93.

Zhang, Xiaohong, and Xiaofeng Chen. "Data security sharing and storage based on a consortium blockchain in a vehicular ad hoc network." *IEEE Access*, 7 (2019): 58241–58254.

Zhaojun, Lu, Liu Wenchao, Wang Qian, Qu Gang, and Liu Zhenglin. "A privacy-preserving trust model based on blockchain for vanets." *IEEE Access*, 6 (2018): 45655–45664.

Zhou, Zhenyu, Caixia Gao, Chen Xu, Yan Zhang, Shahid Mumtaz, and Jonathan Rodriguez. "Social big-data-based content dissemination in internet of vehicles." *IEEE Transactions on Industrial Informatics*, 14, no. 2 (2018): 768–777.

Zibin, Zheng, Xie Shaoan, Ning Dai Hong, Chen Xiangping, and Wang Huaimin. "Blockchain challenges and opportunities: A survey." *International Journal of Web and Grid Services*, 14, no. 4 (2018): 352–375.

Section III

Blockchain for Cybersecurity and Privacy in Healthcare

9 When Healthcare Services Meet Blockchain Technology

Gokay Saldamli, Pavan H. Ramesh,
Karthika M. S. Nair, Roopashree Munegowda,
Jeevan Venkataramana, and Lo'ai A. Tawalbeh

CONTENTS

9.1 INTRODUCTION

Healthcare is an indispensable part of human life. Technological advancements have improved the standard of living, resulting in providing better healthcare services. Healthcare has established itself as an emerging industry utilizing highly sophisticated medical devices and technology to treat and cure ailments. The emergence of the Internet of Things (IoT) has revolutionized the healthcare industry, enabling patients to monitor their own health. However, despite all these developments, there has been limited advancement in the field of patient data storage and sharing.

Patient health data can be categorized into two types: electronic medical record (EMR) and personal health data (PHD). The EMR is the digital form of the patient's health history and treatment plans. These records are owned and maintained by healthcare providers. The current storage mechanism of EMR is mainly either cloud database or through a centralized database system. These storage mechanisms are mostly controlled by the healthcare providers; the patients only have access to view the data and perform basic scheduling of consultation with the healthcare personnel.

The PHD is the record generated by gadgets and healthcare applications such as Fitbit, Apple Watch, Google Fit, etc. This data is owned and maintained by the patients. The enormous amount of data generated from personal health devices has raised concerns about the secure storage capacity of centralized as well as cloud storage systems.

The current system of exchanging patient health data between various entities inside the healthcare domain is called the health information exchange (HIE) [1]. It can be a healthcare provider sharing the data with another provider or a physician sharing the prescriptions to a pharmacy, so that patients can receive medicines. The HIE aims at increasing the interoperability among different healthcare entities. Currently, the HIE covers only the exchange of EMR.

Based on the survey of all acute care hospitals that are members of the American Hospital Association, only 1.5% of US hospitals have comprehensive electronic records [1]. Surveys and statistical analyses were carried on 3049 acute care general hospitals in the USA to determine the extent of adoption of EHR. The report also showcases the differences in the data stored in EHR. Laboratory results were considered as EMR in majority of hospitals, but physician notes were not frequently implemented. Moreover, there is also a serious lack of government funding or financial assistance, which can be one of the reasons for the non-adoption of EMR.

The PHD is not included, and moreover, it is not considered for treatment by the physicians. Since PHD is generated by the patients, there is always a possibility of tampering the data. There is no infrastructure developed to assure the physicians regarding the legitimacy of PHD.

In this work, we aim to find a realistic and viable solution for the secure storage and sharing of PHD.

9.2   RELATED WORK

Many theoretical studies are going on in the field of health industry to increase the interoperability between various healthcare providers. To increase interoperability, digitization of records is necessary. Esposito et al. [2] proposed a realistic solution for converting the patient health data in paper format into electronic form by uploading them to the cloud. But cloud poses different problems related to the accessibility and security of data. These problems can be addressed by introducing the concept of blockchain [2]. Gao et al. proposed a system [3] where patient is given full control over the access and transfer of EMR. An attribute-based digital signature is used to ensure the security of EMR. Another study was carried by Liang et al. [4] that aimed to integrate blockchain to medical data sharing to mobile healthcare applications.

The technical report [5] issued by the Institute for Business Value at IBM states that 70% of the industry leaders predict that the application of blockchain in the healthcare domain can provide a secure, decentralized framework for the controlled sharing of patient records and data exchange between different entities in the healthcare domain. Blockchain is developed from the concept of Bitcoin [6], which was introduced as a digital currency. The purpose of Bitcoin is to avoid third-party involvement in financial transactions. It provides transparency, security, and immutability, which ensure the safe storage of sensitive data. However, the core technology and the benefits it provides have far-reaching applications, even in the healthcare industry [3]. The concepts of peer-to-peer networks, use of public and private keys for data security, and hashing for record authentication can be applied in the healthcare domain too.

There should be specific mechanisms or algorithms implemented in blockchain to determine which block can be added and which block shouldn't be. Proof of work (PoW) and the Byzantine fault tolerance (BFT) are the two important consensus algorithms used in blockchain networks to add a new node to the networks. The PoW is implemented in the Bitcoin network. It requires heavy computing powers to derive a specific hash value for the block. The miner who gets that hash value can add a block to the blockchain. In PoW, any node can join the network and involve in mining. Hence, scalability of nodes is excellent. In BFT, each node should know the identities of other nodes in the network. The consensus is arrived upon the majority decision. Block that gathers the maximum vote or consensus of other nodes will be added to the blockchain. However, the scalability of nodes is bad in BFT-based networks because of the intense network communication that needs to be maintained for adding a node. Vukolić et al. [7] explains the difference between BFT and PoW. Depending on the network design and the requirements, one algorithm can be a better choice than the other one. In this work, BFT is better than PoW, because in a private blockchain, only trusted members can join the network, and the network is designed in such a way that all nodes know its peers. In BFT, node scalability can be a difficult problem to tackle as the network size increases. The BFT has never been tested on a network with more than 20 nodes [7], so the scalability result for a larger network is unknown. Research works are going on to resolve these scalability issues. Marandi et al. [8] suggest a parallel state machine replication design to improve the scalability in parallel and distributed networks. If such a design is implemented, a breakthrough in state machine parallelism can be expected in distributed architecture.

Mettler in 'Blockchain technology in healthcare: The revolution starts here' [9] has very clearly explained the different sectors in the healthcare where blockchain can be implemented. The article also gives an example of a Swiss startup health bank that implemented a network where patients are sharing their health data [10]. It also sheds light on further improvements the startup is working on, which closely resemble the goals of our research. Our research focuses on making PHD available to the blockchain network. With the rapid proliferation of mobile devices coupled with healthcare-monitoring services and devices, a large amount of PHD is being generated. This data is patient-centric. This patient-centric data along with the blockchain implementation can be used to provide secure data storage and sharing. BlocHIE is another blockchain-based theoretical design for enabling HIE [11]. In BlocHIE, the data is categorized into two, namely EMR and PHD. Separate blockchains are used for storing each type of data. BlocHIE uses off-chain storage and on-chain verification for privacy and authentication. This system provides a holistic view of patient-generated and hospital-generated health data.

With the emergence of IoT, health monitoring became more patient-accessible. Various researches are going on to ensure the easy adoption of IoT in the healthcare domain. One of the important factors in a large network where information exchange is involved in making various devices is to agree to a common standard. Yuan-Fa Lee [12] showcases the hindrances in exchanging trustworthy information between healthcare devices. Yuan-Fa Lee proposes adapter x73-PHD system for non-health-care devices that do not follow the x73-PHD standards. The fast improvement of mobile computing prompts another idea of a pervasive social network (PSN)-based social insurance. The PSN-based healthcare [13] empowers clients to share information gathered by sensors. The system design is implemented by following two protocols: the first protocol uses IEEE 802.5.6, and the second protocol uses blockchain, which is based on PSN to distribute health information data.

One of the innovations in the medical field is electronic decentralized storage of patient's health records. Smart contract, an application of blockchain, is used to store medical records. The system called Medrec by Azaria et al. [14] briefly discusses the idea of using blockchain to store the medical record. The article does not speak about any security feature that is provided to ensure the security of the records. Because of the highly sensitive nature of health records, security is of prime importance.

Healthcare records are usually very large in size. For example, a digital X-ray can be of a size of at least 20 MB. Storing such large-sized records on the system/blockchain is not a good idea. Each record put in the blockchain is stored by all members in the network. The record storage will consume a lot of memory. To attain a reduced memory space consumption and to develop a good scalable network, off-chain storage of health records is a good solution. InterPlanetary File System (IPFS) is a distributed peer-to-peer file system used for storing records. The IPFS whitepaper [15] explains the design and algorithms that work behind the implementation of IPFS. The IPFS combines the concepts from different distributed file storage systems such as BitTorrent and Git to develop a well-protected, scalable, and innovative distributed file system. Files or records are stored in the IPFS depending on their sizes. Distributed hash tables (DHT) are used for querying and storage of objects. If the records are small, then they are stored directly in DHT, else the hashed values of the identity of nodes that store the health records are stored. The IPFS is still in its nascent stage, and hopefully, it will soon replace HyperText Transfer Protocol (HTTP), marking the end of a centralized data storage mechanism in the Internet. Chen et al. introduces an innovative design to collaborate IPFS and blockchain to provide better storage options [16]. The data storage algorithm in the IPFS, BitSwap, is modified to accommodate storage of large amounts of data. Such a design is of greater importance, considering the growing importance of BigData. The systems [15] and [16] together give an insight into the future of distributed data storage that can replace HTTP in the long run, mainly taking into consideration the requirements of content service providers as well as individual users.

Cryptography ensures the security aspects of data storage in blockchain. Cryptographic techniques such as hashing, encryption, decryption, and digital signatures are widely used in blockchain implementations. Encryption and decryption are used for providing data confidentiality. They ensure the privacy of the user. Only authorized personnel can access the data. Encryption is the process of converting a file into a ciphertext, so that only those personnel who have the key or password can unlock it and access the file. The ciphertext will appear to have no resemblance to the original file. The process of unlocking the ciphertext is called decryption. Advanced Encryption Standard (AES) [17] and Triple Data Encryption Standard are some of the examples of such algorithms. Each algorithm has its own method to convert a file into ciphertext and vice versa. Several cryptographic algorithms have been developed to ensure the data security. Depending on the requirements of the application that has been developed, the choice of algorithms also changes. Encryption and decryption of large files often consume large amount of resources, whether it be time consumption, memory utilization, or CPU utilization. Elminaam et al. [18] have conducted a performance evaluation on various symmetric key algorithms based on different evaluation metrics such as CPU time, encryption time, CPU clock cycles, and battery power. A detailed study on power consumption of various data encryption algorithms was conducted in [19]. Most symmetric algorithms were considered for the study. From both [18] and [19], it can be concluded that different algorithms have different strengths. Blowfish has efficient power consumption, but time consumption is very high. On the other hand, AES showcases a decent performance in all evaluation metrics. In this modern time, a node can be deployed in laptop, mobile phones, personal computers, etc. So, battery life, CPU usage, and time consumption are of utmost importance. One of the major factors for our work is to maintain the privacy of PHD. As a step of ensuring secrecy of data, we have decided on encrypting the PHD with a private key before generating hash of the data, using IPFS. Since the hash values are available to all nodes in the network, any node can retrieve the data using the hash values. However, the data generated from IPFS will be encrypted data. The decryption key should be distributed only to those users who the owner authorizes. The paper 'Protocols for Pubuc Key Cryptosystems' by Ralph C. Merkle provides a comparative analysis of different public key distribution systems in terms of security and privacy [20].

BigchainDB is a decentralized blockchain database. It is the outcome of blockchain technology applied to BigData. It encompasses the qualities of both traditional blockchains and distributed databases. High throughput, low latency, fast querying, decentralized control, and immutability are some of the features of BigchainDB. The capacity of the blockchain network can be increased by increasing the number of nodes [21]. Unlike Bitcoin, there is no PoW in BigchainDB. All the nodes get a chance to propose a block. If it is approved by other nodes, then this block can be added to the blockchain. In BigchainDB, Tendermint [22] is the software used in this work to provide BFT consensus and blockchain functionalities. The block that gets two-thirds of the blocks can be added to the network. Tendermint [22] gives a detailed explanation of the concepts and the various functionalities of the software.

9.3   SYSTEM COMPONENTS AND ARCHITECTURE

With the advent of many healthcare applications and wearable devices, a huge amount of PHD is generated. However, it is not used for active disease diagnosis or prevention. Since EMR is added by healthcare providers, it is accessible only to that healthcare provider who has created and maintained it. Moreover, health data is highly privacy-sensitive, and storing data in public cloud systems increases the risks of malicious attacks and data stealing.

If a patient decides to switch from one healthcare provider to another, then all the patient-related data may not be disclosed to the second healthcare provider immediately. In such a situation, necessity arises to get the health data of the patient again by taking all the tests once again. This results in increased expenses and delays in following up the treatment of patient. To enable data sharing between two different health institutions, there is a need for secure infrastructure. Another important problem that should be focused on is that, if the patient needs treatment in a foreign country, there is a need for universal access to patient records. This can delay the treatment to the patient, which may have severe consequences. Microsoft HealthVault is a third-party vendor that helps patients to store their PHD and give access to others to view the data. Since the data is stored in third-party data centers, it is susceptible to attacks from hackers, who wants to steal the data. Another problem is the authenticity of data. The doctors can be cautious of the data provided by the patient. There are no viable methods to validate if PHD is tampered with or not. Patients can modify data and submit to healthcare providers.

This study aims at providing a solution to these problems by shifting the centralized architecture of the healthcare domain to decentralized distributed architecture. The PHD is stored on a distributed network owned by the patient. The members of the network can be different healthcare providers, insurance agents, etc. The patient is the owner of the data and the network. The doctors and insurance agents can access the data with patient's approval. Thereby, the healthcare is no longer restricted to only centralized healthcare provider system. The introduction of blockchain technology in this scenario brings security, transparency, and authenticity to the data stored by the patients. The transactions in the network can vary fast with the consensus concept in blockchain, and everyone in the network will be aware of what is happening in the network. Information/data is the greatest asset, and by securely sharing it, a fast hassle-free and transparent system that is patient-friendly can be developed.

9.3.1   LACK OF PHD INTEGRATION IN HIE

At present, no steps have been taken by either healthcare providers or national governments to actively include PHD for healthcare. There are devices available in the market to measure cholesterol, blood pressure, glucose level, etc. These can be monitored by patients themselves. However, the medical personnel do not consider this data for treatment or diagnosis. So, even if a patient notes a fluctuation in his blood pressure with his/her personal device, a physician will only take into account the blood pressure readings from certified labs. One of the reasons for the physicians not considering the data from healthcare applications is the lack of standardization. No communication protocols or systems are deployed to collect this data securely and transfer to healthcare providers. There is a need to standardize all the healthcare devices in terms of hardware, communication protocols, system design, etc. [12]. Even though research is going on in this area, practical implementation of these studies has not yet been deployed.

The inclusion of PHD in HIE can save a lot of time for patients as well as physicians and can speed up the entire treatment process.

9.3.2 MINIMAL DATA SHARING ACROSS HIE

As per a survey conducted with the help of US Department of Health and Human Services [23], it has been observed that even though the number of organizations that are willing to support HIE has been increasing with time, there are very few health providers that support active and robust information exchange. One of the reasons is the lack of government funding available to healthcare providers to set up an infrastructure for HIE. The second reason is that no organization or patient wants to pay for data exchange. There should be a very secure way for transfer of data, and no one is ready to incur the expenses. Yet another reason is low adoption rate of EMR. There are many hospitals in the USA that still have not digitalized their patient record storage systems. They still write reports in papers and store in file cabinets. In such a situation, EMR cannot be adopted.

9.3.3 LACK OF PROPER TECHNICAL SECURITY MEASURES

As mentioned in the earlier sections, the lack of secure and robust infrastructure to store the health reports is a major blow to integrate HIE into mainstream healthcare services.

9.3.3.1 Objectives

9.3.3.1.1 Data Security
The use of blockchain to store data ensures the security of data. When a private blockchain network is created, there are certain criteria that should be satisfied for a member to join the network. The members can be doctors, nurses, and other medical personnel of the patient. Necessary proof should be presented to validate the same. All members in the network will be known to the patient and vice versa [24].

9.3.3.1.2 Immutability
Blockchain is an append-only system. Once a record is added to the blockchain, it can never be removed or deleted. So, no one can tamper with the health records or compromise its private nature. All transactions on the blockchain are recorded and timestamped [25].

9.3.3.1.3 Transparency
All members in a blockchain network can view all the records. Before adding or editing a record, all the members in the network should agree on the same. Only after that, a new record can be added. Since all transactions happen with the consent of all members in the network, transparency is ensured. No one can change anything without the knowledge of others [26].

9.3.3.1.4   Ease of Access

Every member of the network keeps an exact copy of the blockchain on their personal computer. If patients want to monitor their health, they can view it on a personal computer or a mobile device. Physicians can also view the records uploaded by another physician [27].

9.3.3.1.5   Interoperability

An implementation of a secure HIE will enable different healthcare providers to exchange data among themselves. This can help in quick diagnosis and treatment of diseases. Such a system can also enable physicians discussing among themselves effective treatment plans for their patients. Thus, HIE can help to achieve interoperability and better communication between different healthcare providers [28].

9.3.3.2   Architecture

The proposed architecture can be divided into three subsystems: user-friendly frontend – BlockHealth web application, Tendermint, and backend storage systems.

As shown in Figure 9.1, our solution is focused on developing a decentralized distributed application that can ensure the origin and authenticity of health records stored in the blockchain. The decentralized distributed stack architecture ensures that even if one node is down, other nodes have the exact copy of the data. Hence, the data is never lost, and moreover, one node cannot make changes in data without the consensus of other nodes. All the transactions are transparent to all users in the private blockchain network. Since BigchainDB is BFT at a time, one-third of the nodes in the network can fail, and still, the system will be running without any issues.

The first layer in Figure 9.1, BlockHealth web application, provides a user-friendly web interface to upload the health documents and store them in the IPFS and then in blockchain. Tendermint acts as an interface to broadcast transactions to all nodes in the private network. It is Tendermint that initiates the consensus process that determines whether a transaction is valid. If the transaction is valid, it will be added to the network; else, it is not.

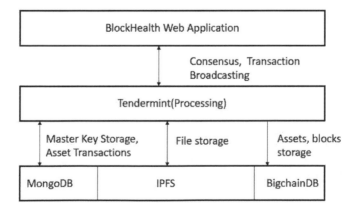

FIGURE 9.1 Decentralized stack architecture.

The third layer of Figure 9.1 showcases the different databases and file systems used for data storage for this application. MongoDB is used for the master key storage and management. The IPFS is used for storing health records, and BigchainDB is used for the storage of assets, blocks, and transactions. All blockchain-related data is stored in MongoDB or BigchainDB.

9.4 SYSTEM DESIGN

The design comprises two sections, as seen in Figure 9.2: the client side and the server side. The client side incorporates steps that start from uploading of file by the user until its conversion to an asset format, and server side is the blockchain network that stores these records. Both server design and client design and their implementation details are described in detail in the following subsections.

9.4.1 ENCRYPTION OF HEALTH RECORDS

Security and privacy are of utmost importance in the healthcare industry. Health records contain highly private data. The application ensures that security and privacy are ensured by encrypting all the records uploaded by the user in the interface. This guarantees that only authenticated members of the network will be able to view the data and use them for analysis and diagnosis purposes.

On the client side, encryption of the records is the first step in making the data secure. The patient/healthcare provider will be responsible for the encryption of data. Authenticated personnel will have the secret key for decryption and can thereby view the records. AES 256-bit algorithm is used for the encryption and decryption of records.

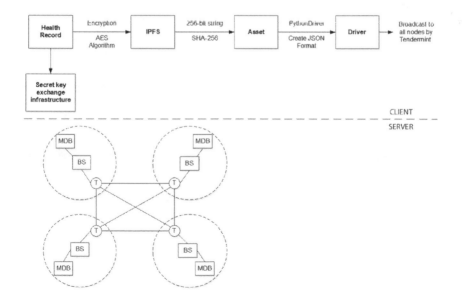

FIGURE 9.2 Overall system design.

9.4.2 STORAGE IN DISTRIBUTED FILE SYSTEM

InterPlanetary File System (IPFS) is used for the storage of health records. It is a distributed system for storing and accessing files. It is a peer-to-peer distributed file system that tries to maintain same file system across all nodes participating in the network, so that it has no single point of failure. The IPFS supports multiple languages. Figure 9.3 shows a code snippet of how to upload files to IPFS, using its Python Application Programming Interface (API) (see Table 9.1 for some of the most used IPFS methods).

The health records are usually large in size (e.g., X.-ray and magnetic resonance imaging scans); therefore, it is not advisable to store such a large chunk of data in the blockchain network. Since all the nodes have the same replica of blockchain network, they will also have same large-sized records stored. This will consume a large amount of memory in each system. To avoid this, once the records are encrypted, they are stored in the IPFS, which is a distributed file system. The advantage of storing the record in IPFS is that, on successful upload of a record, the IPFS will hash

```python
@app.route('/upload', methods=['GET', 'POST'])
def uploadfileAndEncrypt():
        if request.method == 'GET':
                return render_template("uploadFile.html");

        elif request.method == 'POST':
                f = request.files['file'];
                f.save(f.filename);
                print("code completed")
                encryptFile(f.filename, request.form['password']);
                hashVal = ipfsUpload(f.filename+".aes")
                return render_template("displayHash.html", hash=hashVal);


def ipfsUpload(fileName):
        localhost = '127.0.0.1'
        portNumber = 5001
        api = ipfsapi.connect(localhost, portNumber)
        res = api.add(fileName)
        print(res)
        return res['Hash']
```

FIGURE 9.3   IPFS Python API code for uploading files.

TABLE 9.1
IPFS CLI Commands

IPFS Commands	Descriptions
ipfs init	Initiates IPFS in the localhost
ipfs add	Adds a file or directory to IPFS
Ipfs daemon	Initiates IPFS daemon listening to port 5001
ipfs get	Download IPFS objects
ipfs pin	Pin (and unpin) objects to local storage

the record and output a 256-bit hash value as a reference to the record. So, any record of any size is converted to a 256-bit string. This 256-bit hash value is stored in the blockchain.

The following subsections describe the command-line interface (CLI) and web user interface (UI) implementation of IPFS.

9.4.3 Asset Creation and Transfer

Data is stored in the form of assets in BigchainDB. A CREATE transaction is used to register the asset in the blockchain network, as seen in Figure 9.4. Once the asset schema is developed in JavaScript Object Notation (JSON), the asset, along with the signing keys, is sent to the BigchainDB driver to create a transaction. The transaction is validated by both BigchainDB server and Tendermint of the local node and then sent for pre-commit and consensus. After getting more than two-thirds of the votes from the members, the asset can be registered into the blockchain.

The transfer transaction is prepared by passing the asset id to be transferred, public key of the future owner, and 'TRANSFER' string for operation. However, the transaction will be successful only if the fulfillment process is satisfied with the existing owner's private key as a parameter.

```
from bigchaindb_driver import BigchainDB
from bigchaindb_driver.crypto import generate_keypair

bdb_root_url = 'https://127.0.0.1:9984'
bdb = BigchainDB(bdb_root_url)
pulseReadings = {
    'data': {
        'pulseReading': {
            'hashVal':'QmYKk58w8pFbstWfYMT2bY2PkmiFBBRz7MZHyBXHZeqc9H'
            'device':'fitbit'
        }
    }
}

metadata = {
    'identiy': 'required'
    'access time': '20 min'
}
#can also use the member's own public key
myKey = generate_keypair()
prepared_creation_tx = bdb.transactions.prepare(
        operation='CREATE',
        signers=myKey.public_key,
        asset=pulseReading,
        metadata=metadata,
    )

fulfilled_creation_tx = bdb.transactions.fulfill(
        prepared_creation_tx, private_keys=myKey.private_key)

#send to bigchainDb node
sent_creation_tx = bdb.transactions.send_commit(fulfilled_creation_tx)
txid = fulfilled_creation_tx['id']
block_height = bdb.blocks.get(txid=signed_tx['txid'])
```

FIGURE 9.4 JSON format asset creation.

The secret key exchange between two nodes in the network is carried out using Diffie-Hellman key exchange algorithm. Each asset created must have a metadata section that describes the conditions to satisfy to let the owner of the asset share the asset and the period that the owner will allow to the requestor to access the record. Let us consider a scenario where medical personnel wants to view an asset/health record of the patient.

- *Step 1*: The medical personnel initiate the request to view the health record by creating an asset with a set of cipher suite along with the asset id of the record they want to access and send to the patient.
- *Step 2*: The patient selects any one of the cipher suites and transfers the Diffie-Hellman parameters to the medical personnel.
- *Step 3*: The medical personnel calculate the public key and transfers it to the patient.
- *Step 4*: The patient also calculates the public key and sends it to the personnel.
- *Step 5*: The medical personnel encrypt the reason to view the document with the shared secret key and send to the patient.
- *Step 6*: If the patient is convinced, then he/she will share the decryption key for the document encrypted by using shared secret key; if not convinced, the patient sends the reason for rejection.
- *Step 7*: If the personnel have received the decryption key, they can visit the IPFS, download the document using the hash value, and then decrypt it.
- *Step 8*: The patient can change the key and update the blockchain once the allotted time is over.

9.4.4 SERVER DESIGN

As seen in Figure 9.5, the server design comprises BigchainDB node, BigchainDB server, Tendermint, and MongoDB.

9.4.5 BIGCHAINDB NODE

Any computer system with BigchainDB, MongoDB, and Tendermint installed is considered a BigchainDB node. The only requirement is that all the software should be installed successfully, along with Python 3.6. A single node is completely capable of creating assets and storing them in the blockchain. However, without a BigchainDB server network, the user will be pushing assets only to his/her system. A BigchainDB node can be either a virtual machine or a real computer system. In all nodes in the blockchain network, the following ports must be configured to allow both incoming and outgoing communications (Table 9.2).

9.4.6 BIGCHAINDB SERVER

The minimum requirement to deploy a BigchainDB server network is to have at least four BigchainDB nodes up and running. The nodes must share their hostname,

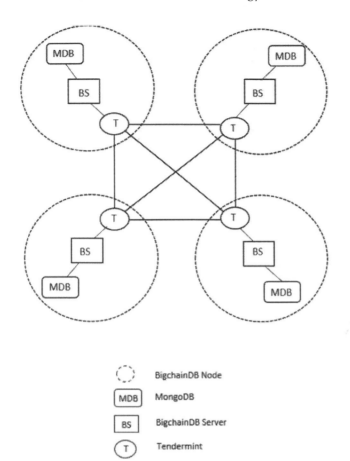

FIGURE 9.5   Server design.

TABLE 9.2
Port Configuration

Protocol	Port	Communication
TCP	22	SSH
TCP	80	HTTP
TCP	443	HTTPS
TCP	26656	Tendermint

public key, and node id with the coordinator of the network. The coordinator will update the genesis file of the Tendermint software with the public key and host-name of the members and share the same file with all members. All members in the network must maintain the same copy of genesis file. To maintain connections between all members in the network, each member must update the config.toml file in Tendermint folder and enter each neighbor's hostname along with the node id in the persistent peers tag. This enables the user to automatically connect to the peers on network start/restart.

9.4.7 TENDERMINT

Tendermint is responsible for enabling blockchain features in a BigchainDB network. It first checks the validity of a transaction. Once successfully validated, Tendermint broadcasts the transaction to all the nodes in the network. Tendermint also plays a very important role in consensus process. Each node gets a chance to put forward a block for inclusion in a round-robin fashion.

9.4.8 MONGODB

MongoDB is a distributed database that stores data in a flexible JSON-like documents. BigchainDB uses MongoDB to query data from the blockchain. BigchainDB, together with MongoDB, provides decentralized control, immutability, and asset autonomy on the top of a distributed database. MongoDB consists of different databases by default after installing BigchainDB software. All blockchain data is stored in BigchainDB.

In BigchainDB, there are many collections with each type of data stored. The mostly used collections are assets, blocks, elections, metadata, transactions, and validators. Assets collection stores all the assets created by the members in the network and stored in the blockchain, as seen in Figure 9.6. Blocks collection stores the blocks committed to the blockchain. Elections collection stores the data regarding the elections carried out to include a new validator/member in the blockchain. Metadata stores the metadata associated with each asset created. Transactions collections stores the data regarding all the transactions that happened between various members in the network. Validators show the list of validators along with their voting power, as seen in Figure 9.7.

```
{
        "_id" : ObjectId("5c02115ac4a72e04f766c255"),
        "data" : {
                "PHD5" : {
                        "hashvalue" : "QmefNyh2PPdLR2X7h2YQg9BDVT2FApSEB93X3xM43
zaTc3",
                        "owner" : "karthika"
                }
        },
        "id" : "b8a5164ee58805c092ea4f59bcc16f5458e86af0cb63280ed54f733e23887945
"
}
```

FIGURE 9.6   Asset display.

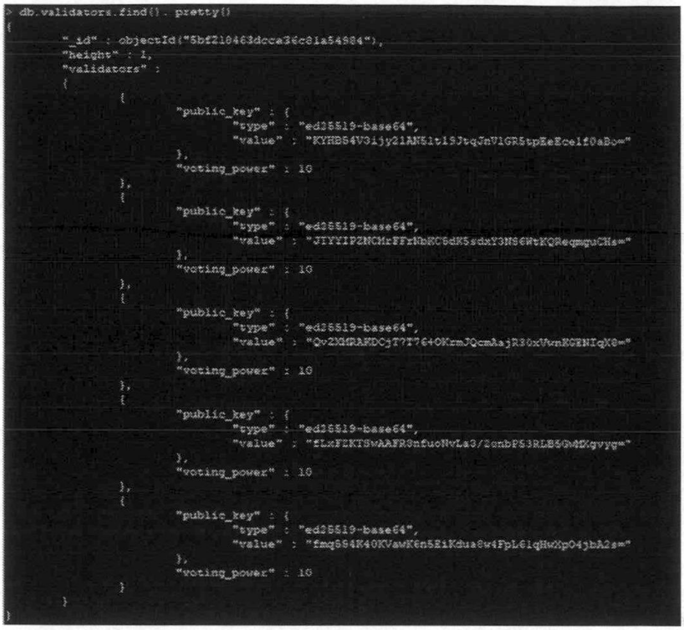

```
> db.validators.find() . pretty()
{
    "_id" : objectId("5bf218463dcca36c81a54984"),
    "height" : 1,
    "validators" :
    {
        {
            "public_key" : {
                "type" : "ed25519-base64",
                "value" : "KYHB54V3ijy21AN51t15JtqJnV1GR5tpEeEceif0aBo="
            },
            "voting_power" : 10
        },
        {
            "public_key" : {
                "type" : "ed25519-base64",
                "value" : "JTYYIP2MCMrFFrNbHC5dK5sdxY3NS6WtKQReqmguCHs="
            },
            "voting_power" : 10
        },
        {
            "public_key" : {
                "type" : "ed25519-base64",
                "value" : "Qv2XdfRAFDCjT7T7640KrmJQcmAajR30xVwnKGENIqX8="
            },
            "voting_power" : 10
        },
        {
            "public_key" : {
                "type" : "ed25519-base64",
                "value" : "fLxFIKTSwAAFR9nfuoNvLa3/2onbPS3RLESGWtXgvyg="
            },
            "voting_power" : 10
        },
        {
            "public_key" : {
                "type" : "ed25519-base64",
                "value" : "fmqS54K40KVawK6n5ZiKdua6w4FpL61qHwXpO4jbA2s="
            },
            "voting_power" : 10
        }
    }
}
```

FIGURE 9.7 Validator details.

9.5 PERFORMANCE EVALUATION

In recent years, several applications have inherited blockchain technology. In order to fit various application specifications, several blockchain platforms have been developed. Some of the blockchain platforms include Hyperledger Fabric, Ethereum, Geth, and Parity. Each of these applications differs on certain features. These changes will help developers understand limitations in the platforms and give an option of choosing a platform that would perform better for their use case. As our proposal involves converting PHD into blocks, a platform that could handle high transaction throughput is needed. BigchainDB is the platform that has the capability of providing high transaction rate with low latency (Figure 9.8). It provides faster indexing and querying data features. The widely popular blockchain software such as Hyperledger Fabric and Ethereum provide smart contract and business logic capability but have the limitation in terms of querying data. These platforms are more suitable for processing, whereas BigchainDB is better for storing structured data. Recently, in order to inherit smart contract features, BigchainDB developers have demonstrated integration solutions with Hyperledger Fabric [29].

The point of benchmarking is to measure the time used for processing the blocks. It includes all processes such as transaction signature checking, database population, validation methods, and so on. The results are reported by Ethereum, in which a machine with a clean database is made to synchronize. The timing performance is measured until the machine imports 1,000,000 blocks. A master node is chosen

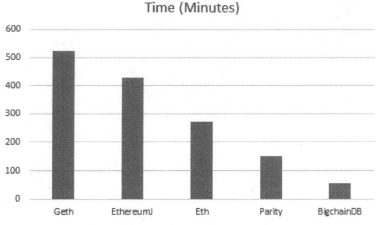

FIGURE 9.8   Comparison of BigchainDB with various platforms running on Ethereum.

and synced with the network. The client to be benchmarked is installed and configured. Parity performed the best in terms of speed and memory [30]. In the case
of BigchainDB, each transaction was of fixed size, ie, 765 bytes. It took less than
56 minutes to insert 1,000,000 transactions into the network. This high-speed performance of BigchainDB is mainly a result of using Tendermint protocol.

In addition, BigchainDB has an experimental parallel validation feature that
allows nodes to use more than one CPU for validation at the same time. This is
a trick that tells Tendermint to consider all transactions incoming as valid, which
decreases the time a node must wait for next transaction. BigchainDB then validates transactions in parallel and discards invalid transactions. This method limits
Tendermint's ability to verify node misbehaviors, but entries into the MongoDB will
be verified by BigchainDB. The comparison of the two ways is plotted as follows.

Figure 9.9 shows that, when the transactions were finalized with Tendermint
validation, it took 9.39 seconds to finalize 99.7% of transactions. Whereas without

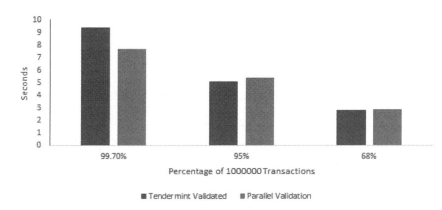

FIGURE 9.9   Parallel validation.

validation, 7.686 seconds were enough for Tendermint to pass the transactions to BigchainDB node. Overall, it took 56 minutes to process all transactions with validity check, whereas it took only 26 minutes without validity check from Tendermint [31].

9.6 CONCLUSION

The proposed system develops a realistic and viable application for the secure storage and sharing of PHD. It can also be used to bridge the gap in data sharing among multiple healthcare providers. With the implementation of such a system, health record management becomes more transparent. The patients gain the ability to track their data. They can view when and who updated their records. The physicians gain access to patient's PHD, thereby arriving at a faster diagnosis. The proposed system is a low-cost alternative, as all the software stack is an open source. Hence, the healthcare providers at the lower end of financial spectrum can develop and maintain such a system.

REFERENCES

1. Ashish Jha, Catherine Desroches, Eric Campbell, Karen Donelan, Sowmya Rao, Timothy Ferris, Alexandra Shields, Sara Rosenbaum and David Blumenthal. "Use of electronic health records in U.S. hospitals." *The New England Journal of Medicine*, 360, 1628–1638, 2009.
2. Christian Esposito, Alfredo De Santis, Genny Tortora, Henry Chang and Kim-Kwang Raymond Choo. "Blockchain: A panacea for healthcare cloud-based data security and privacy?" *IEEE Cloud Computing*, 5, 31–37, 2018.
3. Rui Guo, Huixian Shi, Qinglan Zhao and Dong Zheng. "Secure attribute-based signature scheme with multiple authorities for blockchain in electronic health records systems." *IEEE Access*, 776.99, 1–12, 2018.
4. Xueping Liang, Juan Zhao, Sachin Shetty, Jihong Liu and Danyi Li. "Integrating blockchain for data sharing and collaboration in mobile healthcare applications." *IEEE 28th Annual International Symposium on Personal, Indoor, and Mobile Radio Communications (PIMRC)*. IEEE, 2017.
5. Sean Hogan, Heather Fraser, Peter Korsten, Veena Pureswaran and Ramesh Gopinath. "Healthcare rallies for blockchains: Keeping patients at the center." *IBM Tech Report*, 2016. Available: https://www.ibm.com/downloads/cas/BBRQK3WY
6. Satoshi Nakamoto. "Bitcoin: A peer-to-peer electronic cash system." 2008. Available: http://bitcoin.org/bitcoin.pdf
7. Marko Vukolić. "The quest for scalable blockchain fabric: Proof-of-work vs. BFT replication." *International Workshop on Open Problems in Network Security*. Springer, 2015.
8. Parisa J. Marandi, Carlos E. Bezerra and Fernando Pedone. "Rethinking state-machine replication for parallelism." *Proceedings of the 2014 IEEE 34th International Conference on Distributed Computing Systems (ICDCS)*, pp. 368–377, IEEE, 2014.
9. Matthias Mettler. "Blockchain technology in healthcare: The revolution starts here." *IEEE 18th International Conference on e-Health Networking, Applications and Services* (Health-com), pp. 1–2, IEEE, March 2016.
10. Peter B. Nichol. "The next generation of health IT: Blockchain applications for healthcare." *CIO Magazine*. 17 March 2016. Available: http://www.cio.com/article/3042603/innovation/blockchain- applications-for-healthcare.html

11. Shan Jiang, Jiannong Cao, Hanqing Wu, Yanni Yang, Mingyu Ma and Jianfei He. "Blochie: A blockchain-based platform for healthcare information exchange." *2018 IEEE International Conference on Smart Computing (SMARTCOMP)*. IEEE, 2018.

12. Yuan-Fa Lee. "An interoperability solution for legacy healthcare devices." *IT Professional*, 17, 51–57, 2015.

13. Jie Zhang, Nian Xue, and Xin Huang. "A secure system for pervasive social network-based healthcare." *IEEE Access*, 4, 9239–9250, 2016.

14. Asaph Azaria, Ariel Ekblaw, Thiago Vieira and Andrew Lippman. "Medrec: Using blockchain for medical data access and permission management." *IEEE 2nd International Conference on Open and Big Data (OBD)*, pp. 25–30, Vienna, 2016.

15. Juan Benet. "IPFS—Content addressed, versioned, P2P file system (draft 3)". White Paper. Available: https://github.com/ipfs/papers/raw/master/ipfs-cap2pfs/ipfs-p2p-file-system.pdf

16. Yongle Chen et al. "An improved P2P file system scheme based on IPFS and Blockchain." *Big Data (Big Data), 2017 IEEE International Conference on*. IEEE, 2017.

17. Joan Daemen and Vincent Rijmen. *The Design of Rijndael*. Springer-verlag Berlin Heidelberg, New York, USA, 2002.

18. Diaa S. A. Elminaam, Hatem M. A. Kader and Mohie M. Hadhoud. "Performance evaluation of symmetric encryption algorithms." *IJCSNS International Journal of Computer Science and Network Security*, 8(12), 280–286, 2008.

19. Tingyuan Nie, Lijian Zhou and Zhe-Ming Lu. "Power evaluation methods for data encryption algorithms." *IET Software*, 8(1), 12–18, February 2014.

20. Ralph C. Merkle. "Protocols for public key cryptosystems." *IEEE Symposium on Security and Privacy*, pp. 122–134, IEEE, 1980.

21. BigchainDB GmbH. "BigchainDB: A scalable blockchain database." White Paper, (2016). Available: https://www.bigchaindb.com/whitepaper/bigchaindb-whitepaper.pdf

22. Tendermint documentation. 2019. Available: https://media.readthedocs.org/pdf/tendermint/v0.10.4/tendermint.pdf

23. Julia Adler-Milstein, David Bates and Ashish Jha. "A survey of health information exchange organizations in the united states: Implications for meaningful use". *Annals of Internal Medicine*, 154, 666–671, 2011.

24. Moh'd Abidalrahman, Nauman Aslam, Hosein Marzi and Loai Tawalbeh. "Hardware implementations of secure hashing functions on FPGAs for WSNs." *In Proceedings of the 3rd International Conference on the Applications of Digital Information and Web Technologies (ICADIWT)*. 2010.

25. Lo'ai A. Tawalbeh and Hala Tawalbeh. "Lightweight crypto and security." *Security and Privacy in Cyber Physical Systems: Foundations, Principles and Applications*, vol. 1, pp. 243–261, 2017. Ch. 12.

26. Lo'ai A. Tawalbeh and Waseem Bakhader. "A mobile cloud system for different useful applications." *In 2016 IEEE 4th International Conference on Future Internet of Things and Cloud Workshops (FiCloudW)*, pp. 295–298, IEEE, 2016.

27. Fadi Muheidat, Lo'ai Tawalbeh and Harry Tyrer. "Context-aware, accurate, and real time fall detection system for elderly people." *In 2018 IEEE 12th International Conference on Semantic Computing (ICSC)*, pp. 329–333, IEEE, 2018.

28. Lo'ai A. Tawalbeh and Suhaila Habeeb. "An integrated cloud based healthcare system." *In 2018 Fifth International Conference on Internet of Things: Systems, Management and Security*, pp. 268–273, IEEE, 2018.

29. BigchainDB integrates with hyperledger fabric. 2018. Available: https://blog.bigchaindb.com/bigchaindb-hyperledger-fabricintegration-4c65e5811671

30. Benchmarks for ethereum. 2018. Available: https://github.com/ethereum/wiki/wiki/Benchmarks

31. Performance study: Analysis of transaction throughput in a BigchainDB network. 2018. Available: https://github.com/bigchaindb/BEPs/tree/master/23

10 A Blockchain-Based Secure Data Sharing Framework for Healthcare

Raza Nowrozy, A. S. M. Kayes, Paul A. Watters, Mamoun Alazab, Alex Ng, Mohammad Jabed Morshed Chowdhury, and Omaru Maruatona

CONTENTS

10.1   INTRODUCTION

The inception of the blockchain technology has created new opportunities for businesses to provide high-quality products and services to the market. Healthcare is one of those sectors that can bring potential benefits while integrating with blockchain technology to provide better healthcare services to patients and other associated practitioners. Carson et al. [1] report that blockchain offers numerous short- and long-term benefits for businesses that include the cost saving and complete transformation of business models.

According to Mettler [2], the principles of blockchain technology, such as high transparency, instant access to the information, decentralized services, and convenience, are the major benefits that blockchain technology can bring to the healthcare sector. Initially, blockchain technology was limited to the financial institutions; however, such benefits have been realized by other sectors. Various researchers have attempted to understand it, and they have theoretically conceptualized and proposed frameworks pertaining to the management of business operations for different non-financial sectors and academic institutions [3]. Furthermore, governments have been planning and developing the use of blockchain in the public sector as well [4].

The healthcare industry has its own set of challenges that are unique, so it requires new innovation to overcome the challenges. Bennett [5] pointed out healthcare compliance as one of the major challenges for healthcare institutions and workers. Electronic health records existed before the emergence and diffusion of blockchain technology in various sectors. However, they have admitted security and accessibility issues due to vulnerability of the digital systems [6,7]. It is believed that the blockchain technology, due to its inherent characteristics, has the potentials to overcome healthcare compliance issues in terms of security and accessibility. It can be used to share information with large network of healthcare institutions in an efficient and safer manner (Linn and Koo [8]). Nevertheless, all these aspects of blockchain can only be achieved through the development of a blockchain-based data sharing framework that can be implemented within the healthcare sector for efficient data management and sharing processes.

According to Apriorit (2018), the blockchain technology is designed to protect people and systems from the traditional cyberattacks; however, cybercriminals are developing new attack vectors for hacking blockchain technology.

10.1.1 THE BACKGROUND OF THE STUDY

10.1.1.1 Blockchain

According to Taylor et al. [9], blockchain technology is gaining grounds at a rapid speed in different aspects of information and communication technology. One of the main reasons behind the increasing interest of business is the growth of crypto-currencies such as Bitcoins. However, it is important to note that Bitcoins are just a small portion of the wide-scoped blockchain technology [1].

Peterson et al. [10] defined blockchain technology as a distributed transnational ledger that involves blocks and a set of transactions. The blocks are immutable, which adds benefits to the security of the system. This system is highly decentralized, as the trusted authority can be distributed to many different nodes [11]. The distribution of authority to nodes gives rise to different kinds of blockchain: public blockchain, private blockchain, and consortium blockchain [12].

In public blockchain, all transactions are accessible and visible to all nodes in the network. However, some parts of the blockchain can be encrypted to protect the information. Any individual who lacks considerable security aspects can join such type of blockchain [13]. On the other hand, certain nodes that are authorized by the system can manage the private blockchain. This type of blockchain is usu- ally managed by a single organization and is highly secured [13]. The third type of blockchain is consortium blockchain, which allows a specific group of people to join the network. It is usually utilized by industries and can be managed by more than one organization.

10.1.1.2 Smart Contracts

Carson et al. [1] defined smart contracts as a set of conditions that can be programmed and made part of the blockchain system. Once the conditions in the smart contracts are fulfilled, the transactions are automatically triggered. Smart contracts are codes specifically defined to establish a set of rules on which different parties agree and interact with each other. Smart contracts are of great importance in different sectors, including the medical sector, where it can play a key role in delivering the health records of patients. According to McGhin et al. [14], patients' information is highly sensitive and requires a highly secure system for its transaction. Simple encryption of data is ineffective for the management of patient records.

In the healthcare organizations, the retrieval of patient records is vital for effective and timely medical interventions. However, the patients are required to authorize the access to their health records to different practitioners, which can be obtained through smart contracts. Smart contracts can help in developing and man-aging authorization control, as the necessary requirements for granting access to the recognized personnel can depend on their identity [15]. Moreover, Buterin [16] stated that Ethereum has the potential to assist the healthcare sector in utilizing smart contracts. Smart contracts can be enforced on top of the blockchain, which can validate the conditions and pass the information only when all conditions of smart contracts are fulfilled. Smart contracts not only validate the situations but also can act as an auditing mechanism for sharing of data that can be externally helpful in the healthcare sector.

According to Ekblaw et al. [17], there are three main types of smart contracts in blockchain technology: registrar contract, patient-provider relationship (PPR) contract, and summary contract. The registrar contract is specifically designed for Ethereum platform of the blockchain. The policies that can be coded through the registrar contracts have the potentials to regulate and register new entries into the system. On the other hand, the PPR contract is usually issued between two nodes for storing and managing the medical records. Summary contracts also play a vital role in healthcare-affiliated systems. This type of contract can deal with a list of references pertaining to patients' records. This reference list helps in locating the correct information in delivering accurate and timely information to the healthcare practitioners.

10.1.2 THE OBJECTIVES OF THE SURVEY

The objectives of this survey are as follows:

- Analyze the current limitations in healthcare data sharing
- Analyze the advantages of blockchain over conventional data storage and frameworks
- Review existing blockchain-based data sharing frameworks and identify strengths and weaknesses
- Propose a blockchain-based data sharing scheme for healthcare, given the current security issues and the advantages of blockchain over traditional access control systems

10.1.3 THE SURVEY OUTLINE

The rest of this chapter is organized as follows. The motivation for the survey is discussed in Section 10.2. Current issues of the blockchain-based healthcare technologies and the requirements to build a secure data sharing framework are also discussed in Section 10.2. We discuss the current state-of-the-art blockchain-based data sharing solutions in Section 10.3. Other key findings on a blockchain-based technology are included in Section 10.4. In Section 10.5, we present an in-depth analysis of the open research issues and a new direction for future data sharing framework for healthcare. Finally, we conclude the chapter in Section 10.6.

10.2 RESEARCH MOTIVATION AND GENERAL REQUIREMENTS

10.2.1 RESEARCH BACKGROUND

This research topic is undertaken due to the increasing adoption of technologies such as blockchain technology in different businesses sectors. The healthcare sector is an important private- and public-based sector that requires constant adoption of new technologies to improve their services to patients. According to Carson et al. [1], blockchain technology will be available for adoption on a large scale and will be applicable to the healthcare industry. This can significantly improve the security issues and other complications faced by the healthcare industries while recording, storing, and retrieving patients-related data through electronic means currently utilized on large scales. This research will help to resolve the coopetition paradox related to the development of common standards that can be practiced throughout different industries and institutions within the healthcare sector.

Moreover, Holbl et al. [13] asserted that the implementation of blockchain requires a framework that will help institutions in the healthcare industry manage data for effective, accurate, and timely retrieval of electronic health records. They also claimed that the implementation of blockchain in the healthcare industry will also help in the prescription of drugs for special cases, along with improving supply chain management for effective operations.

10.2.2   HEALTHCARE DATA SHARING FRAMEWORK

In the healthcare sector, the medical records of patients, prescribed drugs, and patients' personal information fall into the category of personally identifiable information (PII). The PII is defined as the information that leads to the identification of an individual or may provide sensitive information of an individual that he or she may not like to reveal. The information such as medical records pertaining to the prescription of the doctor is highly sensitive information and should be protected at all cost unless the patient provides approval for revealing the personal information.

Brodersen et al. [18] argued that with regard to the privacy of blockchain technology, its adoption introduces several limitations. One limitation of blockchain is that even without PII, it can be identified through forensic analysis of network that a certain entity has interacted repeatedly with the other network in a blockchain network. This is due to the pseudonymous property of blockchain technology [17].

According to Ekblaw et al. [17], patients' information is often availed by the hackers owing to its sensitivity. The current electronic database systems based on technologies other than blockchain are efficient; however, they are insecure. In such scenarios, it is important to develop a framework for the implementation of blockchain technology in the healthcare industry, so as to provide an immutable structure for the transaction of data that can be an audit by different individuals.

Moreover, Peterson et al. [10] argued that failure in the provision of effective privacy and security of patient records can lead to severe financial and legal consequences for healthcare organizations. The security of electronic medical records is a challenging task and is a leading cause of efforts undertaken to discourage the sharing of sensitive data. The concepts of security, privacy, and anonymity are extremely important for the healthcare institutions that manage the electronic medical databases, in order to enhance the retrieval of patient data.

Access control is another important issue in the healthcare industry, as authorized access to information protects the data from vulnerability. Maesa et al. [19] stated that blockchain provides an exceptional access control system that can regulate the accessibility to the database. Moreover, it allows the transfer of rights among individuals based on certain situations. They also proposed an architecture that facilitates access to the information of user profile. These access control systems allow the users to selectively hide and expose their information to the third party. This is similar to the online social network, where the users have the same user access as mentioned previously. In the healthcare sector, this option provides the opportunity for the patients to allow the extent of access to their personal information, including PII.

According to Maesa et al. [19], blockchain-based access control systems deal with storing the access control policies, along with storing attributes, and make decisions regarding access control whenever access control request is sent to the system. In addition, in the medical field, importance is placed over the phenomenon of sharing patients' information from the clinical trials [20].

Dubovitskaya et al. [21] described the data sharing mechanism of a blockchain system developed for the healthcare industry (Figure 10.1). The data sharing system is based on consortium blockchain that includes a cloud server that acts as a source of strong information. The cloud systems are connected to the resources of two hospitals that are together through smart contracts. Each hospital has its own local database, where the information is stored. In addition, the membership service plays a key role in registering new users (patients and doctors). In case of registering a new doctor in the database, it is important for healthcare institutions to ensure the registration of a qualified doctor. Therefore, the system is also linked with national practitioner bank to ensure authentication of the information. Moreover, it involves the generation of an encrypted key pair that protects the information.

In addition, Gordon and Catalini [22] described the interoperability system for the healthcare industry involving the sharing of data (Figure 10.2). The system is

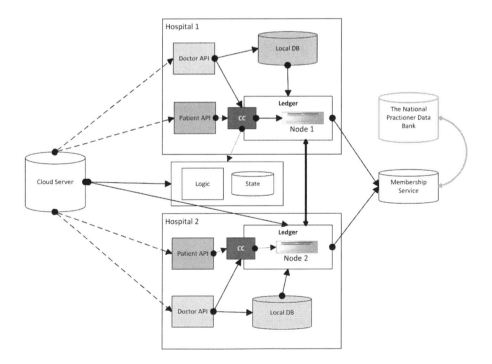

FIGURE 10.1 A solution overview of a data sharing framework between two hospitals. (From Dubovitskaya, A. et al., *AMIA Annual Symposium Proceedings*, American Medical Informatics Association, 2017. With permission.)

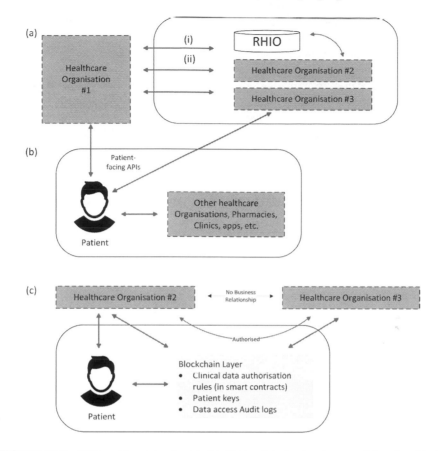

FIGURE 10.2 Different layers involved in healthcare data sharing framework based on blockchain. (a) Example of institution-driven interoperability for clinical Electronic health record data, (b) Example of patient-driven interoperability, (c) Blockchain-enabled patient-driven interoperability. (From Gordon, W.J. and Catalini, C., *Comput. Struct. Biotechnol. J.*, 16, 224–230, 2018.)

broken down into multiple layers, and the relationship between different actors in each layer is analyzed. They mentioned three layers of the system: institution-driven interoperability, patient-driven interoperability, and blockchain-enabled patient-driven interoperability. The three layers of the data interoperability are depicted in Figure 10.2. Moreover, the relationship between the actors can be observed horizontally and vertically throughout the layers of the system.

In the top-most layer of institutional blockchain-enabled patient-driven interoperability, a relationship between the health organization with the Regional Health Information Organization (RHIO) and other healthcare organizations is possible. In patient-driven interoperability, the patient can interact with healthcare organizations, including pharmacy and other institutions through patients-facing API. Whereas, blockchain-based patient-driven interoperability has no business relationship between different healthcare organizations. The relationship can only be developed through official means possible through blockchain technology. This is due to the transparent nature of blockchain technology that protects the privacy of information and offers extra security to patients' records, including sensitive information. All relationships in this system go through patients due to smart contracts and have layers such as clinical data authorization, patients' keys, and credentials for access to data.

Various agencies, including drug-producing companies, are using data sharing to great effect, which is the main objective under observation for this research. Nonetheless, these agencies and related bodies heavily rely on the current centralized systems of electronic health records in the healthcare industry. In addition, this requires a well-developed framework for blockchain system in the healthcare industry, along with incentives for sharing of data and information resources [20].

10.2.3 ISSUES WITH CURRENT DATA SHARING FRAMEWORK IN HEALTHCARE

Based on the current state-of-the-art blockchain-based data sharing frameworks in healthcare, the following are a few research issues (Table 10.1).

TABLE 10.1
Issues with Current Blockchain-Based Data Sharing Framework in Healthcare

Research	Issue
Abouelmehdi et al. [23]	• The security of the data and information resources including those related to the health care industries such as patients' heath record and personal information, is a major issue. • The current electronic database systems in the healthcare industry lacks the security measure to protect the information from hackers and other unauthorized accesses. • It also significantly affects privacy of patients information, which can lead to severe financial and legal consequences.
Esposito et al. [24]	• Data sharing involves a consensus between different parties, such as sharing patients' health records through blockchain-assisted technologies and sharing mediums also requires consensus among the parties. • The development of relevant data sharing policy along with the enforcement of smart contracts. • There are issues with access control in the data sharing platform of the blockchain technology.
Bell et al. [25]	• One of the main issues identified in data sharing application of blockchain for healthcare industry is the lack of consent of patients. • There is also a lack of international standards regarding interoperability of IT services in the healthcare industry.
Meng et al. [26]	• It is necessary to provide a data sharing platform for different entities, such as the practitioners, patients, and administrators. • Administrators should have special rights to oversee the entire system. • Administrators should also have the responsibility of establishing links between different parties and the stored data and information.
Omar et al. [27]	• Proposed a peer-to-peer blockchain-based system for sharing of electronic health records and to ensure a high level of privacy for sensitive data and to add accountability to the process of data sharing. • It is vital to introduce a new framework for the healthcare sector based on the blockchain technology.

10.2.4 REQUIREMENTS FOR A SECURE BLOCKCHAIN-BASED DATA SHARING FRAMEWORK

Numerous researchers have contributed in providing information pertaining to a secure database for the sharing of electronic health records.

The following questions underpin the importance of adopting blockchain technology within healthcare:

- How blockchain technology can be used to protect the sharing of data for improved medical interventions?
- What are the requirements necessary for developing a data storing and sharing mechanism based on blockchain technology for the healthcare sector?

In order to develop a framework for medical data sharing, there are general requirements that need to be followed:

- (R1): A primary need of healthcare system for data sharing is the requirement of a blockchain system for controlling the process for data sharing.
- (R2): Blockchain will act as the main data sharing and controlling mechanism for electronic database system. Moreover, the data involved in these healthcare records are sensitive and private.
- (R3): On top of security, the privacy requirements of different stakeholders also need to be considered. To achieve the previously stated requirements, a new framework for the healthcare industry requires technical compliance for highly secured blockchain system with the help of security token. This can be achieved using credentials that can provide the authorized access to patients' records to doctors and nurses and to other relevant authorities.
- (R4): In addition to basic credentials, other Information and Communication technology (ICT) devices such as biometric verification can also be used to improve the security of such systems.
- (R5): Zyskind and Nathan [28] stated that a high-level privacy can be achieved through various data algorithms that can ensure that the sensitive information cannot be distinguished when compared with other records.
- (R6): Another requirement for the framework pertaining to blockchain technology for patient record is big data management using the cloud system. Since data needs to be stored, the cloud system is by far the most commonly used storage option. It protects the physical space of the healthcare unit and also saves the cost of storage devices (internal storage). However, it has security concerns due to the utilization of third-party for data storage.
- (R7): The blockchain-based data sharing framework can mitigate such security concerns owing to its inherent characteristic of transparency and immutable public ledgers. Moreover, cryptographic algorithms of blockchain technology are difficult to bypass and add security to the blockchain system, which utilizes cloud storage for data management.

10.3   THE CURRENT STATE-OF-THE-ART BLOCKCHAIN-BASED DATA SHARING FRAMEWORKS IN HEALTHCARE

Based on the existing literature, blockchain-based data sharing solutions in healthcare are discussed in this section. Table 10.2 demonstrates eight key blockchain technologies that have been introduced in the last few years.

Peterson et al. [10] provided a blockchain-based approach that resolves the issues related to privacy, security, and incompatibility of data structures. For this purpose, a single source and centralized network system are recommended by the authors, where proof of structure and semantic interoperability are predicted as the best possible blockchain-based approaches to the current problems of the healthcare industry in electronic data sharing and management. They proposed a framework for data entry into patient records by using blockchain technology, including four phases of data entry: transactional distribution, block verification request, signed book return, and new blockchain distribution. In addition, they introduced three algorithms for adding a new block, for proof of interoperability and for minor election. In Algorithm 1 (adding a new block), the transaction process is implemented. The algorithm indicates that

TABLE 10.2

Challenges and Issues for Blockchain-Based Data Sharing Framework in Healthcare

Title	Author	Year	Type
MediBchain: A blockchain-based privacy-preserving platform for healthcare data	Kevin Peterson, Rammohan Deeduvanu, Pradip Kanjamala, and Kelly Boles	2016	Conference
A blockchain-based approach to health information exchange networks	Abdullah Al Omar, Mohammad Shahriar Rahman, Anirban Basu, and Shinsaku Kiyomoto	2017	Journal
BBDS: Blockchain-based data sharing for electronic medical records in cloud environments	Qi Xia, Emmanuel Boateng Sifah, Abla Smahi, Sandro Amofa, and Xiaosong Zhang	2017	Journal
The blockchain technology for healthcare: facilitating the transition to patient-driven interoperability	William J. Gordon and Christian Catalini	2018	Journal
A framework for secure and decentralized sharing of medical imaging data via blockchain consensus	Vishal Patel	2018	Journal
BHEEM: A blockchain-based framework for securing electronic health records	Jayneel Vora, Anand Nayyar, Sudeep Tan-war, Sudhanshu Tyagi, Neeraj Kumar, M. S. Obaidat, and Joel J. P. C. Rodrigues	2018	Conference
MedChain: Efficient healthcare data sharing via blockchain	Bingqing Shen, Jingzhi Guo, and Yilong Yang	2019	Journal
Blockchain-based medical records secure storage and medical service framework	Yi Chen, Shuai Ding, Zheng Xu, Handong Zheng, and Shanlin Yang	2019	Journal

only those blocks with minimum one transaction will be required to sign. The authors introduced the second algorithm for the proof of interoperability, compared with the stored and allowed profiles. If the information is recognized and matches with the profile, the access is utilized for a validation request to the server. Moreover, the algorithm for minor election (Algorithm 3) is demonstrated, where a random number during the signing of the block is used for minor election as a part of mining.

Omar et al. [27] also proposed a framework for sharing sensitive medical records of healthcare organization. The proposed framework is based on peer-to-peer (P2P) transaction of information based on blockchain technology. The entire blockchain system proposed in this research is based on the idea that the patient requires maximum amount of control in such systems and is thus a patient-centric data sharing mechanism.

Xia et al. [29] introduced a blockchain-based data sharing framework for electronic medical records in cloud environments. The proposal can address access control issues that are associated with private and sensitive medical records stored in the cloud. The framework allows access to such medical records only with invited and verified users based on their identities and cryptographic keys.

Gordon and Catalini [22] conducted a research, where they discussed the interoperability issue in blockchain technology. However, in the healthcare industry, a recent trend of patient-based interoperability has emerged, which is difficult to achieve through the conventional electronic data interchange mechanism for data sharing between hospitals and laboratories. Nevertheless, patient interoperability has resulted in privacy and security concerns due to additional access to the system. This research plays an important role in providing evidence for solving the privacy and security concerns due to the emergence of patient-based interoperability, which is necessary for future patient record databases and data sharing systems to be used in the healthcare industry. For this purpose, five useful mechanisms were exploited [22]: data liquidity, data immutability, data aggregation, digital access rule, and patient identity. This research played a crucial role in the identification and resolution of the barriers associated with patient-based interoperability that was specific to the volume of the data, privacy and security of data, transaction of clinical data, and incentives in system for advocating the benefits of data sharing and patient engagement in systems pertaining to sharing of patient's health records. For this purpose, they offered a generic framework that sought to solve the current issues of institutional-based interoperability in the healthcare sector by incorporating patient-based interoperability through blockchain; this was depicted earlier in Figure 10.2. Moreover, they provided the table for the aforementioned five mechanisms with examples related to the healthcare industry, which is provided earlier (Table 10.3).

Patel [30] developed a framework of data sharing of patient records, specifically for the sharing of radiological medical imaging, which is an important part of medical interventions in the healthcare industry. The problems associated with the sharing of information between different departments in a healthcare organization are attempted to be resolved with this cross-domain image sharing framework, with several actors participating as the node in the blockchain network proposed for data sharing. This framework successfully eliminates third-party access to health

TABLE 10.3

Blockchain Mechanisms Related to the Healthcare Industry

Features of Blockchain	Applications in Patient-Based Interoperability
Data liquidity	Data liquidity involves providing the right information to the right person at the right time. This may involve highly sensitive data such as allergies to certain medications and chemical compounds, which can be available on the public blockchain for the correct personnel to avail.
Data immutability	Data immutability through the implementation of the blockchain technology that protects the data from any losses and provides transparent access for auditing the information.
Data aggregation	The blockchain technology that links numerous healthcare institutions that a patient may visit at different times provides data aggregation opportunities to gain a complete picture of the medical record of a patient for effective medical interventions.
Digital access rules	Digital access rule involves the use of smart contracts for accessing their clinical data stored either on-chain or off-chain. For instance, authorizing patients' information for a specific amount of time.
Patient identity	A patient identity, which is useful in storing and accessing information, can be managed by patients through a patient key (public key) based on public key infrastructure. This ensures the healthcare institutions that the authorized personnel, i.e., patient, is actually adding the information and is reliable and trustworthy.

records. The block addition involves the utilization of the cryptographic hash of the previous blocks to ensure data integrity and order of blocks.

Vora et al. [31] proposed another framework pertaining to the electronic data interchange systems based on blockchain technology. The main aim of this framework was to strike a balance between privacy and accessibility to electronic health records to improve the feasibility of blockchain-based systems for the healthcare industry. The authors also provided an architecture of blockchain-based data sharing systems based on Ethereum blockchain.

Shen et al. [32] considered the issues pertaining to the already-established frameworks and data sharing mechanism in the healthcare industry. The efficiency issues and other security and privacy concerns were investigated, and a robust blockchain-based data sharing system framework named 'Medchain' was proposed, which involves the following: the amalgamation of blockchain, the structured P2P networking technique, and the digest chain to overcome the efficiency issues. The framework is based on the session-based healthcare sharing mechanism that attempts to provide higher security assurance to the healthcare institutions and patients. The blockchain structure of the 'Medchain' framework is based on the digest chain system.

Recently, Chen et al. [33] conducted a research, where they focused attention on the development of a system for storing patients' records based on cloud storage option and blockchain technology. This research paper can be used in understanding the basis for improving the storage capabilities of systems based on blockchain system. The framework implemented in this paper is for blockchain systems that restrict absolute power to any of the single actor in the network and eliminate the need for any third party.

10.4 THE KEY FINDINGS OF BLOCKCHAIN-BASED TECHNOLOGIES

This section provides some vital information related to blockchain technology in the healthcare sector. First, the advantages and disadvantages of blockchain technology in data storage and transformation application in the healthcare industry are included. Second, the research related to medical data is discussed. Data sharing by different parties and potential loopholes while using blockchain technology are also discussed. Then, the ownership of data in blockchain setup for the healthcare industry is discussed. Lastly, access control systems are also included as part of this study.

10.4.1 ADVANTAGES AND DISADVANTAGES OF BLOCKCHAIN-BASED TECHNOLOGIES

10.4.1.1 Advantages

According to Gordon and Catalini [22], blockchain offers five main advantages, which make it a better alternative than traditional electronic data interchange systems, including the key features of data liquidity, data immutability, data aggregation, digital access rules, and patient identity. Moreover, Gordon and Catalini [22] stated that blockchain offers a high level of transparency, which is not possible with other database systems.

Moreover, immutability offered by blockchain technology has been utilized by all researchers mentioned in the literature survey, which allows the ability to audit the trail of transactions, specifically for cases of malware attacks. This is to ensure a high-level privacy of sensitive information that is attempted to be shared by the authors based on institutional and patient-based interoperability systems (see Peterson et al. [10]).

10.4.1.2 Disadvantages

According to Patel [30], there are some disadvantages, such as the use of a third-party database (cloud systems), which results in the consolidation of data at a single place, making it a central repository for hackers to steal valuable information. Despite all advantages, privacy is still a major drawback of blockchain-assisted technologies.

Patel [30] argues that information of patients can be accessed owing to transparency, which may result in a violation of trust if smart contracts are not placed in the system. Moreover, the public blockchain system has no filtering mechanism to protect unauthorized access to the information, and hackers could be able to extract a plethora of information that could be used for various purposes.

In addition, the complexity of the processes involved in a blockchain system is also a drawback and can cause complications for developing new application interfaces. Therefore, it is important to develop a user-friendly and simple interfaces for patients and doctors to cover the complexity of the processes and make it a highly adaptable data storage and sharing mechanism for the healthcare industry on a large scale [32].

10.4.2 SECURE DATA SHARING

Blockchain is regarded as one of the emerging technologies for sharing data within hospitals and the healthcare industry. The sharing of information through digital platforms can include blockchain technology along with access control framework for data sharing [34]. Access control plays a monumental role in ensuring data access.

Through a blockchain system, all healthcare institutions linked in a blockchain network can share data, following certain requirements, e.g., through a smart contract [19]. This is to ensure safety and privacy in data sharing through blockchain systems. Different healthcare institutions such as hospitals, clinics, pharmaceutical shops, laboratories, and other organizations can share data in an attempt to improve medical interventions for effective care. Most of the literature available on blockchain applications for data sharing are largely based on medical data.

10.4.3 LOOPHOLES WITHIN THE BLOCKCHAIN TECHNOLOGY

Apriorit [35] stated that cybercriminals usually look for loopholes within the blockchain technology to get into it. Based on this study, five blockchain features that are often targeted are as follows:

- Blockchain network
- User wallets
- Smart contracts
- Transaction verification mechanisms
- Mining pools

In an usual attack on a computer network while targeting a blockchain network, hackers intend to bring down a server by consuming all its processing resources with numerous requests, but during another type of attack, a hacker takes control of multiple nodes in the network, which results in the victim being open to other attacks. These attacks are hard to detect and prevent; however, effective countermeasures such as increasing the cost of creating a new identity among others can be used to prevent these attacks.

Other attacks, such as *Eclipse and Routing* attack and *Time Jacking and Transaction Malleability* attack, exploit vulnerabilities in the blockchain network.

In *User Wallet* attack, cybercriminals use a combination of new methods for finding loopholes in cryptographic algorithms, such as *Dictionary and Phishing* attacks to gain access to the user wallet of a customer. In a dictionary attack, i.e., a dictionary of common passwords such as 'passwordx' or 'passwordxxx' used by victims, criminals create a cryptographic hash of these, and are used to find the credentials to the victim's wallets.

With smart contract being one of the most powerful blockchain tool, no question that it is also the most vulnerable in terms of bugs in the source code being exploited, such as *Virtual Machine* vulnerabilities in exploiting runtime environments. For example, vulnerabilities in the source code would lead to risk to the parties who accept the contract and sign them. Unlike a financial transaction in the real world, a blockchain-based transaction is only complete when all the nodes in the network agree to the transaction, and this vulnerability is also exploited by today's criminals.

10.4.4   DATA OWNERSHIP

The literature survey indicates that the data ownership within blockchain-based frameworks that are associated with healthcare industries depends on the fine details of the frameworks. One of the key indicators of the data ownership in blockchain system is data interoperability. The actors with the highest data interoperability in a data sharing framework have the ownership of data.

In the healthcare industry, one of the main reasons for the lack of implementation of blockchain is the data ownership issue. Based on the patient-driven data interoperability framework for data sharing (see Gordon and Catalini [22]), data ownership is necessary for both patients and the institutions. Whereas, based on the framework proposed by Peterson et al. [10], data ownership completely depends on the institutions.

10.4.5   ACCESS CONTROL

Another key feature in the electronic databases is the access of data and information resources, including the management of data access permissions through the networked database management system. In the literature, there are mainly three broader types of access control systems: role-based access control (RBAC) [36], attribute-based access control (ABAC) [19], and context-aware access control (CAAC) (based on both role and attribute) [37]. More details on access control are given in the following subsections.

10.4.5.1   Attribute-Based Access Control

According to Maesa et al. [19], ABAC model allows access to the database through certain attributes that describe features of the resources, subjects, and environments. It utilizes access control policies based on smart contracts to grant access to the database. Examples of the attributes include the identity of the actors, the identity of the company, and so no.

10.4.5.2   Role-Based Access Control

The RBAC [36] is another type of access control in which access to the system's database is issued based on roles. The user-role and role-permission assignment policies are the main building blocks of the RBAC model. A user by playing a role can access relevant data resources. The access of relevant data to specific individual restricts the flow of information to every individual within an organization. This acts as an adequate security and privacy measure for sophisticated systems such as medical record management systems. The traditional mandatory access control and discretionary access control systems are also implemented according to the ABAC and RBAC policies [38]. However, Cruz et al. [38] stated that there is an element of roles' disguise, which can be used to gain unauthorized access to the system, such as those involved in data storing and sharing in the healthcare industry. This can be prevented with the help of the physical certificates such as cards for identification and passwords.

10.4.5.3 Context-Aware Access Control

Recently, Kayes et al. [37] introduced a new access control solution, called the CAAC, based on both role and attribute, which can be effectively used in today's dynamic environments. The CAAC system can be used to manage the security of blockchain systems, in which the access to the system is provided to the individuals based on role and contextual information [37,39].

The CAAC system involves static and dynamic roles and authorization rights among different users in dynamic environments. This type of access control system is beneficial for the healthcare industry. In particular, the CAAC systems [37,40] can be used to improve data sharing and control unauthorized data access based on contextual conditions [41]. Based on the CAAC state of the art, the following requirements should be considered to implement a blockchain-based CAAC: the relationship-specific data access [42], the situation-specific data sharing [43,44], and the data access according to the imprecise contextual conditions [45]. In today's dynamic and pervasive environments, we can integrate both blockchain and CAAC technologies together to implement more advanced access control systems working toward future implementations of security solutions for data sharing between different parties.

10.5 A BLOCKCHAIN-BASED DATA SHARING FRAMEWORK: GAINS AND OPEN ISSUES

In this section, we first include an overall discussion of different state-of-the-art researches. We then discuss several open research issues related to data sharing. We also highlight the research challenges pertaining to existing access control solutions in the context of data sharing. In addition, we have included several real-world scenarios to realize a new generation of blockchain-based access control for data sharing.

10.5.1 OPEN RESEARCH ISSUES

We identify several open research issues that are not well addressed in the literature while considering privacy, security, and access control challenges.

10.5.1.1 Data Access Through the Blockchain Technology

The authors in the majority of the research papers surveyed in this study agreed on the fact that blockchain can offer better data access and sharing between different parties. Gordon and Catalini [22] considered the Bitcoin-based blockchain as astringent mechanism for data sharing, and consensus through smart contracts is required for restricting the membership. This is also the case for the healthcare sector, apart from the financial institutions. Whereas, Peterson et al. [10] presented the point of view that it depends on other factors such as the access control system preferred for the system. This is also backed by Vora et al. [31]. On the other hand, Patel [30], Chen et al. [33], Omar et al. [27], and Shen et al. [32] considered blockchain-based systems that provide better security on data access control.

The exploitation of the existing roles, attributes, and contexts in databases have already resulted in data breaches and security vulnerabilities, which are causing huge losses to the companies and governments in today's data-driven dynamic environments. Proper access control systems can help in regulating the access of data to certain individuals based on different characteristics. Most common characteristics are attributes, roles, and contexts of a situation. The use of the specific characteristic for providing access to the data based on different scenarios and the access control decisions can be based on organizational policies and legislation. The aforementioned three forms of access control systems can be integrated with blockchain technology for secure data sharing (e.g., for data sharing between different trusted parties within healthcare organization).

10.5.1.2   Data Ownership in the Blockchain Technology

Other than access control, blockchain also can provide better privacy and security measures for data owners. Gordon and Catalini [22], Peterson et al. [10], Patel [30], Omar et al. [27], Vora et al. [31], Chen et al. [33], and Shen et al. [32] considered blockchain technology as pivotal in strengthening data ownership cases of digital assets. Stephen and Alex [46] stated that data ownership in blockchain is more stringent than other available options, especially for the consortium and private blockchain-type system. The high level of trust and transparency fused together with a high sense of data ownership and data access control can make it an attractive option for implementation on a wider scale. However, the limitations currently associated with blockchain technology can create obstacles in its wider-scale implementation.

Dias et al. [47] confirmed blockchain technology as secure in terms of data ownership by stating that it provides data ownership to users, who then allow whether specific information must be shared with others or not.

10.5.1.3   Data Sharing and Interoperability Using
the Blockchain Technology

Collectively, it can be concluded that blockchain technology provides better security for data sharing. Gordon and Catalini [22] reported that the patient-driven interoperability can be achieved through blockchain technology; however, it also can impose new challenges for privacy and data sharing.

Peterson et al. [10], Patel [30], Omar et al. [27], Vora et al. [31], Chen et al. [33], and Shen et al. [32] considered blockchain technology as a valuable addition in providing advanced security to the data sharing mechanism. In addition to the previously stated arguments, Gaetani et al. [48] also supported by arguments that blockchain technology has emerged as a new technology that can provide better security in data sharing owing to its high transparency.

This might be helpful in tracking down the cyberattacks, owing to its ability to provide substantial information for audit. Solanki [49] believed that blockchain provides more secure option in terms of data sharing, owing to the high interaction with the RBAC and CAAC systems. Such an integration of blockchain and access control can help to provide a secure transaction of data and access to specific individuals in an organization.

10.5.1.4 Data Breaches in Healthcare

Esposito et al. [24] indicated that data breaches in the healthcare sector are widely observed. This can lead to the occurrence of different incidents, including disclosure of patient data, loss of credentials, malware, and others. According to Kostkova et al. [50], personal information of patients is a valuable asset for healthcare sector and is also highly sensitive. According to the Health and Human Service breach report, approximately 15 million health records have been hacked or accessed in the course of data breaching recently. According to the reports of the Office of the Australian Information Commissioners, it is identified that over 10 million patients are affected by Australian data breach, in which private health information of patients is one of the most affected sectors in the entire country.

Kim et al. [51] proclaimed that healthcare records of patients are characterized as business record and property of patients; therefore, it is crucial for healthcare providers and organizations to maintain the confidentiality of patient records. Moreover, the process of documentation, sharing, and storing the healthcare data should be executed with the assurance of authentication and taking into consideration other ethical aspects. Although the use of digital platforms and advanced technologies as a blockchain for sharing patient information can enhance the integration of advanced technologies in the healthcare sector. However, privacy, confidentiality, security, integrity are some of the issues to be considered when using the blockchain for data sharing.

10.5.2 The Proposed Blockchain-Based Data Sharing Framework for Healthcare

We present a new generation of access control system for data sharing between different parties. We integrate access control and blockchain technologies together to provide a secure platform.

Emphasizing on the review of the literature and the objectives of the study, including different aspects and implications that are taken into consideration for proposing, designing, and implementing the data sharing framework for healthcare with blockchain technology, we demonstrate a high-level and general data sharing framework for healthcare institute based on blockchain technology in Figure 10.3.

The illustration in Figure 10.3 is a simplistic representation of blockchain-based framework specifically designed for storing and sharing of medical health records.

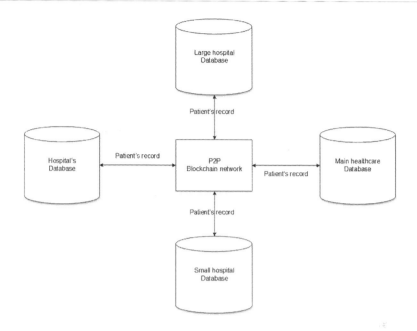

FIGURE 10.3   A blockchain-based data sharing framework for healthcare.

In addition, the healthcare system is designed considering the interaction of various healthcare organizations with the central database, which can be accessed.

The main components in the proposed frameworks include a database for health-care partners, such as clinics, hospitals, and so on. These partners are the main users of this healthcare system powered by blockchain technology. The users either create new information or retrieve the already-existing information from healthcare data-base. All these databases can be linked together with the help of blockchain technology assisted by super peers that can provide P2P interactions with external parties connected in a blockchain network. The blockchain technology for this system can be of any type, i.e., consortium or public.

However, the most favorable type of blockchain-based framework for sharing data among different healthcare partners, which can be accessed by other parties, can be either consortium or public blockchain. Whereas, the clinical database is the local data storage facility of healthcare organizations. The information can later be shared on the main healthcare database, which can be city-, district-, or country-based, depending on the scope of the project. This database will ideally be a cloud-based storage option that allows storage of large amount of data in a convenient manner.

The proposed framework is inspired from the one proposed by Shen et al. [32]. The flow of information for generating new patients' records involves the integration of blockchain technology into the local database, which is then transferred to the main database through the blockchain P2P network. The information stored in the main database is immutable and will be available for further audit. Moreover, the framework requires immutable information that is stored into a relevant database based on blockchain-assisted system.

The following are some advantages of our proposed blockchain-based data sharing framework in the healthcare:

- All information recorded in the blockchain node will be available to the entire network of connected nodes. Thus, all stakeholders can use it following their respective authorities.
- When the doctor writes a prescription, the hospital's pharmacy department will first read it, and then, the stock management department will manage whether backorder is needed to add medical supplies. Meanwhile, in other places, the distributors should update the needs of medicines in the areas that are being reached.
- The pharmaceutical companies will ensure the transparency of the data as a way to manage the associated risk. They can observe and analyze the possibility of fraud.
- From the regulator's point of view, the Ministry of Health can analyze and monitor the possibility of deviations by health service providers such as hospitals and healthcare professionals (e.g., doctors) against excessive prescription.

Overall, the innate characteristics of the proposed blockchain framework can serve and establish a secure channel for data sharing in the healthcare sector.

10.6 CONCLUSION AND FUTURE RESEARCH DIRECTIONS

This literature review provides a key overview of the existing blockchain technologies and relevant concepts that resulted in the generation of a new data sharing framework. The key research related to blockchain technologies for data sharing in the healthcare industry is discussed. The information pertaining to the existing blockchain technologies and algorithms is discussed. In addition, the advantages and disadvantages of blockchain technology, secure data sharing and data ownership mechanisms, and access control systems have been discussed. All this information would result in the achievement of the objective of the research and in the development of a new blockchain-based data sharing framework capable of being used in the healthcare organization.

One possible future direction that can be adopted by future researchers can be implementation of blockchain-based data storage mechanism for management of data. While blockchain-based frameworks are open to cyberattackers with sophisticated attack mechanisms, a large portion of these attacks can be prevented by creating awareness through professional blockchain experts.

REFERENCES

1. Carson, B., Romanelli, G., Walsh, P., Zhumaev, A.: *Blockchain Beyond the Hype: What is the Strategic Business Value.* McKinsey & Company, New York, USA, (2018).
2. Mettler, M.: Blockchain technology in healthcare: The revolution starts here. In: *2016 IEEE 18th International Conference on e-Health Networking, Applications and Services (Healthcom),* IEEE (2016) 1–3.

3. Chowdhury, M.J.M., Colman, A., Kabir, M.A., Han, J., Sarda, P.: Blockchain as a notarization service for data sharing with personal data store. In: *Trust-Com/BigDataSE 2018*, IEEE (2018) 1330–1335.
4. Berryhill, J.: New opsi guide to blockchain in the public sector—Observatory of public sector innovation observatory of public sector innovation, https://oecd-opsi.org/new-opsi-guide-to-blockchain-in-the-public-sector/, 17 July 2019.
5. Bennett, K.M.: Healthtech: How blockchain can simplify healthcare compliance. *Washington and Lee Journal of Civil Rights and Social Just* **25** (2018) 287.
6. Tang, M., Alazab, M., Luo, Y.: Big data for cybersecurity: Vulnerability disclosure trends and dependencies. *IEEE Transactions on Big Data* (2017).
7. Tang, M., Alazab, M., Luo, Y., Donlon, M.: Disclosure of cyber security vulnerabilities: Time series modelling. *International Journal of Electronic Security and Digital Forensics* **10**(3) (2018) 255–275.
8. Linn, L.A., Koo, M.B.: Blockchain for health data and its potential use in health it and health care related research. In: *ONC/NIST Use of Blockchain for Health-care and Research Workshop*. Gaithersburg, Maryland: ONC/NIST. (2016) 1–10.
9. Taylor, P.J., Dargahi, T., Dehghantanha, A., Parizi, R.M., Choo, K.K.R.: A systematic literature review of blockchain cyber security. *Digital Communications and Networks* in press.
10. Peterson, K., Deeduvanu, R., Kanjamala, P., Boles, K.: A blockchain-based approach to health information exchange networks. **10**(9) (2016) e003800.
11. Angraal, S., Krumholz, H.M., Schulz, W.L.: Blockchain technology: Applications in health care. *Circulation: Cardiovascular Quality and Outcomes* **10**(9) (2017) e003800.
12. Kikitamara, S., van Eekelen, M., Doomernik, D.I.J.P.: Digital identity management on blockchain for open model energy system. *Unpublished Masters Thesis-Information Science* (2017).
13. Hölbl, M., Kompara, M., Kamišalić, A., Nemec Zlatolas, L.: A systematic review of the use of blockchain in healthcare. *Symmetry* **10**(10) (2018) 470.
14. McGhin, T., Choo, K.K.R., Liu, C.Z., He, D.: Blockchain in healthcare applications: Research challenges and opportunities. *Journal of Network and Computer Applications* **135** (2019) 62–75.
15. Ouaddah, A., Abou Elkalam, A., Ait Ouahman, A.: Fairaccess: A new blockchain-based access control framework for the internet of things. *Security and Communication Networks* **9**(18) (2016) 5943–5964.
16. Buterin, V., et al.: A next-generation smart contract and decentralized application platform, https://github.com/ethereum/wiki/wiki/White-Paper (visited on 10 October 2016) (2014).
17. Ekblaw, A., Azaria, A., Halamka, J.D., Lippman, A.: A case study for blockchain in healthcare: Medrec prototype for electronic health records and medical research data. *Proceedings of IEEE Open & Big Data Conference* **13** (2016) 13.
18. Brodersen, C., Kalis, B., Leong, C., Mitchell, E., Pupo, E., Truscott, A., Accenture, L.: Blockchain: Securing a new health interoperability experience. In: *Accenture LLP*, Accenture, Chicago (2016) 1–10.
19. Maesa, D.D.F., Mori, P., Ricci, L.: A blockchain based approach for the definition of auditable access control systems. *Computers & Security* **84** (2019) 93–119.
20. Shrestha, A.K., Vassileva, J.: Blockchain-based research data sharing framework for incentivizing the data owners. In: *International Conference on Blockchain*, Springer, Cham, Germany (2018) 259–266.
21. Dubovitskaya, A., Xu, Z., Ryu, S., Schumacher, M., Wang, F.: Secure and trustable electronic medical records sharing using blockchain. *AMIA Annual Symposium Proceedings* **2017**, (2017) 650, American Medical Informatics Association.

22. Gordon, W.J., Catalini, C.: Blockchain technology for healthcare: Facilitating the transition to patient-driven interoperability. *Computational and Structural Biotechnology Journal* **16** (2018) 224–230.
23. Abouelmehdi, K., Beni-Hssane, A., Khaloufi, H., Saadi, M.: Big data security and privacy in healthcare: A review. *Procedia Computer Science* **113** (2017) 73–80.
24. Esposito, C., De Santis, A., Tortora, G., Chang, H., Choo, K.K.R.: Blockchain: A panacea for healthcare cloud-based data security and privacy? *IEEE Cloud Computing* **5**(1) (2018) 31–37.
25. Bell, L., Buchanan, W.J., Cameron, J., Lo, O.: Applications of blockchain within healthcare. *Blockchain in Healthcare Today* **1** (2018) 1–7.
26. Meng, W., Tischhauser, E.W., Wang, Q., Wang, Y., Han, J.: When intrusion detection meets blockchain technology: A review. *IEEE Access* **6** (2018) 10179–10188.
27. Al Omar, A., Rahman, M.S., Basu, A., Kiyomoto, S.: Medibchain: A blockchain based privacy preserving platform for healthcare data. *International Conference on Security, Privacy and Anonymity in Computation, Communication and Storage*, Springer (2017) 534–543.
28. Zyskind, G., Nathan, O., et al.: Decentralizing privacy: Using blockchain to protect personal data. *2015 IEEE Security and Privacy Workshops*, IEEE (2015) 180–184.
29. Xia, Q., Sifah, E., Smahi, A., Amofa, S., Zhang, X.: Bbds: Blockchain-based data sharing for electronic medical records in cloud environments. *Information* **8**(2) (2017) 44.
30. Patel, V.: A framework for secure and decentralized sharing of medical imaging data via blockchain consensus. *Health Informatics Journal* **25**(4) (2018) 1398–1411.
31. Vora, J., Nayyar, A., Tanwar, S., Tyagi, S., Kumar, N., Obaidat, M.S., Rodrigues, J.J.: Bheem: A blockchain-based framework for securing electronic health records. *2018 IEEE Globecom Workshops (GC Wkshps)*, IEEE (2018) 1–6.
32. Shen, B., Guo, J., Yang, Y.: Medchain: Efficient healthcare data sharing via blockchain. *Applied Sciences* **9**(6) (2019) 1207.
33. Chen, Y., Ding, S., Xu, Z., Zheng, H., Yang, S.: Blockchain-based medical records secure storage and medical service framework. *Journal of Medical Systems* **43**(1) (2019) 5.
34. Lau, E.: Decoding the hype: Blockchain in healthcare-a software architecture for the provision of a patient summary to overcome interoperability issues. *Master's Thesis* (2018).
35. Berryhill, J.: Blockchain attack vectors: Vulnerabilities of the most secure technology, https://www.apriorit.com/dev-blog/578-blockchain-attack-vectors, 1 November 2018.
36. Sandhu, R.S., Coyne, E.J., Feinstein, H.L., Youman, C.E.: Role-based access control: A multi-dimensional view. *Tenth Annual Computer Security Applications Conference*, IEEE (1994) 54–62.
37. Kayes, A., Rahayu, W., Dillon, T., Chang, E., Han, J.: Context-aware access control with imprecise context characterization for cloud-based data resources. *Future Generation Computer Systems* **93** (2019) 237–255.
38. Cruz, J.P., Kaji, Y., Yanai, N.: Rbac-sc: Role-based access control using smart contract. *IEEE Access* **6** (2018) 12240–12251.
39. Kayes, A., Han, J., Colman, A.: ICAF: A context-aware framework for access control. *ACISP* **7372** (2012) 442–449.
40. Kayes, A., Rahayu, W., Dillon, T.: Critical situation management utilizing iot-based data resources through dynamic contextual role modeling and activation. *Computing* **101**(7) (2018) 743–772.
41. Kayes, A., Han, J., Colman, A.: An ontology-based approach to context-aware access control for software services. *International Conference on Web Information Systems Engineering*, Springer (2013) 410–420.

42. Kayes, A., Han, J., Colman, A., Islam, M.S.: Relboss: A relationship-aware access control framework for software services. *OTM Confederated International Conferences "On the Move to Meaningful Internet Systems"*, Springer (2014) 258–276.
43. Kayes, A., Han, J., Colman, A.: Po-saac: A purpose-oriented situation-aware access control framework for software services. *International Conference on Advanced Information Systems Engineering*, Springer (2014) 58–74.
44. Kayes, A., Han, J., Colman, A.: An ontological framework for situation-aware access control of software services. *Information Systems* **53** (2015) 253–277.
45. Kayes, A., Rahayu, W., Dillon, T., Chang, E., Han, J.: Context-aware access control with imprecise context characterization through a combined fuzzy logic and ontology-based approach. *OTM Confederated International Conferences "On the Move to Meaningful Internet Systems"*, Springer (2017) 132–153.
46. Stephen, R., Alex, A.: A review on blockchain security. *IOP Conference Series: Materials Science and Engineering* **396**, IOP Publishing (2018) 012030.
47. Dias, J.P., Ferreira, H.S., Martins, Â.: A blockchain-based scheme for access control in e-health scenarios. *International Conference on Soft Computing and Pattern Recognition*, Springer (2018) 238–247.
48. Gaetani, E., Aniello, L., Baldoni, R., Lombardi, F., Margheri, A., Sassone, V.: Blockchain-based database to ensure data integrity in cloud computing environments. https://eprints.soton.ac.uk/411996/,%20University%20of%20Southampton,%20UK. 2017.
49. Solanki, N., Huang, Y., Yen, I.L., Bastani, F., Zhang, Y.: Resource and role hierarchy based access control for resourceful systems. *2018 IEEE 42nd Annual Computer Software and Applications Conference (COMPSAC)* **2**, IEEE (2018) 480–486.
50. Kostkova, P., Brewer, H., de Lusignan, S., Fottrell, E., Goldacre, B., Hart, G., Koczan, P., et al.: Who owns the data? open data for healthcare. *Frontiers in Public Health* **4** (2016) 7.
51. Kim, K.K., Joseph, J.G., Ohno-Machado, L.: Comparison of consumers views on electronic data sharing for healthcare and research. *Journal of the American Medical Informatics Association* **22**(4) (2015) 821–830.

11 Secure Anti-Counterfeiting Pharmaceuticals Supply Chain System Using Composable Non-Fungible Tokens

Ahmad Sghaier Omar and Otman Basir

CONTENTS

11.1 INTRODUCTION

The pharmaceutical industry has one of the most complex supply chain systems, where it includes different stakeholders, starting with the manufacturers and ending at the pharmacy store and with many oversight bodies involved. The security of supply chain in pharmaceuticals is considered more important than in many other industries, where a breach in the supply chain of pharmaceuticals can cause failure in delivering the required health service, which will have severe and direct impact on patients' health and life.

A prominent issue affecting the pharmaceutical industry is drug counterfeiting. The market value of counterfeit, substandard, and gray market medicines is estimated to account for up to $200 billion per year [1]. In sub-Saharan Africa, the World Health Organization (WHO) estimates that around 116,000 people die yearly due to ineffective malaria medication [2]. The counterfeit and substandard medicines are also contributing to hundreds of millions of extra costs in healthcare systems, owing to the failure to treat patients right at the first time.

The two main reasons for drug counterfeiting are the high margin that can be gained and also the loose supply chain system in pharmaceutical industry. A drug bottle or container will change ownership from manufacturer to wholesaler, distributor, and then pharmacist, before it reaches the patient. The issue of tracking and verifying a genuine product becomes more difficult once it reaches the retailer and pharmacy and enters into what is called the post supply chain.

In current supply chain systems, fragmented systems exist, and this results in less information to be shared between different stakeholders. For example, in post supply chain, manufacturers have limited or zero knowledge about their products, and a drug recall will usually not reach the end patient directly. Also, regulatory authorities and insurance companies have very limited visibility on the system, where medication adherence becomes very difficult to achieve.

Many industry bodies identify that healthcare supply chain systems have the following five pain points:

- *Visibility*: It pertains to the capability of having global view on products from manufacturing till the end customer.
- *Traceability*: It relates to the capability to monitor products and their associated events, through the supply chain, and metadata associated with any product.
- *Flexibility*: Considering the example of a recall, this pain point addresses how efficient and adaptable a supply chain system is to abrupt events and issues, with the least operational costs.
- *Compliance*: It means to ensure adherence to the standards and policies imposed by regulatory authorities, specifically in relation to traceability and anti-counterfeiting.
- *Governance*: In the case of healthcare supply chain system, with many different stakeholders managing the stakeholder relationship and building the required trust among the involved parties to reduce risks and streamline the process, is a significant hurdle.

To combat these issues, regulatory bodies introduced compliance policies such as the Falsified Medicines Directive (FMD) in the European Union (EU) [3] and the Drug Supply Chain Security Act (DSCSA) in the US [4]. The aim is to build an interoperable electronic system to define a unique identifier for each sealable drug package and enable tracing and tracking of prescription drugs as they are distributed in the supply chain in the US and the EU. These regulations are developed to enhance the capability in fighting drug counterfeiting, stolen products, and drugs manufactured in substandard formula.

Other efforts focus on introducing sensing technologies and the use of the Radio Frequency Identification (RFID) and Near Field Communication (NFC) tags to provide the feature of electronically reading the unique identifiers of each package. The tracing and tracking requirements are streamlined using RFID and NFC tags; however, cloning of these tags can still take place, and counterfeit and substandard products still reach end customers. However, ensuring one global view and boosting the level of trust are still an issue in addition to the lack of interoperability and capability of disseminating events between those systems utilizing different standards.

The authors suggest in this work the use of the blockchain distributed ledger technology, specifically the Ethereum Request for Comment 721 (ERC-721) nonfungible tokens (NFTs) [5], to employ a compatible approach to the DSCSA and FMD regulations and adhere to the requirements of building unique identifiers, providing the capability of tracing and tracking on both single-item level and lot level and also providing visibility among all parties, with high level of trust between parties with no prior trusted relationship.

This chapter is structured as follows. Section 11.2 describes the current status of drug counterfeiting solutions and technologies and the DSCSA and FMD regulations. Section 11.3 introduces the blockchain technology and the ERC-721 standard for tokenization. Section 11.4 describes the details of the proposed solution. Finally, Section 11.5 concludes the work.

11.2 SUPPLY CHAIN IN PHARMACEUTICALS

Supply chain management systems in pharmaceutical industry is one of the most sophisticated and sensitive verticals. It contains different streams and many participants. The chain starts with drug manufacturers that can be brand manufacturers or generic manufacturers, where the latter focus on manufacturing generic compounds that are used by other manufacturers. In pharmaceuticals, manufacturers manage the distribution of drug products from the point of production to the drug wholesalers and, in certain cases, even to dispensers, especially for hospitals.

Another stream in drugs supply chain can include a direct distribution between manufacturers and government agencies, especially of vaccines and drugs falling under certain assistance programs. The last segment in drugs supply chain is called post supply chain, and it is the segment between the retailer (e.g., pharmacy) and the end customer (patient). This segment lacks better tracing and tracking capabilities and has more risk of increase in counterfeit products reaching the end customers.

The pattern of technology use driven by tightly imposed regulations and policies have dominated how supply chain systems are shaped. The most recently developed regulations in the US and the EU are bringing potential implications and introduce the need for smart and intelligent packaging and require increasing use of the Internet and other technologies to meet the requirements of tracing, visibility, and compliance.

11.2.1 DSCSA AND FMD POLICIES

Both DSCSA and FMD mandate that the originators of drugs in the supply chain represented by manufacturers and packagers are required to provide a unique verifiable identifier for each package, and those identifiers are printed as two-dimensional barcode labels and attached to each package and lot [3,4]. Both share many similarities in the type of data needed to build the unique identifier. The DSCSA require the use of the National Drug Code (NDC) that is interchangeable with Global Trade Item Number (GTIN) in the EU FMD. Both also require that each label contains the lot number, the expiry date, and a serial number for each package. The aforementioned data is considered the metadata for each single package.

The FMD regulation takes a step further by introducing the requirement for the dispenser (e.g., a pharmacy) to ensure the verification of use of each sealable package. The FMD and DSCSA also define the set of the business processes that a product could possibly experience throughout the product life cycle based on the GS1 supply chain rules to include all events starting from the time of origin until the drug being dispensed, which require that third-party logistics providers (3PLs) to perform verification and decommissioning activities and store that in the system with high level of trust in performing those operations.

Highlighting those issues and regulatory requirements, the authors suggest a blockchain-based system that offers a viable solution to simplify the logistical process and enable quality control throughout the supply chain. The next section describes the technology and the fit to supply chain regulations. They suggest a system for supply chain members to authenticate drugs as they move from one entity to another.

The proposed decentralized blockchain-based system allows its members to authenticate products and identify and record how entities authenticate products each time to build a complete distribution history, which can help in identifying rogue actors and tighten security throughout the supply chain. The authors view that the system is to be used for offering tracking on custody relating to the record of organizations, entities, and locations that have had physical possession of the drug and tracing of ownership that records the change of drug ownership till the end customer.

11.3 BLOCKCHAIN AND DISTRIBUTED LEDGER TECHNOLOGY

Blockchain is defined as a distributed shared digital ledger for transactions. It employs public key cryptography in forming the identity and pseudoanonymity of all participants and decentralized consensus algorithms to maintain the ledger intact and to verify any transaction. The distributed ledger is made through combining a number of transactions in a block and hash their content with the hash value of the previous block to construct the hash value of the new block. This happens for each newly generated block, except for the genesis block.

Blockchain technology has emerged in the last few years as the power horse for distributed decentralized applications, and it has gained substantial momentum in many industries, including financial services, auditing, supply chain, and Internet of

Things (IoT). Over the past few years, an entire ecosystem of new and many startups and companies has developed different blockchain applications. These applications feature new decentralized platform that provides fast and secure means of handling domain-specific transactions in healthcare, postal service, IoT, digital marketing, supply chain, and others.

11.3.1 ETHEREUM BLOCKCHAIN

Among the widely adopted blockchain platforms is Ethereum, and it is a blockchain architecture with an associated state database, capable of storing programs and their state. These programs are commonly referred to as smart contracts. A smart contract can be deployed by any Ethereum user, and it has a function-based interface or application binary interface. Once deployed, the smart contract can be referenced by its address, which is a cryptographic identifier. To access a smart contract function, a user calls the smart contract function by sending a transaction to its address as the destination and with the data payload of the transaction containing the function signature and input parameters. Calling a function causes the miners of the network to execute the program and update its state. A smart contract can hold and send the native value token Ether and can furthermore call functions of other smart contracts [6].

Ethereum's main feature is to provide a Turing Complete coding system, where theoretically, code can be put with any logic into an Ethereum smart contract, and it will be run by the whole network Ethereum Virtual Machine (EVM). The EVM's computation capabilities are prevented from abuse by allocating a token (Gas) against each computation, so computation power is paid for. The ecosystem of Ethereum blockchain-based solutions is made of the Ethereum network composed of number nodes (can be either public or private).

11.3.2 SMART CONTRACTS AND TOKENIZATION

Smart contracts in Ethereum are implemented in one of the supported languages (Serpent and Solidity) with defined user interface through libraries [7]. Recently, the introduction of smart contracts brought an added value to the blockchain ecosystem, where generation of tokens to augment the transactional process of a system has become a mainstream, and in the years 2017–2018, as the cryptocurrency market witnessed an explosion in the number of new tokens introduced to support applications of energy trading, prediction markets, messaging apps, and many more.

This has been largely attributed to the standardized and well-defined ERC-20 token standard, authored by Fabian Vogelsteller and Vitalik Buterin in 2015 [8]. In addition to ERC20 tokens, which are considered fungible (interchangeable) tokens, NFTs also started to become a main asset exchanged on blockchain platforms, based on the ERC-721 token standard [5]. That includes examples of game cards and other tradable collectible assets such as CryptoKitties, Decentraland, and DotLicense [9]. The main difference between these two types of tokens is summarized by the fact that ERC-20 tokens are the class of identical interchangeable tokens, more of a fiat currency example, while ERC-721 NFT is the class of unique non-interchangeable tokens. The main feature of NFTs is that they represent owner-ship over digital or physical assets, which include a diverse list of assets such as real estate, unique artwork, virtual collectables, unique pictures of kittens, and collect-able cards. This makes NFTs distinguishable, and their ownership is trackable on individual basis. The NFTs also provide the capability to associate metadata to each unique token for identification purposes.

The authors suggest that the features that NFTs offer can establish the verifiable immutability and authenticity required in addition to other features such as building unique and related identifiers on both the drug package and lot levels. The NFTs also provide simple means for transfer of ownership, revocation, and metadata rep-resentation. Those features are well mapped to previously listed drug supply chain processes.

11.3.3 BLOCKCHAIN MATCH TO SUPPLY CHAIN REGULATIONS

One of the main features of blockchain is its immutability, since the recorded trans-actions are irreversible and permanent. For example, the change in the balance of an account is not done through updating a balance field; rather, each new transaction, combined with other transactions, is used to form a block that will be validated and distributed as well as linked to the previous block.

Immutability ensures that written transactions and data are unchangeable and boost the trust level among network participants, even without prior knowledge of each other. Another feature is the provenance feature, where an item can be traced to its very first origin. This provides a very powerful tool for auditing and the capabil-ity of tracing drug to even identify the original compounds used in manufacturing.

11.3.4 BLOCKCHAIN USAGE IN SUPPLY CHAIN

The authors surveyed the use of blockchain to enable supply chain applications, which have received significant attention from many small and big companies to employ blockchain in enhancing supply chain processes of tracing and tracking and also in combating the distribution of fake and counterfeit products. Significant proj-ects include IBM and Walmart partnership in the project called Food Trust network, which connects participants across the food supply chain through a permissioned, permanent, and shared record of food system data [10]. In logistics, IBM and Maersk also partnered to launch a freight network that digitizes and tracks shipment transac-tions worldwide, with two major shipping companies joining a few months ago [11]. Other companies are building blockchain-based supply chain solutions for luxury items, such as the latest announcement by the fashion giant LVMH to build a prov-enance platform for its brands such as Luis Vuitton and Christian Dior [12].

A few other startups are also building general-usage supply chain, tracing and tracking and anti-counterfeiting solutions. The list includes Verisart, Provenance, and VeChain [13–15]. Many of these solutions focus on art and luxury items, and there is a limited evidence of the existence of solutions targeting pharmaceuticals. To the best of the authors' knowledge, the only hint in the industry to the use of block-chain for drugs supply chain is the MediLedger project led by the drug giant Pfizer

TABLE 11.1

Blockchain and NFT Match to Drug Supply Chain Policies

Feature	DSCSA	FMD	Blockchain
Tracking	Item and lot level	Item and lot level	Composable NFTs
Unique identifier	NDC, lot number, expiry date, serial number	GTIN, lot number, expiry date, serial number	Token metadata
Events	Drug manufacturing, purchase, dispensing	Custom	NFT change of ownership and other events records
Data perseverance	Required	Required	Immutability
Origin Tracing	Required	Required	Provenance
Trust level	High	High	In-built features of immutability and provenance

and implemented by a California startup, Chronicled Inc. [16], using JP Morgan's Ethereum-variant platform (Quorum) to launch a supply chain system for drugs and medicines, with no further implementation details released [17] (Table 11.1).

In this chapter, the authors propose a system that utilizes the blockchain technology and the ERC-721 standard of NFT tokens as a solution for enhancing tracing and tracking in drugs supply chain and combating drug counterfeiting. This work is an extension of the authors' previous work on the use of a decentralized identity management framework for smartphone anti-counterfeiting [18]. The authors here extend the work by introducing, for the first time, based on our best knowledge, the employment of the ERC-721 and NFTs for tokenizing drug sealable packages and providing supply chain processes through extensions to the ERC-721 defined interface. The authors suggest a composable structure for the NFT tokens that can enable tracing on package level, lot level, and even pallet level, with support for the DSCSA and FMD policies.

11.4   COMPOSABLE NFTs FOR DRUG SUPPLY CHAIN

In this section, an overview of the proposed solution will be presented. Particularly, the main system requirements are first highlighted and then a description of the proposed composable NFTs is given. Through the detained description, snippets and pseudocodes of the implemented smart contracts are presented with a description of the procedures used among different stakeholders in the supply chain. Figure 11.1 describes the overall system components.

11.4.1   COMPOSABLE NFTs

ERC-721 is established as the de facto standard for creating NFTs in Ethereum blockchain and other blockchain platforms. The ERC-721 standard is used to represent unique, digital assets that range from collectible digital cards to real estate and art and luxury items. It defines the token-related functions, such as token name or

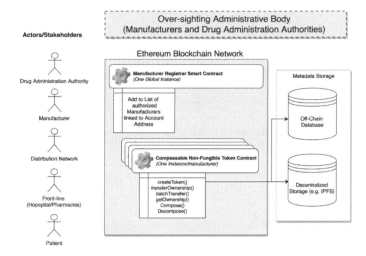

FIGURE 11.1 System components.

identifier, symbol, total supply of tokens, balance of a specific token, ownership of a token, approve of take of ownership, transfer of ownership, and token metadata. It also defines major events related to ownership management, which are transfer and approval.

In our work to evaluate the use of ERC-721 to represent sealable packages and identify each package as NFTs, a major gap was identified, which is related to the policy of requiring that tracing and identification should be achieved at both package level and lot level. An ERC-721 token is mapped to a single item, with no relationship among different tokens. The authors investigated the use of composition of tokens under parent token to represent this relationship.

Based on the research, a promising proposal has been evaluated by the authors, which is the Ethereum Improvement Proposal (EIP-998) for composable NFTs [19]. The EIP-998 is an extension to the ERC-721 to enable the building of composable tokens, such that it is possible to compose lists or trees of simple NFT tokens that have a common ownership relation. The entire composition can be transferred with one transaction by changing the root owner of the composite NFT token.

Before further explaining the different functions by the proposal, we first explain the concepts of NFT token ownership, transfer of ownership, and approve functions.

11.4.1.1   NFT Tokens Ownership

The ERC-721 ownership is determined by an array of token indexes (tokenIds) that is mapped to the owner Ethereum address. The token ownership can be queried against any tokenId and returns the owner Ethereum address. Transfer of ownership is performed by changing the owner address value from the old owner to the new owner, given that certain assertions are validated to ensure that the transfer-of-ownership action is performed by the authorized owner. The ERC-721 also enables adding delegated actions, such that the owner can approve certain addresses to be able to perform transfer of ownership on its behalf. This delegation feature is necessary to enable multiple actors to have access to the tokens and perform the certain supply chain processes assigned. Listing 11.1 shows the details of the ownership functions and how they are implemented.

LISTING 11.1   NFT TOKEN OWNERSHIP FUNCTIONS

```
mapping(uint256 => address) private tokenOwners;
mapping(uint256 => bool) private tokenExists;
// Query Token Ownership
function ownerOf(uint256 _tokenId)
constant returns (address owner) {
    require(tokenExists[_tokenId]);
    return tokenOwners[_tokenId];
}
// Transfer of token ownership
function transfer(address _to, uint256 _tokenId){
    address currentOwner = msg.sender;
    address newOwner = _to;
    // Perform assertion before transfer
    require(tokenExists[_tokenId]);
    require(currentOwner == ownerOf(_tokenId));
    require(currentOwner != newOwner);
    require(newOwner != address(0));
    // Perform transfer actions
    removeFromTokenList(_tokenId);
    balances[oldOwner] -= 1;
    tokenOwners[_tokenId] = newOwner;
    balances[newOwner] += 1;
    // Record transfer event in Blockchain for auditing
    Transfer(oldOwner, newOwner, _tokenId);
}
// Delegate authority of invoking transfer actions
function approve(address _to, uint256 _tokenId){
    // Perform assertion before delegating
    require(msg.sender == ownerOf(_tokenId));
    require(msg.sender != _to);
    // Add delegation
    allowed[msg.sender][_to] = _tokenId;
    // Record approve event for auditing and tracing
    Approval(msg.sender, _to, _tokenId);
}
```

11.4.1.2   Operations of Composable NFTs

Composable NFTs provide a simple way to form composite assets on the Ethereum blockchain; those assets are still utilizing the same concept of ERC-721 but with the capability to link between parent tokens and child tokens. The targeted use case in this work utilizes composable NFTs in tracing and tracking drugs in the supply chain goods that are either composed or decomposed along the supply chain, for example, a sealable package in a lot or a generic compound origin used in a specific drug.

Composable NFTs, according to the EIP-998, can be formed in the top-down or bottom-up approach. For this scenario, we implement a top-down approach, where the parent token is the lot and the child token is the package, with traceability feature from top-down and bottom-up directions. The need for implementing tracing in both directions is introduced to satisfy different supply chain processes.

To highlight the need for tracing in both directions, we look at two examples. A recall event will usually start by the manufacturer and with the main parameter being the lot number. In this case, the lot number is an identifier for the parent token; thus, the recall action should be able to result notifications of owners (distributors/retailers/consumers) of affected packages belonging to that lot. On the other side of the chain, a customer querying about a specific package issues the query based on the child token identifier; yet, for transparency, the customer should be able to see the transfer of ownership happening on the lot level to confirm adherence to certain policies.

Our proposal to use composable NFTs to perform drug supply chain procedures according to the FMD and CSDSA regulations is simplified in a series of actions that we describe and defined hereafter, as well the key requirements for the proper operation of the following proposed approach:

1. Access to token minting and creation is granted only to the legitimate manufacturers that will assume the original ownership of a drug.
2. The manufacturer can create tokens in batches.
3. The smart contracts are able to generate the required randomness for the identifiers.
4. Storing of metadata is done in easily readable and accessible format.
5. Capability to perform operations of composition and decomposition on tokens.
6. The required events by both regulations to enable tracing, tracking, and querying change of ownership and origin shall be recorded on-chain.
7. Visibility on information to all stakeholders and capability of invoking queries.

For the first item, bootstrapping the network is assumed to be performed to ensure that only legitimate manufacturers are able to create tokens and therefore ensure the provenance feature and capability to trace drug item change of ownership since the origin. This requirement is necessary to eliminate non-authorized access and combat counterfeiting. The authors assume the role of a system administrator to handle manufacturers' registration. The possibility of decentralized verification of the legitimacy of manufacturers is not within the scope of this work, but the authors envision the use of a blockchain solution based on Decentralized Identifiers (DIDs) [20], in a similar approach to the Verifiable Organization Network (VON) deployed by the Province of British Columbia in Canada to register business entities [21].

The second requirement is to ensure efficient operation and thereby reduce the cost of token creation, while the third to allow portability where metadata is assigned to each token and can be retrieved using the tokenId. the token metadata representing package or lot attributes are stored off-chain using off-chain database with possibility to choose a decentralized storage such as IPFS. The fourth and requirement is a mandate in the FMD regulation, and it is ensured through the use of a hashing function that digests the metadata provided in addition to a timestamp to generate a random serial number for each token.

To ensure the capability to provide tracing and tracking on package and lot level, the proposed composable NFTs require that the smart contract should provide two functions that perform the function of compositions and decomposition. The first will construct a composite asset from a number of child tokens or amend child tokens to an existing composable NFT and update the parent field of the child tokens with the tokenId of main composable NFT. The decomposition function dismantles a composable NFT and voids the parent token relationship to the child tokens.

To meet the requirements of preserving the events initiated by different stakeholders in the supply chain and to ensure visibility among them, the implemented smart contracts utilize the 'events' feature in Ethereum to register all actions performed by the actors through the supply chain. All these events are stored on-chain for visibility and indexed using tokenId, manufacturer, owner, and a timestamp to allow easy retrieval and querying capability. The overall process of establishing and building the composable NFTs representing the drug packages is as follows:

- An authority is assigned the role of an administrator to approve all registration requests by manufacturer and thus boost the trust level of the network.
- Manufacturers utilize a token generation smart contract for batches of drugs with main parameters required as lot number, CDN/GTIN, expiry date, and manufacturer details (name, country of origin, manufacturing facility, etc). The token generation smart contract generates the serial number required by the regulation, which is used as the NFT tokenId.
- The tokenId is generated using a Keccak hashing function that consumes as input all the supplied resources in addition to the current timestamp to ensure uniqueness and randomness.
- A composition function is called to form a composable token representing a lot.
- On an event of selling or in general transfer of ownership of drugs from one entity to another, a batch transfer function is called.
- In the event of dispensing, a simple transfer of ownership function is called to change the owner parameter of the tokens to the end user.

11.4.2 Details of Smart Contract Implementation

This section details the implemented smart contracts that are developed to fulfill the previously mentioned requirements. The implementation requires two smart contracts: the first is the manufacturer registrar (MR) and the second is the composable NFT manager (CNFT).

11.4.2.1 MR Smart Contract

The MR smart contract implements the functions for managing the information of manufacturers, including the functions of manufacturers enrollment and manufacturer verification. The current implementation assumes a permissioned ledger, where the existence of an oversight body to act as an administrator for the MR smart contract is necessary. The drug administration authority is the default actor that can assume the administrator role.

The administrator role requires the validation of the submitted manufacturer information to ensure that the root of the process is kept intact and boost the trust relationship among all other parties. By ensuring a verifiable and validated identity of the manufacturer, the origin of all drug tokens creation is ensured to be intact and no counterfeiting. The authors do not propose a fully decentralized approach, since the nature of the application requires authority oversight. However, the authors suggest that in case of the existence of a DID and verifiable credential network similar to the VON network, [21], for manufacturers, the MR smart contract can leverage that for validating manufacturers' registration requests.

Algorithm 1: Manufacturer Smart Contract

Input: Manufacturer Information and Ethereum Address, Admin EA
Result: Manufacturer Ethereum Address (*EA*) Added to Authorized List *L*
procedure MRCONTRACTCREATION(AdminEA)

> *Owner* ⇐ *AdminEA*;

procedure ENROLLMANUFACTURER(Manufacturer Info) Manufacturer submit enroll request;
if *information provided complete* **then**
> **if** *Admin Approval* **then**
>> *L* [*L, EA*];
>> Event (*EA, Name, Timestamp*);
>
> **else**
>> Ignore;
>
> **end**

else
> Ignore;

end

Algorithm 1 shows the pseudocode of the MR smart contract: the smart contract includes the owner variable, which is assigned to the administrator, where, upon invoking the smart contract creation, the owner variable is assigned to the administrator Ethereum address. A manufacturer submits an enrollment request, including the parameters such as manufacturer name, country, license number, and Ethereum address. The manufacturer enrollment process requires a validation step by the administrator to approve the request and commit the manufacturer Ethereum address in the list of authorized manufacturers. Listing 11.2 is a snippet of the MR smart contract that shows the main variables and data structures used.

**LISTING 11.2   MANUFACTURER REGISTRAR SMART
CONTRACT VARIABLES**

```
contract MR {
    address admin;
    struct assignee {
        address assignee;
        uint8 privileges;
    }
    struct manufacturer {
        address ea;
        bytes32 name;
        bytes16 country;
        bytes32 license;
        uint8 reputation;
    }
    Constructor {
        admin = msg.sender;
    }
    ...
}
```

11.4.2.2   Composable NFT Smart Contract

The composable tokens CNFT smart contract is created by each manufacturer. The CNFT smart contract is an extended version of the ERC-721 standard, with two main functions added, which perform the functions of (de)composition of the composite assets. The CNFT smart contract also adds main variables such as root-Owner and childTokens to allow traversing the ownership of composable tokens in top-down and bottom-up directions.

The CNFT smart contract, in addition to the (de)composition, functions four other main functions:

- *createToken()*: For a new batch of drugs, the manufacturer invokes this function to generate the NFT tokens for each package and calls the composition function to generate a composite asset for the lot.
- *transferOwnership()*: To support tracing and tracking, the CNFT smart contract extends the transfer function in Listing 11.1, to include the capability to reflect change of ownership of all child tokens as well as the rootOwner. This function should be called for each shipping, selling, or dispensing event in the supply chain management.
- *batchTransfer()*: This function supports transferring batches of packages that belong to the same lot or pallet. The function iterates through the list of tokenIds for all packages need to be transferred and perform the (de) composition steps required to update ownership details.
- *getOwnership()*: This is a query that will traverse the composable NFT to return the single token owner as well as the root owner token.

The composable tokens' CNFT smart contract is created by each manufacturer. The CNFT smart contract is an extended version of the ERC-721 standard, with two main functions added, which perform the functions of (de)composition of composite assest. Algorithm 2 show the NFT batch transfer function. The CNFT smart contract also adds main variables such as rootOwner and childTokens to allow traversing the ownership of composable tokens in top-down and bottom-up directions. Listings 11.3 and 11.4 show the details of the create token function and batch transfer function.

Algorithm 2: NFT Batch Transfer Function

Input: [tokenIds...], fromAddr, toAddr
Result: Updated list of childTokens in original and destination CNFTs
if *fromAddr == requestSender* l*isApproved(requestSender)* **then**
   for $i \leftarrow 0$ **to** *tokenId.length* 1 **do**
      tokens[fromAddr] ⇐ *[tokens[fromAddr], pop(tokenId)]*;
      tokens[toAddr] ⇐ *[tokens[toAddr], tokenId]*;
      tokens[tokenID][toAddr].owner = fromAddr;
      tokens[tokenID][toAddr].rootOwner = fromAddr;
   end
else
   Ignore;
end

LISTING 11.3   CREATE TOKEN FUNCTION

```
function createToken(bytes32 cdn, bytes16 lotNumber,
uint32 expiryDate) public returns
     (uint256) {
        require (msg.sender == adminAddress);
        tokenCount++;
        tokenId = keccak256(cdn, lotNumber, expiryDate,
        block.timestamp);
        tokenIdToTokenOwner[tokenCount] = msg.sender;
        tokenOwnerToTokenCount[msg.sender]++;
        emit (tokenId, cdn, lotNumber, msg.sender);
        return tokenId;
}
```

LISTING 11.4 BATCH TRANSFER FUNCTION

```
function batchTransfer(address fromAddr, address toAddr,
uint256[] tokenIds) external
    {
    // Perform necessary assertions
    require(_to != address(0x0), "ensure that destination
    address is non-zero.");
    require(fromAddr == msg.sender ||
    operatorApproval[fronAddr][msg.sender] == true);

    for (uint256 i = 0; i < tokenIds.length; ++i) {
        uint256 id = tokenIds[i];
        tokens[fromAddr] = tokens[id][fromAddr].sub(id);
        tokens[toAddr] = tokens.add(tokensId[id]);

    }

    // MUST emit event to register that on-chain
    emit TransferBatch(msg.sender, fromAddr, toAddrs,
    tokenIds);

}
```

11.4.2.3 Proof-of-Concept Environment

The proposal implements a proof of a concept for this tool to be used in drugs supply chain traceability systems that adhere to the DSCSA and FMD requirements. The implementation was performed in a testbed, where the smart contracts were deployed on a private Ethereum node with the following specifications: Dell OptiPlex 7010, with Intel Core i5 Quad, 3.20 GHz processor, 4 GB main memory, and 64-bit Windows 7 Professional OS. The proposed tool still requires performing thorough evaluation to discuss questions regarding system's total cost of ownership, scalability, and privacy.

The cost of the system is considered to be affected by the Gas paid for performing each transaction, however that is the case for a public Blockchain. The expected deployment scenario is an enterprise system and a permissioned Blockchain configuration.

11.4.3 LIMITATIONS AND FUTURE WORK

Among the main limitations is the issue of scalability, pertaining to the capability of handling creation of batches of new items. Our proposal tested the creation of 100 tokens in a single transaction; however, further testing is required to assess the trade-off between the number of tokens created in single transaction and the cost associated.

The administration of the network and governance is also a factor that need to be further investigated. This also includes the need to devise a mechanism to boost the network in the initial phase and establish the reputation of the different parties.

Finally, privacy is a main concern, especially when the ownership of the product reaches the end customer. The authors' future work looks at investigating the use of zero-knowledge proof algorithms such as the zk-SNARK algorithm to provide full privacy over the records of ownership.

11.5   CONCLUSION

In this chapter, we present the use of blockchain technology and the NFTs to establish a supply chain tool in the pharmaceutical industry that matches the requirements imposed by the FMD-EU and DSCSA-US regulations. The specifications to implementing the related smart contracts that enable to work as an anti-counterfeiting solution for smart phones are based on the standard ERC-721 NFT definition, with the extension of enabling building top-down composable tokens.

The FMD and DSCSA timeline of full deployment in year 2023 and need for interoperability, combined with the drawbacks of current tracing systems that are fragmented, are addressed in our proposal. The proposed solution provides features of tracing/tracking and ability for building unique identifiers represented by NFT tokens. The proposed use of NFT tokens in the form of composable tokens enables tracing capability in both package and lot level. We demonstrated the ability to perform tracing of drugs from point of production through the distribution channels and at the retailer, with the possibility to extend it to support tracing even on the origin of compounds used.

REFERENCES

1. United States Department of Commerce. "2016 Top Markets Report: Pharmaceuticals." [Online] Available: http://trade.gov/topmarkets/pdf/Pharmaceuticals Executive Summary.pdf.
2. World Health Organization. "1 in 10 medical products in developing countries is substandard or falsified." November 2017 [Online] Available: www.who.int/news-room/detail/28-11-2017-1-in-10-medical-products-in-developing-countries-is- substandard-or-falsified
3. European Parliament and Council. "The Falsified Medicines Directive." [Online] Available: https://ec.europa.eu/health/sites/health/files/files/eudralex/vol-1/dir201162/dir201162en.pdf
4. US Food and Drug Administration. "Drug Supply Chain Security Act." [Online] Available: www.fda.gov/drugs/drug-supply-chain-integrity/drug-supply-chain-security-act-dscsa
5. W. Entriken, D. Shirley, J. Evans and N. Sachs, ERC-721 Non-Fungible Token Standard 2018. [Online] Available: https://github.com/ethereum/EIPs/blob/master/EIPS/eip-721.md, Accessed on: 25 November 2018.
6. V. Buterin. "Ethereum: A next-generation smart contract and decentralized application platform." *Ethereum Foundation*, 2014. [Online] Available: https://github.com/ethereum/wiki/wiki/White-Paper, Accessed on: 5 December 2016.

7. G. Wood. "Ethereum: A secure decentralised generalised transaction ledger." 2014. [Online] Available: http://gavwood.com/paper.pdf, Accessed on: 8 December 2017.

8. F. Vogelsteller and V. Buterin. "ERC 20 Token Standard," 2015. [Online] Available: https://github.com/ethereum/EIPs/blob/master/ EIPS/eip-20.md, Accessed on: 25 November 2018.

9. Non-fungible token (NFT) Market, [Online] Available: https://nonfungible.com. Accessed on: 25 July 2018.

10. IBM Food Trust "IBM Food Trust Expands Blockchain Network to Foster a Safer, More Transparent and Efficient Global Food System." October 2018. [Online] Available: https://newsroom.ibm.com/2018-10-08-IBM-Food-Trust-Expands-Blockchain-Network-to-Foster-a-Safer-More-Transparent-and-Efficient-Global-Food-System-1

11. IBM "TradeLens: How IBM and Maersk Are Sharing Blockchain to Build a Global Trade Platform." November 2018. [Online] Available: www.ibm.com/blogs/think/2018/11/tradelens-how-ibm-and-maersk-are-sharing-blockchain-to-build-a-global-trade-platform/

12. Yahoo Finance "LVMH, ConsenSys, Microsoft announce AURA, to power luxury industry with blockchain tech," May 2019. [Online] Available: https://finance.yahoo.com/news/lvmh-consensys-microsoft-announce-aura-100008984.html

13. Verisart Certify and verify artwork instantly. [Online] Available: https://verisart.com/

14. Provenance Every product has a story. [Online] Available: www.provenance.org/

15. VeChain "The World's Leading Blockchain Application Platform Driven by Enterprise Adoption." VeChain. [Online] Available: www.vechain.com/

16. Linking the physical world to the Blockchain, Chronicled. [Online] Available: www.chronicled.com/

17. MediLedger "Project an Open and Decentralized Network for the Pharmaceutical Supply Chain." [Online] Available: www.mediledger.com/

18. A. Sghaier Omar and O. Basir. "Smart Phone Anti-counterfeiting System Using a Decentralized Identity Management Framework," *CCECE2019: 2019 IEEE Canadian Conference of Electrical and Computer Engineering*, presented in May 2019.

19. M. Lockyer, N. Mudge and J. Schalm. ERC-998 Composable Non-Fungible Token Standard, July 2018. [Online] Available: https://github.com/ethereum/EIPs/blob/master/EIPS/eip-998.md, Accessed on: 18 October 2018.

20. Decentralized Identifiers (DIDs) v0.13. [Online] Available: https://w3c-ccg.github.io/did-spec/, Accessed on: May 2019.

21. Verifiable Organizations Network. [Online] Available: https://vonx.io/

Section IV

*Blockchain for Cybersecurity
and Privacy in Payment Systems*

12 Application of Cryptocurrencies Using Blockchain for E-Commerce Online Payment

Kayode Adewole, Neetesh Saxena, and Saumya Bhadauria

CONTENTS

12.1 INTRODUCTION

E-commerce is conducting business and purchases online over the internet. E-commerce is done worldwide, and new technologies make the transactions much more easy, secure, and sophisticated. There are many online payment methods in e-commerce, such as credit/debit card payment, direct debit payment, electronic funds transfer, electronic wallet payment, smart cards, and cryptocurrency payment (4.1 Electronic Payment Systems [EPS] n.d.). Blockchains and cryptocurrencies are growing areas, and hence, they are being implemented in many applications.

Cryptocurrency is digital money or virtual money that is encrypted using cryptography for security. It is decentralized and is transferred between peers using a public ledger called blockchain. Bitcoin is the first cryptocurrency. Blockchain is the main ledger that records and saves all activities on a cryptocurrency, along with information about the owners. A cryptocurrency transaction is finalized only when it is added to the blockchain. The payment transactions done with cryptocurrencies through blockchains are secure, as they are decentralized, do not need a third party for transactions, have no risk of exchange, and are faster (Martucci 2018).

Many banks and financial institutions are exploring it in areas such as payments, asset registries, regulatory reporting, Know Your Customer (KYC), digital currency exchange, experimentation with digital security, gifts, and many others. Some banks and financial institutions experimenting with blockchains are ANZ bank, Citibank, BNP Paribas Barclays Bank, EBA, Deutsche Bank, NASDAQ, and DBS bank (Know more about Blockchain: Overview, Technology, Application Areas and Use Cases 2018).

12.1.1 SECURITY ISSUES

Phishing and pharming are the general security issues with e-commerce payments. Security issues related to cryptocurrencies and blockchains are time-jacking attacks,

'>50%' attacks, attacks on wallet software, double-spending attack, and selfish mining. These security attacks require fixations in cryptocurrency and blockchain protocols and architecture, besides external security measures. It also has legal, governance, and data management safety implications. This chapter addresses these security issues and available existing solutions to overcome them (Vyas & Lunagaria 2014).

12.1.2 RESEARCH PROBLEM

The online payment process is being widely used due to the increased use of e-commerce transactions. New technologies such as blockchains are finding their way as a payment medium in online transactions. However, they are under evolution in many applications, since the risks and security concerns in implementation are not yet known. This chapter explores employing blockchains as an online payment source, potential security problems, and the available solutions to overcome them. This study helps to locate where problems can arise in blockchain payments and hence look for problematic areas in the future. This study will also benefit from understanding the financial process in online transactions.

The aim of this research is to study the process of using blockchains technology as an online payment medium and to find out the security issues that can arise in such an implementation process. The research objectives are as follows:

- What are the security issues related to online payment process using Blockchains?
- Can the attack be classified?
- Find out the existing solutions for the identified security concerns.

This chapter provides intuitive and comprehensive insights to the basics of cryptocurrency and blockchain technology. It covers all background aspects and the issues related to online payment process (with or without blockchain). Further, in context of online transactions, the security and privacy attributes of blockchain are characterized. At a later stage, the attacks targeting the blockchain are discussed, and their effects with possible defense mechanisms are identified.

12.2 LITERATURE WORK

This section discusses background study, possible security issues with the blockchain, and the existing solutions.

12.2.1 BACKGROUND STUDY

12.2.1.1 Online Payment Process in E-Commerce

Transactions between buyers and sellers in e-commerce comprise request for information, quotation of prices, placement of orders, payment processing, and notifications. All these operations need a high level of confidentiality, authenticity, security, and protection of privacy (Niranjanamurthy & Chahar 2013).

Online payments are not directly processed by shopping sites but generally employ payment gateways. The payment gateways or transaction enablers establish business relationship with financial institutions to accept online payment for their merchant clients. PayPal, Google Checkout, and Authorize.Net are some of the major payment gateways used worldwide (Acosta 2008). Information transaction during payment processing between a customer and the merchant website should be in a secured manner.

Cryptocurrency is a digital or virtual currency created and stored electronically in blockchains. Encryption techniques (cryptography) are used to create funds and regulate and verify the transfer of funds. It is not regulated or controlled by any bank or government and hence is decentralized. Popular cryptocurrencies are Bitcoin, Ethereum, Litecoin, Dash, and Peercoin. Cryptocurrencies have low transaction fees, offer identity protection, and are risk-free for sellers. However, they are volatile due to the fluctuating exchange rates and their newness into the market (What is cryptocurrency – And how can I use it? 2018). Cryptocurrency transactions are recorded in a digital public ledger called blockchain or distributed ledger. Each record or a series of records on the blockchain is called a block. Every user transaction in the network creates a block and is verified by all users of the network, which is then added to the blockchain. A block cannot be changed once verified and added. Those users working to record the transactions are called miners, and they are paid in tokens for the services rendered.

12.2.1.2   Blockchain as an Online Payment Method

12.2.1.2.1   Cryptocurrencies and Blockchain Technology

Cryptocurrencies are digital money that have found their way in many applications, including banking and e-commerce. Blockchain is the building blocks of the master ledger that records cryptocurrency transactions. This section discusses the concepts of blockchain, its architecture, the key elements, its working principle, and the difference between blockchains and traditional databases. Cryptocurrency is digital money or virtual money that is encrypted using cryptography for security. It is decentralized and transferred between peers using a public ledger called blockchain. Cryptocurrencies can be exchanged for fiat currencies in special online markets. They have a variable exchange rate with the world's major currencies such as USD, British Pound, and European Euro. They have only a very finite supply (Martucci 2018).

The blockchain of a cryptocurrency is a master ledger that records and stores all transactions and activities over that currency, along with owner information. Identical copies of blockchain are stored in every node of cryptocurrency's software network run by a group of individuals called miners. The miners pick up transaction records, verify their legitimacy, and generate new blocks by executing cryptographic functions. The blocks are added to the previous blocks in the blockchain and are irreversible. Each cryptocurrency holder has a private key to authenticate their identity and to exchange their units (Jaag & Bach 2016). A blockchain is a distributed ledger formed by all completed transactions of cryptocurrencies in a network. It serves as a single source of truth of a network. A blockchain is composed of a chain of data packages or blocks. A block comprises multiple transactions. The first block is called the genesis block. Besides transactions, each bock consists of the following (Nofer et al. 2017):

- A timestamp
- The hash value of the previous block or the parent – has unique value and changes when blocks in a chain are changed
- A nonce, which is a random number to verify the hash

A blockchain system has a number of nodes, each of which has a local copy of the ledger. The nodes communicate with one another to gain agreement with one another to add a blockchain. The process of gaining this agreement is called consensus. When a chain is added, it is recorded in the ledger in all the nodes, gaining it the name of the distributed ledger. Once a record of a transaction is added in the blockchain, it cannot be changed or removed. This property is called immutability.

The right to perform transactions in a blockchain works on two models, namely permissioned and permissionless models. Users must be enrolled in a blockchain to perform transactions in a permissioned blockchain. Any person can perform transactions in a permissionless blockchain, but they can operate only on their own data (Cloud Customer Architecture for Blockchain 2017). The distributed ledger system helps the blockchain to carry out its tasks, even if a node is broken down. This increases trust in the system. Intermediaries are eliminated in the blockchain architecture, and hence, data security is fostered.

12.2.1.2.2   How Blockchain Works

The blockchain is a shared ledger that stores transaction information in a distributed network of non-trusted peers. The transactions are performed by people in a blockchain through their computers, called nodes. Each block in a blockchain references the previous one and contains data, its own hash, and a hash of the previous block. Hash is a value generated from a string of text, using a mathematical function, and is unique. Though hash algorithm ensures the security of a block and blockchain, a process called proof of work (PoW) is also used to mitigate corruption and enhance security. It is a process of producing data that is hard to produce but easy for others to verify. The miners must complete a PoW or mathematical problem, for a block to be accepted by network participants. On average, performing PoW calculations and adding a new chain to the block take about 10 minutes.

Blockchain wallets are digital wallets where users can store their cryptocurrencies using the unique wallet ID. The wallet is composed of an address, called a public key, and a private key, called the secret. A wallet generates paired public and private keys that ensure the safety of transactions.

Anyone can send a transaction by using the public key to the address of the receiver. The owner of the wallet alone, who has the private key, only can access that transaction. Three principle technologies combine to create a blockchain, namely (1) private key cryptography, (2) a distributed network with a shared ledger, and (3) an incentive for servicing the network's transactions and record keeping. Identity in a blockchain is created by a combination of public and private cryptographic keys. The combination of these keys provides a strong digital signature, leading to strong ownership. The miners perform transactions and create blocks, which are sent to every node. The block is validated using PoW by the nodes and gets added to the blockchain, and ledger is updated. The nodes or miners get rewarded for these activities in the form of cryptocurrencies, which are added to their digital wallet (Bauerle 2018). Payment gateways are also integrated into the transaction process. They scan the blockchain to confirm the transaction.

12.2.1.2.3 Elements of Blockchain

The building blocks of blockchain and the underlying technology behind blockchain transactions show that this is not a single technique but is a combination of cryptography, mathematics, algorithm and economic model, a combination of peer-to-peer (P2P) networks, and application of distributed consensus algorithm forming an integrated multifield infrastructure construction. Blockchain technology is essentially composed of six elements, given as follows (Lin & Liao 2017):

- *Decentralized*: Blockchain does not rely on a centralized node, but the data can be recorded, stored, and updated in a distributed manner.
- *Transparent*: The records and blocks are transparent, making blockchain trustworthy
- *Open source*: Most blockchains are open to everyone. People can check records publicly and use blockchain technologies to create any application.
- *Autonomy*: Nodes are updated by consensus without any user intervention. The trust of safe data transfer and update is placed on the entire system and not just on a single person.
- *Immutable*: All records are reserved forever and cannot be changed unless somebody takes control of more than 51% nodes simultaneously.
- *Anonymity*: Data transfer and transactions can remain anonymous, since only blockchain addresses are needed for access and transfers.

12.2.1.2.4 Characteristics of Blockchain

Blockchain implementations aim for scalability and concurrency and want to ensure no single point of failure. They include pluggable components such as databases and other consensus mechanisms. Their successful implementations come from multilevel confidentiality, privacy through multichannel communication, multiple subledgers, and multiple stakeholders. Blockchains have several characteristics that affect their architecture and implementation (Cloud Customer Architecture for Blockchain 2017):

- *Cryptography*: The trust and validity of blockchain transactions are due to the cryptographic proofs and mathematical computations between various trading partners.
- *Immutability*: Blockchain transactions cannot be deleted or altered.
- *Provence*: The origin of every transaction in a blockchain can be traced.
- *Decentralized computing infrastructure*: Nodes are capable of making independent processing and computational decisions, irrespective of the decisions of their peer nodes.
- *Distributed platform*: This platform handles transactions such as exchanging value, assets, and other entities.
- *Decentralized database*: Each participating party/miner has access to the distributed database at all times, without a central intermediary.
- *Shared and distributed ledger*: The ledgers can be private, public, or semi-private/public. They can be shared among participants with privacy. The ledger entries are time-ordered and have cryptographical and computational architecture.

- *Software development platform*: Blockchain uses the peer-to-peer (P2P) architecture of blockchain-based application programming interface (API)s in their software development platforms. Since the ledger is digital, intelligent, and programmable, contracts could be designed.
- *Peer-to-peer network*: Participating nodes communicate with each other directly, without the need for a central node.
- *Cloud computing*: Cloud computing platforms are used by blockchains. They enable to use large amounts of resources for data storage and can bring flexible and scalable processing resources for data analysis.
- *Wallet*: It is a secured data storage location for user credentials such as user ids, passwords, certificates, and encryption keys.

12.2.1.2.5   Types of Blockchain

Blockchain technologies can be broadly classified into following three types (Lin & Liao 2017):

- *Public blockchain*: A public blockading is an open-ended permission-less network where anyone can participate without permission, execute consensus, and maintain the shared ledger. Everybody can check and verify the transactions in a public blockchain and can also participate in the consensus process. Examples are Bitcoin and Ethereum. Public blockchain has the advantage of being more secure. The disadvantages are low privacy, less eco-friendly, and requirement of huge computational power and energy (How Blockchain Architecture Works? 2018)
- *Consortium blockchain*: This is a hybrid blockchain that is partly private and partly public. The ability to read and write transactions is extended to some nodes, which also control the consensus process. This type of blockchain exhibits properties of the node of authority, can be chosen in advance, data can be open or private, has partnerships such as business-to-business, and can be seen as partly decentralized. Examples are HyperLedger and R3CEV.
- *Private blockchain*: Private blockchain is a permissioned network, which requires an invitation to participate in the network. These networks put a restriction on entry of participants. It operates like a centralized database system that restricts access to users. Examples are Bankchain and Ripple.

12.2.1.2.6   Multi Cryptocurrency Payment Gateway

Cryptocurrency payment gateway is a decentralized payment platform through which users can send and receive payments in multiple cryptocurrencies. The payment gateway reduces the number of intermediaries involved in a transaction. It also aims to increase the use of digital coins. Cryptocurrency payments made through these decentralized payment gateways are much more secure and are less vulnerable to malicious attacks. They also facilitate global transactions in multiple cryptocurrencies between suppliers, distributors, businesses, and customers at a lower cost. Besides payment transactions, some blockchain-based payment gateways, such as ErosCoin, give a whole ecosystem. The payment gateways also aid in making smart contracts. In-chat payment feature and free P2P mass payments are other facilities from ErosCoin (Pauw 2017).

These blockchain payment gateways, for instance, ErosCoin, accept more than 500 types of cryptocurrencies. The other benefits of the gateway are convenience, speed, and cost saving. The payments are completed in 15–20 seconds to anywhere in the world, as against 3–4 days taken by a traditional payment gateway. The multi cryptocurrency acceptance platform eliminates the need for separate applications for various cryptocurrencies (Pauw 2017).

12.2.1.2.7 Difference Between Blockchains and Databases

In a traditional payment system, for instance, in a merchant-bank transaction, the data on a payment is recorded in the bank as well as in the merchant's database. The question that arises here is whether the blockchains have similar or different databases. There are many types of traditional databases such as relational databases, key-value stores, columnar databases, document databases, and graph databases. The databases can be centralized in a single location or can be distributed over many sites and connected by a computer network. The blockchain concept is similar to the distributed database architecture. Distributed database partitions larger information retrieval and divides problems into smaller ones. A user is not aware of the database network topology or database distribution across various nodes. The connected nodes need not be homogenous in a distributed database (Peters & Panayi 2015).

In a distributed database, modifications done at one location are propagated to the various nodes through a 'master-slave' approach. Updates to the master database are propagated to the slaves. There is one problem here – when two copies of the data get modified by different write commands simultaneously. A blockchain can be viewed as such a distributed database that can prevent such issues. A blockchain network will reject a transaction from a node where the balance has already been spent by another node. This is one of the differences between databases and blockchains.

Another difference is that blockchains have the ability to create self-enforcing contracts. Each node can solve a large set of complex problems to add a block to the blockchain, and they themselves act as built-in virtual machines. The traditional databases are only data storage points and not smart contracts (Peters & Panayi 2015).

12.2.1.3 Cryptocurrency Transactions Using Blockchain Payment in E-Commerce

Cryptocurrency adaption has made international transactions easier by minimizing the cost and processing time. To send or receive cryptocurrency, a cryptocurrency wallet is needed. There is also another option of using a point-of-sale (PoS) machine. The merchant account is integrated into the PoS. A cryptocurrency wallet is a software program that stores the public and private keys of users and interacts with various blockchains to send or receive money. Unlike a traditional wallet, this digital wallet does not store money but only the keys or addresses. When a person sends a digital currency, they are signing off ownership of the coins to the recipient's wallet's address. They send the funds to the recipient's public key address. To unlock the sent funds, the private key stored in the recipient's wallet must match with the public address sent by the recipient. If they match, the currency balance in the sender's wallet will decrease and that of the recipient will increase. There is no exchange of real coins. A transaction record or block is created in the blockchain. Software wallets are desktop, online, and hardware (Cryptocurrency Wallet Guide: A Step-By-Step Tutorial 2018).

The steps of sending/receiving cryptocurrency are as follows (How to Send and Receive Cryptocurrency 2018):

- Create a digital wallet.
- Add merchant's public key to the wallet.
- In the wallet, enter the public key of the merchant and the amount to be sent. PoS can be integrated into the merchant'
- At the receiving end, this public key will be matched with the merchant's private key. If they match, the transfer is made.

If the transfer is done in person, it can be done by scanning the QR code from the sender's mobile with the wallet of the receiver, and the transaction is completed.

12.2.1.4   Pros and Cons of Using Blockchain as an Online Payment Source

E-Commerce would like to offer more payment options to customers to attract them to do business with them. The popularity of cryptocurrencies is making them acceptable as one of the payment sources. Many market leaders have started to accept cryptocurrency as payment. Important among them are Microsoft, Sears, Tesla, Shopify and PayPal. In Japan alone, it is estimated that over 250,000 businesses accept Bitcoins (Vivo 2018). Cryptocurrencies have their own benefits and disadvantages.

12.2.1.4.1   Benefits

The benefits of using cryptocurrencies in business are many, some of which are defined hereunder (Abner 2015; Dumitrescu 2017; Vivo 2018):

- *Personal data protection*: The chances of the retailer undergoing cyberattack in a blockchain transaction is very less and hence the risk of losing financial and personal data. The risk happens only when hackers get access to private keys.
- *Lower transaction fees*: The transaction fees of cryptocurrencies are lower than that of credit cards. Transaction $100 with a credit card would cost $3.37, whereas it would cost only $0.61 in a blockchain transaction for the same value, meaning that credit card is 5.5 times costlier. In these transactions, the speed at which users receive money depends on the fees paid. Since the processing power is distributed across the network, the owners make money by charging fees from users to allow their transactions.
- *Faster processing time*: The transactions can take place at a near-instant speed, and hence, there is less waiting time between sales and payment clearance.
- Payment Card Industry (PCI) compliance is not required, as businesses do not carry the costs or responsibilities that come with processing sensitive information from customers, like credit cards.
- The transparency of transaction activities eliminates the need for businesses to produce documents about activities.
- *Protection from chargeback fraud*: Chargeback fraud occurs when a customer makes an online purchase with a credit back and then requests

the issuing bank for a chargeback after receiving the goods. In a traditional payment, since it takes 2–3 days for the payment to go to the merchant, the payment does not reach him for the goods purchased, due to chargeback request from the customer. This type of fraud cannot happen with blockchain payments, as the payment is made immediately.

- *Immune to inflation*: The monetary inflation of cryptocurrencies has been steadily decreasing and will stop when it reaches its maximum limit of 21 million coins.
- *Increase in new customer traffic*: Customers who want to experiment with cryptocurrencies will want to shop with it.
- *More repeat customers*: Owing to the conveniences it offers, the cryptopayments will attract more customers.
- Cryptocurrencies have gained legitimacy on Wall Street owing to investments from major organizations into it, such as Fortress Investment Group, New York Stock Exchange, Pantera, and Goldman Sachs.

12.2.1.4.2 Disadvantages

The disadvantages of cryptocurrencies and blockchains are defined as follows (Abner 2015; Dumitrescu 2017):

- *Volatile market*: Cryptocurrencies market is very volatile, and it can go up and down within a few hours. Transactions have to be done only when their value increases, to avoid losses.
- *Poor security*: Cryptocurrency programmers are not security experts but are from finance and development background. They need a different skill to understand hackers, and hence, security risks arise. Poor security leads to losing files and losing money from the entire wallet.
- *Lack of solid anonymity*: The blockchain transactions and centralized services such as wallets and exchanges are not completely anonymous. Using statistical techniques and pattern analysis, the profiles of at least 60% of blockchain users can be revealed.
- *Prone to scams*: The private key gives access of the wallet to the owner. If it is lost, even the owner cannot open it. Many scams amounting to over 10 million dollars have been reported with cryptocurrency transaction between 2011 and 2014, for example, high-yield investment programs such as Ponzi schemes, mining investment scams, deposits in 'scam wallets', and exchange scams.
- *New cryptocurrencies can obsolete older ones*: New cryptocurrencies are being constantly developed, and they come with new technologies and improvements. Bigger players such as master cards have plans of introducing cryptocurrencies, and when they do so, they will come with a bigger network and improved technology. This leads to a lower market capitalization for other competitors.
- *Trust as a saving point*: People, especially the older generation, are reluctant to use cryptocurrencies as a saving. The computations and complex algorithms also make it difficult for people to understand its working, and hence, they are reluctant to use this as a savings option.

Many of the blockchain features match the needs of online payment infrastructure, namely (Kulkarni 2017):

- *Security*: Distributed processing prevents manipulation of records, thereby preventing fraud and security breach.
- *Processing speed*: Distributed ledger helps to connect all parties for faster processing of payment.
- Traceability
- Global registry in public ledger

Benefits of using blockchain technology in online payments are as follows (Know more about Blockchain: Overview, Technology, Application Areas and Use Cases 2018):

- Each and every record in a blockchain is validated, and hence, payment is secure and reliable.
- All transactions are authorized by miners, and hence, they are immutable and prevented from hacking.
- No central authority is needed for blockchain P2P transactions.
- Decentralized technology and hence is independent of government regulations, making it more flexible.

Challenges in adopting blockchain technology for online payments are as follows (Daisyme 2018; Know more about Blockchain: Overview, Technology, Application Areas and Use Cases 2018):

- *High technology standards*: High standards are needed for security, robustness, and performance of blockchains.
- *Upgrading regulations and legislations*: New legislations have to be defined to integrate blockchains into the financial market infrastructure.
- *Managing operational risk*: Operational risk should be minimized when moving to the new payment system, which will also require that the traditional system is set up as the fallback system.
- *The complexity of technology*: It is difficult for an average person to understand.
- *Huge network size*: Hundreds and thousands of nodes are required for blockchains to work in unison. This makes these systems vulnerable to attack and corruption.

12.2.2 RELATED WORK

12.2.2.1 Major Security Issues in Using Blockchain for Online Payment

12.2.2.1.1 Security Risks

Security risks that can arise in using blockchain for online payment (Vyas & Lunagaria 2014; Distributed Ledger Technology in Payment, Clearing and Settlement 2017) are as follows:

- *Resilience and reliability*: Multiple nodes are provided to provide reliability and continuous operation. However, this can also provide additional entry points for malicious actors, who can compromise the integrity and confidentiality of the ledger.

- Continuous technological advancements can render the current crypto-graphic tools obsolete and ineffective. Integration of distributed ledgers into the existing infrastructure can also lead to security breaches and threats.
- Should be operationally scalable, depending upon requirements.
- Legal framework need not provide settlement finality always.
- Distributed ledgers pose legal risks if a settlement's arrangement is ambiguous.
- Time-jacking attacks, when the attacker posts inaccurate timestamp on a block.
- Online wallets are more prone to distributed denial-of-service (DDoS) attacks.
- '>50%' attack, when a miner or group of users acquire more than 50% of computing power and can self-reverse transactions.
- Double spending, when the attacker makes more than one transaction, using a single coin.
- Selfish mining, where a group of users can obtain revenue more than their mining power.

12.2.2.1.2 Security Threats

As with the other payment methods, blockchain payment systems also have security threats and concerns. The security issues are briefed as follows (Vyas & Lunagaria 2014; Lin & Liao 2017):

- *Attacks on wallet software*: Wallets are used by cryptocurrency customers to manage the currencies owned by them. Online wallets are more vulnerable to security attacks than offline wallets. Hence, they need to be encrypted and backed up off-line. The DDoS attacks are potential threats for online wallets.
- *Time-jacking attacks*: The time counter of a node in the network is altered by the attacker, and this deceived node may accept an alternate blockchain. The consequences are double spending and waste of computational resources.
- *'>50%' attack*: This is one of the major threats to a blockchain network and happens when a user or group of users gets hold of more than 50% of computing power in mining. They do this by getting hold of the 'nonce' value in a block. They can then execute, modify, and self-reverse transactions and prevent the mining of valid blocks.
- *Double spending*: Double-spending attack is the one where an attacker makes more than one transaction with the same coin, resulting in invalidation of the 'honest' transaction and validating the 'fraud' transaction. An attacker makes a transaction with a coin and, simultaneously, another transaction with the same coin is done to another address. By varying the timestamp, the second fraud transaction can be made as a real one. Blockchain peers will not accept two transactions with the same input. They will validate only the first one reaching them, and hence, the fraud transaction will be validated and the original one will not be confirmed.
- *Selfish mining*: It allows a pool of sufficient size to obtain revenue larger than its mining power. The attacking miners will force honest miners to perform wasted computations. The selfish miner will keep their blocks private, will secretly bifurcate their blockchain, and will earn more revenue.

- *Fork problems*: Fork problem is related to decentralized node version agreement when the software upgrades. This is an important problem, as it involves a wide range of blockchain. When a new version of blockchain software is incorporated, consensus rule in nodes also changes. So, there are new nodes as well as old nodes in a blockchain network. Problems arise in getting consensus between old nodes and new nodes during transactions between them. The agreement or consensus between old and new nodes is not compatible.

Hard fork problem occurs when the old node verification requirement is stricter than the new node. Soft fork problem occurs when the new node verification requirement is stricter than the old node (Mosakheil 2018). Besides these, there are many other security threats. A summary of the security threats, the location of their attack or the vectors, and the reason due to which that attack could occur are represented in Table 12.1.

TABLE 12.1

Taxonomy of Blockchain Security Threats

Security Threats	Attack Vectors	Cause
Double-spending threats	Race attack	Transaction verification mechanism
	Finney attack	Transaction verification mechanism
	Vector 76 attack	Transaction verification mechanism
	Alternative history attack	Transaction verification mechanism
	51% attack	Consensus mechanism
Mining/pool threats	Selfish mining/block-discard attack	Consensus mechanism
	Block-withholding attack	Consensus mechanism
	Fork-after-withhold attack	Consensus mechanism
	Bribery attack	Consensus mechanism
	Pool hopping attack	Consensus mechanism
Wallet threats	Vulnerable signature	Elliptic Curve Digital Signature Algorithm (ECDSA) flaws – Poor randomness
	Lack of control in address creation	Public nature of the blockchain
	Collision and pre-image attack	Flaws in ECDSA, Secure Hashing Algorithm 256 (SHA256), and RACE Integrity Primitives Evaluation Message Digest (RIPEMD) 160
	Flawed key generation	Flaws in implementing ECDSA
	Bugs and malware	Client design flaws
Network threats	DDoS attack	External resources, contracts underpriced operations
	Transaction malleability attack	Flaws in blockchain protocols – transaction ID
	Time-jacking attack	Flaws in blockchain protocols – timestamp handling
	Partition routing attack	Flaws in Internet routing – routing manipulations

(Continued)

TABLE 12.1 (*Continued*)
Taxonomy of Blockchain Security Threats

Security Threats	Attack Vectors	Cause
	Delay routing attack	Flaws in Internet routing – routing manipulations
	Sybil attack	Structured P2P network limitation – forge identities
	Eclipse attack	Flaws in blockchain protocols – outgoing connections
	Refund attack	Flaws in BIP70 payment protocol – Bitcoin refund policy
	Balance attack	Consensus Mechanism
	Punitive and feather forking attack	Consensus Mechanism – blacklisting transactions
Smart contacts threats	Vulnerabilities in contracts source code	Program design flaws
	Vulnerabilities in EVM bytecode	Ethereum Virtual Machine (EVM) design flaws
	Vulnerabilities in blockchain	Program design flaws
	Eclipse attack on smart contact blockchain	EVM design flaws
	Low – level attacks	Underprice operations

12.2.2.2 Existing Solutions for Blockchain-Based Payment Systems

Existing resolutions for security issues identified in the earlier section are discussed briefly in this section. The recently developed solutions will be discussed.

12.2.2.2.1 Attack on Wallet Software

A wallet stores the digital credentials of cryptocurrency holdings and allows the user to access and spend them. Software wallet attacks can be in the form of loss of private keys or signature forgeries, leading to loss of digital money. Barber et al. (2012) proposed the idea of 'Super-Wallet' to address the user concern, which is split across multiple computing devices. The super-wallet acts as the user's 'personal bank', where most of the user's coins are stored. Besides this, the user also carries a sub-wallet in the smartphone. User can withdraw small amounts of money from super-wallet into sub-wallet, whenever needed. User can spend money from the smartphone itself and need not go to super-wallet. Even if a smartphone is lost or attacked by malware, only a small amount of money will be lost. The larger amount is still secure in super-wallet and can be spent through a multitude of devices. Constant backup of wallet file helps to overcome accidental loss or data destruction. Wallet backup is done similar to other cryptographic assets, owing to the secrecy. It is also complex due to the continual creation of keys. Another way of protecting a wallet is to encrypt it by using a strong password and replicating the resultant ciphertext. Password-based encryption can be online, offline, or trusted paths (Barber et al. 2012).

12.2.2.2.2 Time-Jacking Attacks

The network time is used to validate new blocks to the blockchain. An attacker announces inaccurate timestamps and alters a node's time counter and deceives it to accept a block from another blockchain instead of a block from its own network. This attack is a theoretical vulnerability. This issue could be overcome by defining acceptable timestamp ranges based on previous block timestamps. Other solutions are as follows (Boverman 2011):

- Using the node's system time for timestamps instead of network time.
- Maximum initial attack window is between 70 and 140 minutes. This is short ened to 30 and 60 minutes, thereby restricting the networks node time to within 30 minutes. This method cannot entirely reduce attacks but can reduce them.
- Blocking untrusted peers and having a secure node can reduce the extent of attack but will not resolve the global time agreement problem.
- Increasing confirmations before accepting a transaction.

12.2.2.2.3 >50% Attacks

51% attack is an attack on the blockchain network by a group of miners controlling more than 50% of a network's mining hash rate. Such an attack is hypothetical and has not known to have occurred. There is a possibility of such attacks happening in the future, even with less than 50% computing power (Vyas & Lunagaria 2014).

12.2.2.2.4 Double Spending

Double spending is signing over the same coin to two users. It is the highest-occurring attack in cryptocurrencies. To prevent double spending of the same coin, cryptocurrencies rely on a hash-based PoW scheme, where users are prevented from double spending through a distributed time-stamping method. Even otherwise, double spending occurs mostly in fast payment scenarios, where payment is done within 30 seconds, whereas it takes nearly 10 minutes to verify a cryptocurrency transaction (Karame et al. 2012).

Karame et al. (2012) discuss three methods of detecting double spending in cryptocurrencies, namely (1) using a 'Listening' period, (2) inserting observers in the network, and (3) forwarding double-spending attempts in the network.

In the first method, a 'listening' period of a few seconds is employed to detect double spending of coins before delivering them. Since every transaction takes a few seconds to propagate to every node in the network, the network checks if any node attempts to double spend the coin that was previously received. The second method is to insert an observer node, which would directly relay all transactions that are received by the nodes. The third method proposes that cryptocurrency peers forward all transactions that try to double spend the same coins in the network.

12.2.2.2.5   Selfish Mining

Selfish mining is possible for any conniving group of miners. Currently, the threshold at which selfish mining is effective is close to zero. The cryptocurrency network is modified using a backward-compatible protocol, to raise this threshold limit to one-fourth, so that when all non-selfish miners adopt it, it will benefit them (Eyal & Sirer 2013).

12.2.2.2.6   Fork Problems

Forking is duplication of a blockchain history when there is a conflict between rules of old and new nodes. The nodes of a blockchain have been programmed to follow that blockchain whose PoW difficulty is the largest. It discards blocks from other forks. The discarded blocks are called orphan blocks. This problem is resolved by collecting transactions on the discarded branches into blocks in the existing branches (Barber et al. 2012).

12.2.2.3   Classification of Blockchain Attacks

The blockchain attacks can be of many types – legal, financial, cyber warfare, Public Relation (PR) attacks to spoil the good name, and hybrid attacks. They are employed to slow down cryptocurrency development, adoption by businesses and common use, and reduce the infrastructure. A tabulation of the attacks is shown in Table 12.2. Though it shows currencies such as Bitcoin, the attacks are applicable to any cryptocurrency (CryptoBullsAdm 2018).

12.2.2.4   Cryptocurrency Policies and Regulations to Make Online Payments

Money transactions are regulated by individual governments, banking authorities, and international bodies to maintain validity and prevent frauds and scams. Since cryptocurrencies are also a form of currency, but digital, they also have to undergo a similar procedure. The efforts on regulation, the involved bodies, and the extent to which they have been able to govern and regulate cryptocurrencies are discussed in this section (Jaag & Bach 2016).

- Cryptocurrencies are hard for the government, as they do not have any central point of access, making it difficult for law enforcement. Since the system is anonymous, money holdings cannot be seized. Accounts cannot be frozen in the decentralized systems, as in traditional banking systems.
- Owing to their decentralized nature, the transactions can be done across borders. Hence, regulations have to be coordinated across countries.
- Institutions and companies offering services related to cryptocurrencies can be regulated, as they have a central point of access. For example, currency exchanges that act as a payment gateway between traditional currencies and cryptocurrencies can be forced to abide by regulations such as anti-money-laundering law.
- The first guidance related to the regulation of these digital money services was issued by the Financial Crimes Enforcement Network (FinCEN) in the USA in March 2013. Individuals who use cryptocurrencies to sell and purchase goods do not fall under FinCEN but only businesses such as cryptocurrency exchanges. Miners and software providers do not fall under this regulation.
- Business license of cryptocurrency activities was issued by New York State Department of Financial Services in August 2015. Several Bitcoin companies stopped their businesses due to these regulations.

TABLE 12.2

Classification of Attacks on Bitcoin

	Possible Attacks on Bitcoin	Probability of Such Attack in the Next 10 years	Possible Damage if the Attack Was Successful	Probability × Damage
Legal attacks	Ban of Bitcoin by a small country	High	Low	Medium
	Legal persecution of a major Bitcoin merchant	High	Low	Medium
	Public persecution of a prominent Bitcoin figure	High	Low	Medium
	Oppressive taxation of Bitcoin by a major power	Medium	Medium	Medium
	A UN/WTO-level legal attack on Bitcoin	Low	High	Medium
	Ban of Bitcoin by several major powers (US, EU, and China)	Low	Medium	Medium
Cyberwarfare	Large-scale attack on Bitcoin merchants	Medium	Medium	Medium
Attacks to slowdown the Bitcoin adoption	Hack of a major Bitcoin merchant	High	Low	Medium
	Mass digital surveillance to steal private keys/de-anonymize users	Medium	High	High
	Large-scale attack targeting Bitcoin users	Medium	Medium	Medium
PR attacks	Influencing the public opinion to associate Bitcoin with crime (drugs, etc.)	High	Low	Medium
	Spreading FUD about Bitcoin in the media	High	Low	Medium
	large-scale leak of user information from a major Bitcoin merchant	High	Low	Medium
	Creation of a competing state-supported crypto	Medium	Medium	Medium

(Continued)

TABLE 12.2 (Continued)
Classification of Attacks on Bitcoin

	Possible Attacks on Bitcoin	Probability of Such Attack in the Next 10 years	Possible Damage if the Attack Was Successful	Probability × Damage
Financial attacks	Pumping funds into a competing centralized crypto o make it the biggest	High	Medium	High
	Large-scale market manipulation to spread FUD about Bitcoin	High	Medium	Medium
Hybrid attacks	Creating a similarity named altcoin to confuse users	High	Low	Medium
	Astroturfing social and political opposition to Bitcoin (r/buttcoin, etc.)	High	Low	Medium
	Gaining control over a major Bitcoin community	Medium	Medium	Medium
	Splitting up a major Bitcoin community	High	Low	Medium
Cyberwarfare	Creating a flood of transactions with the goal of slowing down the network	High	Medium	Medium
	Sybil attack on nodes	High	Low	Medium
	DoS attacks on nodes	High	Low	Medium
	Time-jacking of nodes	High	Low	Medium
	A majority attack by state-sponsored miners	Medium	Medium	Medium
	Using some zero-day exploit of the client code to disturb the network	Low	High	Medium
Attacks to reduce the efficiency of the Bitcoin infrastructure	Using some zero-day exploit in the Bitcoin-related cryptography	Low	High	Medium
	Malicious modification of transactions on the Internet Backbone level	Low	High	Medium

(Continued)

TABLE 12.2 (*Continued*)
Classification of Attacks on Bitcoin

Possible Attacks on Bitcoin	Probability of Such Attack in the Next 10 years	Possible Damage if the Attack Was Successful	Probability × Damage
Hybrid attacks			
Compromising the code with a carefully designed hidden vulnerability	Low	High	Medium
A country-wide filtering of Bitcoin traffic	Medium	High	High
Forcing a major CPU or OS provider to implement relevant vulnerabilities	Medium	High	High
Forcing a major soft-/hardware wallet provider to implement vulnerabilities	Medium	Medium	Medium
Gaining direct control over a major soft-/hardware provider	Medium	Medium	Medium
Attacks to slowdown the bitcoin development			
Hybrid attacks			
Gaining direct control over a major miner by a state-sponsored entity	High	Medium	High
Preventing necessary upgrades from being implemented	High	Medium	High
Manipulating a part of the community into supporting a malicious fork	High	Medium	High
Gaining direct control over an influential dev	Medium	Medium	Medium
Hijacking admin rights in a major code repository	Low	Low	Low
Killing or incapacitating an influential dev	Low	Low	Low

12.2.2.5   Abuses of Blockchain Technology

Blockchain technology is decentralized, anonymous, and distributed and is termed safe from hacking. However, loopholes have been found, and this technology has also been abused. Some of the abuses of blockchain technology are discussed in this section.

12.2.2.5.1   Links to Child Abuse Content

German researchers found that anonymous persons are using Bitcoin's blockchain to store and link to child abuse images. Besides storing financial data, blockchains can also be used to store links and files. A total of 59 files were found to contain images or links to child abuse. Spending blockchain may not require a copy of blockchain, but mining techniques require that it be downloaded. A total of 112 countries trading with cryptocurrencies consider possessing such content as illegal (Claburn 2018).

12.2.2.5.2   Sex, Drugs, and Related Illegal Activities

The anonymity provided by cryptocurrencies has led to its use in the illegal trade of drugs, hacks and thefts, illegal pornography, and even murder-for-hire. There is also the potential to fund terrorism, launder money, and avoid controls. Cryptocurrencies have facilitated the growth of 'darknet' online marketplaces. The FBI recently seized $4 million Bitcoins from one such marketplace named 'Silk road', explaining the enormity of the problem. 'Silk Road' was found to conduct business mostly in drugs and weapons (Foley et al. 2018).

12.2.2.5.3   Tax Evasion

Owing to the anonymous nature of cryptocurrencies, there is the possibility of tax evasion. Some users have also reported the theft of their cryptocurrencies. Major retailers such as Microsoft and Dell are accepting Bitcoin currencies. Bitcoin is used by many parties, and its wide use has eliminated its need to get converted into traditional currency by intermediaries or exchanges and integrate it with the real economy. This lack of intermediaries also helps in tax evasion, since the USA employs only intermediary-based tax-enforcement mechanisms (Ruppert 2017).

12.2.2.5.4   Money Laundering

Cryptocurrencies present the risk of money laundering. They are not linked to a person's identity and only depend on the private key to connect to the wallet or account. There is also no central record-keeping that financial institutions can check. Individuals also need not have to rely on intermediaries for money transfers. All these give advantage to people to transfer a large amount of money to anonymous accounts (Sharma 2018).

12.2.2.5.5   Terrorism

Terrorists evolve tactics to adapt and break the barriers imposed on their activities by security and intelligence forces. They always need funds to support their activities. The volatility and anonymity of cryptocurrencies have made it to be used to fund terrorists. In June 2016, the online propaganda forum of Salafi Jihadist Group Mujahedeen Shura Council, a terrorist group, added the option of donating in 'Bitcoin' in its campaign. This showed that the terrorist group is well equipped to receive cryptocurrencies, convert it to fiat currencies, and use it for buying and selling. Terrorist groups are only at the infant stage of receiving cryptocurrency payment, but this should be curbed at the initial stage itself (Thein 2017).

12.3   RESEARCH METHODOLOGY

Research methodology lays out the systematic plan to conduct research. It describes how the sample, measures, and analysis work together to attain the research objectives. This section explains the method by which research is carried out, the source of research data, data collection methods, and data analysis methods. This research provides an understanding of the application of cryptocurrencies in E-commerce online payment. It proposes to attain this in following two parts.

12.3.1   QUALITATIVE AND QUANTITATIVE RESEARCH

The responses of the general public will be collected through a questionnaire on their understanding of cryptocurrencies, the associated risks on security and privacy, and their view of cryptocurrencies as an investment option. The responses are analyzed quantitatively to find if cryptocurrencies are being favored as a secure payment and investment choice. The security and privacy issues expressed by the public will be studied qualitatively to find resolutions to overcome them from the existing literature. The concerns expressed by the general public on making cryptocurrencies as an investment option are qualitatively analyzed, and resolutions are found from the literature to address them.

12.3.1.1   Qualitative Method

Qualitative data refers to texts, words, and sounds collected from users or from the literature. In this research, data responses from cryptocurrency users are only numerical in nature, and no textual data is collected. Similarly, the secondary literature analysis is conducted on predefined subjects such as security issues in cryptocurrency usage and abuses of blockchain technology. Hence, the qualitative method of data collection is not employed in this research. However, secondary data are qualitatively analyzed to substantiate and counter user responses and to provide responses for research questions on security issues and abuses of the blockchain technology.

12.3.1.2 Quantitative Method

Quantitative data deal with measurable numbers, quantities, and values and are expressed in numerical form. The questionnaire responses are recorded in numerical values. These responses are analyzed using existing literature to arrive at meaningful interpretations and results. The purpose of this research is also to identify trends in the problems faced by cryptocurrency users, who may be new or experienced users.

12.3.2 DATA COLLECTION METHODS

Data collection is the process of gathering data on variables of study in a systematic method to answer defined research questions. Data collection falls into two categories: primary data and secondary data. Primary data is original in nature and is collected for the first time. Primary data is collected through instruments such as surveys, questionnaires, telephone, mail, and direct interviews, where responses of participants are recorded, characterized, and analyzed. Secondary data is the data collected from previously publishes sources such as books, journals, online portals, and others (Data Collection 2017). This research involves the collection of both primary and secondary data.

Primary data collection can be quantitative or qualitative. Quantitative methods are based on calculations, with inputs from closed-ended questions. Qualitative research methods are not based on mathematical calculations but are associated with words, sounds, emotions, and other non-quantifiable elements (Data Collection 2017). The data collection method for this research is based on a closed-ended questionnaire, where responses will be collected in numbers. The questionnaire will also invite comments from the respondents, which are qualitative in nature. Hence, both qualitative and quantitative research methods will be employed for this work.

Besides the questionnaire, this research work also employs secondary data collection in the form of literature, books, journals, and other sources. The literature is on recommendations for using blockchain as an online payment medium and resolutions to overcome security issues due to blockchain payments and attacks. Literature is also collected pertaining to the blockchain technology itself, on improving its application as a payment medium, risks and opportunities for systems using blockchain technology, and preventing abuses of the blockchain technology.

12.3.2.1 Primary Data – Questionnaire

Primary data will be collected through a questionnaire. Sample population that has an understanding of cryptocurrencies is selected to give responses to the questions. The sample size would be 100 numbers.

The questionnaire has questions on the users' willingness to adopt cryptocurrencies as a payment medium and investment and their opinion on threats to cryptocurrencies. The questionnaire has 15 questions. The variables in the questionnaire can be independent or dependent. Since the data are dependent on users' response, they are dependent variables.

The variables employed to collect data in the questionnaire are of different types, such as binary, nominal, ordinal, interval, and ratios. Binary, nominal, and ordinal variables are called categorical variables (Types of Variables – Categorical 2017). A binary variable has two mutually exclusive choices. When the variable has more than two choices to select from, it is called a nominal variable. A variable that has categories that can be put in a logical order is called as an ordinal variable. Interval and ratios are called continuous variables (Types of Variables – Continuous 2017). Interval variable is one where the variable choices are ordered and the level between each category is equal and static. Ratio variable is similar to the interval but has a clear '0' point, and the differences between them are comparable.

12.3.2.2   Secondary Data

Secondary data is collected from storage sources that may or may not be published. The data should be reliable, suitable, and adequate. Secondary data is used in this research for two purposes.

For the first purpose of qualitatively analyzing the questionnaire responses, secondary data from journals, books, web material, public records, and many other sources are used. Primary data is the key resource for this research, and secondary data is used as supplementary, wherever necessary (Methods of data collection – Primary and Secondary data 2016).

The second purpose of employing secondary data is to undertake a theoretical study on resolutions for (1) security problems in using blockchains as a payment source in e-commerce applications, (2) attacks on blockchain networks, and (3) abuses of blockchain technology. This part does not focus on the problems faced by users but focusses on the existing resolutions available to overcome these problems.

12.3.3   Research Sample

This research focusses on issues with cryptocurrencies and corresponding resolutions, and hence, people who have knowledge on cryptocurrencies will be suitable to answer the questionnaire. The sample population is selected with great care. The respondents should have some basic knowledge about cryptocurrencies, blockchains, their applications, security issues, and the future potential of cryptocurrencies. Blockchains are ledgers that record cryptocurrency transactions. Common users are not aware of what goes in blockchains. Hence, questions on blockchains are not included in the questionnaire. People in the age group of 25–40 years will be more interested in learning and experimenting with the latest technologies and applications. Hence, people who are familiar with cryptocurrencies and in the age group of 25–40 years, from various professions, are selected for administering the questionnaire. The sample size of 20–25 numbers is considered appropriate to get enough data for qualitative and quantitative analyses.

12.3.4 Data Analysis

The process of extracting relevant information from the collected data is called data analysis. Data analysis identifies common patterns in data responses and critically analyzes them to attain research objectives. The questionnaire responses are quantitatively analyzed. Secondary literature is qualitatively analyzed to critique questionnaire responses and provide resolutions for cryptocurrency security issues, attacks, and abuses.

Quantitative data analysis is the process of converting data into numerical forms and analyze them for making interpretations. Each question and its responses are analyzed individually to infer results from the numerical responses. Theoretical literature is also used to substantiate the interpretations. No explicit statistical tools are needed for this data analysis.

Qualitative data are non-numerical in form. Qualitative data analysis is not performed on primary data in this research. It is basically opinions and resolutions from existing secondary literature on issues identified from user responses in questionnaire and research objectives. This is essentially the procedure of document studies, where documents are studied to understand issues and resolutions to these issues.

The security and privacy issues expressed by the public will be studied qualitatively to find resolutions to overcome them from existing literature. The concerns expressed by the general public on making cryptocurrencies as an investment option are qualitatively analyzed, and resolutions are found from literature to address them. Besides, resolutions for research questions are also found out.

12.3.5 Ethical Considerations

In this research on cryptocurrencies, a few practices were followed, keeping in mind the end goal to not disregard the moral practices of research. They are as follows:

- Participants of the research are people familiar with cryptocurrencies.
- Full assent ought to be gotten from the exploration members who take up the questionnaire.
- Research scope ought to be straightforward to the members and research's subtle elements ought to be clearly conveyed to them.
- Research questions should be relevant to the participant's field and knowledge, as well as with the scope of research (only cryptocurrencies and blockchains).
- The privacy rights of the participants should be protected.
- Research information from members relates to this research only.
- Research data are confidential and should be protected from manipulation.
- Participants ought to be treated with pride and regard.
- They should have enough time to understand and answer the questionnaire.
- Literature used should be original content and from authenticated resources.
- All sources used in this research are properly referenced to keep away from plagiarism.

12.4   RESEARCH FINDINGS

12.4.1   RESULTS OF DATA ANALYSIS

The data analysis involves two parts – (1) analyzing responses from the questionnaire and finding resolutions for problems reported, and (2) finding resolutions for security issues and blockchain abuses that were identified in the literature review, from secondary literature. The second part is addressed by presenting resolutions from relevant literature on the identified issues, whereas the first part works on questionnaire responses. The outcome of the questionnaire responses is briefed out in this subsection.

The questionnaire was on the practical use of cryptocurrencies, common people's familiarity with them, their concerns about the digital currency, and their opinion on using it as an investment option. The responses were collected from 100 professionals across multiple occupations, in the age group of 15–40 years. The questionnaire consisted of 15 closed-end questions, where the respondent recorded his/her option by selecting one or multiple choices. There were no open-ended questions that invited open responses. Based on the recorded responses, the issues faced by the common public were identified, and their possible resolutions were studied from the secondary literature.

The collected responses show that the majority of the population is aware of cryptocurrencies, but only one-third of them have actually used them. In total, 58% of the respondents would like to try out the digital currencies, but their main reason is to know what it actually is and not because they are confident to use it. More than 70% of them said that they know that cryptocurrencies can be used for online shopping and bill payments, but the only lesser population is aware of other applications. Most of them are hesitant to use cryptocurrencies due to poor security, and lack of data protection is their chief concern in terms of security.

The respondents are skeptical about cryptocurrencies having a long-term future. Nearly 80% of them do not consider cryptocurrencies as an investment option and also would not like to invest in Initial Coin Offering (ICO) from a company. ICO is a process where companies sell their cryptotokens in exchange for Bitcoin and Ethereum to raise funds. Even if the digital currencies are comparable with gold, they are not willing to invest in cryptocurrencies in the present. They are afraid that cryptocurrencies do not have future, are subject to scams, and are illegitimate. These threats and potential resolutions are also studied using literature in the next chapter. Resolutions for questionnaire responses are analyzed and discussed in detail.

12.4.2   ANALYSIS AND DISCUSSION OF QUESTIONNAIRE RESPONSES

The questionnaire on cryptocurrencies had questions on cryptocurrencies related to respondents' awareness of cryptocurrencies, their applications, their concerns on security, and their opinion on using the digital currencies as an investment option.

There were 15 questions answered by 100 respondents. The questions were of multiple-choice type. Depending on the question, one or more options could be selected as answers. Each of the questions is quantitatively analyzed in this section. The responses are critically studied and analyzed, wherever necessary, with secondary literature and are shown in Figure 12.1.

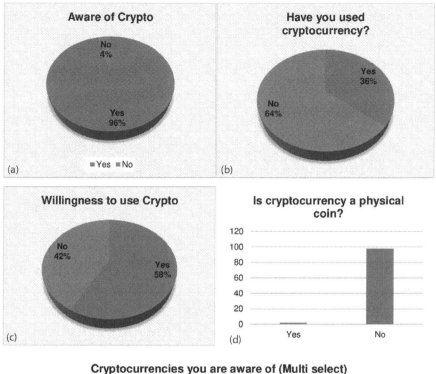

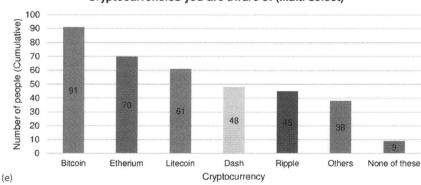

FIGURE 12.1 Questionnaire responses (left-to-right, top-to-bottom) on (a) awareness of cryptocurrencies, (b) Have you used cryptocurrency? (c) Are you willing to use cryptocurrency? (d) Is cryptocurrency a physical coin? (e) What are the cryptocurrencies you are aware of?

(*Continued*)

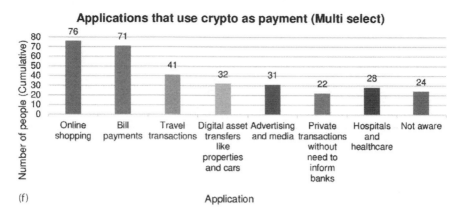

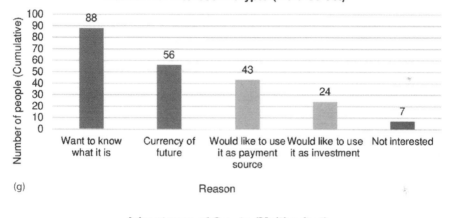

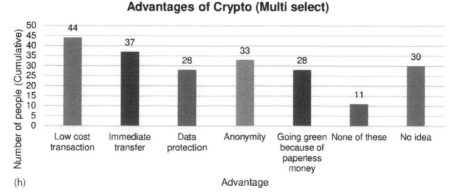

FIGURE 12.1 (Continued) Questionnaire responses (left-to-right, top-to-bottom) on (f) Do you know about the applications where cryptocurrencies can be used as payment? (g) What makes you take an interest in cryptocurrency? (h) What do you think are the advantages of cryptocurrencies? (*Continued*)

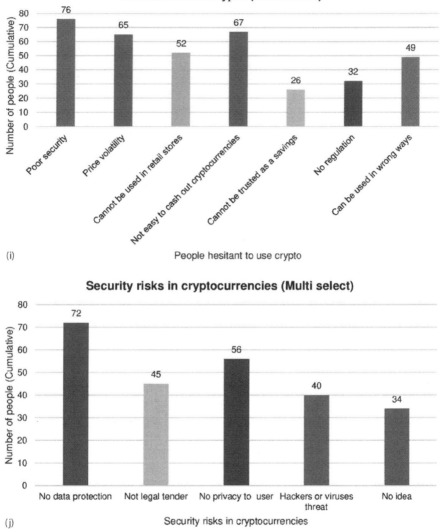

(i)   People hesitant to use crypto

(j)   Security risks in cryptocurrencies

FIGURE 12.1 (Continued) Questionnaire responses (left-to-right, top-to-bottom) on (i) Why are you hesitant to use cryptocurrency? (j) What do you feel are the security risks in cryptocurrencies?

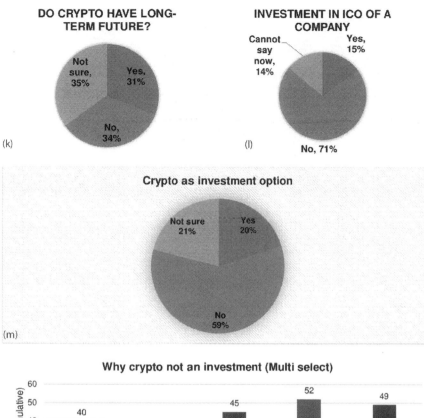

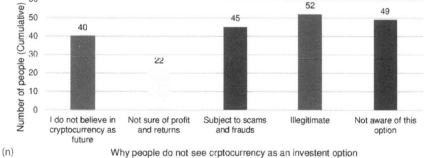

FIGURE 12.1 (Continued) Questionnaire responses (left-to-right, top-to-bottom) on (k) Do you think cryptocurrencies have long-term future?, (l) Will you invest in ICO from a company? (m) Do you consider cryptocurrencies as an investment option? (n) Why do you not see cryptocurrency as an investment option? and

Crytpo compared with gold

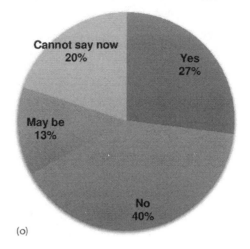

(o)

FIGURE 12.1 (Continued) Questionnaire responses (left-to-right, top-to-bottom) on (o) Cryptocurrencies are more or less compared with gold rather than with money or stock exchange. If it is in par with gold, will you invest in it?

Following is a list of the questions asked to the participants, along with their responses:

Question 1: Are you aware of cryptocurrencies? (1) Yes and (2) No
Response: Response shows that 96% of them are aware of cryptocurrencies. This makes the sample population a proper fit to answer rest of the questions.
Question 2: Have you used cryptocurrency? (1) Yes and (2) No
Response: Response shows that only 36% or about one-third of the sample population has used cryptocurrency. This shows that the currency has not made a good entry into people's desks.
Question 3: Are you willing to use cryptocurrency? (1) Yes and (2) No
Response: 58% have expressed their willingness to use cryptocurrencies, which is a positive sign. This is 22% in addition to those who have used cryptocurrency and hence will be new users.
Question 4: Is cryptocurrency a physical coin? (1) Yes and (2) No
Response: Respondents said that it is a physical coin, showing that they are not aware of the characteristics of cryptocurrency. A total of 98% of the sample population have some basic idea about the digital currency, which is a sign in its favor.
Question 5: What are the cryptocurrencies you are aware of? (Mark all that apply) (1) Bitcoin, (2) Etherium, (3) Litecoin, (4) Dash, (5) Ripple, (6) Others, and (7) None of these.
Response: 96% said that they are aware of cryptocurrencies in question 1. Of them, 91% said that they are aware of Bitcoin. This is a multiselect question to find how any currencies people are aware of. Ethereum and Litecoin are

the next popular currencies, followed by Dash. This response shows that people have made an effort in getting to know the available cryptocurrencies in the market.

Question 6: Do you know about the applications where cryptocurrencies can be used as payment? (Mark all that apply) (1) Online shopping, (2) Bill payments, (3) Travel transactions, (4) Digital asset transfers like properties and cars, (5) Advertising and media, (6) Private transactions without having the need to inform banks, (7) Hospitals and healthcare, and (8) Not aware.

Response: This question is important, as it tests the awareness of people about using cryptocurrencies practically. The survey is interested in knowing if the knowledge of people is just basic or if they have ideas of the applications of the digital currency. If they are aware, they will move on to the next step of using it in real time early in the near future. A total of 76% of people are aware of its use in online shopping and 71% about its use in bill payments. The other applications are known by 30%–40% of the people, which is a good sign to show their awareness. Though they may be motivated to apply it in real-life applications, still it is a long step toward that goal.

Question 7: What makes you take an interest in cryptocurrency? (Mark all that apply) (1) Want to know what it is, (2) Currency of future, (3) Would like to use it as a payment source, (4) Would like to use it as an investment, and (5) Not interested.

Response: This question wants to know the real interest of people toward cryptocurrencies, as this leads to other areas such as payment and investment option. In total, 88% said they want to know what it actually is. Though 36% said they have actually used in question 2 and 52% have expressed their willingness to use it in question 2, the real reason to pursue it lies behind the interest in knowing it. A total of 76% of people are aware of its application in online shopping, but only 46% said here that they will use it as a payment source. So, there are some inhibitions for them to use it, which is found out in the questions that will follow. Only 24% said that they will use it as an investment. Though cryptocurrencies have been touted as the currency of the future, only 56% think so.

Question 8: What do you think are the advantages of cryptocurrencies? (Mark all that apply) (1) Low-cost transaction, (2) Immediate transfer, (3) Data protection, (4) Anonymity, (5) Going green because of paperless money, (6) None of these, and (7) No idea.

Response: The number of responses got toward the advantages of cryptocurrencies is quite surprising. Only people who have used it said that it is a low-cost transaction and gets transferred immediately. The other responses are only about 30%. A total of 30% agreed that that they have no idea at all about the advantages. The responses cannot be straightforward compared with other questions, as they are of a multiselect type, and the same person could have selected more than one option. Hence, no single pattern can be got from the number of responses.

Question 9: Why are you hesitant to use cryptocurrency? (Mark all that apply) (1) Poor security, (2) Price volatility (unstable and depends on demand), (3) Cannot be used in retail stores, (4) Not easy to cash out cryptocurrencies to fiat money, (5) Cannot be trusted as a savings, (6) No regulation, and (7) Can be used in wrong ways such as money laundering, tax evasion, and terrorism.

Response: 76% of people site poor security as the reason for not willing to use cryptocurrency-based payments. The other major reasons are that their application is limited, and they cannot be used as a payment medium in the frequently visited retail stores, price volatility of cryptocurrencies, difficulty in cashing out cryptocurrencies to fiat money, and fear of being used in wrong ways. All these concerns are prevalent from previous experiences. Safety measures have to be improved, as is discussed in security resolutions discussed in Section 5.3. The currency has to be stabilized to reduce volatility. The profound way to avoid abuses of technology is to instigate strong universal regulations, and this lack of regulation is a concern expressed by 32% people for their hesitation in using cryptocurrencies. Steps to reduce these issues will go a long way in encouraging the common public to use cryptocurrencies for online trading.

Question 10: What do you feel are the security risks in cryptocurrencies? (Mark all that apply) (1) No data protection, (2) Not legal tender, (3) Can be traced back and hence no privacy to the user, (4) Hackers or viruses can wipe out Blockchain network, and (5) No idea.

Response: This question is to find what the common people perceive as security risks in using cryptocurrencies. Despite the claim of cryptocurrencies that they are secure and tamperproof, owing to their decentralized nature, there have been many instances of security attacks, leading to questions among the users. It is no wonder that people attributed security concern as the main reason for their hesitation in using cryptocurrencies. A total of 72% of the people say that there is no data protection, and 56% say that there is no privacy to the user, as all transactions are made public. The transparency is a feature boasted by the cryptocurrency as a key feature in its security provision, and this cannot be compromised because the users want privacy. This requires education on users' part. A total of 45% feel that it is not legal render due to not having strict regulations, and 40% say there is a threat of hackers, which is a genuine reason. A total of 34% say that they have no idea, as they could not understand the working and the characteristics of cryptocurrencies. The security concerns expressed will be discussed with real-life examples in Section 5.2, and the security resolutions will be covered in Section 5.3.

Question 11: Do you think cryptocurrencies have a long-term future? (1) Yes, (2) No, and (3) Not sure.

Response: Opinion is divided on whether cryptocurrencies have long-term future. Ironically, only about one-third of the sample say that it has a long-term future; even though 58% are willing to use crypto, 56% say it is the currency of future, and 43% would like to use it as a payment source. About one-third say that it does not have a long-term future, and another one-third say that they are not sure. Hence, through user response, it cannot be deduced how cryptocurrencies will fare in the future.

Question 12: Will you invest in ICO from a company (fundraising where the public can buy cryptocoins similar to shares)? (1) Yes, (2) No, and (3) Cannot say now.

Response: ICOs are sold to investors as tokens to acquire legal tender or other cryptocurrencies. This is considered an investment just like shares. In question 9 on hesitation in adopting cryptocurrencies, 26% of respondents said that it cannot be trusted as savings. In question 10 on security risks, 45% opined that there is no legal tender for cryptocurrencies, and two-thirds of respondents said that they do not believe that cryptocurrencies have a long-term future. At this backdrop, it is only logical that the respondents would not be willing to invest in ICOs, as they do not trust them and have no legal tender. In this question, only 15% are willing to invest in ICOs, whereas the other 85% are either undecided or are not willing to invest in ICOs.

Question 13: Do you consider cryptocurrencies as an investment option? (1) Yes, (2) No, and (3) Not sure.

Response: This is a direct question on whether the respondents will invest in cryptocurrencies, rather than ICO tokens. Again, only 20% said that they will make an invest, whereas the other 80% are either undecided or not willing. People willing to invest in ICO were 15%, whereas those willing in cryptocurrencies were 20%. There is not much difference. Hence, it can be summed up that people do not consider investment in cryptocurrencies as a viable option.

Question 14: Why do you not see cryptocurrency as an investment option? (Mark all that apply) (1) I do not believe in cryptocurrency as future, (2) Not sure of profit and returns, (3) Subject to scams and frauds, (4) Illegitimate, and (5) Not aware of this option.

Response: These questions ask for reasons from people as to why they do not see cryptocurrencies as an investment option. Forty people say that they do not believe in cryptocurrency as future, and 52 see it as illegitimate. Though this may contradict people's opinion on their willingness to use cryptocurrencies, it can be inferred that security risks play a major role in people's decision making. Forty-nine people are not even aware that it can be used as an investment. Awareness of cryptocurrencies, its characteristics, and its applications will play a major role in influencing people's decision on considering it as an investment.

Question 15: Cryptocurrencies are more or less compared with gold rather than with money or stock exchange. If it is in par with gold, will you invest in it? (1) Yes, (2) No, (3) Maybe, and (4) Cannot say now.

Response: Gold has always been considered a safe and reliable investment owing to its characteristics of price appreciation, stabilization, and legal tender. Cryptocurrency developers are proposing this digital currency in par with gold. The questionnaire wanted to know if cryptocurrency can be considered in par with gold, will people make an investment into it.

The responses show that willingness to invest has improved slightly but not considerably. Twenty people say that they cannot say now and would like to see its performance in the future. Hence, it can be safely concluded that efforts from cryptocurrency manufacturers and standard regulations will help to bring people's trust over them and will help in its investment and adoption.

12.4.3   ANALYSIS OF RESULTS

The key concern in online payment is a security issue, with blockchain method being no exception to it. The security issues in blockchain payment methods and earlier solutions for those security issues were studied in the literature review section. Recent solutions on security issues for blockchain-based payments are discussed. This research work presents findings using literature on the following:

- *Security issues arising out of blockchain attacks*: Finding ways of attack and classifying the attacks
- Find out if any blockchain attacks have been successful, and if so, how did they succeed
- Resolutions to overcome security problems while using blockchain as an online payment source in e-commerce applications
- Classification of abuses on blockchain technology
- Preventing abuses of blockchain technology

12.4.3.1   Types and Classification of Blockchain Attacks

The types and classification of blockchain attacks were studied in the literature review chapter. The major types of attacks identified were attacks on cryptocurrency wallet, time-jacking attacks, 51% attack, double-spending attacks, selfish mining, and fork problems. Some of these attacks were said to be hypothetical in the early phases of cryptocurrency foundation but were later found to have occurred in reality. Attacks such as time jacking led to other types of attacks such as double spending. The occurrence of these attacks in real time is discussed in the next subsection.

The attacks on cryptocurrencies can be classified into the following categories:

- Attacks to slowdown cryptocurrency adoption
- Attacks to reduce the efficiency of cryptocurrency infrastructure
- Attacks to slow down the development of cryptocurrencies

Some attacks have a high probability of getting executed, while some do not. The damage could be less or very high (CryptoBullsAdm 2018). At this outset, the blockchain attacks that were successful are studied in the next section.

12.4.3.2   Are Any Blockchain Attacks Successful, and How Did They Succeed?

The characteristics of blockchain technology such as distributed and decentralized consensus, trust-free transactions without any intermediaries, immutability distributed ledger, embedded cryptographic mechanisms, and anonymity were supposed to make it a breakthrough technology for registering, recording, verifying, and managing transactions and hence capable of preventing frauds and attacks (Xu 2016). However, hackers were able to find loopholes in the technology and used them to carry out various types of attacks. The attacks were considered hypothetical, but many of them were executed practically. This section discusses the types of attacks that were carried out successfully and the way in which they succeeded.

12.4.3.2.1   Attack on Wallet Software

Cryptocurrencies are difficult systems to hack, and hence, customers are targeted. Customers are supposed to be more responsible in a decentralized financial services system. Client software exploits such as theft of wallet are one of the client-side attacks employed. The first wallet attack on Bitcoin cryptocurrency was reported in June 2011 by Symantec at the Bitcoin Bubble, which was done by a malware Infostealer.coinbit. When this Trojan is run, it searches for Bitcoin wallets in Windows machines and emails the information to the attacker through a server in Poland. Another similar but much more complicated Trojan DevilRobber targets Mac machines, where it destroys wallet files, collects system information, and collects username and passwords. In this case, even encrypted wallets could not prevent the malware from stealing their wallet contents. A solution to overcome this issue is encrypting wallet private keys with the Advanced Encryption Standard symmetric key algorithm (Latifa et al. 2017).

TABLE 12.3

Malicious Attacks on Blockchain and Their Defensive Measures

Malicious Attack	Definition	Defensive and Preventive Measures
Double spending	An individual makes more than one payment using one body of funds.	The complexity of the mining process
Record hacking	Records in the ledger are modified or fraudulent transactions are inserted into the ledger.	Distributed consensus
51% attack	A single miner node with more computational resources (51%) than the rest of the network nodes dominates the verification and approval of transactions.	Detection techniques; wide adoption of the blockchain technology
Identity theft	The private key of an individual is stolen.	Identify relevant blockchain
Illegal activities	Parties transact illegal goods or commit money laundering.	Detection techniques; laws and regulations
System hacking	The programming codes and systems that implement blockchain are compromised.	Robust systems and advanced intrusion detection methods

12.4.3.2.2 Time Jacking

Time jacking is executed by altering the timestamp of a network node and deceiving it to forming an alternate blockchain. Consequences of this process are an increase in the chances of double spending and wastage of computational resources. This attack is a theoretical vulnerability, and no cases of time-jacking attack have been reported so far (Hypothetical Attacks on Cryptocurrencies 2018). However, three cases of 51% attack in April and May 2018 reported by privacy-centric digital currency Verge (VxG) showed that the attack was executed by altering the timestamp of the target node. A malicious miner was able to mine blocks with spoofed timestamp, deceiving the network to think that the new block was mined an hour ago and added it to the blockchain. The next mined block was also added immediately to the network. The attacker was able to mine one block per second in this manner and accumulated 250,000 VxG in the first attack on April 4, 2018 (Lielacher 2018).

12.4.3.2.3 51% attack

51% of attacks or majority attacks occur when miner(s) control more than 50% of the network's hashing power, so that they can create a fork of the network and make a double-spend attack. The attacking miners can reverse and erase transaction history and can prevent new blocks from confirming. Since 51% attack requires a lot of computing power to execute, they are mostly restricted to smaller coins and blockchain networks. 51% attack is not due to security flaws or vulnerabilities but is a result of the manipulation of technology.

An example of this majority attack is the attack on Krypton (KR) network, using a dual-prolonged approach, which combined majority hashing power with a DDoS to artificially increase the relative hashing power of the attacking party. During this attack, about 21,000 KR was stolen from the KR network, which was sent to Bittrex and exchanged for Bitcoin. The attackers then reversed the transaction by rolling back the blockchain and took away the Bitcoins. Since a majority attack on the Bitcoin network will require large computing power, it was theoretically assumed that such an attack will not take place. However, it was proved wrong when in July 2014, Ghash.io, one of the popular Bitcoin mining pools, exceeded the 51% hashing power of the total bitcoin network. Though they did not make any attack, they showed that majority attacks are possible in a network as big as Bitcoin and Ethereum (Spirkovski 2018).

12.4.3.2.4 Double Spending

Double-spending attack is one where the attacker makes more than one transaction with the same coin. An example of a double-spending attack on Bitcoin Gold (BTG) shows the involvement of a 51% attack, resulting in double spending. BTG lost $17.5 million in this attack on May 16, 2018 (Osborne 2018). BTG found out that double-spending attacks were launched against BTG exchanges rather than individuals. The team reported that an unknown party who had access to large amounts of hash power used 51% attack to carry out 'double spending' attacks. A total of 51% attacks force reorganizations in the blockchain. In double-spending, confirmed transactions are reversed, and the money is spent again. Double spending also prevents miners from mining valid blocks (Osborne 2018).

12.4.3.2.5   Selfish Mining

Selfish mining is one of the major attacks in blockchain networks. Selfish mining is one where a miner successfully mines a block but does not broadcast it to other miners. The miner can keep on adding blocks to his secret block, creating a chain. In a blockchain network, the longest chain is considered as the correct one. Hence, the blocks of other miners with small chains are invalidated and become orphaned. A selfish miner makes transactions with the hidden chain before they are invalidated. In essence, they have never paid for their purchases. Monacoin blockchain was attacked in Japan by trying to send it to exchanges outside of Japan to exchange it with other coins, before the hidden chains are revealed in the blockchain. The malicious miner had about 57% hash rate or computing power to execute selfish mining. The attack was identified on May 18, 2018, but the crypto-coin authorities stated that the miner has been trying to exploit for about 6 months (Gutteridge 2018).

12.4.3.2.6   Fork Problems

A fork is a divergence in a blockchain when part of a network has different views on transaction history than another part of the network. The fork can occur naturally or can be purposefully introduced. Forks can be introduced by miners or cryptocurrency users. Blockchains were very long and were managed by a few people. They were split or forked, so that many people could work on small chains. Large cryptocurrencies split or fork their currencies to generate new ones. For instance, Bitcoin underwent a fork on October 24, 2017, to create a new coin namely BTG cryptocurrency. This was created with the aim of allowing more people to mine BTG with less powerful machines. Expert opinion is divided on whether a fork is good or bad for a blockchain (Kharpal 2017).

12.4.3.3   Resolutions to Overcome Security Problems with Blockchain Online Payment

Some of the major security problems in blockchain networks were discussed in the literature review. Their occurrence in the real world was substantiated with evidence in the previous section. Some latest resolutions to overcome security issues are discussed in this section. Irrespective of the type of attack, general resolutions such as detection technologies, identity for blockchains, regulations, and wide adoption of the technology are some ways of securing blockchains. Also, the recent resolutions for some types of attacks have been discussed.

12.4.3.3.1   General Resolutions

Detection Technologies. Techniques such as machine learning and data-mining algorithms can be used in applications that detect fraud and intrusions in block-chain trading. Supervised machine learning approaches such as deep-learning neural networks, support vector machines, and Bayesian network can help to find outlier behavior (Xu 2016).

Identity Blockchain. Identity is protected by private keys in a blockchain, thereby making it vulnerable to digital identity theft. Loss of key leads to loss of identity in the network. Identity and reputation system in a blockchain network can be built by using measures such as fingerprint records and tracking life events such as birth, schooling, purchasing homes, buying cars, and opening bank accounts.

Regulation. Administrative functions by the government are eliminated in blockchain owing to its decentralized consensus and anonymous characteristics. However, these characteristics can give rise to maliciousness and illegality. Government bodies and lawmakers across the world should cooperatively develop and implement laws, policies, and regulations to govern blockchain applications.

Wide Adoption. Mechanisms and protection technologies associated with blockchain technology can work effectively only when the technology is widely adopted by the majority of the society (Xu 2016).

Various malicious attacks in blockchain and the potential strategies to encounter them are shown in Table 12.3.

12.4.3.3.2 Attack on Wallet Software

Some measures of securing cryptocurrency wallet are as follows (Latifa et al. 2017; Rajput 2018):

- Encryption of private keys of wallet with Advanced Encryption Standard symmetric-key algorithm.
- *Combination of private keys and multisignature security*: Multilevel authentication is operated by users.
- *Hardware wallet storage*: Securing through cold storage by storing the coin values in a hardware wallet. This method does not require an Internet connection and is called an offline method.
- Backing up entire wallet, encrypt backups, using multiple locations to backup wallet data, and regular backup.

12.4.3.3.3 Time Jacking

Attacks like time jacking have had near-zero occurrences, and hence, no new techniques have been developed to overcome that attack. Since it is always associated with double spending, most of the security measures for double spending also holds good for time-jacking attacks.

12.4.3.3.4 51% Attack

Many techniques are in use, and many more are being explored to counter 51% attack. One such technique is delayed PoW (dPoW) mechanism, which stores backups of the blockchain onto the cryptocurrency ledger. This mechanism takes a snapshot of every blockchain to record the balance of each and every address. This snapshot is written into the security services' main chain, whose snapshot is also taken. All this information is saved in a block in the blockchain. This process occurs every 10 minutes. An attacker has to alter the currency as well as security services' network before altering or destroying the backups of blockchain within a window of 10 minutes. There is not enough time to launch a successful 51% attack. This dPoW mechanism acts as two-factor authentication (Pigeon 2018).

12.4.3.3.5   Double Spending

The time between transaction broadcasting and its publication in a block is called zero-confirmation transaction. Pérez-Solà et al. (2017) proposed a model to overcome double-spending attacks occurring on zero-confirmation transactions. Through this model, the attacker will be punished to attempt double spending, as he will face the risk of losing a large number of Bitcoins greater than the amount of double spending. This solution especially benefits fast-payment scenarios.

12.4.3.3.6   Selfish Mining

Selfish mining is the major type of attack, and hence, many solutions are being explored and put in place to prevent and overcome this type of attack. Heilman (2014) proposed a defense mechanism against selfish mining by raising the minimum power required to selfishly mine profitably from 25% to 32%. This solution uses unforgeable timestamps to make sure that a particular block was generated not beyond the timestamp. This model offers incentives to miners of selfish mining cartel to leak information on compromised infrastructure. Hence, the selfish miners will evade from cooperating for selfish mining. Another way of overcoming selfish mining is to increase the threshold level at which selfish mining is effective (Eyal & Sirer 2013). The current threshold is close to zero. The authors proposed a backward-compatible modification that raises the threshold of the cryptocurrency to one-fourth.

12.4.3.3.7   Fork Problems

Forks can be regarded as a necessary evil, as the advantages they bring in are more compared with the negative changes. According to Adams (2018), forks can be considered equal to a software or protocol update to blockchain network. Forks are formed as a result of technical disagreements, to reverse transactions in blockchain, and to add new features or functionality to the network. Forks bring in negative consequences such as infighting and collision between miners and developers of a cryptocurrency. Hence, a thorough understanding of the forking process and the reason for forking are needed to judge if the impact of forks is positive or negative on a cryptocurrency at a given point of time.

12.4.3.3.8   Preventing Abuses on Blockchain Technology

The literature review showed that blockchain technology undergoes abuses such as links to child abuse content, tax evasion, money laundering, links to drugs, financing illegal activities, and terrorism. The ways of preventing these abuses are being explored. One of the major factors that contributes to these types of abuses is a lack of international regulation of cryptocurrencies and blockchain networks.

Different countries look upon cryptocurrencies in a different manner for taxation purpose. For instance, Israel taxes cryptocurrency as an asset, Switzerland as foreign currency, Argentina as subject to income tax, Bulgaria as a financial asset, and so on. This is only one example to show the different perspectives of different countries on cryptocurrencies, making it difficult to regulate under one roof and policy (Global Legal Research Directorate Staff 2018).

To avoid abuses by participants of cryptocurrency, the concerned states must issue regulations on the subject to avoid the negative effects on the economy and international institutions. In the absence of state regulation, the cryptocurrency market has to implement self-regulation on the use of cryptocurrencies to avoid abuses and attacks (Cryptocurrencies: International Regulation and Uniformization of Practices 2017).

12.5 CONCLUSION AND FUTURE WORK

Cryptocurrencies have evolved as an online payment medium over the course of years since their inception as digital currencies. This chapter studied one area of its application, namely e-commerce payment. Similar to traditional online payment, payment with cryptocurrencies also has issues, main among them being security concerns. The major security concerns were identified and discussed in the literature review. Resolutions to overcome security concerns were studied using literature and presented as results of the study.

The research employed a questionnaire on cryptocurrencies to know the extent to which people are willing to use it and the reasons for their unwillingness. The results showed that security concerns and digital currencies not being legal tender are the main reasons for people's hesitation in adopting cryptocurrencies for applications. The resolution for abuses of blockchain technology is to have a centralized global regulatory body. Presence of universal governance will subside fears of cryptocurrencies not being legal tender. The fear of illegitimacy holds back people's investments in cryptocurrencies, and a central governance system will help in overcoming people's fears and attract investments.

The responses showed security issues as the main reason for users' unwillingness in adopting cryptocurrencies as a payment medium. Resolutions are continuously being developed, and employing appropriate ones will help to tide over this problem. Another point of study here is to know if cryptocurrencies have a future, and this was judged by people's views on it being an investment option. This idea of investment did not sit well with the respondents. They quoted security concerns and cryptocurrency not being legal tender as the main reasons for not investing in the digital currency. Security resolutions were discussed earlier in this chapter. Proper regulations and global policies will make cryptocurrencies a reliable and stable currency, so that people will not hesitate to use it. This idea has also been discussed in resolutions to overcome abuses of blockchain.

This research work has studied the security attacks and abuses on cryptocurrencies. The major security issues were discussed, and resolutions were found only for those issues. Besides these attacks, there are many other security issues. All these attacks and abuses could be studied as a separate research subject. Similarly, an extensive study of cryptocurrency resolution is another area of research.

REFERENCES

"*4.1 Electronic Payment Systems (EPS)*". n.d. Available from: http://ocw.metu.edu.tr/pluginfile. php/354/mod_resource/content/0/Lecture_4.pdf.

Abner, B. 2015. The pros and cons of using bitcoin for payments. *The Business Journals*. Available from: www.bizjournals.com/bizjournals/how-to/technology/2015/08/the-pros-and-cons-of-using-bitcoin-for-payments.html [9 July 2018].

Acosta, K.K. 2008. *Online Payment Process, E-Business technologies*. Available from: https://webuser.hs-furtwangen.de/~heindl/ebte-08-ss-Online-Payment-Process-Kathleen.pdf.

Adams, C. 2018. *Everything You Need to Know About Cryptocurrency Forks*. Available from: www.investinBlockchain.com/cryptocurrency-forks.

Barber, S., Boyen, X., Shi, E., & Uzun, E. 2012. Bitter to better-how to make bitcoin a better currency. *Lecture Notes in Computer Science*, 7397, 399–414, Springer-Verlag. Available from: https://eprints.qut.edu.au/69169/1/Boyen_accepted_draft.pdf.

Bauerle, N. 2018. *How Does Blockchain Technology Work?* Available from: www.coindesk.com/information/how-does-Blockchain-technology-work/ [9 July 2018].

Boverman, A. 2011. *Timejacking & Bitcoin*. Culubas. Available from: http://culubas.blogspot.com/2011/05/timejacking-bitcoin_802.html.

Claburn, T. 2018. *Bitcoin's Blockchain: Potentially a Hazardous Waste Dump of Child Abuse, malware, etc.* Available from: www.theregister.co.uk/2018/03/19/ability_to_dump_illegal_content_in_bitcoins_Blockchain_puts_participants_in_peril/ [10 July 2018].

"*Cloud Customer Architecture for Blockchain*". 2017. Cloud Standards Customer Council. Available from: www.cloud-council.org/deliverables/CSCC-Cloud-Customer-Architecture-for-Blockchain.pdf.

"*Cryptocurrencies: International Regulation and Uniformization of Practices*". 2017. Available from: www.uncitral.org/pdf/english/congress/Papers_for_Congress/29-DOLES_SILVA-Cryptocurrencies_and_International_Regulation.pdf.

CryptoBullsAdm. 2018. *Classification of Attacks on Bitcoin*. Available from: https://cryptobulls.info/classification-attacks-bitcoin [10 July 2018].

"*Cryptocurrency Wallet Guide: A Step-By-Step Tutorial*". 2018. Available from: https://blockgeeks.com/guides/cryptocurrency-wallet-guide [9 July 2018].

Daisyme, P. 2018. *Issues with Blockchain Security*. Available from: www.business2community.com/tech-gadgets/issues-Blockchain-security-02003488.

"*Data Collection*". 2017. research-methodology.net. Available from: https://research-methodology.net/research-methods/data-collection/ [22 July 2018].

"*Distributed Ledger Technology in Payment, Clearing, and Settlement*". 2017. Bank for International Settlements 2017. Available from: https://www.bis.org/cpmi/publ/d157.pdf.

Dumitrescu, G.C. 2017. *Bitcoin—A Brief Analysis of the Advantages and Disadvantages*. Available from: www.globeco.ro/wp-content/uploads/vol/split/vol_5_no_2/geo_2017_vol5_no2_art_008.pdf.

Eyal, I., & Sirer, E.G. 2013. *Majority Is Not Enough: Bitcoin Mining Is Vulnerable*. Available from: https://arxiv.org/pdf/1311.0243.pdf.

Foley, S., Karlsen, J.R., & Putniņš, T.J. 2018. *Sex, Drugs, and Bitcoin: How Much Illegal Activity Is Financed Through Cryptocurrencies?* Available from: www.law.ox.ac.uk/business-law-blog/blog/2018/02/sex-drugs-and-bitcoin-how-much-illegal-activity-financed-through [10 July 2018].

Global Legal Research Directorate Staff. 2018. *Regulation of Cryptocurrency Around the World*. Available from: www.loc.gov/law/help/cryptocurrency/world-survey.php#eu.

Gutteridge, D. 2018. *Japanese Cryptocurrency Monacoin Hit by Selfish Mining Attack*. Available from: www.ccn.com/japanese-cryptocurrency-monacoin-hit-by-selfish-mining-attack.

Heilman, E. 2014. *One Weird Trick to Stop Selfish Miners: Fresh Bitcoins, A Solution for the Honest Miner*. Available from: https://eprint.iacr.org/2014/007.pdf.

"*How Blockchain Architecture Works? Basic Understanding of Blockchain and Its Architecture*." 2018. Zignuts Technolab. Available from: www.zignuts.com/blogs/how-Blockchain-architecture-works-basic-understanding-of-Blockchain-and-its-architecture/ [9 July 2018].

"*How to Send and Receive Cryptocurrency*". 2018. Cryptocurrency Facts. Available from: https://cryptocurrencyfacts.com/how-to-send-and-receive-cryptocurrency [9 July 2018].

"Hypothetical Attacks on Cryptocurrencies". 2018. Blockgeeks. Available from: https://blockgeeks.com/guides/hypothetical-attacks-on-cryptocurrencies.

Jaag, C., & Bach, C. 2016. *Blockchain Technology and Cryptocurrencies: Opportunities for Postal Financial Services*. Swiss Economics Working Paper 0056. Available from: http://cryptecon.org/wp-content/uploads/2016/08/0056JaagBach.pdf.

"Know more about Blockchain: Overview, Technology, Application Areas and Use Cases". 2018. MEDICI. Available from: https://gomedici.com/an-overview-of-Blockchain-technology.

Karame, G.O., Androulaki, E., & Capkun S. 2012. Double-Spending Fast Payments in Bitcoin. In *CCS'12 Proceedings of the 2012 ACM Conference on Computer and Communications Security*, 16–18 October 2012, Raleigh, North Carolina, 906–917. Available from: www.eecis.udel.edu/~ruizhang/CISC859/S17/Paper/p9.pdf.

Kharpal, A. 2017. *Bitcoin Splits Again, Creating a New Cryptocurrency Called Bitcoin Gold that Then Plunged 66%*. CNBC. Available from: www.cnbc.com/2017/10/25/bitcoin-gold-price-plunges-what-is-hard-fork.html.

Kulkarni, A. 2017. *Blockchain; Applications in Payments*. Available from: www.european-paymentscouncil.eu/news-insights/insight/Blockchain-applications-payments.

Latifa, E., Ahemed, E.K.M., Mohamed, E.G., & Omar, A. 2017. Blockchain: Bitcoin Wallet Cryptography Security, Challenges and Countermeasures. *Journal of Internet Banking and Commerce*, 22(3). Available from: www.icommercecentral.com/open-access/Blockchain-bitcoin-wallet-cryptography-security-challenges-and-countermeasures.pdf.

Lielacher, A. 2018. *More 51% Blockchain Attacks Expected*. Available from: https://bravenewcoin.com/news/more-51-Blockchain-attacks-expected.

Lin, I., & Liao, T. 2017. A Survey of Blockchain Security Issues and Challenges. *International Journal of Network Security*, 19(5), 653–659. Available from: https://pdfs.semantic-scholar.org/f61e/db500c023c4c4ef665bd7ed2423170773340.pdf.

Martucci, B. 2018. *What Is Cryptocurrency—How It Works, History & Bitcoin Alternatives*, SparkCharge media, LLC. Available from: www.moneycrashers.com/cryptocurrency-history-bitcoin-alternatives/ [25 May 2018].

"Methods of Data Collection—Primary and Secondary Data". 2016. BBAlmantra. Available from: www.bbamantra.com/methods-of-data-collection-primary-and-secondary-data/ [22 July 2018].

Mosakheil, J.H. 2018. Security Threats Classification in Blockchains. Thesis submitted to: *St. Cloud State University—The Repository at St. Cloud State*. Available from: http://repository.stcloudstate.edu/cgi/viewcontent.cgi?article=1093&context=msia_etds.

Niranjanamurthy, M., & Chahar, D. 2013. The study of E-Commerce Security Issues and Solutions. *International Journal of Advanced Research in Computer and Communication Engineering*, 2(7). Available from: http://www.ijarcce.com/Upload/2013/july/69-o-Niranjanamurthy%20The%20study%20of%20ECommerce%20Security%20Issues%20and%20Solutions.pdf.

Nofer, M., Gomber, P., Hinz, O., & Schiereck, D. 2017. Blockchain. *Business & Information System Engineering*, 59(3), 183–187. Available from: www.cs.unibo.it/~montesi/CBD/Articoli/2017Blockchain.pdf.

Osborne, C. 2018. *Bitcoin Gold Suffers Double Spend Attacks, $17.5 million lost*. ZDNet. Available from: www.zdnet.com/article/bitcoin-gold-hit-with-double-spend-attacks-18-million-lost.

Pauw, C. 2017. *Multi Cryptocurrency Payment Gateway, Explained*. Cointelegraph. Available from: https://cointelegraph.com/explained/multi-cryptocurrency-payment-gateway-explained.

Pérez-Solà, C., Delgado-Segura, S., Navarro-Arribas, G., & Herrera-Joancomartí, J. 2017. *Double-Spending Prevention for Bitcoin Zero-Confirmation Transactions*. Available from: http://eprint.iacr.org/2017/394.

Peters, G.W., & Panayi, E. 2015. *Understanding Modern Banking Ledgers through Blockchain Technologies: Future of Transaction Processing and Smart Contracts on the Internet of Money.* Available from: https://arxiv.org/pdf/1511.05740.pdf.

Pigeon, D. 2018. The Anatomy of a 51% Attack and How Komodo can help Prevent One. Available from: https://komodoplatform.com/51-attack-how-komodo-can-help-prevent-one.

Rajput, M. 2018. *Valuable Steps to Make Your Bitcoin Wallet Safe and Secure.* Available from: www.globalsign.com/en/blog/steps-to-make-your-bitcoin-wallet-safe-and-secure.

Ruppert, P. 2017. Privacy, Tax Evasion, and the Development of Cryptocurrencies. *Georgetown Law Technology Review*, 1(2), 398. Available from: www.georgetownlawtechreview. org/privacy-tax-evasion-and-the-development-of-cryptocurrencies/GLTR-04-2017.

Sharma, T.K. 2018. *How Does Bitcoin Money Laundering Work?* Blockchain Council. Available from: www. Blockchain-council.org/Blockchain/how-bitcoin-money-laundering-works [10 July 2018].

Spirkovski, Z. 2018. *Strength in Numbers: A Brief History of 51% Attacks.* Crypto-News.net. Available from: www.crypto-news.net/strength-in-numbers-a-brief-history-of-51-attacks.

"*Types of Variables—Categorical*". 2017, University of Minnesota, Available from: https:// cyfar.org/types-variables-categorical.

"*Types of Variables—Continuous*". 2017, University of Minnesota, Available from: https:// cyfar.org/types-variables-continued-0.

Thein, A.Z.P. 2017. *Cryptoterrorism: Do Cryptocurrencies Facilitate Terrorism?* marketMogul. Available from: https://themarketmogul.com/cryptoterrorism-far-cryptocurrencies-come-financing-terror/ [10 July 2018].

Vivo, M.D. 2018. *Why and How to Accept Cryptocurrency on Your Website.* Singe Grain. Available from: www.singlegrain.com/Blockchain/why-and-how-to-accept-cryptocurrency-on-your-website/ [9 July 2018].

Vyas, A.A., & Lunagaria, M. 2014. Security Concerns and Issues for Bitcoin. *International Journal of Computer Applications (IJCA)*, 10–12. Available from: https://pdfs. semanticscholar.org/4751/e99514948c2cbef0f6e4a12e65c72f75ae8.pdf.

"*What Is Cryptocurrency—And How Can I Use It?*" 2018. FinderUS. Available from: www. finder.com/what-is-cryptocurrency.

Xu, J.J. 2016. Are Blockchains Immune to All Malicious Attacks? *Xu Financial Innovation*, 2(25). Available from: https://pdfs.semanticscholar.org/780c/d51bdf55183f3d-440d8e7d84b17526c08d5e.pdf.

13 Smart Contracts for Contract Management
A Retention Payment System

Salar Ahmadisheykhsarmast, Ferda Özdemir Sönmez, and Rifat Sönmez

CONTENTS

13.1 INTRODUCTION

Blockchain technologies provide a secure, decentralized, immutable, transparent, and reliable environment for storage and transfer of digital assets. Smart contracts go one step further and enable computerized transaction protocols that execute terms of a contract (Szabo, 1996) on blockchain, including the automated transfer of digital assets. Autonomy, decentralized, and self-executing features of the smart contracts minimize reliance on lawyers, banks, and other intermediaries, resulting in savings in transaction fees and administrative costs and expedite the transaction process (Crosby, Nachiappan, Pattanayak, Verma, & Kalyanamaran, 2016; Fanning & Centers, 2016).

One of the main innovations of smart contracts is their capability of automated and secure execution of the contract conditions through a decentralized consensus, with no need for a central authority or a trusted intermediary. Hence, smart contracts enable the automated transfer of funds when certain contract conditions are satisfied. The smart contracts also require the contract conditions to be represented as a code that leads to elimination of uncertainties in the contract for preventing potential disputes.

This book chapter aims to discuss and demonstrate the advantages of smart contracts for providing a secure and trustworthy platform to improve the traditional contract management process. A decentralized application (DApp) to execute retention clauses of a typical project contract is presented for contract management. Retention is the total amount withheld from the progress payments to provide the client with some security in case the contractor does not correct the defects at project completion or during the warranty period. In general, a portion of the retention is paid to the contractor during project completion and remaining is paid after the warranty period. In some contracts, partial payment of the retention for the parts of the work completed is permitted. Even though payment of retention is very crucial for the contractor's cash flow, the common procedure for retention payment is not very efficient and may take up to 60 days or more after initiation of the partial completion process. Hence, the main objective of the proposed smart contract application is to enable secure and automated payment of the retention for the works completed, as well as secure storage and record-keeping of the project completion documents. The improvements achieved by the application are illustrated through a case study of a real construction project.

The rest of this chapter is organized as follows. In Section 13.2, a brief summary of the blockchain technology along with smart contracts is provided and a literature review of smart contract studies for contract management is included. The proposed smart contract-based retention payment system is presented in Section 13.3, and the case study is included in Section 13.4. The design decisions and security evaluation of the proposed DApp are discussed in Section 13.5. Finally, concluding remarks are made in Section 13.6.

13.2 BLOCKCHAIN, SMART CONTRACTS, AND CONTRACT MANAGEMENT

This section consists of two parts. In the first part, a brief summary of the blockchain technology and smart contracts is provided. In the second part, the applications of blockchain and smart contract technologies in the contract management domain are presented.

13.2.1 BLOCKCHAIN AND SMART CONTRACT, A BRIEF RECALL

Blockchain technology provides a globally consistent distributed database that is formed of a growing list (chain) of records (blocks) that are locked in the chronological order and secured using cryptographic proof and decentralized consensus. The transaction process in the blockchain is demonstrated in Figure 13.1. At the initial stage, an owner of digital asset requests for a transaction by digitally signing a hash of the previous transaction and the public key of the next owner. The request is included in a block and is broadcasted to the parties (nodes) within the blockchain network for verification. Once nodes reach consensus and verify the block, the block is added to the blockchain in a transparent, unaltered, and unremovable way, and the transaction is completed.

The transactions are verified and added to the blockchain by a decentralized consensus process called mining. The original blockchain consensus algorithm used by Bitcoin named proof of work requires the miners (network participants that verify the

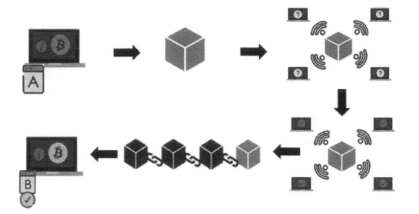

FIGURE 13.1 The transaction process of the blockchain.

transactions) to solve a computationally hard but easily verifiable problem. The first miner that solves the problem presents the solution to the blockchain network. If 51% or more miners verify the solution, a consensus is reached, and the miner that solves the problem is rewarded with cryptocurrencies. In a blockchain, the data is not stored on a central server. Instead, it is replicated and held on all the nodes at the same time. The distribution of data across the network ensures the security of data by not having a single point of failure.

Blockchain was originally introduced for Bitcoin (Nakamoto, 2008) but since then has evolved to other DApps such as smart contracts (Alharby & Moorsel, 2017). Smart contracts can not only enable storage and transfer of digital assets such as a standard blockchain but also present a platform for automated execution of agreements, including transfer of digital assets. Hence, smart contracts provide a secure, decentralized, immutable, transparent, and reliable environment for execution of the terms of a contract as automated computerized protocols.

Automated execution of contract clauses on the secure and trustworthy smart contract platform presents numerous advantages for improving the traditional contract management process. Since smart contracts are executed through code, the ambiguity and misunderstandings are eliminated (Christidis & Devetsikiotis, 2016). Hence, disputes resulting from vagueness and late enforcement of the contract could be noticeably reduced (Ahmadisheykhsarmast & Sonmez, 2018). Smart contracts also provide an innovative and secure platform for automated execution of payment terms in the contract, such as progress payments, payments for materials on-site, or retention payments to reduce the payment uncertainties. The potential of blockchain and smart contracts for contract management is mentioned in numerous researches and is discussed in the next section.

13.2.2 BLOCKCHAIN AND SMART CONTRACTS IN CONTRACT MANAGEMENT

Blockchain and the smart contract technologies have significant implications for contract management of projects. Automating the payment process by considering the payment clause of the contract could be referred to as an example of transaction within the system. As the outlined contract milestones are reached and payments are made, they are recorded in such a way that neither party can repudiate, remove, and manipulate the record (Icertis, 2019).

The blockchain technology accompanied by the building information model (BIM), provides a powerful tool for keeping the records of the BIM during the design and construction phases (Shou, Wang, & Wang, 2015; Wang, Wu, Wang, & Shou, 2017) ensures accuracy of information through immutability and identification of the person making changes along with the details of the changes to allow better recording and tracking of the data (Stougiannos & Magneron, 2018). Blockchain integrated with BIM may enable addressing existence BIM challenges such as traceability and data ownership by providing change tracking, as well as provenance tracking (Nawari & Ravindran, 2019). As a result, the environment provided by the blockchain could maximize the efficiency of the collaborative design process and integrated project delivery strategies. In addition, blockchain presents a promising method to address cybersecurity threats such as storage device failures, information corruption and disruption of BIM operations by abuse of authorized access, and malicious intent of involved participants, which can affect BIM workflow and its connected systems. The proof of delivery, which is secured and transparent via blockchain, can also be used as a contract document management tool.

Blycha (2019) proposed the idea of recording the delivery dates of the materials and performing automated payment of them by smart contracts when they are delivered to the predetermined location. Applying the blockchain technology in supply chain phase of the construction projects may significantly increase the performance of the supply chain management (Li, Greenwood, & Kassem, 2018). Pilagos (2019) presented an example in which the weather data retrieved from the weather sensor on-site is used as an input to the smart contract, which enables compensation of weather events according to the contract conditions.

The immutable nature of blockchain provides an environment in which the compliance information can be stored securely (Icertis, 2019). The certificates related to the materials and site quality checks can be recorded, stored, and shared through the participants within the blockchain system (Penzes, 2018). Hence, blockchain can also be utilized for quality assurance (Wang et al., 2017) for confirming the project quality requirements specified in the contract and the specifications.

One of the key application areas of smart contracts for contract management is the assurance of security of payment for equipment, materials, and services. Hence, smart contracts present a major opportunity to eliminate or reduce payment delays and related trust issues in the industry. In the procurement phase, the payment regarding the materials and equipment could be embedded into a smart contract and could be automatically transferred when the materials and equipment are delivered to the site; hence, the need for the letter of credit (a document that is provided by the bank to guarantee the payment) could be eliminated (Ahmadisheykhsarmast & Sonmez, 2018). Smart contracts with embedded funds are also proposed for the construction phase of the projects for eliminating payment issues and to improve the efficiency of the contract administration process (Cardeira, 2015; Wang et al., 2017; Mason 2017; Li & Kassem, 2019).

Even though numerous researches have highlighted the importance of smart contracts for contract management, very few have developed DApps to illustrate their benefits. Within this context, the main objective of this book chapter is to present a smart contract-based retention payment system.

13.3 RETPAY SYSTEM

The proposed system named Retention Payment (RETPAY) is a smart contract application that aims to reflect a common use case, both in construction management and in other management domains. In this part, while the business logic and terminologies are described textually, the design of the system will be provided through the use of top-level architecture design description, including the selected technologies; the flow of activities; the changes on the sample data with respect to system activities; description of code parts via pseudocoding; and end-user interface screenshots.

RETPAY provides a DApp for payment of retention to the contractor by the client for the works completed. RETPAY is mainly designed for the project contracts in which partial completion and partial payment of retention are allowed. RETPAY not only enables automated payment of retention but also performs storage and record-keeping of the project completion data on a secure, reliable, and trustworthy blockchain platform. The top-level design that shows the main flow of activities of RETPAY is presented in Figure 13.2.

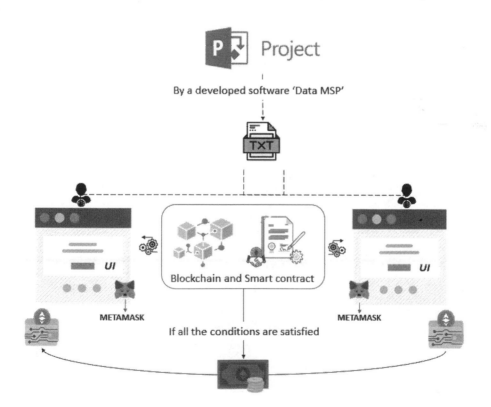

FIGURE 13.2 RETPAY process.

In RETPAY, the contract conditions related to the retention payment for partial completion are coded as a smart contract. The retention payments for each work are also embedded in the smart contract. The smart contract is deployed on the Ethereum blockchain, which is the most widely used blockchain supporting smart contracts (Li et al., 2017). Once completion of a work is confirmed by the contractor and client, RETPAY transfers the retention amounts of the works completed from client's account (wallet address) to the contractor's account (wallet address) and stores the partial completion data on the blockchain.

RETPAY consists of two modules. The first module is add-on software that was developed to capture data from Microsoft Project 2019, using the C# language and Visual Studio 2019 platform. Microsoft Project software is commonly used for project management in numerous domains, including the construction sector. The purpose of the first module is to enable the contractors to use their existing project data and software for preparing the list of works completed, to facilitate the data exchange among the proposed system. In the add-on, the contractor first selects a reporting period, marks the works that have been completed, enters their completion dates, and then presses on the 'Prepare List of Works Completed' button, as shown in Figure 13.3. Once the button is pressed, the add-on exports the list of completed works' unique IDs and their completion dates to a TXT file, as shown in Figure 13.3.

The second module of RETPAY is a DApp consisting of two parts: the web part and the smart contract part. The web part is developed using the PHP Laravel 5.8 Framework in the backend and HTML5, CSS3, and JavaScript in the frontend. The smart contract is developed in Remix IDE, using the Solidity 0.5.2 language. For integrating the HTTP web page User Interface (UI) with the Ethereum node and

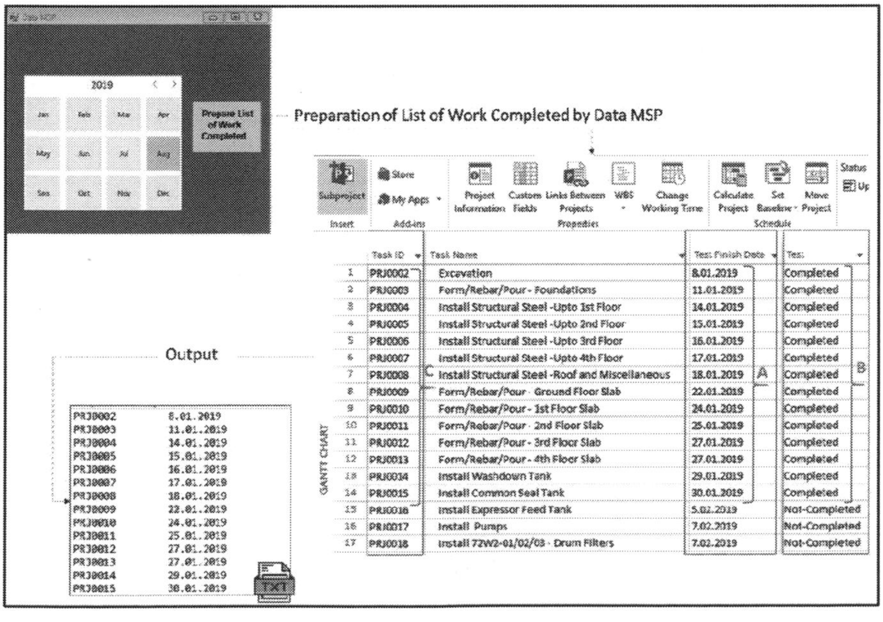

FIGURE 13.3   First module of RETPAY.

```
constructor() public {
    TaskIDs("PRJ0002", 44850*5/100,);
    TaskIDs("PRJ0003", 127430*5/100,);
    TaskIDs("PRJ0004", 267545*5/100,);
    TaskIDs("PRJ0005", 245830*5/100,);
    TaskIDs("PRJ0006", 238432*5/100,);
    TaskIDs("PRJ0007", 214800*5/100,);
    TaskIDs("PRJ0008", 129325*5/100,);
    TaskIDs("PRJ0009", 26830*5/100,);
    TaskIDs("PRJ0010", 18460*5/100,);
    TaskIDs("PRJ0011", 18460*5/100,);
    TaskIDs("PRJ0012", 18460*5/100,);
    TaskIDs("PRJ0013", 18460*5/100,);
    TaskIDs("PRJ0014", 4532*5/100,);
    TaskIDs("PRJ0015", 9618*5/100,);
}
```

FIGURE 13.4 Retention amounts of works embedded into the smart contract.

smart contract, Web3.js is used. MetaMask is used as the user interface for identity management on the Ethereum blockchain. The smart contract is deployed to a virtual Ethereum blockchain, namely Ganache, to test the DApp.

The retention amounts of works are embedded into the smart contract, along with their unique IDs, as shown in Figure 13.4. In the example given in Figure 13.4, 5% of the total costs of works will be transferred from the client's wallet to the contractor's as retention payment after the completion of the works. The contractor will have to login the MetaMask by using his wallet specified in the smart contract to start the partial project completion and retention payment process. The contractor will use the 'Request' button of the second module to request the approval for partial completion and retention payment, as shown in Figure 13.5. The DApp will then check whether the contractor's wallet address is same as the address specified in the smart contract. If the addresses are same, DApp will use the list of completed activities in the TXT file to determine the amount of retention payment in the currency of the contract and in Ethereum based on the latest exchange rate. In retention calculations, DApp checks whether the retention payments of the requested works have been paid previously to prevent double payment, using the latest list of works completed, which are stored on the blockchain, as shown in Figure 13.6.

The DApp will display the total retention amount to be paid for a list of completed works on the contractor's screen. The contractor can change the list of completed works by clicking on the 'Reject' button and then by using the first module. Once the contractor approves the completed works and the retention amount, by pressing the 'Confirm' button, the DApp notifies the client by displaying 'You have a request to approve' message on the client's screen. Notifications are shown from interface (JavaScript) on the information fetched from smart contract.

FIGURE 13.5 Second module of RETPAY.

```
function getIDsAmount(bytes32 _IDs) public view returns (uint) {
  for(uint j = 0; j < PaidIDs.length; j++){
    if(IDsPaid[j] == _ID){
      return (0);
```

FIGURE 13.6 Prevention of double payment in the smart contract.

The DApp requires the client's approval to complete the partial completion and retention payment process for the reporting period. The client will have to login the MetaMask by using his wallet specified in the smart contract to start the approval process. Once the client logs in with the specified wallet, the DApp will display the requested retention payment amount of the client's screen, as shown in Figure 13.5. If the client does not approve the list of works completed and the retention payment amount, the DApp will notify the contractor and will provide the reasons for rejection of the client. If the client approves the completed works, the agreed retention amount for the report period is transferred from the client's wallet to the contractor's wallet, and the list of completed activities that are stored in the blockchain is updated, along with their completion dates. The client, however, has to make sure that there are sufficient funds in her wallet before approval. Once the contractor receives the retention amount in Ethereum, he can convert it into any fiat currency in the local cryptocurrency exchanges.

13.4   VALIDATION OF THE PROPOSED SYSTEM THROUGH A CASE STUDY FOR CONSTRUCTION MANAGEMENT DOMAIN

The proposed RETPAY system is applied to a real construction project, which had a contract with retention clauses similar to the majority of construction projects. The project was a process plant project contracted on engineering procurement and construction bases. As per the conditions of contract, the retention was withheld by the client only for permanent works that are included in the bill of quantities. The issue and approval of partial project completion documents were completed within 20–30 days. The retention for the completed works was paid within 30 days after the approval of partial completion of works. Hence, the retention was paid to the contractor 50–60 days after initiation of the partial completion process, impacting the cash flow of the contractor negatively.

RETPAY was tested for partial retention payment of the case project twice. Each period consisted of a month, which included partial retention payments for the works completed within the specified period. The schedule and cost data of the contractor were available in Primavera software format. Primavera software is also commonly used for scheduling and managing construction projects, along with the Microsoft Project. The cost and activity data in Primavera format were exported to Microsoft Project 2019 to enable the use of the first module. Therefore, the existing project data of the contractor was used in the first module to facilitate data exchange to the DApp. The DApp presented in RETPAY includes general retention payment procedures that can be implemented to the majority of construction projects that include standard partial retention payment clauses. Hence, the DApp was used for the case project without any changes.

Applying the smart contracts for the retention clauses promised a significant potential to reduce the duration of retention payments substantially. The tests of RETPAY on the case project revealed that the retention payments could be made within seconds after the approval from the client. The proposed RETPAY system expedites the payment process and reduces the transaction cost because of the inherited features of the smart contracts. Further, all the retention clauses are enforced by the smart contract. Thus, the need for third party such as banks and lawyers to transact the payments and to execute the contract terms, respectively, are minimized. In addition, all data regarding the transactions and operations are recorded in the blockchain and shared among the contract parties in the secure blockchain environment. Hence, the disputes, misunderstandings, and obscurities among the parties could be significantly reduced. RETPAY also enabled the contractors to use their existing project data for preparing the list of works completed and did not require a long period for the document preparation and approval process for payment of retention.

Despite its advantages, RETPAY has some limitations. One of the main limitations is that it does not lock the funds of the client but rather relies on the availability of sufficient funds in the client's wallet for paying the retention. In case the funds are not available, RETPAY cannot execute the automated payment of retention. RETPAY will also incur deployment and transaction costs, as it uses the Ethereum blockchain. Since RETPAY includes a small size of source code for the smart contract, the deployment cost is insignificant. For example, the deployment and two transactions cost for the case project was \$4.0 at the exchange rate of \$180.0/ Ethereum. There will also be the cost of development if the client wants to develop their own DApp. However, the development cost of the proposed DApp, including the smart contract part, is a minor cost for most of the clients. since it only includes a few basic clauses.

13.5 DISCUSSION OF THE DESIGN DECISIONS AND SECURITY EVALUATION

The architectures of smart contract applications have been manifested in various ways in time. Initially, it was not in a smart contract form, but simply, there were assets to be used for digital transfer. Later, digital assets were taken more seriously and were commonly used for the payment of digital goods such as for the payment of content stream. The basic architecture of smart contract appeared later, with only one party such as landlord remote control of locks passed on payment. Next, smart multiparty contracts arose. The proposed system is an example of a multiparty smart contract architecture. It runs on a distributed environment, namely blockchain. In its current form, it fulfills a single requirement/use case, the retention payment as a part of project contract management. As it is already demonstrated in the case study, retention payment is commonly used in the construction domain, but it is not necessarily specific to this domain. It is seen in all domains where commonly project-based tasks are done with possible partial payments.

Relying on the blockchain network, it is a distributed application and has the inherent advantages and disadvantages. The most well-known risk to blockchain applications is 51% vulnerability. It occurs when one malicious person/group forms the 51% of the blockchain community (Li, Jiang, Chen, Luo, & Wen, 2017). In general, this risk is mainly toward the integrity of blockchain data. Being able to change integrity may result in secondary blockchain risks, such as double spending and criminal activities. The authors believe that the nature of the retention payment would result in the interest of a closed group of related users rather than a vast amount of blockchain users. Thus, having the possibility of 51% risk for this specific application is very low. Another risk for blockchain applications is the risk of security of private keys for the blockchain. This may end up confidentiality problems for both the users and data. This issue, storage of private keys, is depicted more during the description of use of wallets for this application.

The current design relies on the use of web wallets. Other types of wallets are desktop wallets, phone wallets, brain wallets, and hardware wallets. Although the web-based wallets are not as secure as other types of wallets, the ease of use and free (for majority of the web-based wallets), compared with paid hardware wallets, make them convenient to be used in such a prototype system.

MetaMask is chosen in RETPAY prototype design and implementation. The use of MetaMask to store the wallet has some advantages. MetaMask is known to be a secure web wallet. It is open-source; thus, its code is open to be evaluated by a large community of users, currently reaching 1 million active user population. It also allows connection of hardware wallets such as Ledger (Gentilal, Martins, & Sousa, 2017) and Trezor (Boireau, 2018) effortlessly, which would result in increasing the security level of the application instantly.

Unlike some other web browsers, which store the keys in the wallet vendors' server, MetaMask stores the public and private key information on the wallet owner's browser. This results in user having more control over his/her keys. However, it supports limited number of browsers, namely Google Chrome, Mozilla Firefox, Opera, and the newly emerged Brave browser. The users who do not want to store their keys on browsers by the mainstream vendors may choose the latter one or simply reject using MetaMask at all.

The web part of the system relies on the PHP Laravel framework. The prototype is implemented simply and does not benefit the known security features of the Laravel system, such as Laravel Authentication System. However, by default, it benefits from protections for vulnerabilities, such as cross-site request forgery and cross-site scripting, which Laravel provides. Relying on a known platform such as Laravel for the web part of smart contract applications would result in better security for these applications and may allow quick improvement in the overall system by integrating other features of Laravel in the production environment.

Being a distributed application, and by running on a specific platform, blockchain brings additional vulnerabilities to the smart contract applications. Primitive codes caused by either development languages/platforms or lack of experience in distributed application design result in problems that may cause important security issues. Luu et al. (2016) proposed a system called OYENTE, which investigates the smart contract code for vulnerabilities. OYENTE provides an output as a result of this investigation, pointing out possible vulnerabilities such as integer overflow, integer underflow, parity multisig bug, callstack depth attack vulnerability, transaction ordering, timestamp dependency, and re-entrance vulnerability for smart contract applications. This application was also used during the case study, resulting in no significant security-related bug of the listed types.

The business logic of retention payment is not complex. Event-ordering vulnerabilities and time-stamp dependency are two commonly seen business logic-originated vulnerability types in smart contract applications. The proposed smart contract application does not take any action based on timestamps. Thus, it is not prone to the latter vulnerability. However, in order to examine the existence of event-ordering vulnerability, it is necessary to investigate the order of events for this specific use case. Later, there is a numbered list that summarizes these orders of events, where activity four can be followed by either activity 4.1 or 4.2.

1. Contractor uses MS Project add-in to claim the partial completion of project activity(s).
2. Contractor uses DApp to submit this claim to the client.
3. Client sees a completion request on his/her screen.
4. Client checks the request and approves or rejects.
   4.1 Once the request is approved, the retention amount of the approved activities is transferred to the contractor's wallet.
   4.2 If rejected, a pop-up appears on the contractor's screen, and the contractor makes the necessary changes.

Due to dependency on pop-up warnings that act in the order of events, the assortment of owner and contractor events cannot be changed for this use case. Thus, it can be claimed that the business logic of this RETPAY smart contract application is also not prone to event-ordering bugs.

13.6 CONCLUSION

This book chapter presented a pioneering contract management application of smart contracts that enabled automated execution of retention clauses of a typical project contract, as well as storage of project completion and retention payment data on the blockchain. The potential advantages of the new decentralized application were illustrated through a case study of a real construction project. A security evaluation of the proposed application was performed, which revealed that the application does not have any major security-related concerns.

The proposed application and the case study support the fact that smart contract technology provides a secure, reliable, immutable, transparent, efficient, and trustworthy platform not only for automated execution of contract clauses but also for the storage of contractual data. Hence, smart contracts present an innovative alternative for enhancing the traditional contract management process, in particular for automated execution of contract clauses involving payments. The case study revealed that the smart contracts could enable major improvements in the contract management process, by eliminating the need for third parties and reducing fee and payment durations.

The proposed application relies on the availability of sufficient funds in the client's wallet for paying the retention. Future research focusing on a smart contract retention payment application that locks up the funds for retention and releases at completion of the works would enable security of payment of retention. Smart contract-based progress payment applications could be another promising area for future research on contract management to eliminate payment issues in project-based industries, particularly in the construction industry. The smart contract also enables security of payments, which promises an efficient and cost-effective alternative to project bank accounts.

REFERENCES

Ahmadisheykhsarmast, S., & Sonmez, R. (2018). Smart Contracts in Construction Industry. In *5th international Project and Construction Management Conference (IPCMC2018)* (pp. 767–774). North Cyprus: Conference Proceeding.

Alharby, M., & van Moorsel, A. (2017). Blockchain-based smart contracts: A systematic mapping study arXiv preprint arXiv:1710.06372.

Blycha, M. (2019). Smart contracts in the construction industry. Retrieved 2 October 2019 from www.lexology.com/library/detail.aspx?g=78d1740e-bb52-4c67-9135-3d0193a2b2b7.

Boireau, O. (2018). Securing the blockchain against hackers. *Network Security, 2018*(1), 8–11.

Cardeira, H. (2015). Smart contracts and possible application to the construction industry. In *New Perspectives in Construction Law Conference* (Vol. 1). Bucharest.

Christidis, K., & Devetsikiotis, M. (2016). Blockchains and smart contracts for the internet of things. *IEEE Access, 4*, 2292–2303.

Crosby, M., Nachiappan, Pattanayak, P., Verma, S., & Kalyanamaran, V. (2016). BlockChain technology: Beyond bitcoin. *Applied Innovation Review, 2*(6–10), 71.

Fanning, K., & Centers, D. P. (2016). Blockchain and its coming impact on financial services. *Journal of Corporate Accounting & Finance, 27*(5), 53–57.

Gentilal, M., Martins, P., & Sousa, L. (2017). TrustZone-backed bitcoin wallet. In *Proceedings of the Fourth Workshop on Cryptography and Security in Computing Systems* (pp. 25–28). ACM.

Icertis. (2019). How blockchain and smart contracts will change contract management in 2018. Retrieved 10 October 2019 from www.icertis.com/blog/blockchain-smart-contracts-will-change-contract-management-2018/.

Li, J., Greenwood, D., & Kassem, M. (2018). Blockchain in the built environment: Analysing current applications and developing an emergent framework. In *Creative Construction Conference* (pp. 59–66). Ljubljana, UK: Diamond Congress Ltd.

Li, J., & Kassem, M. (2019). A proposed approach integrating DLT, BIM, IoT and smart contracts: Demonstration using a simulated installation task. In *International Conference on Smart Infrastructure and Construction (ICSIC)* (pp. 275–282). Scotland: ICE Publishing.

Li, X., Jiang, P., Chen, T., Luo, X., & Wen, Q. (2017). A survey on the security of blockchain systems. *Future Generation Computer Systems, 107*, 841–853.

Luu, L., Chu, D. H., Olickel, H., Saxena, P., & Hobor, A. (2016, October). Making smart contracts smarter. In *Proceedings of the 2016 ACM SIGSAC Conference on Computer and Communications Security* (pp. 254–269). ACM.

Mason, J. (2017). Intelligent contracts and the construction industry. *Journal of Legal Affairs and Dispute Resolution in Engineering and Construction, 9*(3), 1–6.

Nakamoto, S. (2008). *Bitcoin: A Peer-to-Peer Electronic Cash System.* https://bitcoin.org/bitcoin.pdf.

Nawari, N. O., & Ravindran, S. (2019). Blockchain Technologies in BIM Workflow Environment. In *ASCE International Conference on Computing in Civil Engineering 2019* (pp. 343–352). Atlanta.

Penzes, B. (2018). *Blockchain Technology in the Construction Industry.* Digital Transformation for High Productivity. Scotland: ICE Publishing.

Pilagos, N. (2019). Disrupting the building blocks: Smart contracts and blockchain in construction. Retrieved from www.taylorwessing.com/download/article-disrupting-building-blocks.html.

Shou, W., Wang, J., & Wang, X. (2015). A comparative review of building information modelling implementation in building and infrastructure industries. *Archives of Computational Methods in Engineering, 22*(2), 291–308.

Stougiannos, L., & Magneron, A. (2018). BIM, Blockchain and the Smart Construction Contract. *Mondaq Business Briefing U6.*

Szabo, N. (1996). Smart contracts: Building blocks for digital markets. *EXTROPY: The Journal of Transhumanist Thought* (16), 18, 2.

Wang, J., Wu, P., Wang, X., & Shou, W. (2017). The outlook of blockchain technology for construction engineering management. *Frontiers of Engineering Management, 4*(1), 67–75.

Section V

Blockchain for Cybersecurity
and Privacy in Digital Forensics

14 Ensuring Data Integrity
Towards a Blockchain-Based Platform to Share the Datasets

Takia Islam, D. K. Tonoy Kumar, Sheikh Shah Mohammad Motiur Rahman, Md. Ismail Jabiullah, Mamoun Alazab, and A. S. M. Kayes

CONTENTS

14.1 INTRODUCTION

Recently, sharing the datasets through web-like University of California Irvine (UCI) repository has become momentous. Most of the researches nowadays is value-less without data. In that case, any changes to actual data may lead to wrong path or direction. So, ensuring data integrity has become crucial. On the other hand, blockchain can barely be characterized as a sort of decentralized shared record that utilizes sequential, encrypted, and chained squares to store certain and synchronized information over a shared (peer-to-peer [P2P]) network [1]. It creates data with dispersed accord calculations, stores data with encrypted chained blocks, and controls data with self-executed program contents. Blockchain offers a secure, distributed database that can work without a central authority or manager [2]. Blockchain information arranged through a decentralized P2P network will be confirmed and recorded into blockchain utilizing the accord an instrument [3].

The original blockchain is an open record for fiscal exchanges, with extremely constrained ability to help programmable exchanges [4]. It is an appropriate database that keeps up a persistently developing rundown of exchange data records, cryptographically anchored from altering and correction. The measure of data in our world is quickly expanding. According to an ongoing report, it is assessed that 20% of the world's information has been gathered in recent years [5]. The decentralization and security qualities of blockchain have pulled in specialists to create different applications, for example, smart contracts, distributed Domain Name System (DNS), character administration, and so on [6]. The distributed decentralized data storage will help to reduce the most conventional data failures and blackouts by expanding the security, privacy, and control of the data [7,8]. A decentralized storage network has been established with many benefits.

The core contributions of this chapter are as follows:

- A strong basement of a distributed platform for data scientists or researchers to share their dataset for further research.
- Ensuring the integrity of datasets by decentralization.
- A combination of consortium and public blockchain has been proposed.
- Usage of proof-of-authority (POA) network bridge to interconnect two chains.
- Usage of privacy-preserving searching model to make the data requester more authentic.
- A theoretical foundation of the blockchain-based decentralized storage system.
- A scenario of practical implementation has been discussed briefly.
- The proposed architecture has been compared with traditional storage as well as some recently proposed blockchain-based storage system, and the effectiveness has been established.
- Solve the problems addressed in multiple studies [40–42].
  - Security of datasets source.
  - Datasets' immutability.
  - Future usage of datasets.
  - Maintain the anonymity of datasets.
  - Lifetime of datasets
  - Monetization of the datasets
  - Maintain the quality of datasets
  - Unlock privacy-preserving datasets

14.2 LITERATURE REVIEW

It is rapidly getting to be obvious that blockchain innovation is about much more than just Bitcoin. Recently, quick advancements have been occurring in adjusting the blockchain innovation in different greenfield regions such as smart energy [9], smart cities and the sharing economy [10,11], smart home [13,14], smart government [12], intelligent transport [15], and healthcare [24].

Blockstack [16] presents the idea of virtual chains and proposes a decentralized serverless DNS. Blockstack stretches out to a decentralized public key circulation framework and registry for client identities. Enigma [5,17] is the nearest to our methodology in that it utilizes the blockchain for access control and empowers the sharing of off-chain stored data. However, the information stored by Enigma reaches the logs within the block, without addressing the notable scalability issues. In addition, their framework is not suited for Internet of Things (IoT) stream information.

Christian Esposito et al. [18] proposed a blockchain-based Electronic Medical Records (EMR), Electronic Health Records (EHR), and Personal Healthcare Records (PHR) ecosystem that allows us to acquire a worldwide view of the patient's medical history in an effective, obvious, and lasting way.

For maintaining the integrity of datasets, they proposed a reference integrity metric (RIM) that is maintained by blockchain. In this methodology, there is a central hub that just keeps up references of member repositories, where the datasets are really put away and disseminated. There is another chain of block that maintains member information (such as address and sharing policy) and RIM of datasets, so that the blockchain guarantees data integrity [19].

Saqib Ali et al. [20] designed a decentralized information storage and access framework for PingER, utilizing permissioned blockchain technology. To store health information securely, Huirui Han et al. [24], in their proposed model, utilized a combined form of consortium and private blockchain named as a hybrid blockchain.

14.3 BLOCKCHAIN OVERVIEW AND ARCHITECTURE

Blockchain is a sequence of blocks that are connected through the cryptographic hash and that makes it possible to maintain the integrity of transacted data [23]. Every transaction added to a blockchain is approved by various computers on the Internet. Figure 14.1 shows a part of blockchain. In general, the block header is made up of metadata (Data about data) [24].

The basic blockchain terminologies, different types of blockchain, and comparison among different types of blockchain are demonstrated in Tables 14.1 through 14.3, respectively.

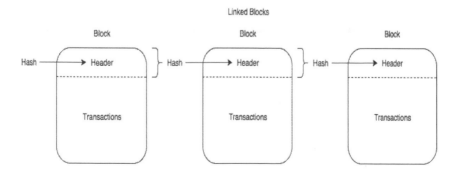

FIGURE 14.1 Blockchain nodes architecture.

TABLE 14.1
Basic Blockchain Terminologies

Blockchain Terminology	Description
Block version	The version number is referred to the software or updating protocol.
Merkle tree root hash	The Merkle tree root hash is a 256-bit hash value of all transactions in a block.
HashPreBlock	It is the previous block hash, which is the value of hash function of the previous block's block header.
Timestamp	Timestamp is a record of the current time.
Bits	Bit indicates a hash value of current target.
Nonce	Nonce denotes a 32-bit random value from 0.
Digital signature	Digital signature is a string of figures that the sender of data can create. Also, it is not possible for anyone to fake. Digital signature is to ensure the authenticity of data sent by the sender. The sender creates a digital abstract of a message by a hash function and afterward encodes the digital abstract by its private key to create a digital signature [24]. At the end of the day, it is guaranteed that the message is sent by the sender, since no one can fake the sender's signature. Moreover, the message is complete [27].
Smart contract	Smart contract is a computer program that runs automatically within the system for the purpose of executing common contractual conditions such as payment terms, confidentiality, and even enforcement. Mainly, it uses the alternative of the third party [28].
Consensus algorithm	Consensus is basically a distributed computing concept that has been used in blockchain in order to provide a means of agreeing to a single version of truth by all peers on the blockchain network. Predominantly, the consensus algorithms are either lottery-based (proof of work and proof of elapsed time) or voting-based (simplified Byzantine fault tolerance) and rely on the unique requirement of the system and level of fault tolerance [21, 22, 29].
Peer to peer	Blockchain network maintains connection (peer to peer) among their nodes through Internet, without central server. Therefore, they are safe from a single point of failure or attack [25].

TABLE 14.2
Types of Blockchain

Types of Blockchain	Description
Public blockchain	Public blockchain protocols are open source by proof-of-work consensus algorithms, and anyone can participate, without permission.
Consortium blockchain	Consortium blockchain shows a blockchain where consensus process is controlled by a prechosen set of nodes. For instance, there is a consortium of 15 monetary foundations, every one of which works as a node, and of which 10 organizations need to approve the new block to influence it to be legitimate.
Private blockchain	In a private blockchain, alter permissions are kept centralized to one organization. Private blockchain is a method for exploiting blockchain technology by setting up groups and members who can check transactions internally.

TABLE 14.3

Comparison of Different Types of Blockchain

Property	Public	Consortium	Private
Consensus determination	All nodes	Selected nodes	A specific institution
Read permission	Public	Public or restricted	Public or restricted
Efficiency	Low	High	High
Centralized	No	Partial	Yes

14.3.1 PROPOSED ARCHITECTURE OF DECENTRALIZED PLATFORM

The proposed architecture is continued in Figure 14.2. It has been observed that in the proposed architecture, two blockchain networks are used such as consortium blockchain and public blockchain. To interact and communicate among the cross-networks, a network bridges POA based on consensus mechanism POA by independent validators [36,37].

In this proposed architecture, all gathered data are eventually recorded in a digital ledger in the form of linked blocks that remain in distributed form. It is very important to maintain data accuracy, data broadcast, and data verification via the data validation process. In this section, we illustrate in detail the working procedure of the proposed architecture, which builds mainly of data transmission, verification, and record.

14.3.1.1 Data Encryption and Distribution

Each validation node in the consortium blockchain network has a pair of the public and private keys. The public key is available publicly in the validation-node network. The private key is used to verify node's identity and operation that it may perform. Since it is a blockchain-based distributed network, therefore, each node

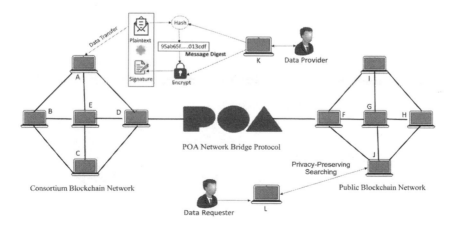

FIGURE 14.2 Proposed blockchain architecture.

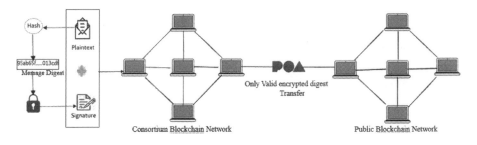

FIGURE 14.3   Dataset validation and broadcast process.

gets the encrypted hash value of the provided dataset and shares it to another node
in the network. The distributed network processes are illustrated in Figure 14.3.

The sharing data consists of plaintext and the encrypted hash value of the same
plaintext (digital signatures). In the encryption mechanism, the new plaintext data
are refined using secure hash algorithm, which produce a message digest. The private key of each validation node encrypts the message digest, forming a digital
signature that decrypts using its public key. Then, the sharing data is broadcast to all
other validation nodes into the consortium network via the communication network.
Trust-based ranking [44,45] can be used to validate the datasets.

14.3.1.2   Data Decryption and Verification

All validation nodes that receive broadcast information need to decrypt the received
information and verify the result, as depicted in Figure 14.4. Again, the plaintext data
must be processed using the same hash algorithm and generating a message digest
1. Otherwise, the signature should be decrypted using its public key and generate a

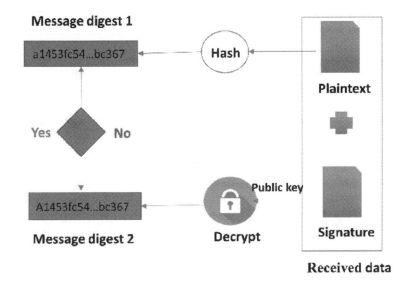

FIGURE 14.4   Data decryption and verification process.

message digest 2. Now compare both digest 1 and digest 2: if both digests are the same, the received information is successfully verified; otherwise, the received information is considered false. After completion of both processes, only valid encrypted data digests are stored into the blockchain-based distributed ledger.

14.3.1.3 Data Provider

Figure 14.5 represents the data provider core elements governing the data profile. For the purpose of storing data securely in blockchain network, a data provider needs to maintain a data profile that includes private key management and storage, which is used to encrypt the hash value of data. The data providers maintain their personal identity, which is automatically verified through smart contract. The data profile needs to link with the data sources via Application Programming Interface (API) access keys, and the data profile should be updated.

14.3.1.4 Data Requester

The data requester core requirements are illustrated in Figure 14.6.

The requester has to join the public blockchain network for searching the required dataset and after that create data request for specific data. This request notification will notify the consortium blockchain network; before releasing the dataset, the validator verifies the requester identity as a researcher. This given information is verified

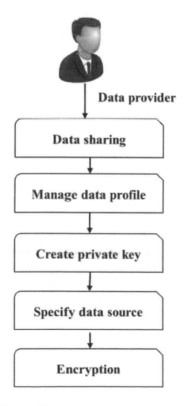

FIGURE 14.5 Data provider profile management.

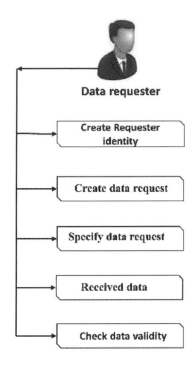

FIGURE 14.6 Data requester.

automatically via smart contract. If the requester is successfully verified by the validation node, then the requester can download the desired dataset. The searching mechanism [39] for creating the request is illustrated in Figure 14.7.

14.3.2 THEORETICAL CONCEPTS OF BLOCKCHAIN IMPLEMENTATION

The consortium blockchain network has been used for validating the data, and then, just encrypted hash value will be broadcast to the public blockchain network via the POA network protocol. Consider an example for better understanding. A data provider Alice wants to share her data with the blockchain network. In order to ensure data integrity and data security, she needs to follow some procedures before uploading dataset. (In a later section, these procedures will be described.) Bob is a data requester. At first, he will join the public blockchain network and then search for dataset with the required keyword, and this keyword matches with the data profile keyword. If he finds the desired dataset, then he will create a data request, but before access, the dataset validation node verifies requester identity as a researcher, based on predefined rules that execute via smart contract automatically.

Now, the main concern is how a data provider and a data requester interact with Ethereum platform-based blockchain network. Both users will need to install web3py. Web3py is a Python library for connecting with the Ethereum blockchain. The system executes the Ethereum protocol, which defines the regulation of communication of nodes with one another as well as with smart contracts over that network.

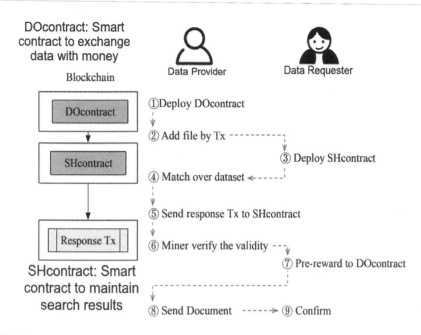

FIGURE 14.7 Privacy-preserving searching model.

If the user wants to provide data or access data, then the protocol requires user's computer to connect to the nodes. There are basic two categories of nodes that user could use in their first approach: local and hosted. A hosted node is a better choice, it is monitored by another person, but the user can easily associate to it and play around with the blockchain all alone.

To access such a hosted node, Infura [38] can be used. When they're done with Infura, they will see a list of networks that they could connect to the main net (the main Ethereum blockchain). After that, they could also connect with the proposed network using the network address.

The principal approach imports the Web3 object and builds up an HTTP connection, and users can explore the data and submit data via the web3 API. For instance, data provider wants to share their data, and they process their data using SHA256 hash algorithm and encrypt the hash value using their private key. After that, they share their encrypted hash and plaintext data from (k) node through Web3 API in the consortium blockchain network (A) node, which is already illustrated in Figure 14.2.

In the same way, the data requester also can access their desired dataset through web3 API. First, they search their required data from (L) node to (J) node and have to create a request for the dataset from node (L), and then, they will be verified as a researcher automatically via smart contract. After successful verification, they could access their desired dataset. A privacy-preserving searching model [39] can be used for searching the dataset.

In the proposed architecture, two Ethereum blockchain networks are used, as illustrated in Figure 14.1. For maintaining communication (data transfer) between two blockchain networks, POA network bridge protocol will be used. The two blockchain network can easily maintain interoperability via this POA network bridge protocol. For connecting with this protocol, each node of the blockchain network has to deploy protocol home address (0xB87b6077D59B01Ab9fa8cd5A1A21D02a4d60D358) that refers to the POA core network.

After successfully deploying home address into two blockchain networks, each node (A, B, C, D, E) and (F, G, H, I, J) two blockchain networks are able to transfer data via POA network bridge. Now, data requester can easily send their data request (L) to (J) and then (D) via protocol, after connected with the public blockchain network as a node. On the contrary, consortium network can easily transfer data from (D) to the public network (F) through POA protocol.

To transfer data from consortium to public blockchain network, we need to copy POA network contract ABI and paste it on the Ethereum node contract section, from where the data will be transferred. After that, we need to put recipient node (F, G, H, I, J) address to the address section and put required data to the data section. For instance, data sending node (D) and recipient node (F) addresses are '0x8527153b4hf57h' and '0x0000673af598gft'. After sending data, it goes to POA network address of '0xd819e948b', and then, later, data will go to the recipient address.

14.4   SECURITY ANALYSIS AND EVALUATION

This section presents security analytics and other strategies to evaluate the proposed architecture.

14.4.1   Tamperproofing

Basically, tamperproofing of data is effective in the blockchain by two things: a cryptographic fingerprint that is unique to each block and a consensus protocol that processes a deal to add a new block in the network. The fingerprint called hash requires huge computing power and time to generate initially, and each block is linked with this hash. So, a hacker competes against the worldwide computing power that makes it very difficult to tamper the data. But, it would be possible if 51% miner agreed to rewrite.

14.4.2   Reliable Storage

Decentralized capacity is relied upon to bring the best properties of blockchain innovation together. The features of decentralized stockpiling will take care of the down-to-earth demand of putting away huge measures of information.

In the proposed architecture, the data provider has ownership of his/her data and the control of using the data. Since all data are stored in a distributed way, the same dataset is kept in every node. It solves the issue of a single point of failure.

14.4.3   Security

While hackers can break into conventional systems and discover every one of the information in a single repository and exfiltrate it or degenerate it, the blockchain makes this unfeasibly hard. The information is decentralized, encoded, and cross-checked by the entire system. When a record is on the record, it is relatively difficult to change or expel without it being seen and nullifying it a signature [27, 28].

Each genuine transaction is affirmed by numerous nodes on the system. To effectively hack blockchain, you would need to hack the vast majority of the nodes all the while, which, however, in fact, conceivable with enough supercomputing force and time, is well past the capacity of cybercriminals today.

Rather than transferring information to a cloud server or putting it away in a single location, blockchain breaks everything into little pieces and appropriates them over the entire network of PCs. To evaluate the proposed blockchain architecture for the dataset sharing platform, the proposed system has been compared and debated with a traditional storage system. Table 14.4 shows the comparison between blockchain and traditional storage [26,32–35].

TABLE 14.4
Comparison Between Blockchain and Traditional Storage

Characteristics	Blockchain-Based Storage	Traditional Storage
Transparency	All the user can see how the blockchain works with time	Traditional storage provides information only after user credentials are authenticated
Integrity	The user can be sure that the data remains unaltered and uncorrupted from the time it was recorded	Traditional storage cannot give a guarantee that data remain unaltered
Performance	Blockchain is considered a slow database; however, it is ideal as a transaction platform	Since the traditional storage has been in existence for decades now, there has been an increase in performance.
Data ownership	Maintained by cryptographic key pairs and native cryptographic algorithm	Established through a central authority
Access control	Inherently identical for all permissioned nodes	Centrally administered
Trust	Native via immutable records	Established via central authority
Database validity	Continuous	Provided only for single instances in time
Privacy and security	Cryptographic authentication	Each row-based enactment from central authority
Concurrency and synchronization	Consensus yields an identical copy	Through complex checking
Reliability and availability	Peer-to-peer network to distribute data replication across all nodes	Potential single point of failure
Transaction creation	Available for all permissioned nodes	Managed via central authority
Fraudulent/malicious change	Almost difficult because all blocks are connected through cryptographic hash	Not available where current keys and check constraints remain insufficient

14.5   DISCUSSION AND COMPARISON BETWEEN EXISTING BLOCKCHAIN APPROACHES

The current research of protecting data on blockchain is concentrated on finding and distinguishing enhancements to the current difficulties and confinements. When a comparison between blockchain and traditional storage has been made, it has been found that the main difference is the central authority. The data ownership is established in blockchain via cryptographic key pair and central authority in traditional storage. The key territory of blockchain is 'open check', which is empowered because of integrity and transparency work. This helps the clients or customers to check every one of the points of interest on the block. They are completely mindful of what is happening in the blockchain. The traditional storage provides details to clients or customers simply after their accreditations are verified. The authority gives just the required data and not all that matters [26].

In one study [30], a private blockchain-based data protection framework proposed to store encrypted data alongside plaintext data. Anyone can access that plaintext data by joining their network. However, in this architecture, two types of blockchain network have been used. One is consortium for verifying the data, and then, only encrypted data are stored into public the blockchain network. The consortium blockchain network will consist of predefined nodes that validate the data. Peer-to-peer connection does not support single point of failure: if any node goes down, then the system continues working, whereas in traditional storage, if any single-point failure occurred, then the system will stop working.

Xia et al. [31] in their research proposed blockchain-based data sharing (BBDS) system that uses permissioned blockchain, which allows access to only invited and verified users. This means that if a user wants to access their data, then the user should have to prove their identities and cryptographic key pairs. The main problem is that, after successful completion of user authentication if the user does not find their required data, then the whole authentication process that has already happened will be useless. To mitigate this problem in the proposed architecture, public blockchain has been used, where anyone can search their required data in encrypted form, and then, they could create a data request. After that, one can verify the requester identity as a researcher; if the requester is verified successfully as a researcher, then the data could be released. Verified data requester could download data from consortium blockchain network.

14.6   CONCLUSION AND FUTURE RESEARCH

To recapitulate, a decentralized distributed data sharing platform architecture using consortium and permissionless (public) blockchain has been proposed and evaluated. The architecture removes the centralized repository concepts. Using blockchain technology, this architecture also ensures data integrity. By actualizing the proposed model, all will have the capacity to store all their documents on an online medium, with no danger of information leakage. It is fascinating to expand this work by completely investigating these in future studies.

Our future work will address the implementation of our proposed architecture. In addition, evaluating machine learning models using DanKu protocol [43] against the datasets will be implemented in the future.

Future scholars can also improve the blockchain-based data sharing by adopting traditional security and access control frameworks, such as security vulnerability model [46] and context-aware access control model [47,48], and working toward future implementations of blockchain-based access control frameworks for secure data access [49], for managing imbalanced data [50], and for data federation through authentication [51]. The future blockchain-based access control approach can be used to tackle different requirements, such as context-specific data access [52], relationship-based data sharing [53], and managing data access by considering imprecise contextual conditions [54,55].

REFERENCES

1. "Intro to Blockchain Technology", https://blockchainhub.net/blockchain-technology, last accessed: 18 October 2018.
2. Angraal, S., Krumholz, H. M., & Schulz, W. L. (2017). Blockchain technology: Applications in health care. *Circulation: Cardiovascular Quality and Outcomes*, 10(9), e003800.
3. Yuan, Y., & Wang, F. Y. (2016). Towards blockchain-based intelligent transportation systems. In *Intelligent Transportation Systems (ITSC), 2016 IEEE 19th International Conference on* (pp. 2663–2668). IEEE.
4. Xu, X., Pautasso, C., Zhu, L., Gramoli, V., Ponomarev, A., Tran, A. B., & Chen, S. (2016). The blockchain as a software connector. In *2016 13th Working IEEE/IFIP Conference on Software Architecture (WICSA)* (pp. 182–191). IEEE.
5. Zyskind, G., & Nathan, O. (2015). Decentralizing privacy: Using blockchain to protect personal data. *In Security and Privacy Workshops (SPW)*, 2015 IEEE (pp. 180–184). IEEE.
6. Liang, X., Shetty, S., Tosh, D., Kamhoua, C., Kwiat, K., & Njilla, L. (2017). Provchain: A blockchain-based data provenance architecture in cloud environment with enhanced privacy and availability. In *Proceedings of the 17th IEEE/ACM International Symposium on Cluster, Cloud and Grid Computing* (pp. 468–477). IEEE Press.
7. Kuo, T. T., Kim, H. E., & Ohno-Machado, L. (2017). Blockchain distributed ledger technologies for biomedical and health care applications. *Journal of the American Medical Informatics Association*, 24(6), 1211–1220.
8. Shafagh, H., Burkhalter, L., Hithnawi, A., & Duquennoy, S. (2017). Towards blockchain-based auditable storage and sharing of iot data. In *Proceedings of the 2017 on Cloud Computing Security Workshop* (pp. 45–50). ACM.
9. Li, J., Greenwood, D., & Kassem, M. (2018). Blockchain in the built environment: Analysing current applications and developing an emergent framework. Diamond Congress Ltd.
10. Rivera, R., Robledo, J. G., Larios, V. M., & Avalos, J. M. (2017). How digital identity on blockchain can contribute in a smart city environment. In *Smart Cities Conference (ISC2)*, 2017 International (pp. 1–4). IEEE.
11. Biswas, K., & Muthukkumarasamy, V. (2016). Securing smart cities using blockchain technology. In *High Performance Computing and Communications; IEEE 14th International Conference on Smart City; IEEE 2nd International Conference on Data Science and Systems (HPCC/SmartCity/DSS), 2016 IEEE 18th International Conference on* (pp. 1392–1393). IEEE.

12. Hou, H. (2017). The application of blockchain technology in E-government in China. In *Computer Communication and Networks (ICCCN), 2017 26th International Conference on* (pp. 1–4). IEEE.

13. Dorri, A., Kanhere, S. S., Jurdak, R., & Gauravaram, P. (2017). Blockchain for IoT security and privacy: The case study of a smart home. In *Pervasive Computing and Communications Workshops (PerCom Workshops), 2017 IEEE International Conference on* (pp. 618–623). IEEE.

14. Lazaroiu, C., & Roscia, M. (2017). Smart district through IoT and Blockchain. In *Renewable Energy Research and Applications (ICRERA), 2017 IEEE 6th International Conference on* (pp. 454–461). IEEE.

15. Yuan, Y., & Wang, F. Y. (2016). Towards blockchain-based intelligent transportation systems. In *Intelligent Transportation Systems (ITSC), 2016 IEEE 19th International Conference on* (pp. 2663–2668). IEEE.

16. Ali, M., Nelson, J. C., Shea, R., & Freedman, M. J. (2016). Blockstack: A global naming and storage system secured by blockchains. In *USENIX Annual Technical Conference* (pp. 181–194).

17. Zyskind, G., Nathan, O., & Pentland, A. (2015). Enigma: Decentralized computation platform with guaranteed privacy. arXiv preprint arXiv:1506.03471.

18. Esposito, C., De Santis, A., Tortora, G., Chang, H., & Choo, K. K. R. (2018). Blockchain: A panacea for healthcare cloud-based data security and privacy? *IEEE Cloud Computing*, 5(1), 31–37.

19. Banerjee, M., Lee, J., & Choo, K. K. R. (2018). A blockchain future for internet of things security: A position paper. *Digital Communications and Networks*, 4(3), 149–160.

20. Ali, S., Wang, G., White, B., & Cottrell, R. L. (2018). A blockchain-based decentralized data storage and access framework for PingER. In *2018 17th IEEE International Conference on Trust, Security and Privacy In Computing And Communications/12th IEEE International Conference On Big Data Science And Engineering (TrustCom/BigDataSE)* (pp. 1303–1308). IEEE.

21. Gramoli, V. (2017). From blockchain consensus back to byzantine consensus. *Future Generation Computer Systems, 107*, 760–769.

22. Christidis, K., & Devetsikiotis, M. (2016). Blockchains and smart contracts for the internet of things. *IEEE Access*, 4, 2292–2303.

23. Al-Megren, S., Alsalamah, S., Altoaimy, L., Alsalamah, H., & Soltanisehat, L. Blockchain use cases in digital sectors: A review of the literature. In: *2018 IEEE International Conference on Internet of Things (iThings) and IEEE Green Computing and Communications (GreenCom) and IEEE Cyber, Physical and Social Computing (CPSCom) and IEEE Smart Data (SmartData)* (pp. 1417–1424). IEEE, Halifax, NS.

24. Han, H., Huang, M., Zhang, Y., & Bhatti, U. A. (2018). An architecture of secure health information storage system based on blockchain technology. In *International Conference on Cloud Computing and Security* (pp. 578–588). Springer, Cham.

25. Guegan, D. (2017). Public blockchain versus private blockchain. https://halshs.archives-ouvertes.fr/halshs-01524440/

26. Zheng, Z., Xie, S., Dai, H., Chen, X., & Wang, H. (2017). An overview of blockchain technology: Architecture, consensus, and future trends. In *Big Data (BigData Congress), 2017 IEEE International Congress on* (pp. 557–564). IEEE.

27. Johnson, D., Menezes, A., & Vanstone, S. (2001). The elliptic curve digital signature algorithm (ECDSA). *International Journal of Information Security*, 1(1), 36–63.

28. Jain, A., Jain, A., Chauhan, N., Singh, V., & Thakur, N. (2018). Seguro digital storage of documents using blockchain.

29. Xu, Q., Aung, K. M. M., Zhu, Y., & Yong, K. L. (2018). A blockchain-based storage system for data analytics in the internet of things. In *New Advances in the Internet of Things* (pp. 119–138). Springer, Cham.

30. Liang, G., Weller, S. R., Luo, F., Zhao, J., & Dong, Z. Y. (2018). Distributed blockchain-based data protection framework for modern power systems against cyber attacks. *IEEE Transactions on Smart Grid.*

31. Xia, Q., Sifah, E. B., Smahi, A., Amofa, S., & Zhang, X. (2017). BBDS: Blockchain-based data sharing for electronic medical records in cloud environments. *Information,* 8(2), 44.

32. Sun, J., Yan, J., & Zhang, K. Z. (2016). Blockchain-based sharing services: What blockchain technology can contribute to smart cities. *Financial Innovation,* 2(1), 26.

33. Motro, A. (1989). Integrity = validity + completeness. *ACM Transactions on Database Systems (TODS),* 14(4), 480–502.

34. Wilkinson, S., Lowry, J., & Boshevski, T. (2014). Metadisk a blockchain-based decentralized file storage application. *Technical Report.*

35. Ethereum, W. G. (2014). A secure decentralised generalised transaction ledger [J]. *Ethereum Project Yellow Paper,* 151, 1–32.

36. "Introducing POA Bridge and POA20", https://medium.com/poa-network/introducing-poa-bridge-and-poa20-55d8b78058ac.

37. "TokenBridge: Connecting Chains", https://poa.network/bridge.

38. "INFURA", https://infura.io/.

39. He, M., Zeng, G., Zhang, J., Zhang, L., Chen, Y., & Yiu, S. (2018). A New privacy-preserving searching model on blockchain. In *International Conference on Information Security and Cryptology* (pp. 248–266). Springer, Cham.

40. "Datum," https://datum.org/assets/Datum-WhitePaper.pdf.

41. "Ocean Protocol: A Decentralized Substrate for AI Data & Services", https://github.com/TraneAI/Whitepaper/blob/master/TraneAi%20-%20TPAI%20Whitepaper.pdf.

42. "TraneAI", https://github.com/TraneAI/Whitepaper/blob/master/TraneAi%20-%20TPAI%20Whitepaper.pdf.

43. Kurtulmus, A. B., & Daniel, K. (2018). Trustless machine learning contracts; evaluating and exchanging machine learning models on the ethereum blockchain. arXiv preprint arXiv:1802.10185.

44. Steele, J., & Agrawal, S. (2012). U.S. Patent No. 8,214,634. Washington, DC: U.S. Patent and Trademark Office.

45. Chung, F., Tsiatas, A., & Xu, W. (2011). Dirichlet PageRank and trust-based ranking algorithms. In *International Workshop on Algorithms and Models for the Web-Graph* (pp. 103–114). Springer, Berlin, Heidelberg.

46. Tang, M., Alazab, M., & Luo, Y. (2019). Big data for cybersecurity: Vulnerability disclosure trends and dependencies. *IEEE Transaction Big Data,* 5(3), 317–329.

47. Kayes, A. S. M. Han, J., Rahayu, W., Dillon, T. S., Islam, Md S., & Colman, A. (2019). A policy model and framework for context-aware access control to information resources. *Computer Journal,* 62(5), 670–705.

48. Kayes, A. S. M., Rahayu, W., Dillon, T. S., Chang, E., & Han, J. (2019). Context-aware access control with imprecise context characterization for cloud-based data resources. *Future Generation Computer Systems,* 93, 237 255.

49. Kayes, A. S. M., Han, J., & Colman, A. W. (2012). ICAF: A context-aware framework for access control. *ACISP,* LNCS, Vol. 7372, pp. 442–449.

50. Ebenuwa, S. H., Sharif, M. S., Alazab, M., & Al-Nemrat, A. (2019). Variance ranking attributes selection techniques for binary classification problem in imbalance data. *IEEE Access,* 7, 24649–24666.

51. Awaysheh, F. M., Cabaleiro, J. C., Pena, T. F., & Alazab, M. (2019). Poster: A pluggable authentication module for big data federation architecture. *SACMAT '19: Proceedings of the 24th ACM Symposium on Access Control Models and Technologies* (pp. 223–225). Toronto, Canada.

52. Kayes, A. S. M., Han, J., & Colman, A. (2013). An ontology-based approach to context-aware access control for software services. *WISE,* LNCS, Vol. 8180, pp. 410–420.

53. Kayes, A. S. M., Han, J., Colman, A., & Islam, Md. S. (2014). RelBOSS: A relationship-aware access control framework for software services. *OTM Conferences—CoopIS*, LNCS, Vol. 8841, pp. 258–276.
54. Kayes, A. S. M., Rahayu, J. W., Dillon, T. S., Chang, E., & Han, J. (2017). Context-aware access control with imprecise context characterization through a combined fuzzy logic and ontology-based approach. *OTM Conferences—CoopIS*, 10573, 132–153.
55. Kayes, A. S. M., Rahayu, W., & Dillon, T. S. (2019). Critical situation management utilizing IoT-based data resources through dynamic contextual role modeling and activation. *Computing*, 101(7), 743–772.

15 Applications of Blockchain in Digital Forensics and Forensics Readiness

Manish Kumar

CONTENTS

15.1   INTRODUCTION

Today, society is living a digital life, where people are more connected with each other. The proliferation of the Internet and smartphones has changed the various aspects of our lifestyle. Time and place are no more constraints. Villages have become cybervillage, the world has become a cyber world, and life has become digital life.

No doubt, technology has uplifted the social life, but history is evident that any technological invention has both pros and cons. Scientists, IT professionals, and software developers, who contributed a lot in the development of the digital life ecosystem, would have never thought that the Internet, smartphone, and social media will become instruments to commit crimes (Kumar and Hanumanthappa, 2015; Kumar, Kumar Singh and Kumar, 2018). As 'cyber' is a popularly known word in our daily life, 'cybercrime' has also become a well-known word for the netizens.

Cybercrime is one of the most significant threats to society now. It is a crime in which electronic gadgets, computers, or Internet-based services are targets of crime (hacking, phishing, and spamming) or are used as a tool to commit an offense. Usually, cybercrime is committed by the technically skilled people; and hence, it is also called white-collar crime. Cybercriminals use their diverse skills to hack bank accounts, steal the confidential data, blackmail innocent people, and stalk or harass the users. There are various types of cybercrime classified based on the nature and objectives of the cybercrime. Some cybercriminals commit the crime individually against individual or organizations for financial or personal gains. Whereas sometimes, it is organized and state-sponsored against a state or a country with bigger objectives.

In a civilized society, when there is a crime, there is a law to curb the crime. If someone exploits the technology or misuses it for personal gain and benefits, state or federal agency must take action as per the law and punish the culprit. However, law can act only when there is evidence. Without a valid evidence, law cannot do justice. Law needs strong support of evidence to act on culprit. Evidence is acceptable in court of law only when it is collected and analyzed in a forensically sound manner.

Digital forensics is a very vast and advanced field dealing with the collection and analysis of digital evidence in a scientifically sound manner, which is acceptable in a court of law. Digital forensics is one of the most important fields in today's digital era, without which controlling cybercrime cannot be imagined. Law enforcement agencies use digital forensics tools and techniques for electronic evidence collection, preservation, analysis, and reporting purposes. As our daily life is heavily dependent on the Internet, smartphones, social network tools, and smart gadgets, all our activities leave behind digital footprints. Digital forensics tools help investigators to collect and analyze these digital footprints in case any unlawful activity is committed. Digital forensics not only help in cybercrime investigation but also help in investigating other types of crime such as economic offenses, civil disputes, terrorist activities, etc.

Though digital forensics is very advanced and mature field, it has many challenging issues. Handling digital evidence poses many challenges because of its volatile and fragile characteristics. It is a big challenge for the investigating agencies to preserve the integrity and authenticity of the evidence collected from heterogeneous digital gadgets for its admissibility in the court of law. Guaranteeing the authenticity of evidences and legality of process and procedure followed throughout the digital forensic investigation is a real challenge for the investigators. Digital evidence management becomes more complicated when multiple agencies and forensics examiners are involved in investigation. The capabilities of blockchain technology, i.e., *immutability, auditability, provenance, integrity, security, and trustworthiness*, make it the most promising solution against the challenges posed by digital forensics. Blockchain can provide robust platform for evidence management and chain of custody.

The chapter is basically focused on applications of blockchain in digital forensics and forensic readiness. Section 15.2 gives a brief idea about digital forensics, followed by a basic understanding of blockchain. In Section 15.3, literature survey is shown, with research gap analysis. A blockchain-based digital forensics framework is discussed in detail with a prototype model in Section 15.4. Forensics readiness with use cases is discussed in Section 15.5, followed by conclusion in Section 15.6.

A mix of different research approaches has been used in the chapter. Forensics products review, recent research papers, journals, articles, and dissertations have been thoroughly analyzed and referred in the chapter. Interviews of the expert forensic examiners and forensics software developers were carried out to understand the weakness in the current system and how blockchain can be used to bridge the gap. A comparative analysis was done between the existing system and the prototype system based on blockchain. Further, a practical implementation and a case study are discussed as proof of concept.

15.2   OVERVIEW OF DIGITAL FORENSICS PROCESS AND BLOCKCHAIN TECHNOLOGY

15.2.1   DIGITAL FORENSICS

Digital forensics is a specialized branch of forensic science. It deals with the electronic evidence collection, preservation analysis, and reporting of the findings in a scientific manner, which should be acceptable in the court. The whole life cycle of the evidence collection and analysis has to strictly adhere to the standard procedure defined by the law. Any deviation in the process can make the whole evidence and its findings unacceptable during the trial in court.

Electronic evidence is the information collected through various digital gadgets and information technology equipment that is suspected and might have been used in crime. It may be laptops, personal computers, smartphones, tablets, servers, network equipment, cloud storage, hard disk, memory stick, etc. Digital evidence is not only used in the prosecution of cybercrime but also used to prosecute all other types of crime.

FIGURE 15.1   Digital forensics investigation stages.

The significant steps of digital forensics, as shown in Figure 15.1, are as follows:

- *Evidence identification*: The first job of an investigating officer is to identify the potential source of evidence. It may be a micro memory card, computer, laptop, play station, iPod, or any other electronic gadget that has the storage capacity.
- *Evidence collection*: Once the potential source of evidence is identified at the crime scene, it has to be seized. It is vital to maintain chain of custody while seizing the device. Chain of custody basically records the sequence of events beginning from seizure of evidence, transfer, analysis, and its disposition in the chronological order. Every minute detail of the crime scene and device details need to be recorded while collecting the evidence.
- *Evidence acquisition*: Once the forensics experts have seized the suspected electronics gadgets and devices from the crime scene, they need to make a copy of the storage media. It is one of the most crucial steps. One of the fundamental requirements of digital forensics is that during the investigation procedure, source of evidence should not be altered or modified. Hence, as a standard procedure, forensics examiner makes the exact duplicate copy of the original evidence storage media and keeps the original device in safe custody. Later, all analysis is done on the duplicate copy of the original storage media seized from the crime scene.
- *Evidence validation*: It is important to validate that the copy of evidence made during the acquisition steps is intact, and there is not a single bit of difference between the original evidence and mirrored copy. Validation of the evidence can be done using hashing. It assures the integrity of the evidence. The evidence will not be accepted if it fails the integrity test during any stage of investigation and prosecution.
- *Evidence extraction and analysis*: Evidence extraction and analysis is a challenging step. Most of the time, the electronic evidence collected is encrypted and password protected. There are various techniques used by the cybercriminal to evade from forensic analysis. They use many antiforensics methods to hide the evidence or sometimes try to completely wipe out the evidence. It is the job of forensics examiners to extract the *encrypted files, deleted files, corrupt files,* or *hidden files* using various tools and techniques. Decrypting, decompressing, carving, and bookmarking are some of the techniques used by forensic experts to extract evidence from multiple sources.

- *Reporting*: Reporting is the last and vital step for the examiner. During the investigation, examiner might have analyzed much evidence from various sources. Examiner needs to present the facts found in analysis in context to the given case. It is essential to understand that when the case history and evidence are handed over to the examiner, he/she is responsible only to analyze the evidence in context to the given case and not beyond that. The report is the final outcome of the whole investigation, which has to be presented in the court. Hence, the statement should be very clear and precise. The authenticity of the report is the most important.

15.2.1.1 Challenges in Digital Forensics

Digital forensics and investigation process work under strict guidelines. Forensic examiner faces many tough situations during seizer of evidence, extraction, and analysis. For every case, investigator needs to collect electronic evidences from various sources. Collectively, the size of this electronic evidence is huge. Collecting and preserving terabytes of electronic evidence for different cases create evidence management issues for law enforcement agencies.

The involvement of multiple organizations and forensics examiner poses challenge for maintaining the chain of custody. Utmost care should be taken to ensure the safety, security, authenticity, and integrity of the evidence. Let us understand the various issues related to evidence management and chain of custody in detail.

15.2.1.1.1 Evidence Management

The traditional evidence management approach is not so practical in handling digital evidence. In today's technological era, volume of data generated every day is mindboggling. HD images, videos, and surveillance camera footage produce mammoth size of data. While investigating any case, investigator may need to collect evidence from various sources. It may be smartphone, personal computers, social network accounts, CCTV camera footage, etc. Collecting and managing these terabytes of data related to an individual case create challenges for the law enforcement agencies. The evidence repository system must protect the evidence from any contamination and ensure the safety and security of evidence from unauthorized access. Electronic evidences are extremely volatile. Once the evidence is contaminated, it cannot be decontaminated.

15.2.1.1.2 Chain of Custody

Investigators must record every activity right from the beginning of the investigation in the chain of custody. It records the steps followed by forensic examiner during the seizure of evidence, transfer, analysis, and disposition in the chronological order. Chain of custody is used to make sure that the standard procedures are followed. If the authenticity of evidence is challenged in court, a chain of custody can be used to defend its authenticity. Along with the chain of custody, it is also advisable to record how evidence was collected and what tools, techniques, methods, and procedures were used in the investigation process.

Most of the organizations are facing a chain of custody issue for electronic evidence. It is very challenging for the organizations to maintain the integrity of the evidence, which usually gives negative outcomes in court trials. Some of the common problems faced by organizations are as follows:

- *Evidence alteration or modification*: Digital evidence may be in the form of electronic documents, images, videos, call records, etc. If the evidence is mishandled during the analysis process, it may corrupt the evidence. Sometimes, evidence manipulation may be intentional. Whatever may be the reason, system should ensure the integrity and authenticity of evidence. The ease with which electronic evidence can be manipulated poses a challenge for the chain of custody.
- *Lack of effective access control*: In many cases, evidence needs to be examined by multiple examiner and multiple organizations. Sometimes, forensic report has to be examined and approved by multiple experts. The traditional evidence access control and report management are not effective enough. The access control system should support for identifying the examiner who has accessed the evidence and time stamping for every activity carried out by the examiner.

Effective evidence management and chain of custody are the most common challenges faced by investigating agencies. Often, the validity and authenticity of evidence are cross-questioned in court. A well-maintained evidence management system and chain of custody are most essential to defend the validity of evidence during the trial.

15.2.2 BLOCKCHAIN TECHNOLOGY

There are many theories behind blockchain. Most people have the impression that the blockchain is developed along with cryptocurrency called Bitcoin. However, the fact is that blockchain and cryptocurrency are two separate technologies. Cryptocurrency is developed by using the blockchain technology.

The initial work on secured data storage in the form of a chain of blocks was first introduced by Stuart Haber and W. Scott Stornetta in 1991. They wanted to make document timestamps to be tamperproof. In 1992, Bayer, Haber, and Stornetta introduced the Merkle tree in their design concept to improve the efficiency of the system (Cebe et al., 2019; Montasari and Hill, 2019).

Bitcoin is one of the most popular applications of blockchain. It was conceptualized by Satoshi Nakamoto in 2008. Nakamoto improved the design by using a hashcash-like method to timestamp blocks without requiring them to be signed by a trusted party and to reduce speed with which blocks are added to the chain. The improved design was implemented by Nakamoto in Bitcoin application to serve as a public ledger to record all the transactions.

In simple words, if we define blockchain, it is a 'Chain' of 'Blocks' (Figure 15.2), where each block contains digital information. Each block is connected with the previous block, forming a chain pattern. Hence, it is called blockchain.

The whole blockchain is distributed over multiple nodes (computer/device), which makes the system more robust. The technique is intended to create a tamper-proof timestamped digital record (Kouzinopoulos et al., 2018; Luciano et al., 2018; Ryu et al., 2019). The transactions and electronic records are processed by a network of users, not by a centralized administrator. The network of users verifies the

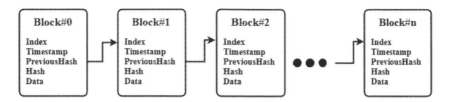

FIGURE 15.2   Blocks in blockchain.

transactional records and reaches a common consensus before adding the data into a blockchain (Wan et al., 2015; Li, Qin and Min, 2019).

Blockchain has several features that make it different from traditional data storage such as a ledger or a relational database. Some of the biggest advantages of blockchain that motivate us to adopt the technology are as follows:

- *Efficiency*: In our day-to-day official activity, we can observe that many documents and important records need a multilevel verification, settlement, and clearance. Blockchain provides a shared ledger, which is a single version of agreed-upon data. It reduces the verification times and helps in quick processing of jobs and settlement.
- *Reliability*: Blockchains are distributed and managed across the nodes (computing device) in a peer-to-peer network. Since the blockchain is distributed among the nodes, it makes it more reliable and fault-tolerant. It also makes the system scalable and robust.
- *Immutable*: The data stored in the blockchain is immutable. Every block in the blockchain is linked with the previous block through hash value. Data modification or alteration will change the hash value of the block, and it will trigger the mismatch of hash value of all the remaining blocks in the blockchain. By storing the data or transaction record in the chronological order, blockchain certifies the unalterability of all operations. It means that when any new block has been added to the chain of ledgers, it cannot be removed or modified.
- *Provenance*: Blockchain provides provenance features. The word provenance is derived from the French word, which means 'to come from'. The provenance feature is one of the most important features of blockchain technology that gives an immutable audit trail for the origin of data or records and their changes over time.
- *Security*: Storing the data on distributed nodes across the network makes the job of hackers difficult. The fraud transaction and data can be added in blockchain only if the majority of computers are compromised in the network. It is practically very difficult for hackers to compromise the majority of the nodes (computers) in the network to do so. It makes the system very secure.
- *Transparency*: Blockchains are shared ledger. Any modification or addition of data is visible to every user (node) in the business network. It makes the overall system very transparent. Nothing can be hidden from any users, and nothing can be added to the blockchain without the user's consensus.

15.2.2.1   Blockchain Variants

Generally, blockchains are classified into three variants: *Public blockchain, private blockchain,* and *federated blockchain.*

15.2.2.1.1   Public Blockchain

If we define in a very simple way, it is a kind of blockchain '*for the people, by the people and of the people*'. Anyone in the public domain can access the public blockchain. The user can participate in reading/writing and auditing the blockchain. The public blockchains are not in the control of a single authority. These types of blockchains are more open and transparent. Since there is no single authority to control the administration of the blockchain, the decisions are taken by various decentralized consensus mechanisms.

15.2.2.1.2   Private Blockchain

As the word private makes it self-explanatory, private blockchains are owned by an individual or an organization. The private blockchains are under the control of an individual or an organization. Unlike a public blockchain, in a private blockchain, administrator decides about the access rights and user permissions. Typically, in a private blockchain, the consensus is achieved through selective endorsement. It is based on the concept that network participants have gained permission to be there and that the participants involved in a transaction are able to confirm it (Singh and Singh, 2016; Liu, Chen, and Hu, 2017; Taylor et al., 2019).

15.2.2.1.3   Federated/Consortium Blockchain

Basically, a federated blockchain is a group of companies or individuals coming together. It is cost-effective and fast. Federated blockchain looks like a private blockchain but it is not. In a private blockchain, a single organization has control over the blockchain, whereas in a federated blockchain, a consortium of organization has control over the blockchain. It is a permissioned blockchain, where access and permissions are decided by consortium.

The comparative analysis of three different types of blockchains is shown in Table 15.1.

There are various platforms such as Ethereum, IBM Hyperledger, Multichain, Hydrachain, Ripple, Open Chain, etc., available for blockchain application development. Each one has its advantages and disadvantages. Technical discussion about various software platforms for blockchain development is out of the scope of this chapter.

15.2.3   Advantages of Using Blockchain in Digital Forensics Process

The digital forensics process has many open challenges. However, blockchain cannot address all the issues. Table 15.2 shows the list of challenges faced in each stage of the digital forensics process and their feasible solution using blockchain technology.

TABLE 15.1

Public vs. Private vs. Federated Blockchain

	Public Blockchain	Private Blockchain	Federated/Consortium Blockchain
Access	• Anyone	• Single organization (owner)	• Multiple organizations
Participants	• Permissionless • Anonymous	• Permissioned • Known participants	• Permissioned • Known participants
Security	• Consensus mechanism • Proof of work/proof of stake	• Pre-approved • Voting/multiparty consensus	• Preapproved • Voting/multiparty consensus
Transaction speed	• Slow	• Medium and Fast	• Medium and fast

TABLE 15.2

Digital Forensics Challenges and Feasible Solution Using Blockchain

Forensics Phases	Current Challenges	Blockchain Promising Solutions
Evidence identification[a]	• Obscure physical area • Decentralize information • Duplicated information • Cross-jurisdiction	N/A
Evidence collection	• Multitenancy[a] • Cross-jurisdiction[a] • Large volume of data[a] • Encrypted data[a] • Deleted or hidden data[a] • Chain of custody • Evidence management	Blockchain cannot provide the solutions for all the issues related to evidence collection. However, it can effectively address the issues of evidence management and chain of custody.
Evidence acquisition	• Password protected device[a] • Customized hardware and embedded system[a] • Customized file systems[a] • Encrypted storage media[a] • Chain of custody • Evidence management	Blockchain cannot provide solutions for all the issues related to evidence acquisition. However, it can effectively address the issues of evidence management and chain of custody.
Evidence preservation	• Chain of custody • Evidence safety and security • Evidence integrity	Preserving the electronic evidence on the blockchain-based platforms can guarantee the safety, security, integrity, and effective chain of custody.
Evidence access control and examination	• Absence of log framework • Coordination issues for multiexaminers and multiorganizations	A blockchain-based evidence management system can provide effective access log. It can also provide smooth platform for evidence sharing among multiorganizations and multiexaminers.

(Continued)

TABLE 15.2 (*Continued*)
Digital Forensics Challenges and Feasible Solution Using Blockchain

Forensics Phases	Current Challenges	Blockchain Promising Solutions
Reporting	• The authenticity of the report • Collaborative report through multiexaminers and multiorganizations	Forensic reports managed through blockchain platform can ensure the authenticity of report. It will also bring transparency in collaborative reports through common consensus.

ᵃ Blockchain cannot provide feasible solutions for the challenges.

15.3 BACKGROUND AND LITERATURE REVIEW OF THE EXISTING WORKS

There are very limited research papers, book chapters, and dissertations available on applications of blockchain in the digital forensics domain. Most of them have proposed a model based on blockchain, whereas few papers have discussed a prototype model build on the concept. The research and development on this topic are in a very infant stage and are yet to witness a success story.

Lone and Mir (2019) have proposed forensic-chain: a blockchain-based digital forensics chain of custody. The objectives of the authors are to build a tamperproof chain of custody for digital forensics. A prototype of a blockchain-based digital forensics chain of custody is discussed in the paper. The prototype is developed using Hyperledger Composer.

Bonomi, Casini, and Ciccotelli (2018) have proposed a blockchain-based chain of custody (B-CoC). The work presented in the paper mainly focuses on the evidence management to guarantee its suitability, integrity, and traceability of the owner. The paper discusses the prototype implementation of B-CoC architecture based on Ethereum. Authors have also presented the performance evaluation of B-CoC, which is able to sustain realistic workload with acceptable overhead.

Ryu et al. (2019) have proposed a blockchain-based forensics framework for IoT environment. The IoT environment includes smart grid, smart home, smart appliances, smart car, smart industry, sensors, etc. The research presented in the paper basically focuses on forensics readiness, so that in case of any cybercrime, it can ease the investigation. The author has presented the proof of concept using the simulated model of prototype using the Ethereum private network platform.

Al-Khateeb, Epiphaniou, and Daly (2019) have briefly discussed the admissibility of digital evidence in a court of law and the importance of chain of custody. The research work presented in the paper focuses on the implementation of chain of custody using distributed ledger. The authors have also presented the practical scenario that how chain of custody preserved on blockchain makes the overall system forensically ready and enables better investigation.

Li, Qin, and Min (2019) have presented the work focused on evidence identification, preservation, analysis, and presentation recorded in the chain of blocks.

TABLE 15.3
List of Major Digital Forensics Challenges Addressed by Researchers

Author(s)	Challenges Addressed	
Lone and Mir (2019)	Chain of custody	√
	Evidence management	×
	Evidence access control	×
	Report management	×
Ryu et al. (2019)	Chain of custody	√
	Evidence management	×
	Evidence access control	×
	Report management	×
Al-Khateeb, Epiphaniou, and Daly (2019)	Chain of custody	√
	Evidence management	×
	Evidence access control	×
	Report management	×
Li, Qin, and Min (2019)	Chain of custody	√
	Evidence management	×
	Evidence access control	×
	Report management	×
Bonomi, Casini, and Ciccotelli (2018)	Chain of custody	√
	Evidence management	√
	Evidence access control	×
	Report management	×

The authors have briefly discussed the importance of collecting digital evidence, maintaining its integrity, and provenances across jurisdictional borders. The authors have also proposed IoT Forensic Chain (IoTFC), which can deliver a guarantee of traceability and track provenance of evidence items. The IoTFC significantly increases the trust of examiners by providing transparency. Table 15.3 gives a quick review of the challenges addressed by researchers.

Intrinsic characteristics of blockchain can provide a solution for some of the major challenges of digital forensic process, i.e., chain of custody, evidence management, evidence access control, and report management.

As mentioned earlier, very limited work is done on the application of blockchain in the digital forensics domain. Most of the researchers have focused on the chain of custody using blockchain, whereas evidence management, access control, and report management are yet to be addressed.

15.4 BLOCKCHAIN-BASED DIGITAL FORENSICS FRAMEWORK

Blockchain has many potential features to transform the digital forensics investigation process in various ways. Digital forensics investigation goes through multilevel process. Many times, multiple agencies and expert examiners are involved in a single case investigation. There are always possibilities of evidence tampering and mishandling (Billard, 2018; Lone and Mir, 2019; Ricci, Baggili and Breitinger, 2019). Each organization and expert involved in the investigation need to verify and validate the evidence as a standard practice. The involvement of multiple organizations and multiple forensics experts in the investigation process makes it difficult to maintain the chain of custody and preserve the integrity of evidence. Overall, it also increases the investigation time.

Before we discuss how blockchain can address the issues of digital forensics, we need to first understand if do we really need blockchain? If yes, what types of blockchain would be suitable? Figure 15.3 shows steps to ascertain the need of blockchain and helps to identify the types of blockchain to be implemented.

Since multiple stakeholders are involved in a forensic investigation, it is clear from Figure 15.3 that we need blockchain. As far as the category of blockchain is concerned, it can be private permissioned or federated blockchain.

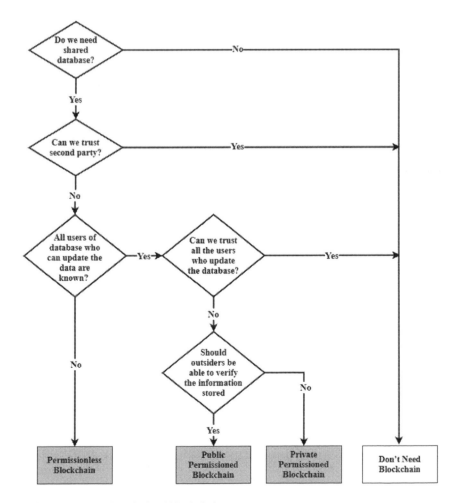

FIGURE 15.3 Need analysis of blockchain.

The current digital forensics investigation process needs a technological solution to improve the following:

- Process efficiency
- Transparency in the investigation
- Evidence management, security, and authentication
- Reliability in maintaining the chain of custody
- Authentic expert report

Blockchain has all the potential features to satisfy the above requirements. Blockchain can greatly improve the overall efficiency of the process. It can improve transparency, trust, security, reliability, and authenticity.

The next section briefly discusses the architecture of blockchain-based digital forensics investigation process and framework. The prototype model is developed using hyper ledger fabrics. The objective of this chapter is to give an idea about the blockchain-based investigation process framework to the reader. Hence, to keep the chapter simple and easily understandable, process flow and architecture are discussed in detail. However, programming code and screenshots are kept away from inclusion in this chapter.

15.4.1   Overall Architecture

There are many stakeholders involved in the investigation process. Major stakeholders are as follows:

- *Investigating organization*: Normally, the investigation is initiated by law enforcement agencies. However, since digital forensics is also used in civil cases, investigation may be initiated by a regulating authority, auditing organization, and other legal body.
- *Court*: Court is a government organization to adjudicate the legal dispute in accordance with the rule of law. The court needs forensic evidence to deliver justice.
- *Defense*: In civil or criminal prosecution, under the common law, accused has the right to raise a defense to avoid civil or criminal liability.
- *Investigating officer*: Investigation officer is the person in charge to investigate the case. Investigating officer collects the evidence and hands it over to the forensic lab for analysis.
- *Prosecution*: It is the legal party responsible for presenting the case in a criminal trial against an individual accused of breaking the law.

It is not feasible to build a single system based on blockchain to integrate the entire process, fulfilling the requirements of every stakeholder. Different organizations and entities have different work processes and cultures. Combining the whole process on single platform will make the system very complicated. It will also raise performance, scalability, and maintainability issues.

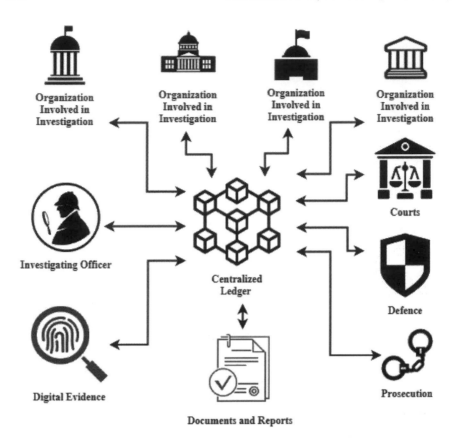

FIGURE 15.4   Blockchain-based digital forensics investigation framework.

Understanding the complexity of the system, we found that modular approach would be feasible to develop the system. In our prototype model, we have divided the work into two core modules. These modules focus on evidence management and chain of custody. The overall architecture shown in Figure 15.4 is a federated blockchain. Only authorized users and organizations have access to it.

15.4.1.1   Evidence Management and Access Control

The blockchain-based architecture shown in Figure 15.5 provides a robust platform for evidence management and access control. The module is divided into two submodules.

15.4.1.1.1   Electronic Evidence Storage

Digital forensics analysis is carried out on the image copy of data acquired through physical evidence seized from the crime scene. During the data acquisition process, hash key (using MD5, SHA1) of the image copy is also generated to validate the integrity of the evidence. Both evidence files and hash key of evidence

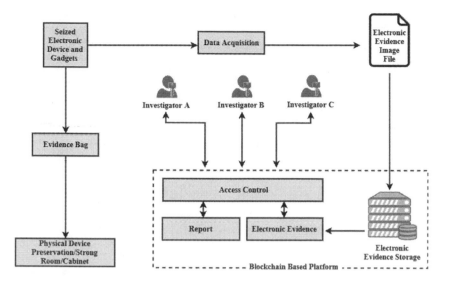

FIGURE 15.5   Blockchain-based evidence management and access control.

need to be stored on the evidence server. While adding the new evidence file into server, hash key is recalculated and matched with the hash value supplied along with the evidence. Evidence file is added to the evidence server only when hash value matches. Each evidence file is assigned with unique ID prefix with case ID. Only an investigator/examiner having valid credentials can upload the evidence file into server. On successful uploading the evidence file into evidence server, a timestamp, user ID, evidence ID, evidence hash key, case ID are stored in the blockchain.

15.4.1.1.2   Examiner Access Control

It is difficult to control access to digital evidence. Digital evidence can be easily copied and transmitted, which makes monitoring and access control challenging. In the prototype system, each forensics examiner and organization is provided credentials to access the evidence; whenever any examiner accesses the evidence, a timestamp, along with examiner ID and evidence ID, is stored in the blockchain. Once the examiner logs out from system, again the timestamp, examiner ID, evidence ID, duration of access, and evidence hash key are stored in the blockchain. Each time examiner logs out, evidence hash key is generated and verified with the evidence original hash key. The reason behind storing the hash key on every logout is to ascertain the accountability of users in case of evidence tampering.

15.4.1.1.3   Report

Forensics report is the outcome of the analysis. Examiner can create a new report, edit the existing report, and endorse the report. Each report is stored with unique ID prefixed with the case ID. Whenever a new report is created, examiner ID, timestamp, and case ID are stored in the blockchain. Subsequently, for any examiner who accesses the report, examiner ID, timestamps, and types of operations (read, modify, and endorsement) are stored in the blockchain.

The evidence management and access control module has the following features:

1. Digital evidence can be stored on the blockchain platform. It makes the evidence untamable and secure.
2. Multiple organizations or examiner involved in the investigation can easily access the evidence stored on the blockchain platform. In case of any mishandling and tampering of the evidence, responsible user or organization can be easily identified.
3. Any evidentiary facts or expert reports can be easily shared with respective organizations or examiner. Since the records are maintained on the blockchain platform, they can be trusted as free from any forgery or mala fide alteration.

15.4.1.2　Chain of Custody

Chain of custody is the process of handling evidence. It records the evidence-handling process right from the seizure of evidence to its presentation in the court of law and its disposition. During the entire investigation, process evidence is handled by many organizations and many examiners. There are many possibilities of evidence tampering. It is important that the entire process of evidence search and seizure is recorded in the chronological order. The prototype model of blockchain-based chain of custody, as shown in Figure 15.6, makes it immutable and trustworthy.

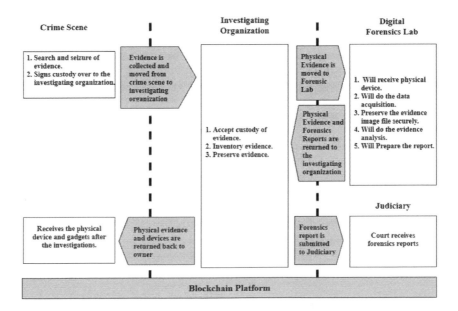

FIGURE 15.6　Blockchain-based chain of custody.

The proposed blockchain-based chain of custody platform, as shown in Figure 15.6, basically focuses on recording the movement (transaction) of physical device, digital evidence, forensic reports, etc.

1. As soon as the search and seizure process begins, the details of the physical devices and gadgets can be recorded on the blockchain platform. The investigating officer can login the platform with valid credentials and create a case ID. After successfully creating the case ID, details of the seized physical device, video, and still photos of seizure procedure, investigator ID, etc. can be stored into system.
2. Once the details of physical evidence are entered into the system, unique ID is generated for each device. Devices are tagged with the unique ID and kept in safe custody. Inventory of physical evidence is maintained on the blockchain platform. Any movement of physical evidence is recorded on the blockchain platform, along with the date of access, investigator ID, case ID, etc.
3. Physical evidence is transferred to a forensic lab for data acquisition. Once the data acquisition is done successfully, the physical evidence is returned to the investigating agency for safe custody. The entire activity of physical device movement is recorded in the blockchain system. It is not advisable to do any forensic analysis on primary evidence (physical device) directly. All the analyses need to be carried out on the evidence image copy. The digital evidence copy is stored in the evidence server with a unique ID prefixed with case ID, as shown in Figure 15.5.
4. After completing the forensic analysis, report is prepared and stored in the repository with a unique ID prefixed with case ID. The forensics report is provided to the investigating agency. The movement and report are also stored on the blockchain.
5. The investigating agency needs to submit the forensics report to court during the trial. The movement of report and the detail of its access are recorded on the blockchain platform.
6. Physical evidence may be handed over back to its owner. However, the decision of returning the physical evidence back to its owner depends on various factors. In case the physical evidence is returned to owner, it is recorded on the blockchain platform with the respective case ID and evidence inventory system.

15.4.2 BENEFITS OF BLOCKCHAIN-BASED DIGITAL FORENSICS FRAMEWORK

Evidence management and chain of custody are crucial parts of the investigation process. In case of any claim on the authenticity of evidence in the court of law, a chain of custody is the one vital proof of record to defend the authenticity of the evidence. Till now, various manual forms and formats are commonly used by the investigating officer to record the chain of custody. Further, the chain of custody form is signed by the investigating officers and witnesses. Maintaining the evidence movement details and the chain of custody on the blockchain platform significantly improve the following features:

- *Integrity*: Forensics processes need to ensure that evidence integrity is maintained throughout the investigation process. Immutable features of blockchain maintain the integrity of evidence. Evidence tampering is virtually eradicated with the implementation of evidence retaining using blockchain.
- *Evidence traceability*: When the investigation officer seizes any gadget or device, it has to be handed over to the forensic lab. The examiner would like to know how the evidence was seized, and investigation officer may be interested to know the whereabouts of the seized devices. Movement of the evidence can be recorded in the blockchain. The digital certificate for the evidence movement could be updated in the blockchain. The complete movement of the evidence can be tracked any time, which increases the transparency in evidence handling.
- *Evidence sharing among multiple organizations*: Investigation process involves many organizations. Evidence needs to be handled by multiple organizations to do the examination. Evidence management and evidence sharing can be done through blockchain.
- *Smart document management*: There are many stakeholders who may be interested in the investigation report. All the documents related to the case, i.e., case diary, witness report, evidence analysis report, and any other documents relevant to the case can be stored in blockchain-based smart document repository. Smart document management greatly reduces the investigation time. Since smart documents will be consistently validated by stakeholders and users on the network, authenticity of the records is maintained.
- *Verifiability*: Any stakeholder involved in the process of investigation can view the whole chain of evidence handling. It helps them to know the status of investigation at any point in time.
- *Increased process efficiency*: By adopting the blockchain technology, the overall investigation process is very fast and efficient. It reduces the multiple verification and authentication process and saves time and money.

15.5 FORENSICS READINESS

Now, almost all organizations are dependent on information technology. Cyberattack and cybercrime are common incidents to occur in any organization. Most of the organization takes preventive measure to protect themselves from such incidents. However, in case of any such unwanted or unforeseen incident, an organization needs to recover and continue the day-to-day operations. The organization must have a strategic plan for incident response, disaster recovery, and business continuity.

Apart from business continuity and recovery issues, there are many other issues such as regulatory compliance, business ethics, insurance claim, and legal matters that crop up and need to be addressed carefully. During the course of the investigation, claims may arise against the organization, an employee, or even third-party service providers.

Digital evidence becomes most important when such issues arise. Blockchain is a promising technology that makes the organization's digital data forensically ready.

Forensics readiness is the capability of an organization to effectively and efficiently use the digital evidence in case of incident to minimize the cost and time of the investigation. It is important for the organization to have an appropriate level of capabilities to preserve, protect, and analyze digital evidence (Bariki, Hashmi and Baggili, 2010; Watson and Jones, 2013). Evidence preserved by the organization in forensically sound manner would be helpful in any employee disciplinary matters, legal dispute, tribunal, or court of law.

15.5.1 Forensic Readiness Using Blockchain – Use Cases

Almost all sectors such as banking, finance, health, education, law and order, and government secretariat are witnessing the applications of blockchain in a very creative way. It is making the overall system very transparent and secure. It is also giving the forensic readiness edge to the system. It may not be feasible to discuss all different types of use cases in this chapter. However, two use cases are discussed here to give a little familiarity to the reader about the creative use of blockchain to make the system forensically ready.

15.5.1.1 Automatic Traffic Violation Monitoring System Using Blockchain

Most of the countries are implementing automatic traffic enforcement and fine traffic system. With the advancement in technologies, it is possible to automize the detection of traffic violations with the help of advanced CCTV cameras. These cameras automatically detect the speed limit violation, red light signal violation, lane discipline violation, etc. The camera captures the high-resolution images, which are transferred to centralize server, where experts with the help of image analytics and video analytics software identify the vehicle registration details and raise the penalty/fine ticket.

A blockchain-based traffic violation monitoring system is shown in Figure 15.7. The entire process starting from image capture to identification of vehicle registration details goes through multiple stages. The image captured through CCTV is vital to be retained as evidence. The system shown in Figure 15.7 supports both the blockchain-enabled traffic-monitoring camera and the legacy traffic-monitoring camera.

1. A blockchain-enabled traffic monitoring camera detects traffic violations and captures the images of the incidents. The camera automatically generates the hash value of the captured image and stores it on the blockchain platform.
2. The legacy traffic monitoring camera transmits the captured images of incident to the control center. The control center generates the hash value of the images and stores it on the blockchain platform.

Many times, authenticity of the evidence is challenged in court. Blockchain-based storage of CCTV footage and still images makes the entire system very trustworthy and secure. In case of legal proceedings, it significantly helps in expediting the process and disposing of the matter.

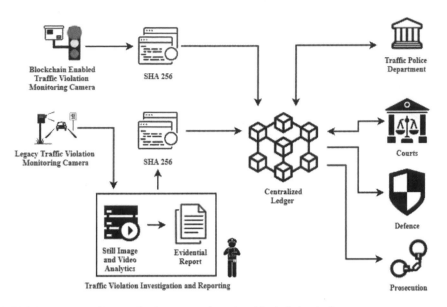

FIGURE 15.7   Traffic-monitoring system based on blockchain platform.

Since many organizations may be involved in the entire process of raising the penalty ticket, legal proceedings, and disposing of the case, a blockchain-based platform makes it a seamless process. It saves time and money for the government organization and significantly improves the trust of all stakeholders.

15.5.1.2   Blockchain-Based Cyberattacks and Incident Response Management System

Cybersecurity is one of the primary domains where applications of blockchain are extensively explored. Many companies working in cybersecurity domain are designing and developing their products, keeping blockchain in core. Attackers are continuously evolving their attack patterns. There are many sophisticated and stealthy attacks that are challenging to detect at the right time. Sometimes, attackers are successful in deleting or modifying the log reports. It makes impossible for the investigator to trace the origin of attack or understand the attack patterns.

Blockchain could potentially help to improve cybersecurity. The platform provides data security and can detect fraudulent activities through consensus mechanism. Because of its intrinsic characteristics, it ensures immutability, transparency, auditability, and operational resilience.

Auditable characteristic of blockchain is one of the major advantages that provides forensic readiness. Storing the user access control information and activity logs on blockchain platform provides an edge to the system. In case of any cyberattack, blockchain-based activity logs would help the forensics examiner to rely upon the logs and investigate the incident. Access control information and logs stored on

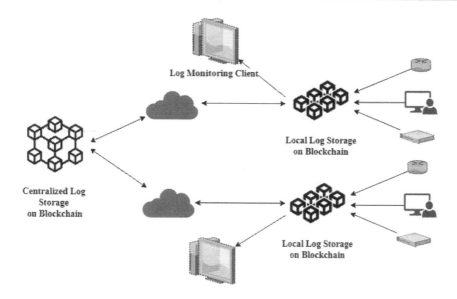

FIGURE 15.8   Blockchain-based network log management system.

non-blockchain platform cannot be trusted for the incident's investigation. It can be compromised and can always mislead the forensic investigator.

An example of a blockchain application for log management and incident analysis is presented in Figure 15.8. The objective of the presented architecture is to help the administrator to detect normal threat as well as advanced persistent threats (APT) and attacks.

Most of the network security devices and monitoring systems focus on real-time detection. However, the attackers are changing their attack techniques now. They spread their attacks over a long period of time (sometimes 2–3 months or more). Such types of attacks are called APTs, where attackers remain undetected for a long period of time. It is difficult for a network admin to analyze the network logs of such longer period of time and trace the attackers or understand attack patterns.

Generally, the organization preserves logs for a limited period of time. In such a scenario, detecting and analyzing the APT attacks may not be possible. If the attackers are clever enough, they will try to delete or corrupt the logs to remove all their footprints. Blockchain-based log preservation makes the system foolproof and secure from all such types of threats (Kumar, Kumar Singh and Kumar, 2018).

The overall architecture of the cloud-based log management system using blockchain is shown in Figure 15.8. There are four major functional components in the system.

1. *Log generator devices*: These are the devices that generate logs and store them in the local blockchain log server.
2. *Local log server*: The local log server collects the logs from various log generator devices connected in-network or sub-network. The local log

server stores the log in local blockchain-based server. The log data is further processed and normalized in the standard format to be pushed in cloud server for long-term storage and easy analysis. The local log server uploads the log to a centralized server in batches, based on schedule or as and when specific threshold value is reached. The threshold value can be set in terms of log size or in terms of number of log records.

3. *Logging cloud server*: The logging cloud server is based on blockchain. It collects the log from local log servers belonging to different subnetworks and stores it using blockchain for long-term archival and analysis.

4. *Log-monitoring clients*: These are local hosts that are used by an administrator to monitor and analyze the log data from local server as well as from the cloud server.

The overall objective of the architecture shown in Figure 15.8 is to build a robust log management system using blockchain. It will not only help organizations to detect different types of attacks but will also empower them to detect or analyze any internal threats or malicious activity by their employees.

15.5.2 BENEFITS OF FORENSIC READINESS

* *Fast Investigation*: Data and transactional records stored in blockchain platform ease the job of forensic examiners. Blockchain records are more trustworthy than the data and records stored in traditional databases. Significant time is saved in verifying the authenticity of record. Overall, it also saves the cost of investigation.

* *Prevention from Insiders Attack*: Organization is vulnerable from their own employees. Once employees are aware that the transaction records and activities are recorded in blockchain, they are deterred from carrying out any mischievous activities for the fear of being caught.

* *Cost Reduction for Regulatory Compliance*: Most of the organizations work under some regulatory authority. Regulatory authorities always need authenticated compliance reports from the organizations. Digitizing the process of regulatory compliance on blockchain would make the process smooth and trustworthy. It will significantly save the audit time and prevent the organization to indulge in any fraudulent activities.

* *Good Corporate Governance*: Implementation of information system management policies such as forensics readiness garner goodwill for the organization. It increases the trust of all stakeholders and significantly helps the regulatory authority and law enforcement agencies in case of any incident.

15.5.3 FORENSIC READINESS PLANNING GUIDELINES

No doubt, forensics readiness gives edge to organization's information system, but thorough analysis is needed before its implementation. Blockchain may seem to be a promising solution to provide forensics readiness, but it requires strategic planning for implementation. Some of the guidelines that can be followed are as follows:

1. Identify the digital records, which are important as evidence in case of any dispute
2. Identify the potential source of evidence
3. Identify the requirements for evidence preservation
4. Design and develop a blockchain-based platform to preserve the digital record transactions and access controls
5. Ensure that the system satisfies legal and other statutory compliance
6. Periodically review and upgrade the system based on changes in legal and statutory compliances

15.5.4   LEGAL ACCEPTANCE OF BLOCKCHAIN EVIDENCE – GLOBAL SCENARIO

The data and records are stored in the blockchain in such a way that it maintains the integrity of historical data and detect tampering. The technological architecture of the blockchain system satisfies most of the industry standards and modern laws. Hence, as a standard practice, top leading business organization, industry, academia, and government organizations around the world started adopting blockchain. The promising features of blockchain technologies have prompted many countries to amend or create the law to legitimate blockchain digital records in court and government proceedings. Let us look at the recent adoption of blockchain in some of the countries.

15.5.4.1   United States

In 2016, the US state of Vermont passed a law to welcome the use of blockchain data in the courtroom. In 2017, Arizona state amended the existing legislation on electronic records and recognized the blockchain record as a valid evidence. This amendment recognized a signature secured through blockchain technology as an electronic signature; a record or contract secured through blockchain technology as an electronic record; smart contract as valid; and ownership and other rights in interstate or foreign commerce as remaining valid if subsequently secured by blockchain technology. The Vermont legislature published a report stating, 'Providing legal recognition of blockchain technology may create a "first mover" advantage with the potential to bring economic activity surrounding the development of blockchain technology to Vermont'. Further, the states of Ohio, Hawaii, and many other states in the United States have introduced the law to accept the use of blockchain records in the court when accompanied by digital signature. Some of the states have taken the initiative to start a pilot project to study the benefits of blockchain for different industry sectors and are in the process of legalizing it.

15.5.4.2   China

In 2018, China Supreme People's Court has made blockchain records admissible in the court. Traditionally, the court was dependent on third-party notary organizations to authenticate the evidence. Now, the court has accepted blockchain as a new method for verifying the evidence, which is more efficient, secure, convenient, and low in cost. Apart from legalizing the acceptance of blockchain record, the Supreme People's Court in China has also taken a major initiative to embraced blockchain technology for the storage and authentication of digital evidence while processing legal disputes through digital court system. China has set up its first Internet court in Hangzhou in 2017. Hangzhou is the first court to recognize blockchain assets evidence, while Beijing and Guangzhou are getting ready to do the same.

15.5.4.3   United Kingdom

Recently, the UK's Ministry of Justice has announced a pilot project to introduce the blockchain-based evidence system. The objective of the project is to streamline and simplify the court processes involving digital evidence. It will solve the challenges of digital evidence sharing among organizations, evidence and smart record management, and maintaining the authenticated audit trail. The system is intended to maintain the chain of custody on blockchain platform in the chronological order to capture how digital evidence has been created/accessed/modified, by whom, and from which location. Recording of chain of custody in a secure and chronological order will enable reconstruction and trace the sequence of events.

15.5.5   BLOCKCHAIN AND LEGAL CHALLENGES

Though blockchain satisfies many legal compliances, it still faces some of the challenges in the court of law. Traditional digital evidence and blockchain-based evidence are different in characteristics. Acceptance of blockchain-based evidence is possible either with the amendment in current law or by providing some exceptions to the blockchain evidence.

15.5.6   THE HEARSAY CHALLENGE

Though the blockchain data is virtually incorruptible, blockchain records or evidence might be challenged in a court of law's inadmissible hearsay. It is commonly defined as 'an out-of-court statement offered to prove the truth of the matter asserted therein'. In some of the courts, hearsay evidence is inadmissible unless an exemption to the hearsay rule applies.

For example, to prove that Tom was in town, the attorney asks a witness, 'What did Susan tell you about Tom being in town?' Since the witness's answer will rely on an out-of-court statement that Susan made, if Susan is unavailable for cross-examination, the answer is hearsay. A justification for the objection is that the person who made the statement is not in court and thus is insulated from cross-examination.

Legal experts have also argued that since the entries in blockchain ledger are the direct result of human action, so the blockchain record might fail the Lizarraga-Tirado test. All countries have their own law for the admissibility of evidence in the court of law. From time to time, these laws have been amended. Most of the countries consider digital records and electronic evidence as valid evidence, with some extra measures. As far as admissibility of blockchain records are concerned, several countries are amending their laws to give admissibility of the blockchain records in court.

There is positive progress toward the acceptance of blockchain evidence. However, legal experts and practitioners must be prepared to address hearsay challenges and ensure that blockchain evidence can be authenticated. The organization that is implementing the blockchain should also be prepared to explain the benefits of blockchain to the court. It should be able to convince the court about how blockchain records are maintained and why it is exceptionally reliable and trusted.

15.6 CONCLUSION

Digital forensics is a challenging field. It deals with digital evidence. Once the digital evidence is contaminated, it cannot be reproduced, and hence, it requires utmost care in evidence handling. Intrinsic characteristics of blockchain, i.e., security, authenticity, integrity, transparency, and suitability, make it the best choice to be adopted in the investigation process. It improves the stakeholder's trust and reduces the investigation cost tremendously. In this chapter, we discussed the challenging issues of digital forensics and how blockchain can be used to overcome the challenges. The chapter also focused on the forensics readiness using blockchain and the critical issues of admissibility of blockchain evidence in the court of law. Though blockchain seems to be very promising technology to satisfy many requirements, implementation of blockchain is a costly affair. The initial cost of implementation of blockchain technology will be a bit heavy on organizational budget. We also have to understand that mere implementation of blockchain may not serve the purpose. It should satisfy the requirement of business process, statutory compliance, and legal compliance.

REFERENCES

Al-Khateeb, H., Epiphaniou, G. and Daly, H. (2019). Blockchain for Modern Digital Forensics: The Chain-of-Custody as a Distributed Ledger. In: H. Jahankhani, S. Kendzierskyj, A. Jamal, G. Epiphaniou and H. Al-Khateeb, eds., *Blockchain and Clinical Trial*. Berlin, Germany: Springer.

Bariki, H., Hashmi, M. and Baggili, I. (2010). Defining a Standard for Reporting Digital Evidence Items in Computer Forensic Tools. In: *2nd International ICST Conference on Digital Forensics & Cyber Crime (ICDF2C)*. Berlin, Germany: Springer, pp. 78–95.

Billard, D. (2018). Weighted Forensics Evidence Using Blockchain. In: *International Conference on Computing and Data Engineering (ICCDE 2018)*. New York: ACM, pp. 57–61.

Bonomi, S., Casini, M. and Ciccotelli, C. (2018). B-CoC: A Blockchain-Based Chain of Custody for Evidences Management in Digital Forensics. *CoRR*, [online] abs/1807.10359. Available at: https://arxiv.org/pdf/1807.10359.pdf.

Cebe, M., Erdin, E., Akkaya, K., Aksu, H. and Uluagac, S. (2019). Block4Forensic: An Integrated Lightweight Blockchain Framework for Forensics Applications of Connected Vehicles. *IEEE Communications Magazine*, 56(10), pp. 50–57.

Kouzinopoulos, C., Spathoulas, G., Giannoutakis, K., Votis, K., Pandey, P., Tzovaras, D., Katsikas, S., Collen, A. and Nijdam, N. (2018). Using Blockchains to Strengthen the Security of Internet of Things. In: *International ISCIS Security Workshop: Euro-CYBERSEC 2018*. Springer.

Kumar, M. and Hanumanthappa, M. (2015). Cloud based intrusion detection architecture for smartphones. In: *International Conference on Innovations in Information, Embedded and Communication Systems (ICIIECS 2015)*. IEEE, pp. 1–6.

Kumar, M., Kumar Singh, A. and Kumar, T. (2018). Secure Log Storage Using Blockchain and Cloud Infrastructure. In: *9th International Conference on Computing, Communication and Networking Technologies (ICCCNT)*. IEEE, pp. 1–4.

Li, S., Qin, T. and Min, G. (2019). Blockchain-Based Digital Forensics Investigation Framework in the Internet of Things and Social Systems. *IEEE Transactions on Computational Social Systems*, pp. 1–9.

Liu, Y., Chen, H. and Hu, F. (2017). A blockchain-Based Verification for Sharing Data securely. In: *International Conference on Progress in Informatics and Computing (PIC), Nanjing, 2017*. IEEE, pp. 249–253.

Lone, A. and Mir, R. (2019). Forensic-Chain: Blockchain Based Digital Forensics Chain of Custody with PoC in Hyperledger Composer. *Digital Investigation*, 28, pp. 44–55.

Luciano, L., Baggili, I., Topor, M., Casey, P. and Breitinger, F. (2018). Digital Forensics in the Next Five Years. In: *13th International Conference on Availability, Reliability and Security (ARES 2018)*. ACM, pp. Article 46, 14 pages.

Montasari, R. and Hill, R. (2019). Next-Generation Digital Forensics: Challenges and Future Paradigms. In: *2019 IEEE 12th International Conference on Global Security, Safety and Sustainability (ICGS3)*. IEEE, pp. 205–212.

Ricci, J., Baggili, I. and Breitinger, F. (2019). Blockchain-Based Distributed Cloud Storage Digital Forensics: Where's the Beef? *IEEE Security & Privacy*, 17(1), pp. 34–42.

Ryu, J., Sharma, P., Jo, J. and Park, J. (2019). A Blockchain-Based Decentralized Efficient Investigation Framework for IoT Digital Forensics. *The Journal of Supercomputing*, 75(8), pp. 4372–4387.

Singh, S. and Singh, N. (2016). Blockchain: Future of Financial and Cyber Security. In: *2nd International Conference on Contemporary Computing and Informatics (IC3I)*. IEEE, pp. 463–467.

Taylor, P., Dargahi, T., Dehghantanha, A., Parizi, R. and Choo, K. (2019). A Systematic Literature Review of Blockchain Cyber Security. *Digital Communications and Networks*, in press.

Wan, X., He, J., Liu, G., Huang, N., Zhu, X., Zhao, B. and Mai, Y. (2015). Survey of Digital Forensics Technologies and Tools for Android based Intelligent Devices. *International Journal of Digital Crime and Forensics*, 7(1), pp. 1–25.

Watson, D. and Jones, A. (2013). *Digital Forensics Processing and Procedures*. Rockland, MA: Syngress.

16 RESCHAIN
A Futuristic Solution for Avoiding Fraudulence in Real Estate Environment

Gulshan Kumar, Rahul Saha, G. Geetha, and Mamoun Alazab

CONTENTS

16.1 INTRODUCTION

Real estate is an influential business paradigm in the present world of economy. The scenic beauty; comfortable rooms in a prominent location; basic facilities such as healthcare, recreation, and entertainment; and obviously a good social impact are always desired by all humans. These needs have flourished the real estate business around the globe. 'Real estate has rewarded investors with strong returns in a world of falling interest rates and established business models. The positive outlook for the global economy is an encouraging sign that the rewards will continue for some time to come' [1]. With a global economy perspective, real estate is both an opportunity and challenge but is changing positively the economic equations of global markets. Not only the residence but also industrial establishments are closely connected with real estate values. The rigorous development in real estate environments has elevated the total real estate investment; sales volume surged 49% q-o-q to $6.7 billion for the second quarter of 2019, according to a report by Cushman and Wakefield, with a commercial investment dealing of worth $3.5 billion, which made up 52% of the total amount [2]. The growth is shown in Figure 16.1.

Besides its ample perspective in future and socioeconomic calibrations, real estate businesses also face some serious problems of fraudulence [3,4]. Various false cases have been reported worldwide, in which stakeholders, including both buyers and sellers (investors as general), are at risk. Along with that banking provisions also get a hitch back, as the investors are connected to the commercial banks for loaning purposes. Moreover, crowdfunding is another strategy that has been popular in recent years from real estate perspective. Eventually, such crowdfunding is also facing some hazards due to lack of security [5]. Some of the general problems for real estate environment include approval and regulatory compliances, lack of clarity in land titles, speculation in land and prices, finance problems, billing requirements, political influences, and many more [6]. Apart from these developmental problems, some specific fraudulent problems that exist include mortgage fraud, foreclosure fraud, title fraud, value fraud, income and employment fraud, air loans, etc. [7,8]. Therefore, to avoid these frauds, real estate requires some mechanism

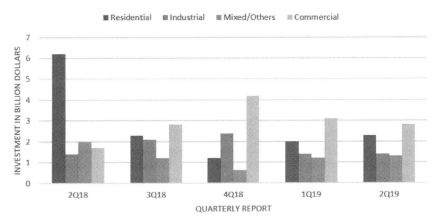

FIGURE 16.1 Investment in real estate in different quarters. (From Tay, T., Investment sales jump 49% q-o-q to $6.7 bil in 2Q2019, EdgeProp Singapore, available at: www.edge-prop.sg/tags/cushman-wakefield, 2019.)

that can provide a fair process of real estate business development and transactions. Thus, we have come with a proposal called 'RESCHAIN', which is a blockchain-based real estate business model.

Blockchain is a very promising technology in the present world [9]. The decentralized and transparent features have attracted all other domains of technical and non-technical, government, and non-government organizations to check out its feasibilities for their respective purposes. Thus, blockchain has been widely accepted by industries, organizations, and academicians. It has also synthesized impactful business model, which is applicable in various business solutions [10]. Therefore, in our proposal, we have explored the feasibility of blockchain implication in real estate transactions and information sharing. The objectives of the proposed concept are as follows:

- To provide a transparent approach for real estate properties
- To develop an open and distributed system for all real estate stakeholders for completion of a project and identification of the cause factor of any incident
- To smoothen the government's and bank's monitoring process on legal and illegal real estate properties

The rest of the proposal is organized as follows. Section 16.2 describes the feasibility of blockchain applications. Section 16.3 explains the proposed approach of 'RESCHAIN'. Section 16.4 analyzes the theoretical benefits, and finally, Section 16.5 concludes with future aspects.

16.2   RELATED WORK

Blockchain application in the real estate business domain is unobserved till date. Being in its infant stage with its potentialities, various applications have embraced blockchain significantly. Therefore, in this section, we have briefly reviewed such application zone to obtain a view of wide acceptance of blockchain and to identify its scope in real estate business. We have identified some of the major domains where blockchain has proved its influence and efficiency.

16.2.1   E-COMMERCE

The requirement of comfortable and 'smart' life and the inclusion of Internet of Things (IoT) have emphasized the growth of e-commerce. It has also provided its influence in the global economic structure. Further, blockchain application in e-commerce has added a cap of benefits with fairness and transparency, which is accepted globally [11].

16.2.2   E-HEALTHCARE AND BIOMEDICAL

One of the most prominent applications of blockchain has been observed in e-healthcare and biomedical. Along with a comfortable life, humans also require some beneficial and smart health services. Various researches have been executed in this domain. Some important work and summarizations are found in [12–15].

16.2.3 SUPPLY CHAIN MANAGEMENT

Supply chain management and import-export always have been a crucial part of cross-border countries and the socioeconomic-political growth of a country. Few research works have been oriented to this direction to examine the feasibility of blockchain in trading and supply chain management. Some influential works are discussed in [16,17]. Moreover, the agricultural chain, from farm to mouth, is also being researched recently [18].

16.2.4 CYBERSECURITY

The digitally evolving world is also concerned about its data security. Blockchain has shown its positive and efficient impact on this aspect and has provided various solutions for providing security in cyber paradigm. Some of the important solutions are discussed in [19,20].

Apart from these majorly identified domains of blockchain applications, some other important application-based solutions have been carved by blockchain technology. Its future directions, applications scope, and problems are rigorously researched in recent years [21].

The previous discussion on blockchain applications signifies a clear fact that blockchain has a vast potential in various applications for its distributed architecture, decentralized vision, and a transparent transaction with controlled methods of access. Therefore, we have explored the feasibility of it in real estate and have identified it as a beneficial approach to be considered.

16.3 PROPOSED CONCEPT

RESCHAIN is a blockchain-based proposed solution to avoid frauds in real estate environment. It maintains decentralized distributed and transparent ledger of property information, which is accessed by different stakeholders with proper credentials. The real estate business and information system deal with various stakeholders, who have their own set of tasks and responsibilities. In the present scenario, the stakeholders of a real estate are not able to monitor the development process or even transaction processes directly online, and only manual vigilance is in process. Therefore, it will be very much useful when blockchain provides a mean of real estate status. Table 16.1 summarizes the stakeholders and their basic responsibilities and functions in a real estate environment. This table helps us to functionalize the blockchain in real estate.

When a seller wants to sell or a buyer wants to buy a real estate property, he has to join the RESCHAIN with his wallet credentials. After joining the network, he can initiate a transaction for the required property. The other stakeholders such as government, bank, and other buyers or sellers (if it is in second through or third through the property) must verify the details of the property and validate it. The government checks the legalization and property compliance, bank examines the loan and financial

TABLE 16.1
Functions of Stakeholders Considered for RESCHAIN

Stakeholders	Functions
Government	Monitoring and tax control
Land acquirers	Purchase of land and maintenance as per government compliances and banking
Buyers	Banking, land information gathering, and networking
Builders	Banking, third-party perspective, connecting suppliers, and partnership
Suppliers	Raw material supply and supply chain management
Bank	Transaction management among other stakeholders

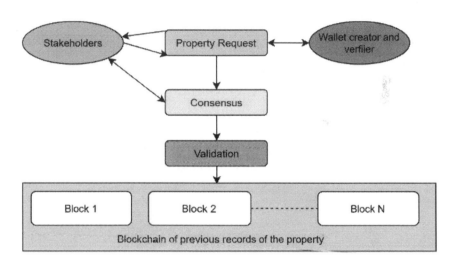

FIGURE 16.2   RESCHAIN system model.

encounters, and other buyers and sellers provide the status feedback. The cumulative validation ensures that the property is genuine. Similarly, validation of the buyers and sellers can also be executed to ensure that the buyer or the seller is genuine and not having any previous fault. The overall system model is shown in Figure 16.2.

The processes for RESCHAIN are as follows:

Step 1: Stakeholder requests for initiating a block of the query (property request) with his/her wallet id.

Step 2: The stakeholder's wallet is verified.

Step 3: Stakeholders participate in consensus for property validation.

Step 4: Once the decision is to reach, the status of the property is added in RESCHAIN. We have also considered that each property should have a unique ID for distinguishing among various properties.

In the following subsections, we have explained the modularization details of the proposed approach.

16.3.1 WALLET CREATION

In the proposed system approach, we have considered that each of the stakeholders willing to take part, as any of the roles listed in Table 16.1, need to be registered with the blockchain process with their details. The information they need to share while in the registration phase must include at least two social identity proof; for example, Indians provide Adhaar card, voter id card, driving license, or passport as proof of identity. Once they are registered and proofs are verified, stakeholders need to apply for wallet assignment process, as shown in Figure 16.3. This wallet assignment process deals with a generation of public-private key combinations, so that each of the stakeholders uses those keys as per the cryptographic applications' requirement. Moreover, each wallet has a wallet id W_{ID} to identify the corresponding stakeholder. This W_{ID} also works as pseudoidentity of the stakeholder. W_{ID} is generated by applying hash function on the social identity proof. We can use any candidate cryptographic hash function (we have selected SHA-512) for the process. The private information such as name, location, and social identity proofs is all mapped to W_{ID} to protect the privacy of the users. Further, the private key is generated, taking random b bits from the hashed output concatenated with timestamp. The public key is generated by the ring modulo operation on the private keyring generator.

$$\text{Private key of User } (U_{PR}): \prod_{b=rand()} SHA-512\left(\text{Social Identity Proof}\right)$$

$$\in G_1 \times G_1 \to G_1$$

$$\text{Public key of User } (U_{PUB}): \left(\check{G} \times SHA512\left(\text{Social Identity Proof}\right)\right) \bmod p$$

where, G_1 is a group of ring elements; p is large prime with the condition of $1 < p < b$, and $\check{G}$ is the generator of G_1.

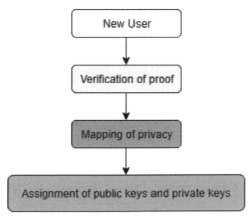

FIGURE 16.3   Wallet assignment process.

Therefore, as per the proposed concept, the wallet consists of: $\{W_{ID}, U_{PUB}, U_{PR}\}$, where U_{PUB} and U_{PR} are the public and private keys, respectively, of the stakeholder U_i.

16.3.2 BLOCK GENERATION

Each of the property is considered a block of transactions. For example, a real estate is established with a series of processes such as buying of land, raw materials purchase, government dealing, construction, and many more. So, all such transactions of processes can be bundled in a single block and are distributed in the RESCHAIN network as a RESCHAIN block, as shown in Figure 16.4.

It may happen that all the stakeholders are not part of RESCHAIN at the very beginning. Therefore, initiation of a successful blockchain can be done by any of the stakeholders, and other stakeholders can join the network, as applicable. Once blocks are generated, pseudoidentity is provided to the block by hash function, which is kept transparent and public. This hash serves two purposes: pseudoidentity and integrity of the block data. Any change in the data is to be done by the consensus approach.

16.3.3 CONSENSUS PARTICIPATION

Once any transaction on the block by any stakeholder is initiated, the initiator broadcasts the request of block B_{Req}. Upon receiving the request message, the stakeholders (e.g., in Figure 16.5, the existing stakeholders are S1, S2, S3, and S4) of that particular block start the verification through the consensus protocol and permit the initiator for further access of the information. If the initiator needs any information, only required information is shared by checking the privacy of the stakeholders. This privacy management has been kept for our future research work. If the initiator needs to add any information or block, the stakeholders come to a decision of consensus, and the block is added in RESCHAIN. The process has been shown in Figure 16.5.

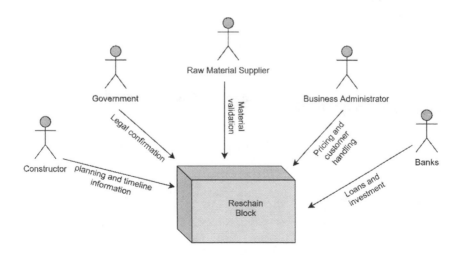

FIGURE 16.4 RESCHAIN block generation.

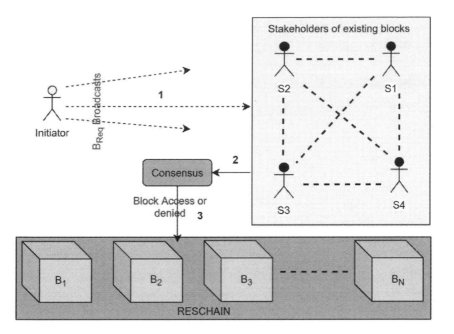

FIGURE 16.5 Logical interpretation of consensus participation.

16.4 THEORETICAL BENEFITS

Blockchain for real estate acquisition must be open and public, without any hindrance to analyze the usage of the requests. It additionally aims to provide security services such as measurability, access control, confidentiality, and privacy.

16.4.1 MEASURABILITY

A distributed blockchain that contains property records, documents, pictures, and proofs has the information storage perspective and information output limitations for suitable viewing of a record to an authenticate user. Moreover, the view access is separate for various stakeholders; for example, government should be allowed to view all records to approve or disapprove the properties' legalization aspects, whereas the buyer or seller should only have the access about the report by government and is not required to check the reports of supplier or builders in depth. The historical information about a property is beneficial to confirm the present status.

16.4.2 ACCESS CONTROL

Blockchain provides an access control mechanism to authenticated users through its wallet provision. The stakeholders who are sharing the information must have access to their own information and management in what manner their information is to be shared. The users of RSECHAIN are to be assigned with a collection of access permissions while writing to the chain. All stakeholders must collaborate and cooperate for audit management in timely manner.

16.4.3 CONFIDENTIALITY AND PRIVACY

RESCHAIN contains data about properties in a state or a country. Therefore, confidentiality and privacy are much more important while implementing. The wallet keys are used for this purpose. Pseudoanonymity is used through wallet ID for the stakeholders. While storing data in RESCHAIN, stakeholders use the encryption technique Rivest–Shamir–Adleman (RSA) and hashing technique SHA-512. The generation of the keys processes through randomization, which makes the keys secure. Therefore, confidentiality is maintained in RESCHAIN. SHA-512 provides one-way cryptographic hash and therefore provides pseudoanonymity and integrity of RESCHAIN data.

16.4.3.1 Bidding Option

RESCHAIN is also able to include an open bidding option for buying and selling properties. As a result, the bidding will be more transparent, and the eligible owner will have the rights of the bid properties. We shall include this option as our future work.

16.4.3.2 Traceability

As the stakeholders are connected in this blockchain, the development of a property and its corresponding suppliers can be recorded. If any mishappening occurs, traceability of the feature will be easier, and the real guilty will be behind bars.

16.4.3.3 Decentralization

RESCHAIN is decentralized, i.e., no stakeholder has full control over any property information. Rather, they have to execute a consensus protocol to confirm the information for a property. Thus, the political influence or brokers' indulgence can be avoided.

16.4.3.4 Government Perspective

RESCHAIN includes the government sector as its one major stakeholder. As a result, it can easily monitor the development phases and processes of properties, their legalization, and taxation accountability. This will help in removing the biasness of the government and non-government employees in real estate environment.

16.4.3.5 Banking Perspective

Real estate is closely related to banks, as investors take a loan from banks for their properties' acquisition. Some of the investors try to camouflage and continue business without repaying to the banks, and thus, banks face loss. Therefore, RESCHAIN will also help to maintain the accountability on the inventors' balance sheet specifically in real estate environment. This will reduce the loss incurred to banks, as in consensus process, banks can verify the previous loan status of the stakeholder.

Therefore, we can see that the implication of blockchain in a real estate environment has enough potential, and thus, both our government and society can be reformed with good ethics and morality.

16.5 CONCLUSION

The real estate business is in boom of development everywhere; it has also initiated country collaborations. Keeping this socioeconomic growth in mind, we have to be concerned about its negative impact, due to some immoral stakeholders. Such negative impact even leads to death toll sometimes. Therefore, we have initiated this proposal to evolve the real estate business domain with the implementation of blockchain. The solution, called RESCHAIN, is advantageous in providing various benefits individually and collectively. The government, banks, and the stakeholders all will be obtaining benefits from it. In our extended work of this solution, we shall implement it technically with Amazon blockchain as a service and will measure the potential technical features. Further, the bidding provision can also be added with the solution as an add-on service to RESCHAIN. Privacy and data parsing in blockchain are also to be explored for better management of data privacy.

REFERENCES

1. www.pwc.com/gx/en/industries/financial-services/assets/pwc-etre-global-outlook-2018.pdf.
2. Tay, Timothy, Investment sales jump 49% q-o-q to $6.7 bil in 2Q2019, EdgeProp Singapore, 2019, available at: www.edgeprop.sg/tags/cushman-wakefield, accessed on 5 July 2019.
3. van de Bunt, Henk, and Karin van Wingerde, We are all going to be rich. A case study of the Dutch Real Estate Fraud, *The Routledge Handbook on White-Collar and Corporate Crime in Europe*, Chapter: 19, Publisher: Routledge, Editors: Judith van Erp, Wim Huisman & Gudrun Vande Walle, pp. 304–317, 2015.
4. Anatomy of a real Estate Fraud: A Case Study, 2015, available at: www.bridgfordlaw.com/articles/anatomy-of-a-real-estate-fraud-case-a-case-study/, accessed on 5 July 2019.
5. Garcia-Teruel, Rosa M., A legal approach to real estate crowdfunding platforms, *Computer Law & Security Review*, 35(3), 2019, pp. 281–294.
6. Real Estate Sector: Problems and Regulations, available at: https://iasscore.in/economy/real-estate-sector-problems-and-regulations-, accessed on 5 July 2019.
7. Shunnar, Thaer and Barry, Michael, Tracking fraudulent activities in real estate transactions, *FIG Working Week 2011: Bridging the Gap Between Cultures*, 2011.
8. Real estate Fraud, available at: www.legalmatch.com/law-library/article/real-estate-fraud.html.
9. Lu, Yang, The blockchain: State-of-the-art and research challenges, *Journal of Industrial Information Integration*, 15, 2019, pp. 80–90.
10. Morkunas, J., Vida, Paschen, Jeannette and Boon, Edward, How blockchain technologies impact your business model, *Business Horizons*, 62(3), 2019, pp. 295–306.
11. Li, Ming, Shen, Leidi, and Huang, George Q., Blockchain-enabled workflow operating system for logistics resources sharing in E-commerce logistics real estate service, *Computers & Industrial Engineering*, 135, 2019, pp. 950–969.

12. Drosatos, George and Kaldoudi, Eleni, Blockchain applications in the biomedical domain: A scoping review, *Computational and Structural Biotechnology Journal*, 17, 2019, pp. 229–240.
13. McGhin, Thomas, Raymond Choo, Kim-Kwang, Zhechao Liu, Charles and He, Charles, Blockchain in healthcare applications: Research challenges and opportunities, *Journal of Network and Computer Applications*, 135, 2019, pp. 62–75.
14. Abujamra, Ramzi and Randall, David, Blockchain applications in healthcare and the opportunities and the advancements due to the new information technology framework, *Advances in Computers*, Elsevier, 115, 2019, pp. 141–154.
15. Saha, Rahul, Kumar, Gulshan, Rai, Mritunjay Kumar and Kim, Hye-Jin, A security provisioned blockchain architecture for multipurpose health information, *International Journal of Advanced Science and Technology*, 116, 2018, pp.141–150.
16. Helo, Petri and Hao, Yuqiuge, Blockchains in operations and supply chains: A model and reference implementation, *Computers & Industrial Engineering*, 136, 2019, pp. 242–251.
17. Xiwei, Xu, Qinghua, Lu, Yue, Liu, Zhu, Liming, Yao, Haonan and Vasilakos, Athanasios V., Designing blockchain-based applications a case study for imported product traceability, *Future Generation Computer Systems*, 92, 2019, pp. 399–406.
18. Zhao, Guoqing, Liu, Shaofeng, Lopez, Carmen, Lu, Haiyan, Elgueta, Sebastian, Chen, Huilan, Boshkoska, and Mileva, Biljana, Blockchain technology in agri-food value chain management: A synthesis of applications, challenges and future research directions, *Computers in Industry*, 109, 2019, pp. 83–99.
19. Kumar, Nallapaneni Manoj and Mallick, Pradeep Kumar, Blockchain technology for security issues and challenges in IoT, *Procedia Computer Science*, 132, 2018, pp. 1815–1823.
20. Taylor, Paul J., Dargahi, Tooska, Dehghantanha, Ali, Parizi, Reza M., Choo, Kim-Kwang Raymond, A systematic literature review of blockchain cyber security, *Digital Communications and Networks*, 2019 (in press).
21. Casino, Fran, K. Dasaklis, Thomas and Patsakis, Constantinos, A systematic literature review of blockchain-based applications: Current status, classification and open issues, *Telematics and Informatics*, 36, 2019, pp. 55–81.

Index

Note: Page numbers in italic and bold refer to figures and tables, respectively.